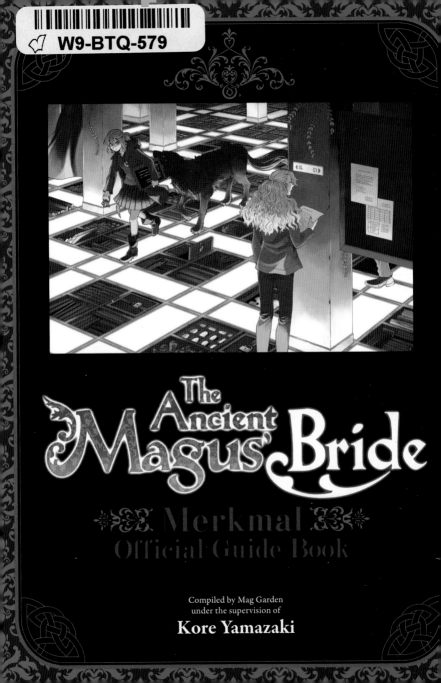

The Ancient Magus' Bride

Merkmal
Official Guide Book

Compiled by Mag Garden
under the supervision of
Kore Yamazaki

Illustration Gallery

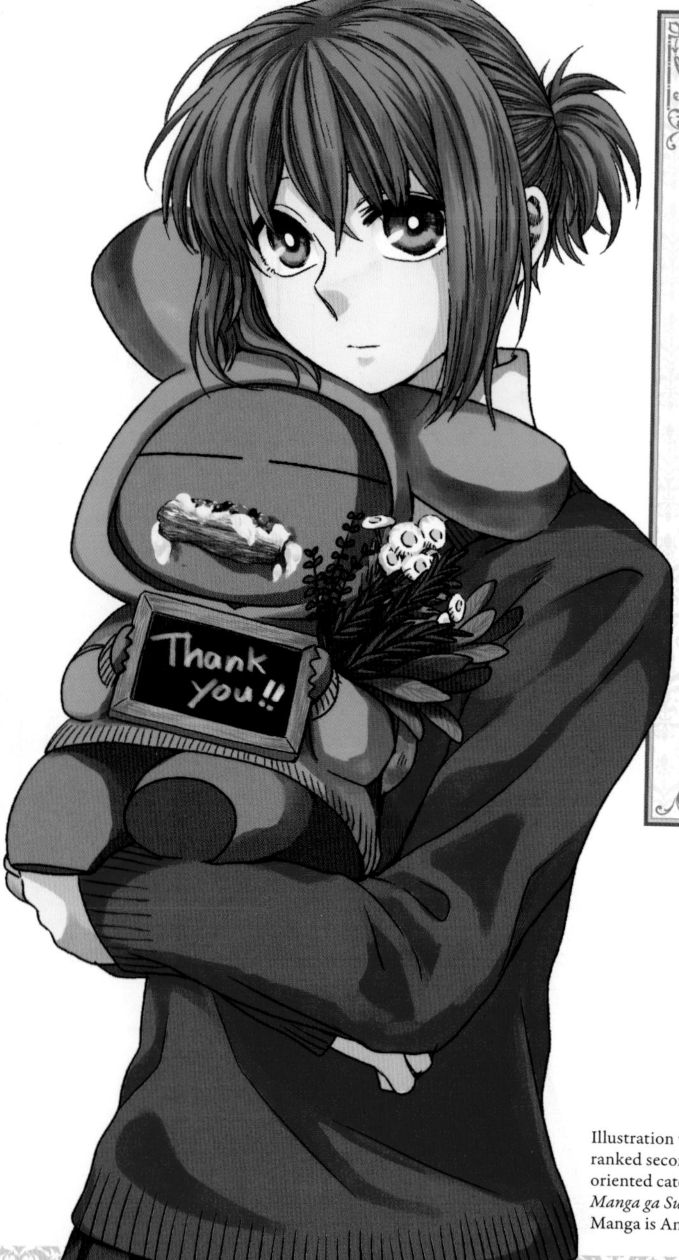
Thank you!!

Illustration to celebrate being ranked second in the male-oriented category in *Kono Manga ga Sugoi!* 2015 (This Manga is Amazing! 2015).

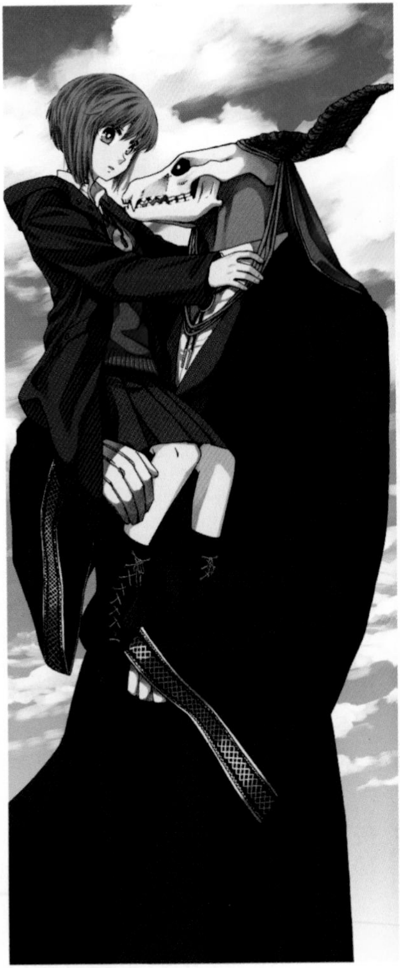

Art for standing signboards at bookstores.

Bookmark art for the collaborative fair FANTASTIC3.

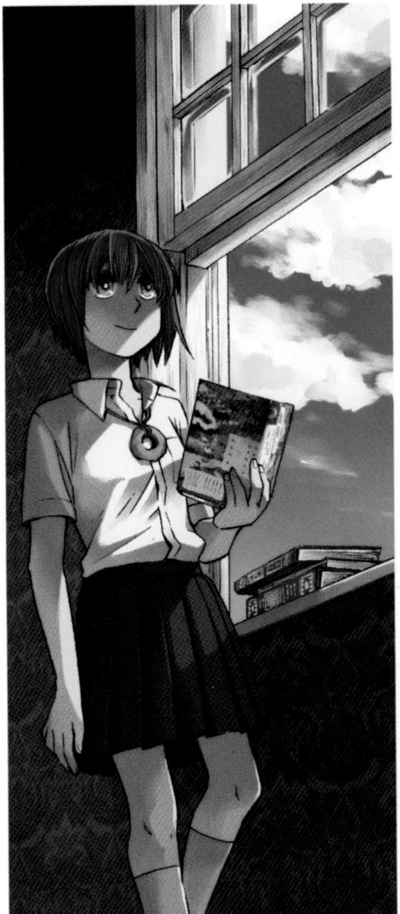

Art to support the third volume of *Hanaoni Tobira no Sakaimeya-san* (The Border Shop at Flower Demon Gate).

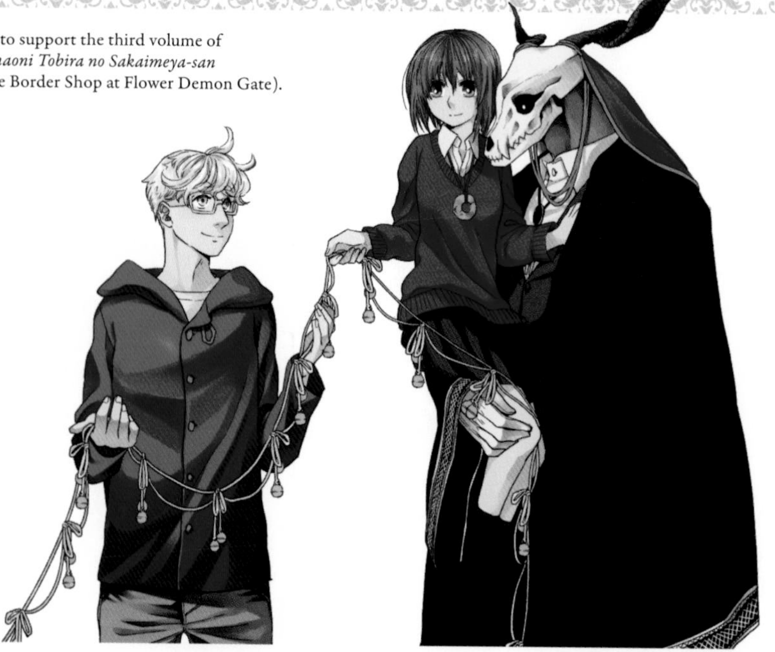

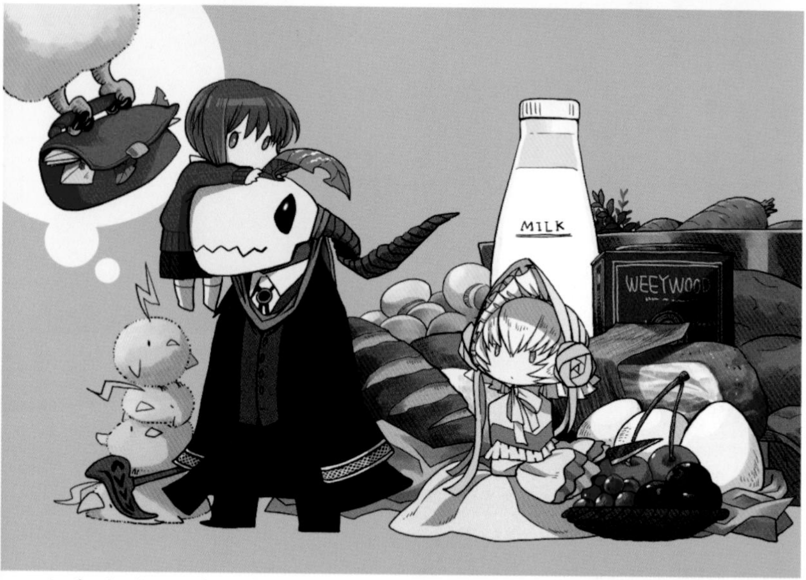
MILK
WEEYWOOD

Art for the alternate dust jacket included with the November 2014 issue of *Gekkan Comic Garden*.

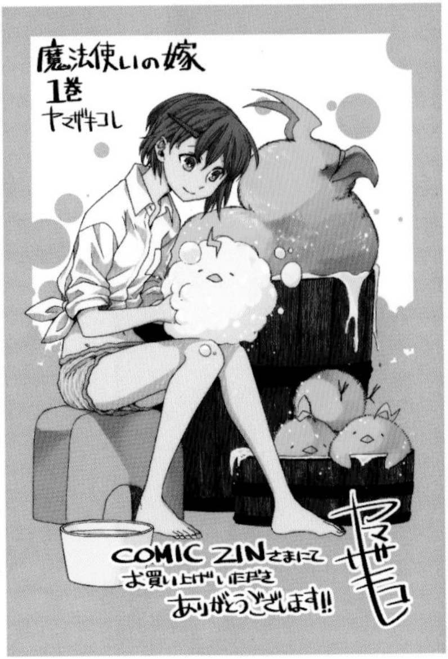
魔法使いの嫁
1巻
ヤマザキコレ
COMIC ZINさまにて
お買い上げいただき
ありがとうございます!!
ヤマザキコレ

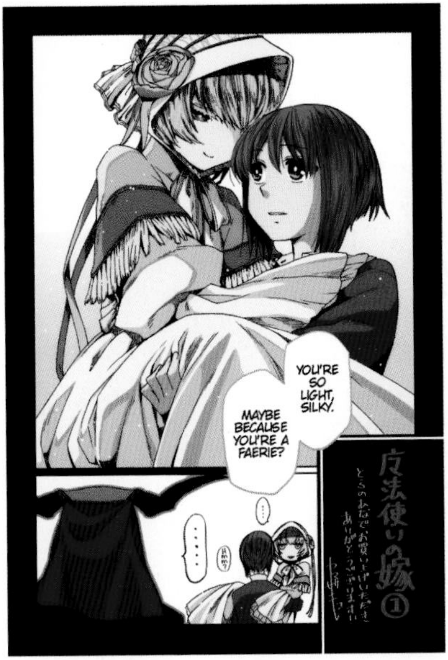
YOU'RE SO LIGHT, SILKY.
MAYBE BECAUSE YOU'RE A FAERIE?
魔法使いの嫁①
とらのあなでお買い上げいただき
ありがとうございます
ヤマザキコレ

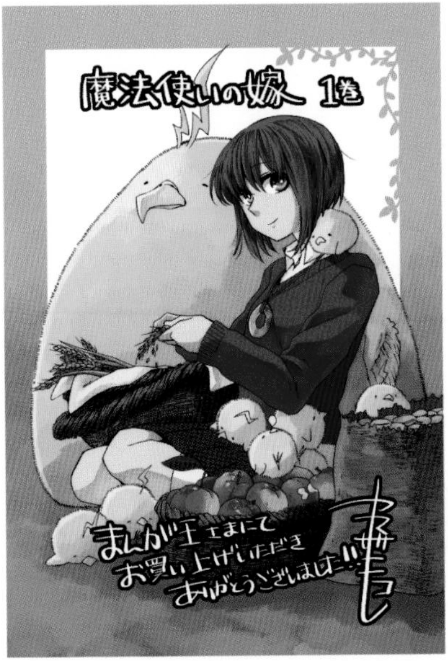
魔法使いの嫁 1巻
まんが王さまにて
お買い上げいただき
ありがとうございます!!
ヤマザキコレ

Merkmal

UPPER RIGHT
Volume 1 retailer illustration card:
"Thank you for your purchase at Comic Zin!"

UPPER LEFT
Volume 1 retailer illustration card:
"Thank you for your purchase at Toranoana!!"

LOWER LEFT
Volume 1 retailer illustration card:
"Thank you for your purchase at Mangaoh!!"

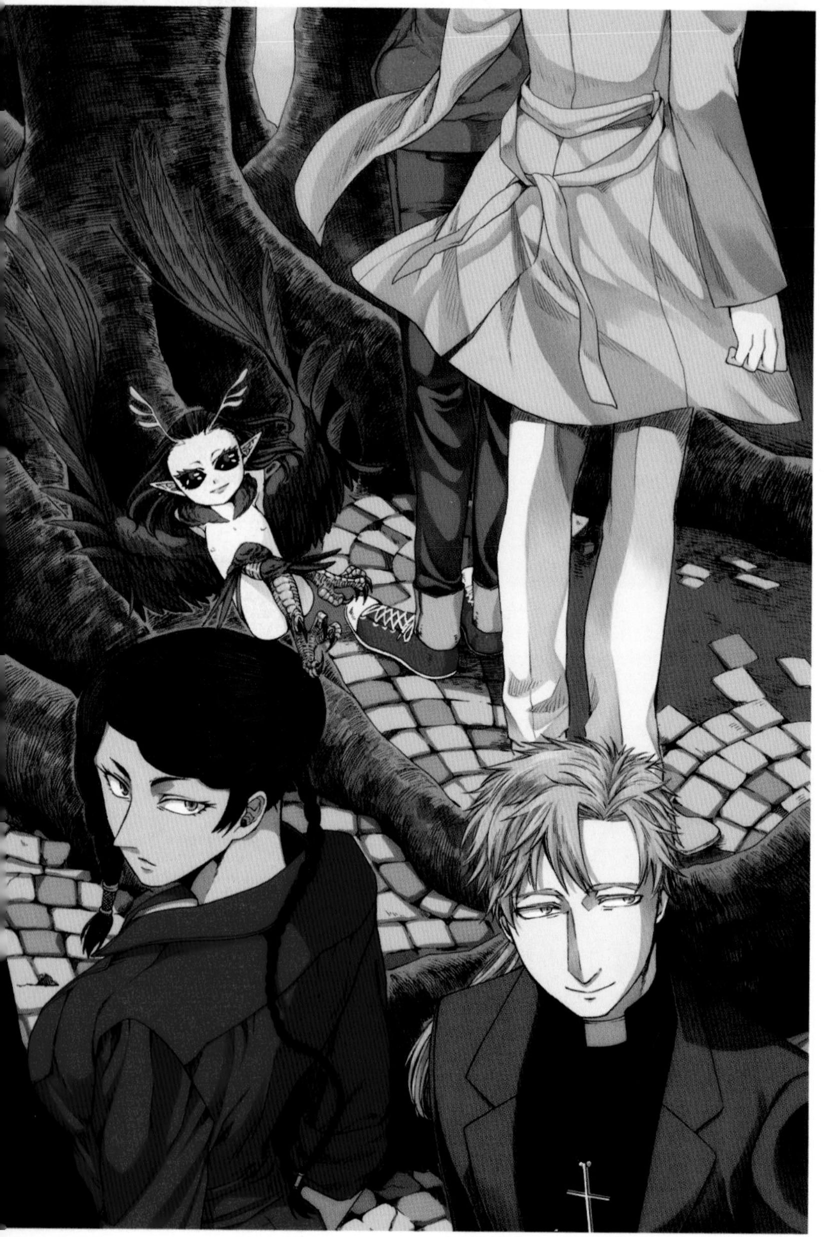

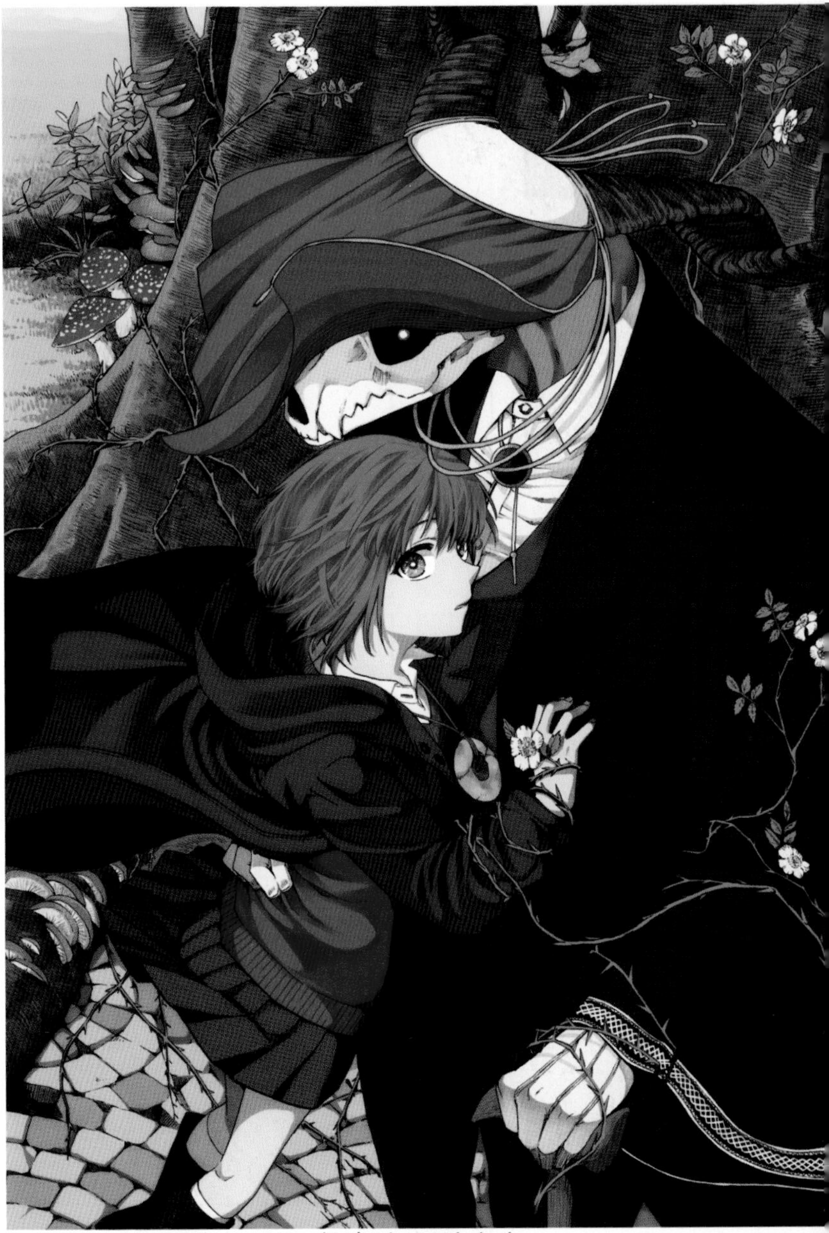

Leaflet for purchasers of *The Ancient Magus' Bride* Vol. 1 at Melonbooks.

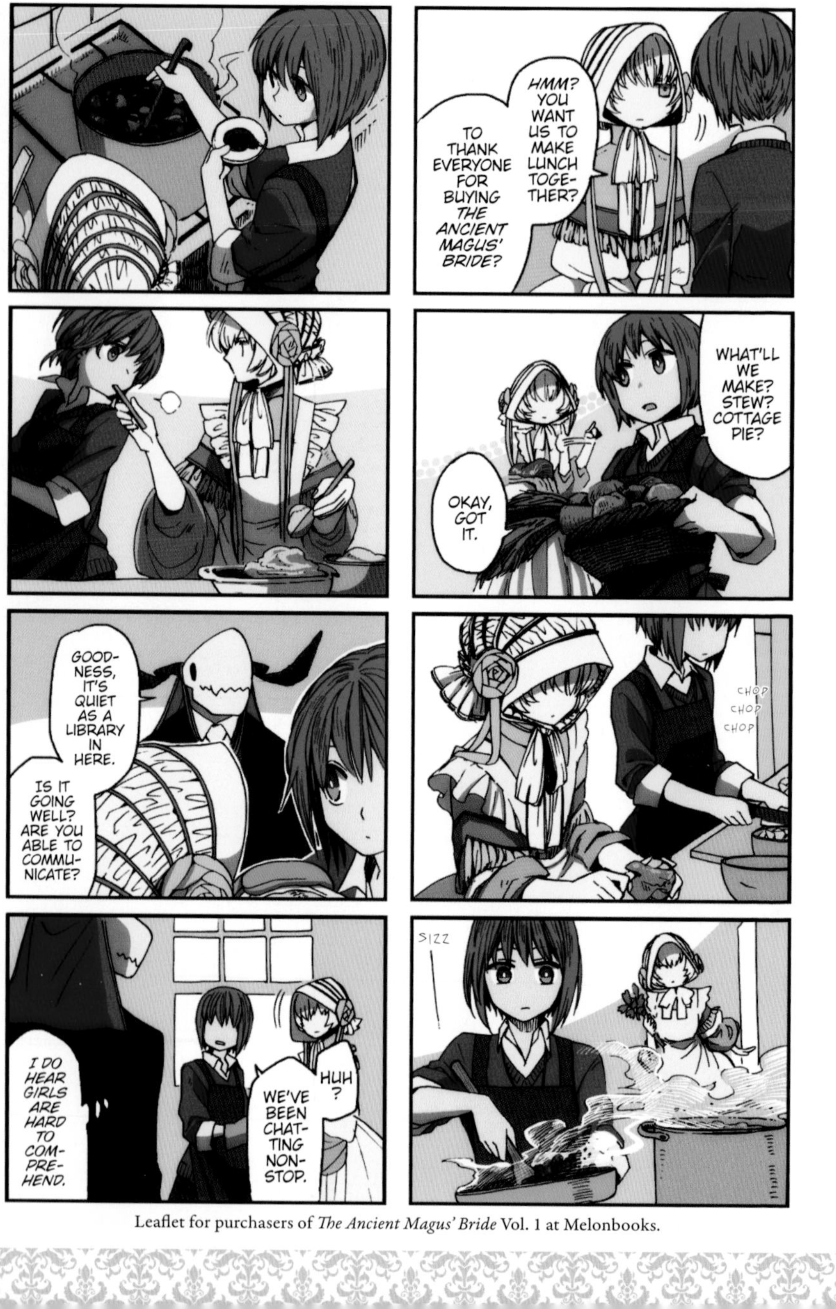
HMM? YOU WANT US TO MAKE LUNCH TOGE-THER?
TO THANK EVERYONE FOR BUYING *THE ANCIENT MAGUS' BRIDE?*
WHAT'LL WE MAKE? STEW? COTTAGE PIE?
OKAY, GOT IT.
CHOP CHOP CHOP
GOOD-NESS, IT'S QUIET AS A LIBRARY IN HERE.
IS IT GOING WELL? ARE YOU ABLE TO COMMU-NICATE?
SIZZ
I DO HEAR GIRLS ARE HARD TO COM-PRE-HEND.
HUH?
WE'VE BEEN CHAT-TING NON-STOP.

Leaflet for purchasers of *The Ancient Magus' Bride* Vol. 1 at Melonbooks.

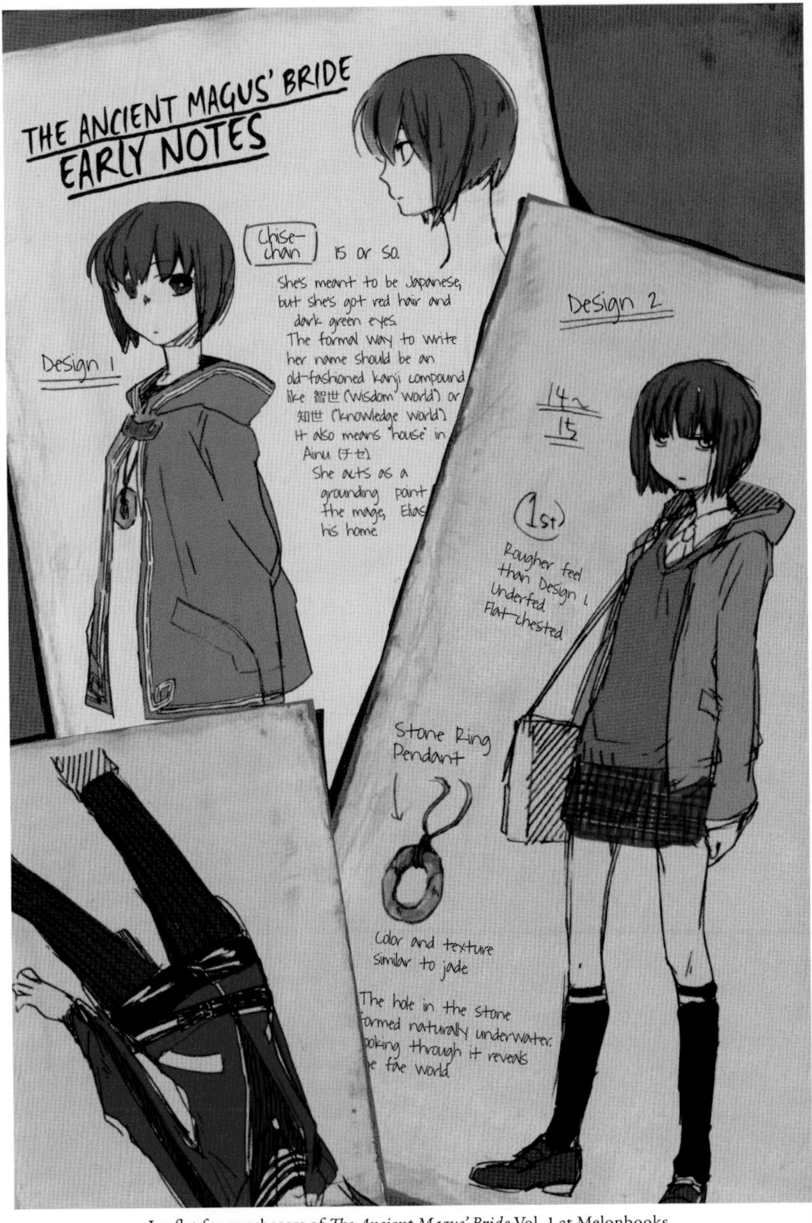
THE ANCIENT MAGUS' BRIDE
EARLY NOTES
Chise-chan
15 or so.
She's meant to be Japanese, but she's got red hair and dark green eyes.
The formal way to write her name should be an old-fashioned kanji compound like 智世 ("wisdom world") or 知世 ("knowledge world").
It also means "house" in Ainu (チセ).
She acts as a grounding point the mage, Elias his home.
Design 1
Design 2
14~15
1st
Rougher feel than Design 1. Underfed. Flat-chested
Stone Ring Pendant
Color and texture similar to jade
The hole in the stone formed naturally underwater. ooking through it reveals e fae world.

Leaflet for purchasers of *The Ancient Magus' Bride* Vol. 1 at Melonbooks.

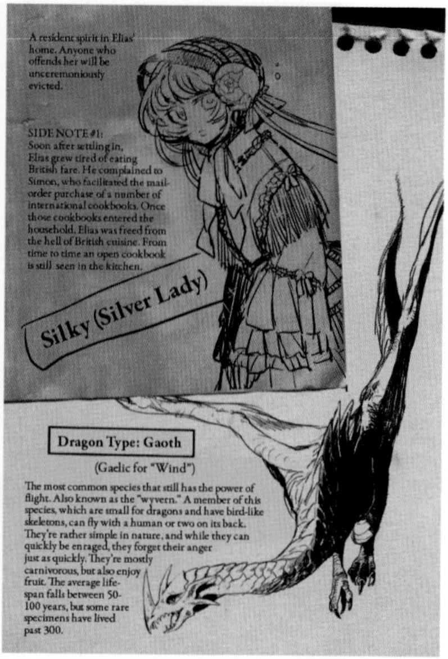
A resident spirit in Elias' home. Anyone who offends her will be unceremoniously evicted.
SIDE NOTE #1:
Soon after settling in, Elias grew tired of eating British fare. He complained to Simon, who facilitated the mail-order purchase of a number of international cookbooks. Once those cookbooks entered the household, Elias was freed from the hell of British cuisine. From time to time an open cookbook is still seen in the kitchen.
Silky (Silver Lady)
Dragon Type: Gaoth
(Gaelic for "Wind")
The most common species that still has the power of flight. Also known as the "wyvern." A member of this species, which are small for dragons and have bird-like skeletons, can fly with a human or two on its back. They're rather simple in nature, and while they can quickly be enraged, they forget their anger just as quickly. They're mostly carnivorous, but also enjoy fruit. The average life-span falls between 50-100 years, but some rare specimens have lived past 300.

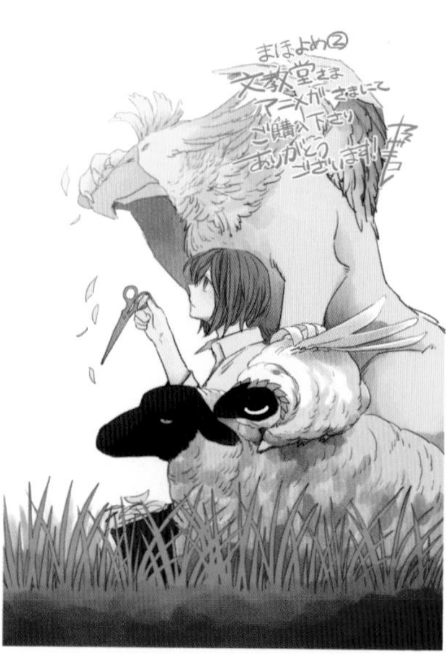
まほよめ②
文教堂さま
アニメガさまにて
ご購入下さり
ありがとうございます！

Merkmal

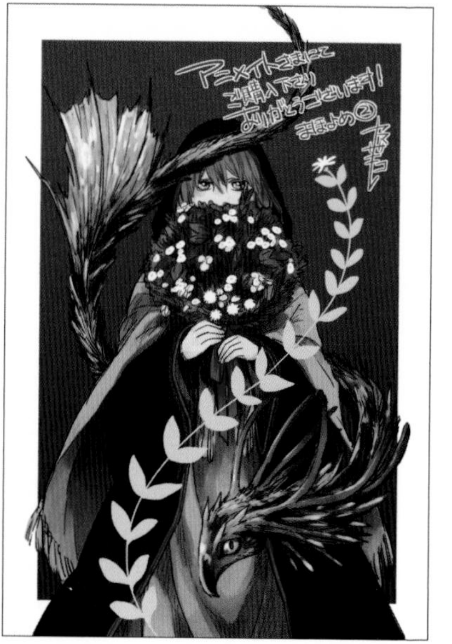
アニメイトさまにて
ご購入下さり
ありがとうございます！
まほよめ②

UPPER RIGHT
Volume 2 retailer illustration card: "Thank you for your purchase at Bunkyodo/Animega!"

UPPER LEFT
Leaflet for purchasers of *The Ancient Magus' Bride* Vol. 2 at Melonbooks.

LOWER LEFT
Volume 2 retailer illustration card: "Thank you for your purchase at Animate!"

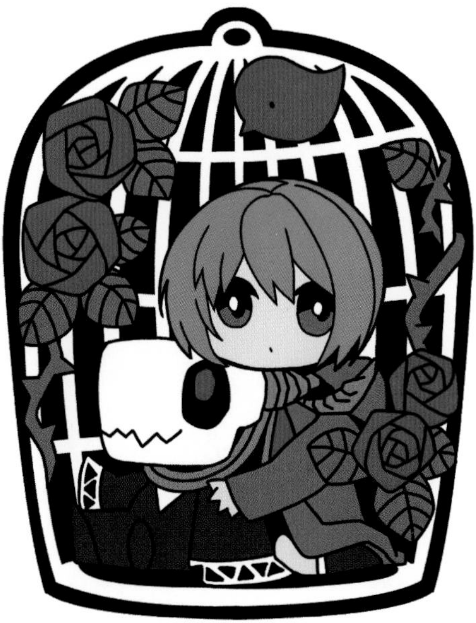

Rubber phone charm included with *The Ancient Magus' Bride* Vol. 3 (Limited Edition).

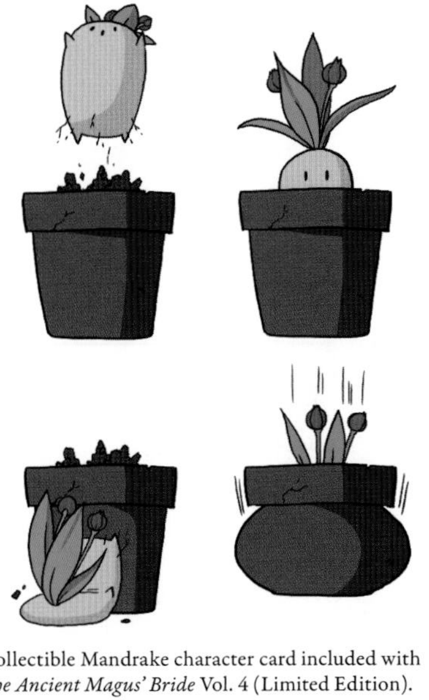

Collectible Mandrake character card included with *The Ancient Magus' Bride* Vol. 4 (Limited Edition).

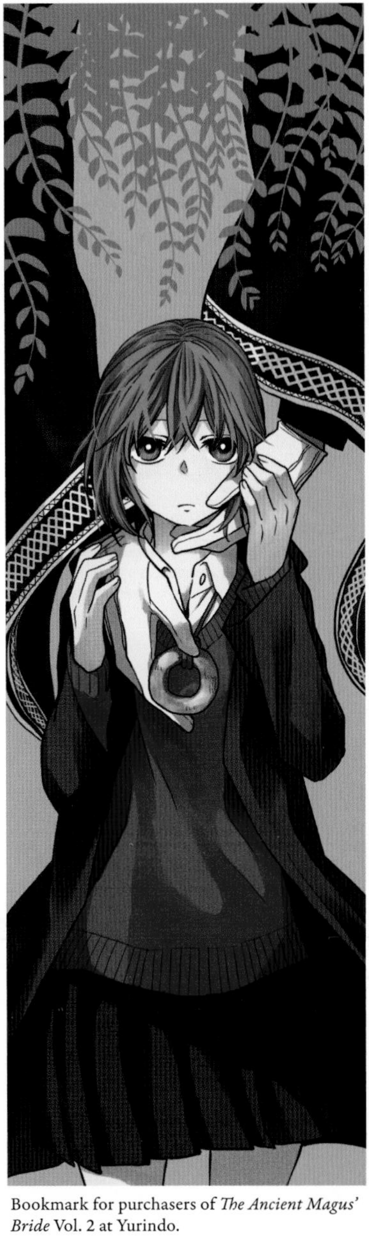

Bookmark for purchasers of *The Ancient Magus' Bride* Vol. 2 at Yurindo.

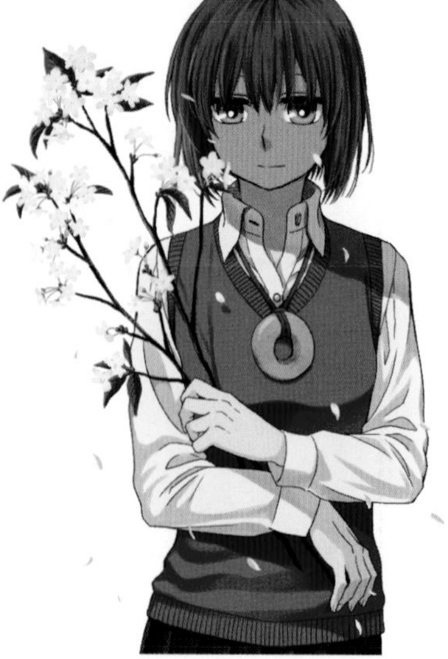

Collectible Chise character card included with *The Ancient Magus' Bride* Vol. 4 (Limited Edition).

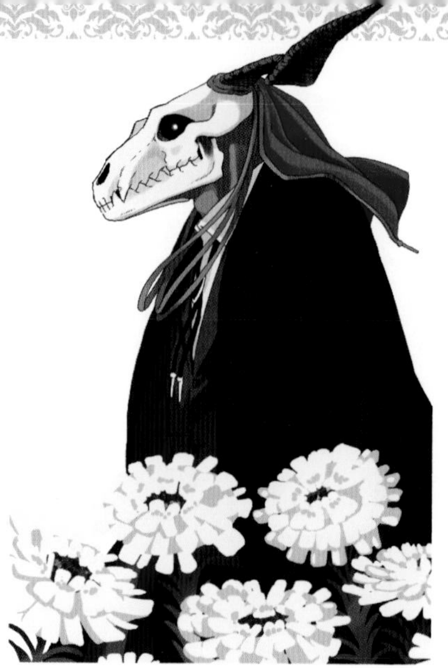

Collectible Elias character card included with *The Ancient Magus' Bride* Vol. 4 (Limited Edition).

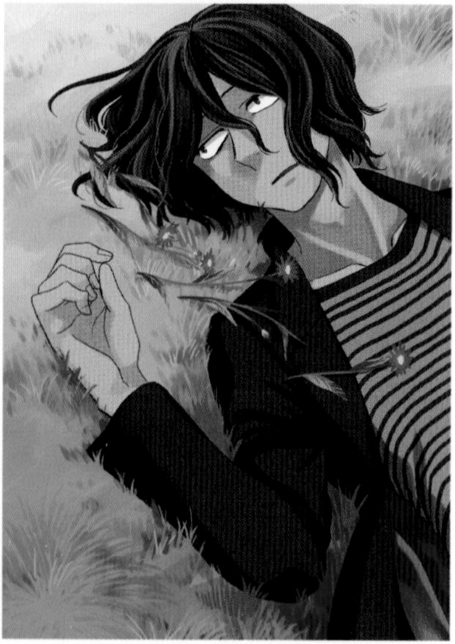

Collectible Ruth character card included with *The Ancient Magus' Bride* Vol. 4 (Limited Edition).

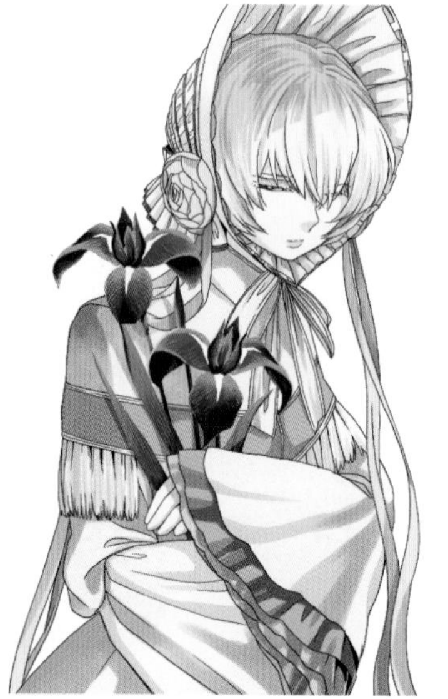

Collectible Silky character card included with *The Ancient Magus' Bride* Vol. 4 (Limited Edition).

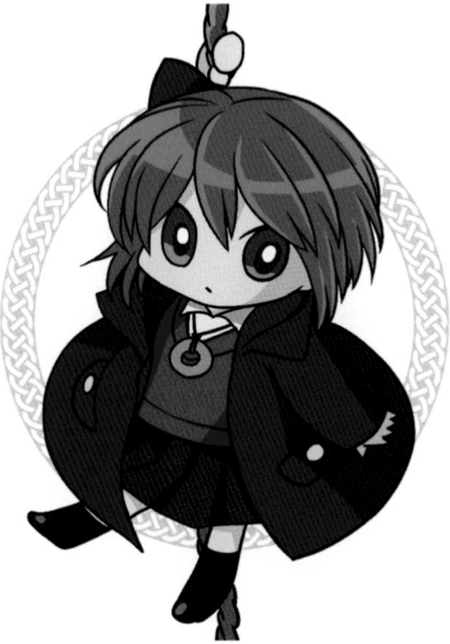

Collectible Chise acrylic charm included with *The Ancient Magus' Bride* Vol. 4 (Limited Edition).

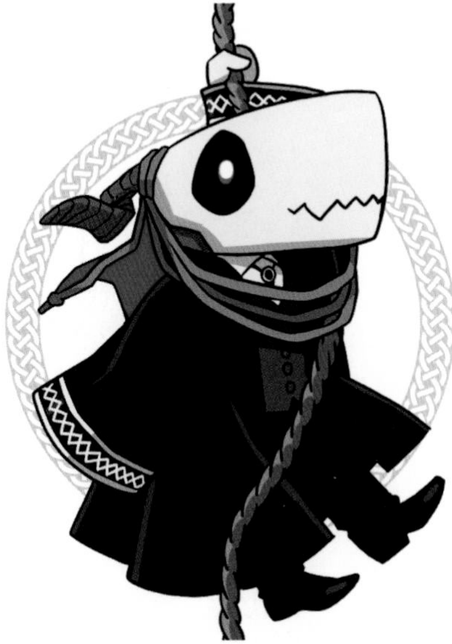

Collectible Elias acrylic charm included with the October 2015 issue of *Gekkan Comic Garden*.

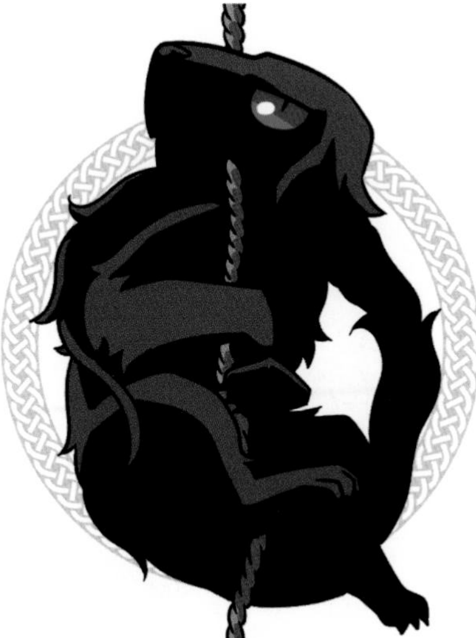

Collectible Ruth acrylic charm included with *The Ancient Magus' Bride* Vol. 4 (Limited Edition).

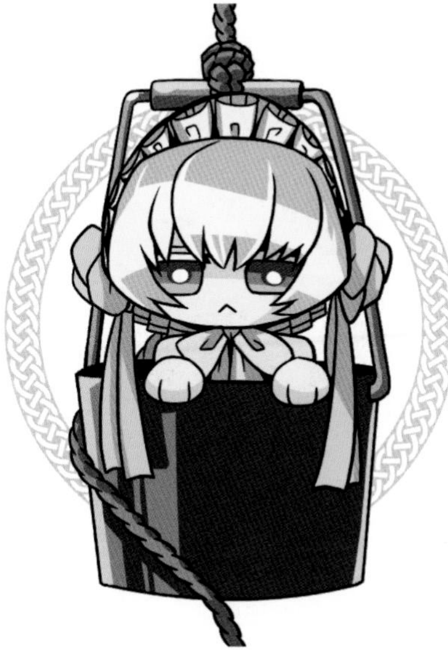

Collectible Silky acrylic charm included with the October 2015 issue of *Gekkan Comic Garden*.

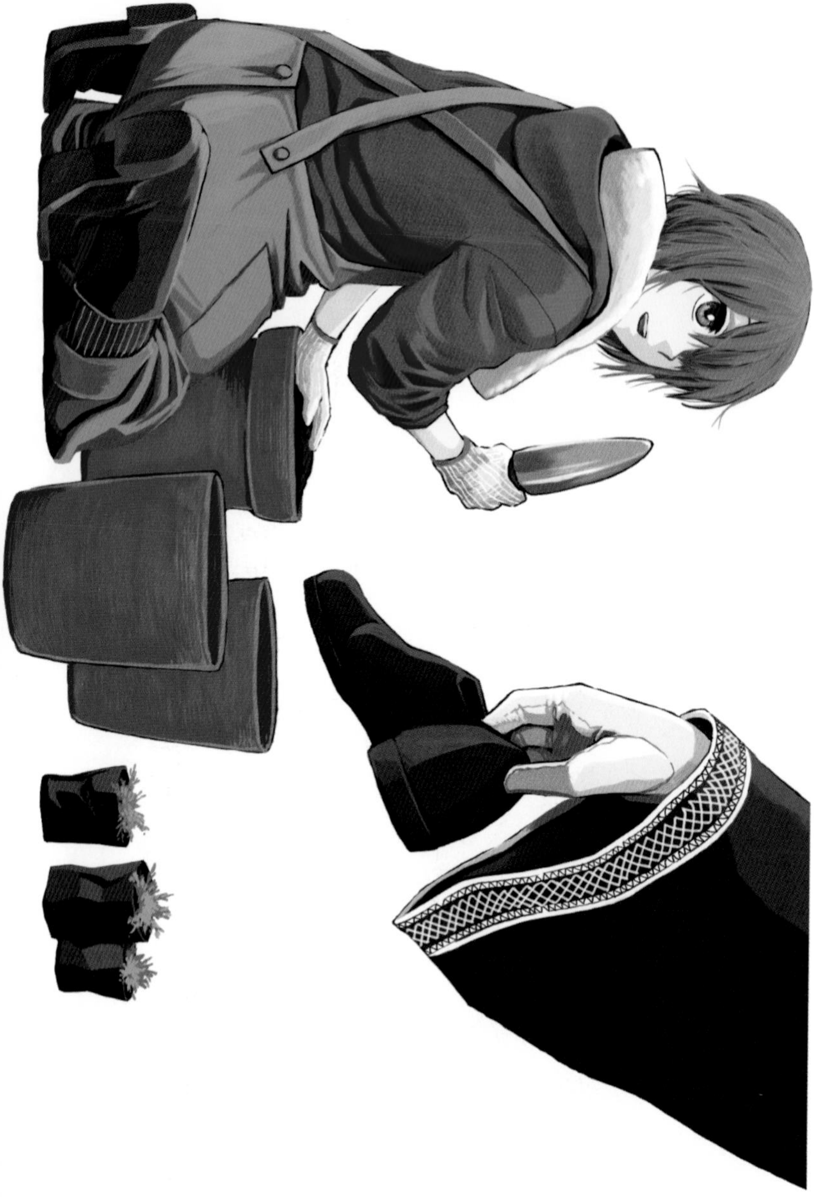

Wraparound illustration for the Radio Drama CD included with *The Ancient Magus' Bride* Vol. 5 (Limited Edition).

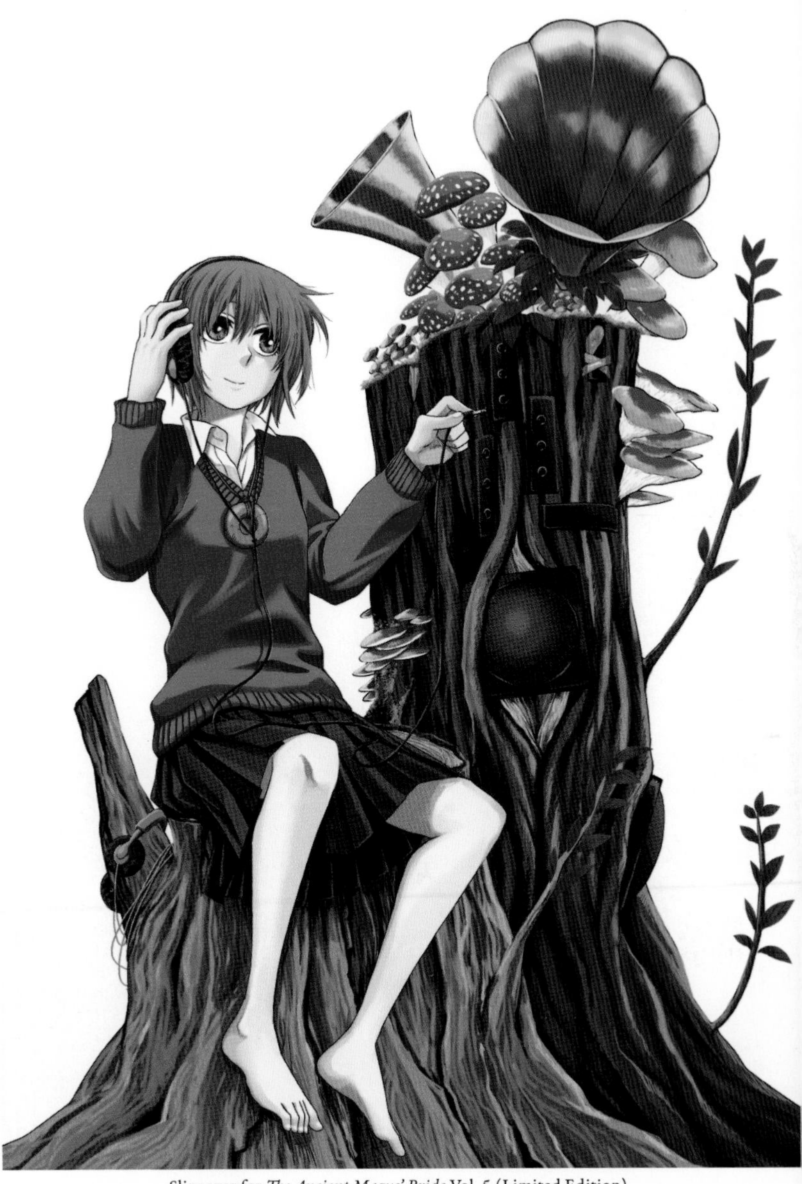

Slipcover for *The Ancient Magus' Bride* Vol. 5 (Limited Edition).

The Ancient Magus' Bride

Merkmal

CONTENTS

1

Characters

The *Ancient Magus' Bride* is full of marvelous characters, and now it's time to get to know them better! This section contains profiles with previously-unrevealed information.

Chise Hatori

Our protagonist. Her ability to see beyond the human world caused her father to leave and her mother to commit suicide. Left alone in the world, she was passed from relative to relative. At fifteen, she puts herself up for auction and is purchased by Elias. As a "sleigh beggy," she has unusual physical traits.

CHISE HATORI	
AGE:	16 (as of Vol. 8)
ORIGIN:	Japan
HEIGHT:	155cm (5′1″)
WEIGHT:	54kg (119lb)
RACE:	Human
SEX:	Female

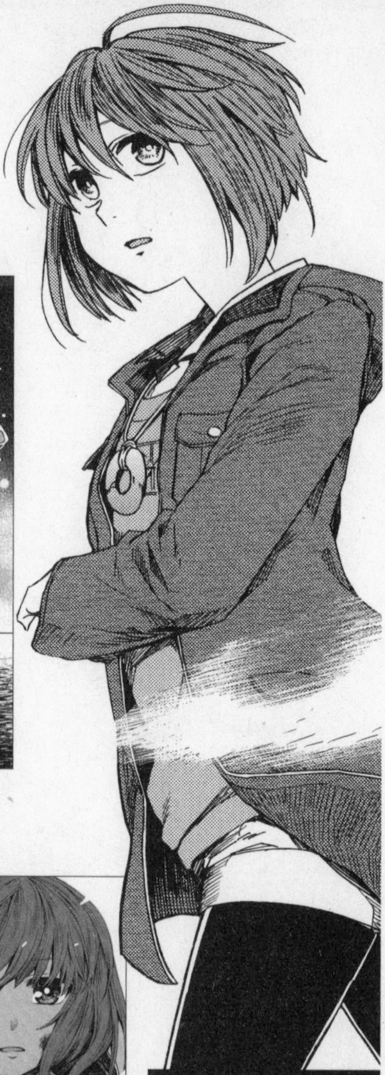

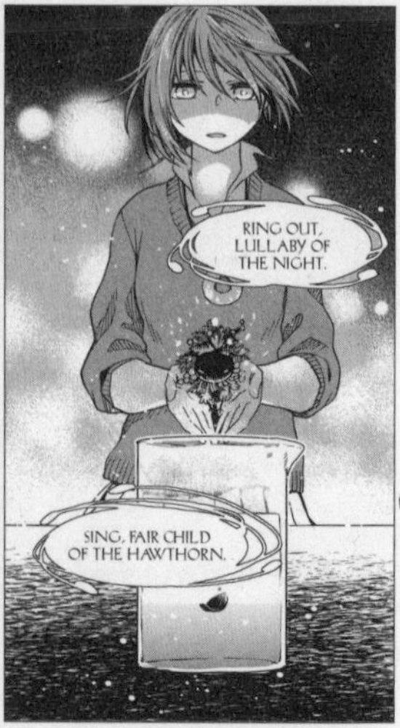
RING OUT, LULLABY OF THE NIGHT.
SING, FAIR CHILD OF THE HAWTHORN.

Upon purchasing Chise, Elias makes her his apprentice. She begins to spend her days training as an apprentice mage.

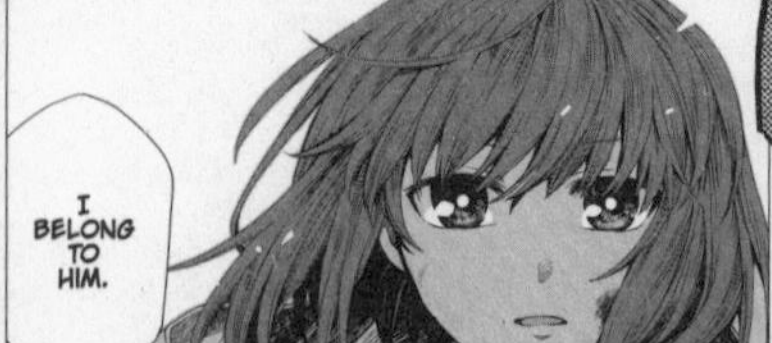
I BELONG TO HIM.

Elias declares that Chise is not only his apprentice but his bride. Although they were brought together by his purchase of her, Chise's growing feelings about him are genuine.

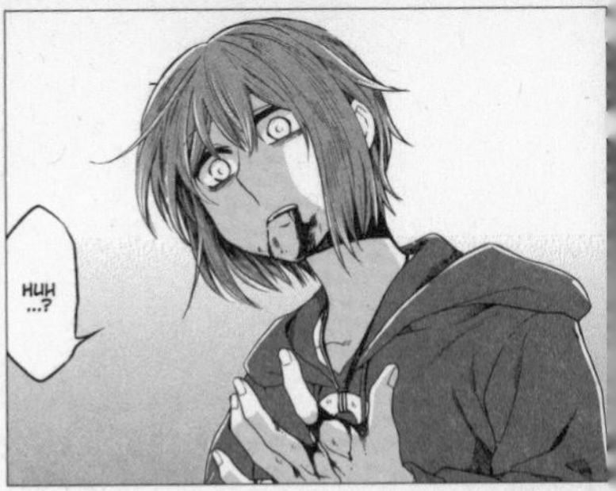
HUH ...?

Sleigh beggy are destined to live brief lives. The heavy strain on their bodies results in symptoms such as coughing up blood and falling into comas from magic loss.

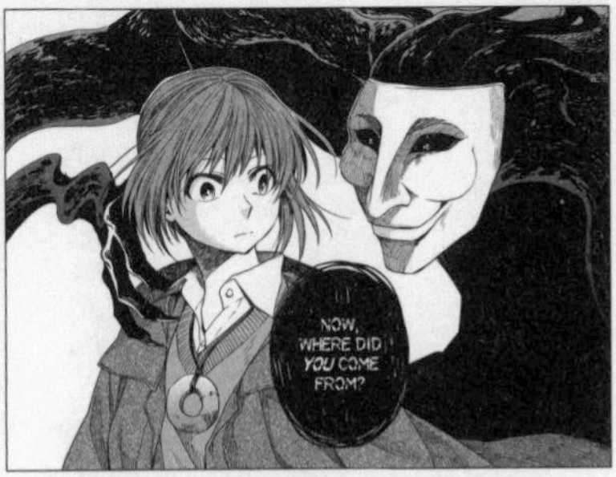
NOW, WHERE DID YOU COME FROM?

Chise's inherent nature attracts the attention of neighbors. Some are unsavory and downright dangerous.

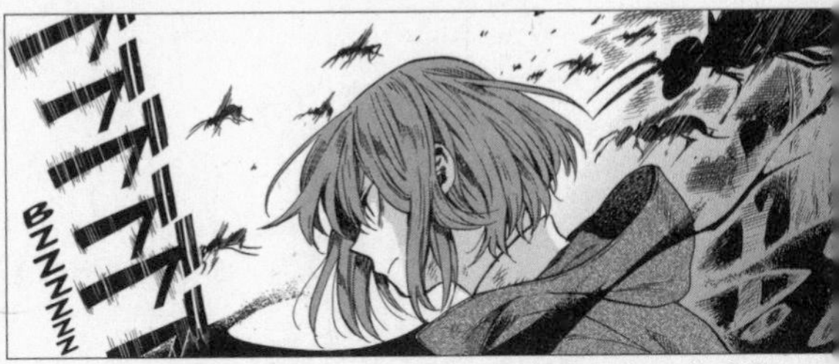
BZZZZZZ

Chise rarely shows how she feels, but it's obvious what she thinks of Cartaphilus' self-centeredness and ego

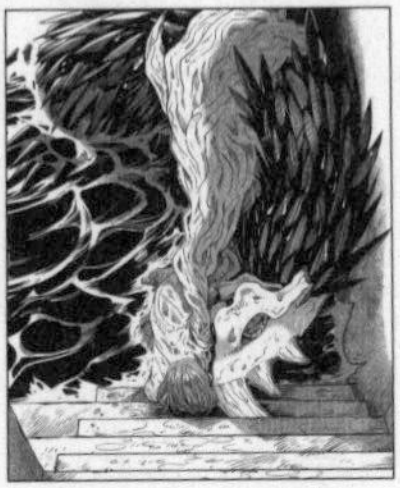

A dragon's curse causes Chise's arm to undergo a dramatic transformation.

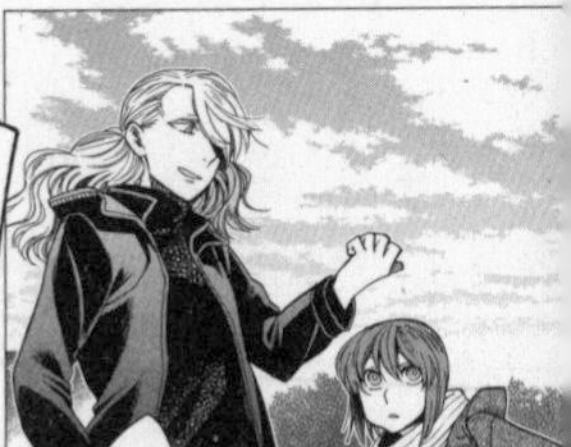
LET'S GET GOING.
YOU'VE GOT A TRAIN TO CATCH! WE'D BETTER MAKE UP OUR MINDS FAST.

Chise and Alice are initially at odds, but their similar roles as apprentices bring them close. Alice is one of Chise few friends.

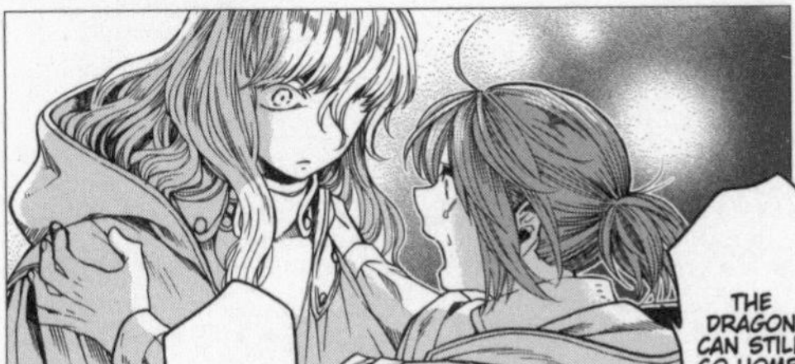
THE DRAGON CAN STILL GO HOME!
SHE WANTS TO GO HOME!
SHE HAS A PLACE TO CALL HOME!

When Chise stands up for something, it's always for someone else's sake. Is it kindness that makes her act on behalf of others, such as a leannán sídhe or a dragon, or something else...?

KNOWN AS
+ **MAGES:** Sleigh Beggy
+ **FAE:** Robin

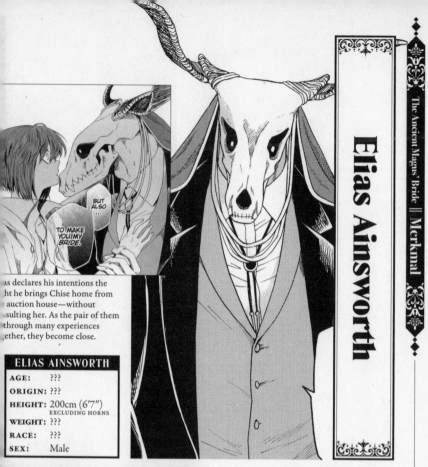

Elias Ainsworth

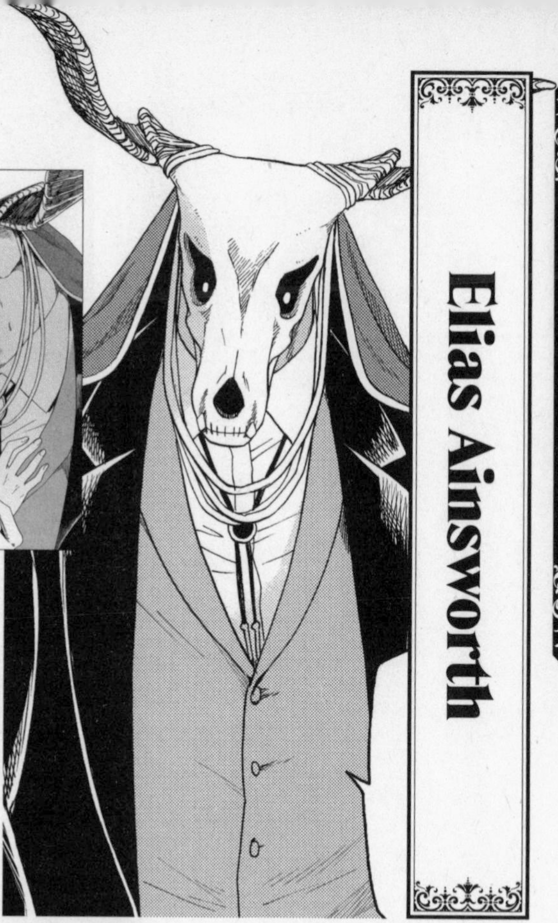

The mage who purchases Chise at an auction. As one of the few remaining true mages, he is monitored by the Church. He buys Chise as an apprentice, but also announces that he intends to make her his bride. He is humanoid, but his head looks like an antlered skull. He is famed as a misanthropic recluse.

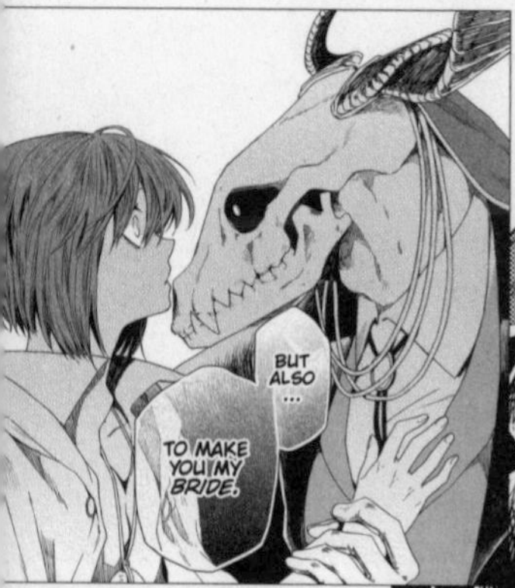
BUT ALSO ...
TO MAKE YOU MY BRIDE.

as declares his intentions the ht he brings Chise home from auction house—without sulting her. As the pair of them through many experiences gether, they become close.

ELIAS AINSWORTH	
AGE:	???
ORIGIN:	???
HEIGHT:	200cm (6'7") EXCLUDING HORNS
WEIGHT:	???
RACE:	???
SEX:	Male

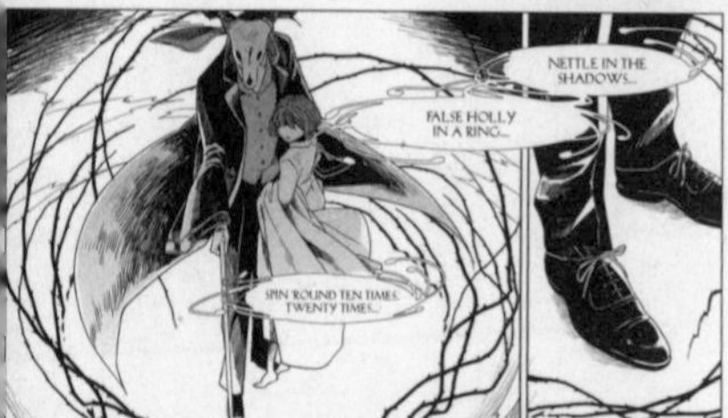
NETTLE IN THE SHADOWS...
FALSE HOLLY IN A RING...
SPIN 'ROUND TEN TIMES, TWENTY TIMES...
SPIN A SPIDER'S WEB ON THAT DISTANT BOUGH.

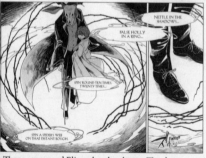

Thorns surround Elias when he chants. They're the reason he's called "the Thorn Mage."

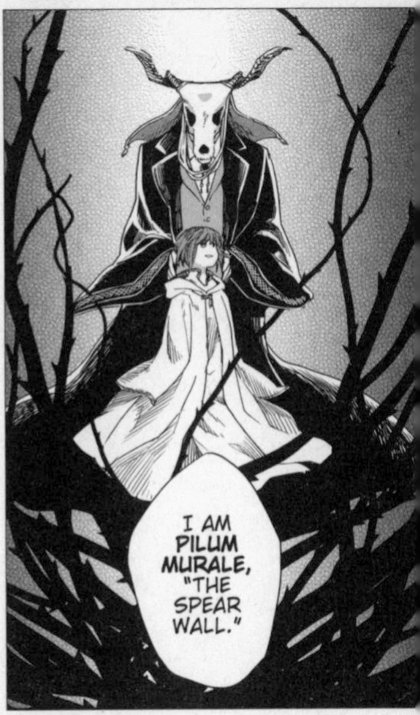
I AM PILUM MURALE, "THE SPEAR WALL."

Elias describes himself as a being of shadow. He is able to use shadows as weapons and can hide within Chise's shadow.

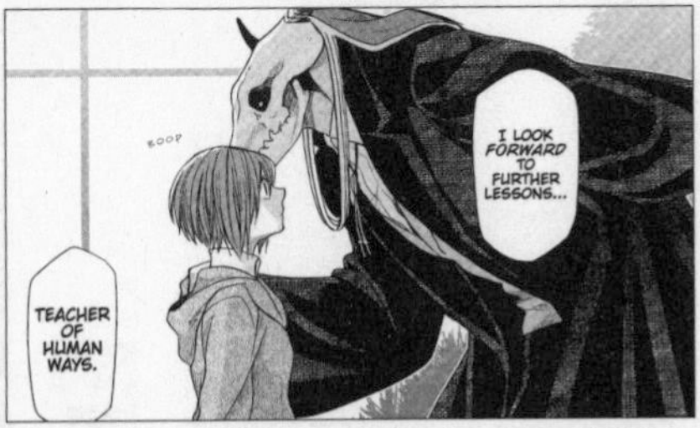
I LOOK FORWARD TO FURTHER LESSONS...
BOOP
TEACHER OF HUMAN WAYS.

Elias welcomes Chise as someone who can teach him human ways and enable him to better understand humans—including Chise herself.

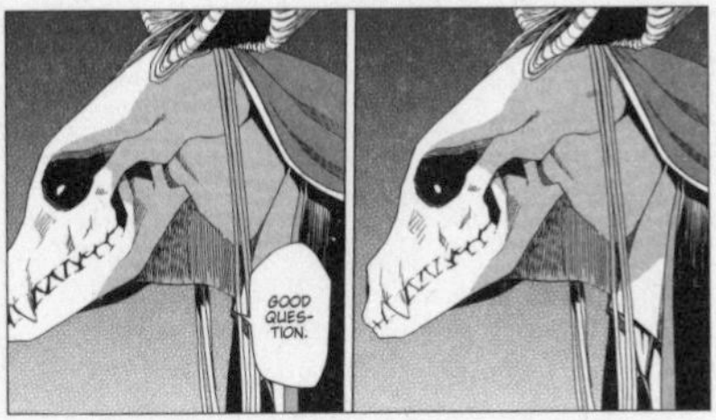
GOOD QUES-TION.

Elias' skull head makes him seem unexpressive, and yet his eyes convey a range of emotions.

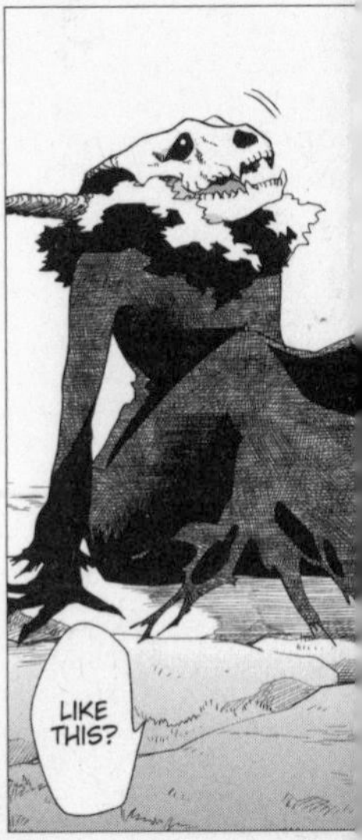
LIKE THIS?

Elias is ordinarily quite tall at two meters, but he can make himself smaller. On the flip sic when driven by rage, he can appear even more terrifying.

ANTHROPOMORPHOSIS

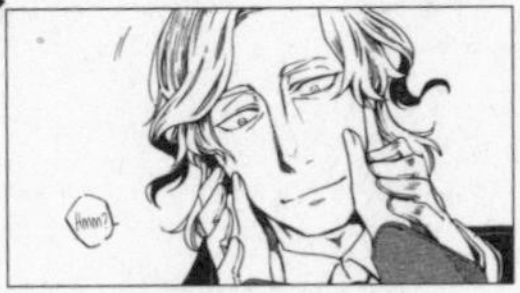
Hmm?

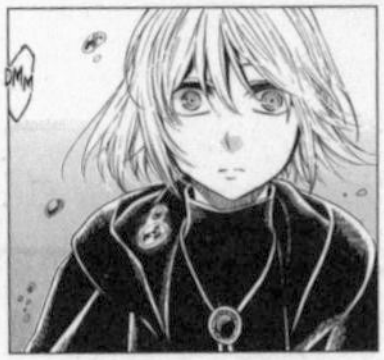

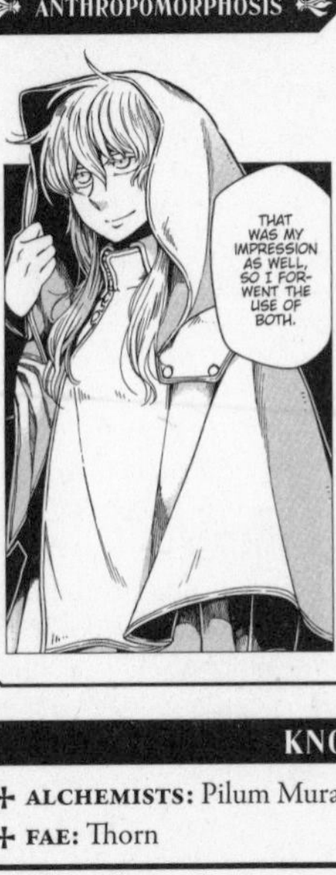
THAT WAS MY IMPRESSION AS WELL, SO I FOR-WENT THE USE OF BOTH.

Elias models his human appearances on people he knows. Simon and Chise are familiar, but who could this be?

KNOWN AS

+ **ALCHEMISTS:** Pilum Murale
+ **OBERON:** Liath Anam
+ **FAE:** Thorn

Simon Cullum

SIMON CULLUM	
AGE:	41
ORIGIN:	England
HEIGHT:	177cm (5′10″)
WEIGHT:	63kg (139lb)
RACE:	Human
SEX:	Male

A pastor charged by the Church with watching over Elias. He lives in the same village as Elias and Chise. Having observed Elias for ten years, he claims to be one of Elias' few human friends. He's not capable of performing magic or alchemy, but he can see "neighbors" such as fairies.

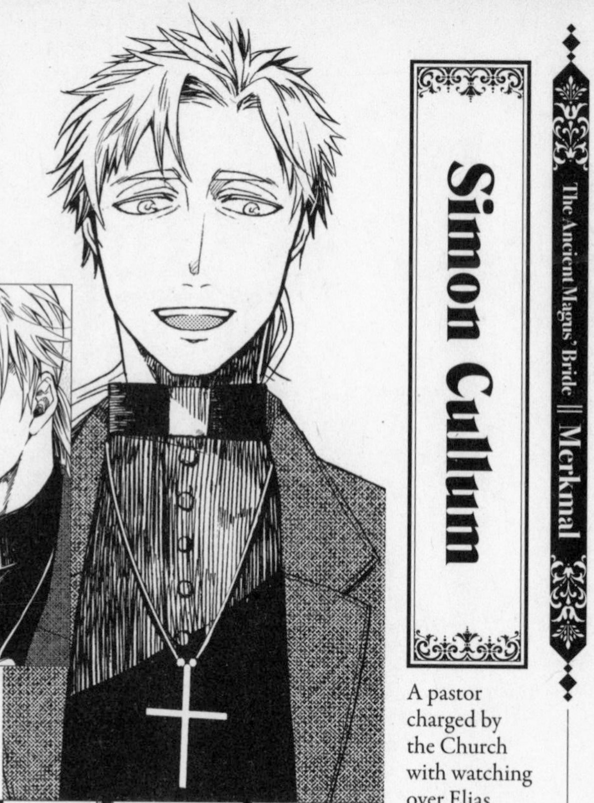

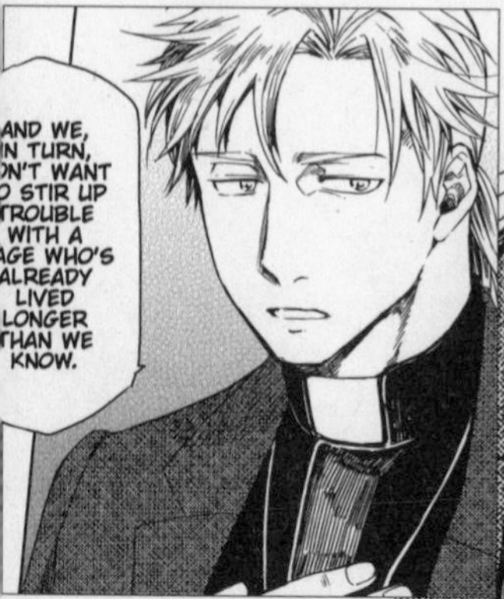
AND WE, N TURN, ON'T WANT O STIR UP TROUBLE WITH A AGE WHO'S ALREADY LIVED LONGER THAN WE KNOW.

Simon is friendly, but when there's something he has to say as Elias' observer, he does his duty. Early in the story, he makes several requests of Elias.

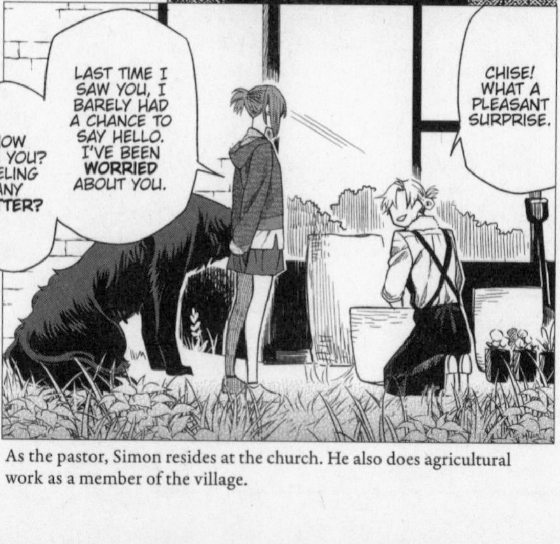
CHISE! WHAT A PLEASANT SURPRISE.
LAST TIME I SAW YOU, I BARELY HAD A CHANCE TO SAY HELLO. I'VE BEEN WORRIED ABOUT YOU.
HOW ARE YOU? FEELING ANY BETTER?

As the pastor, Simon resides at the church. He also does agricultural work as a member of the village.

> SEE AND HEAR THEM, YES, BUT THAT'S THE EXTENT OF MY GIFTS.

Though no alchemist, he can perceive "neighbors."

> TO LEARN TO READ THAT **BONY FACE** OF YOURS, CLOTH OR NO CLOTH.

> I'VE BEEN MONITORING YOU FOR OVER A DECADE! THAT'S PLENTY LONG ENOUGH FOR ME...

Although Simon has been tasked with monitoring Elias, after ten years, he feels he can call Elias a friend.

> YOU WOULDN'T THINK A PRIEST AND A MAGE WOULD GET ALONG...

Unsurprisingly, given their respective situations, Simon and Elias have their share of disagreements.

> HIS MEDICINE IS THE ONLY THING THAT EASES MY COUGH.

Simon takes Elias' medicine for the chronic cough that has plagued him his whole life. Elias' concern for Simon's health and preparation of the medicine offers them a reason to become closer.

> ....

> BAM

> BAM

> I'LL CALL AGAIN ANOTHER TIME.

Ruth tell Simon he "smells funny," and even Silky treats him coldly.

KNOWN AS
✟ **HUMANS, ELIAS:** Simon
✟ **TITANIA:** Disciple of that foreign god

> IF THIS HERMIT TIRES OF YOU, YOU'RE ALWAYS WELCOME AT MY CHURCH.

> YOU CAN LEAN ON ME.

> AHEM!

Whether because of his priestly responsibility or his innate personality, Simon treats Chise, an unexpected newcomer, with kindness.

Lindel

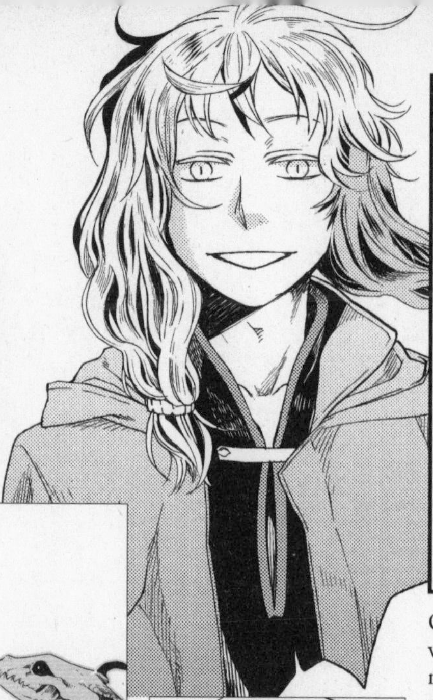

LINDEL	
AGE:	???
ORIGIN:	Finland
HEIGHT:	160cm (5′3″)
WEIGHT:	65kg (143lb)
RACE:	Human
SEX:	Male

One of the world's few mages. He and Elias are friends. He oversees the aerie in Iceland where dragons dwell, making his home there with them and shielding it from the sight of ordinary people. He was the first mage Elias ever met, and they still share a deep bond. He cares for Chise as a grandfather would.

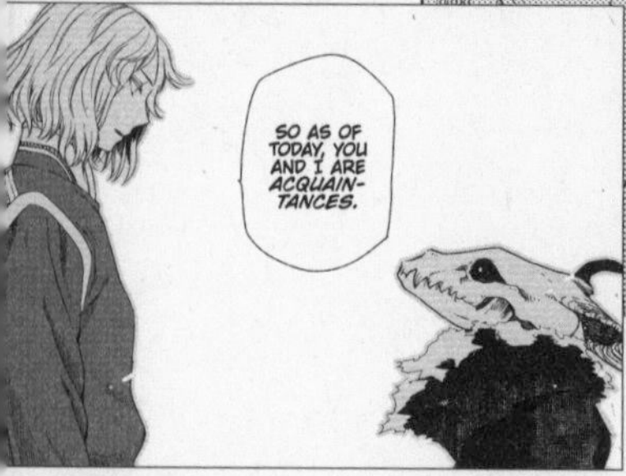
SO AS OF TODAY, YOU AND I ARE ACQUAIN-TANCES.

Lindel's master, Rahab, suggests that he take Elias as his apprentice. Lindel refuses, but does accept Elias as an "acquaintance." Over three centuries later, their relationship is still going strong.

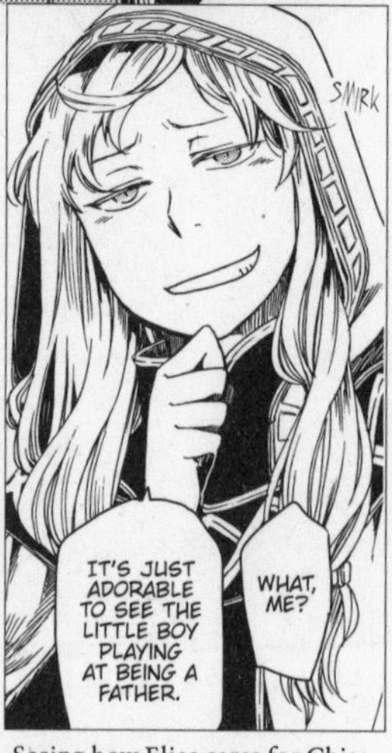
SMIRK
WHAT, ME?
IT'S JUST ADORABLE TO SEE THE LITTLE BOY PLAYING AT BEING A FATHER.

Seeing how Elias cares for Chise, Lindel teases him for "playing at being a father." Still, he calls Chise his granddaughter, and now and then displays similar concern for her.

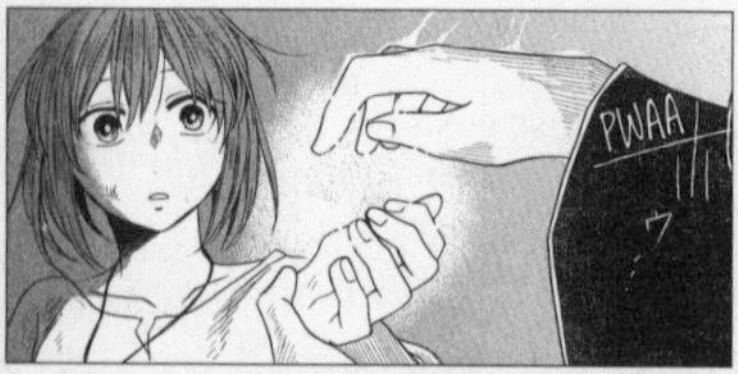
PWAA

As someone with "healing hands," Lindel can immediately heal any wound that is not mortal. Healing hands were once common among mages, but the gift is now all but extinct.

KNOWN AS	
+ MAGES:	Echos
+ RAHAB:	Tree of gatherings

Rahab

Lindel's master, and another of the few remaining mages. Lindel sees her as a "busybody," but she's the one who shows Elias his way when he is aimless. Reaching her home requires a technique for "locating what's been lost," as its whereabouts are unknown.

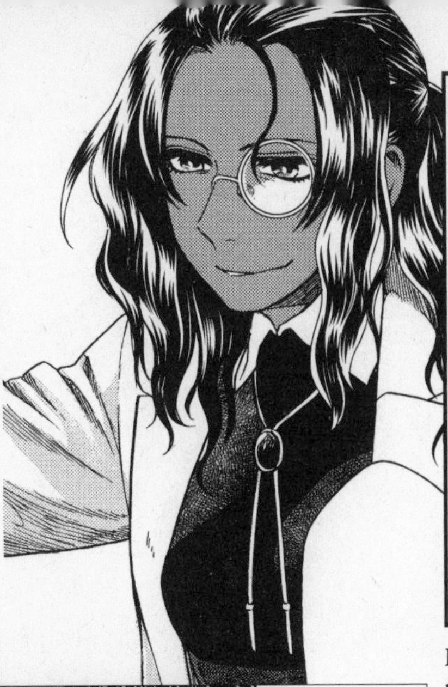

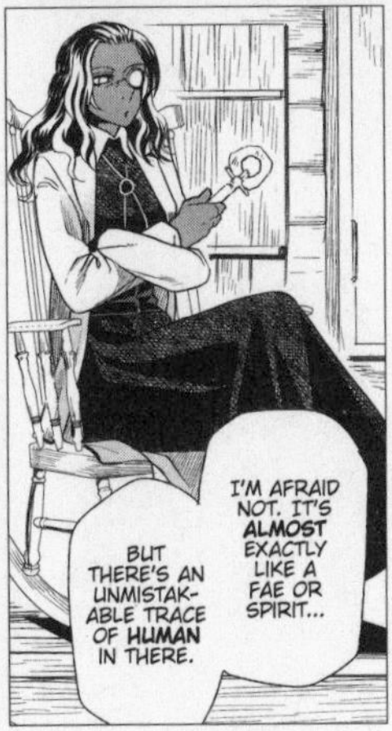
I'M AFRAID NOT. IT'S **ALMOST** EXACTLY LIKE A FAE OR SPIRIT...
BUT THERE'S AN UNMISTAK-ABLE TRACE OF **HUMAN** IN THERE.

At Lindel's request, Rahab tries to discern Elias' nature, but she's unable to pin it down. However, it's clear that Lindel trusts her immensely. She has lived far longer than he has, and has tremendous knowledge.

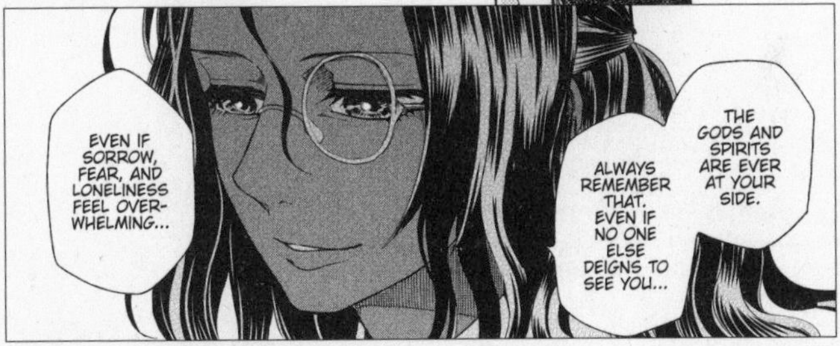
THE GODS AND SPIRITS ARE EVER AT YOUR SIDE.
ALWAYS REMEMBER THAT. EVEN IF NO ONE ELSE DEIGNS TO SEE YOU...
EVEN IF SORROW, FEAR, AND LONELINESS FEEL OVER-WHELMING...

Rahab listens to Elias, who has neither any memory of his past nor knowledge of how he should live his life. She reassures him with advice on how to move forward, with a tender maternal expression.

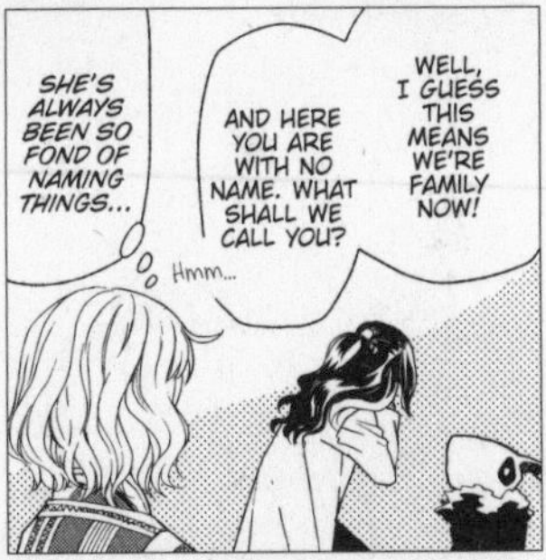
WELL, I GUESS THIS MEANS WE'RE FAMILY NOW!
AND HERE YOU ARE WITH NO NAME. WHAT SHALL WE CALL YOU?
SHE'S ALWAYS BEEN SO FOND OF NAMING THINGS...
Hmm...

Rahab names Elias, much as she once named Lindel, who is otherwise known as "Echos." The name "Lindel" comes from "the tree of gatherings."

RAHAB	
AGE:	???
ORIGIN:	West Asia
HEIGHT:	163cm (5′4″)
WEIGHT:	67kg (148lb)
RACE:	Human
SEX:	Female

KNOWN AS

+ **LINDEL:** Master

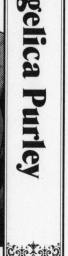

Angelica Purley

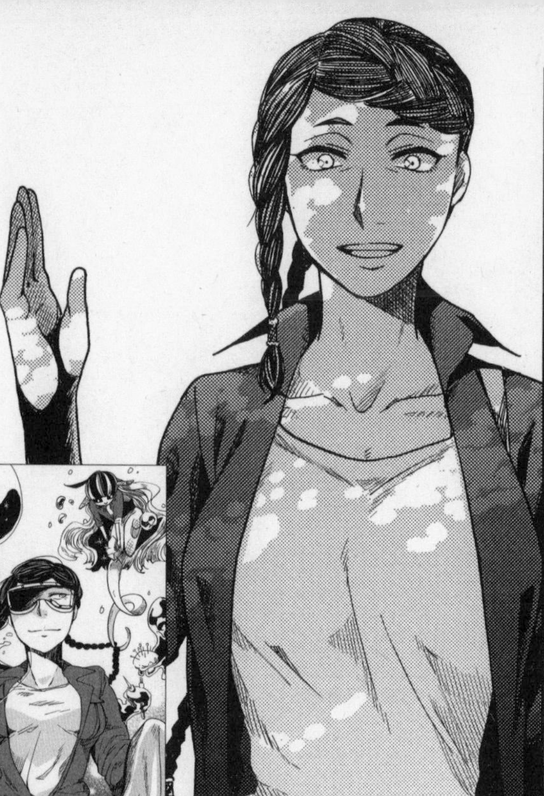

ANGELICA PURLEY	
AGE:	105
ORIGIN:	England
HEIGHT:	170cm (5′7″)
WEIGHT:	68kg (150lb)
RACE:	Human
SEX:	Female

A mage and artificer who runs a shop where she makes and sells tools needed by mages and alchemists. Her father was also an artificer of magus crafts, so she has known Elias since she was small. She is married to an ordinary human, David, and has one daughter, Althea.

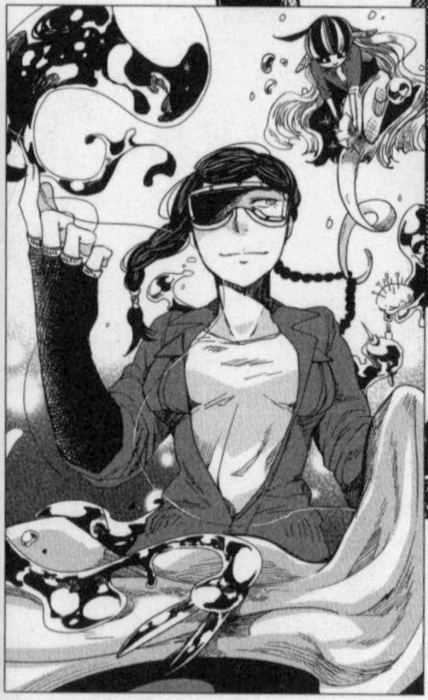

Angelica not only makes magus crafts people commission from her but fine-tunes them so they're customized for their users.

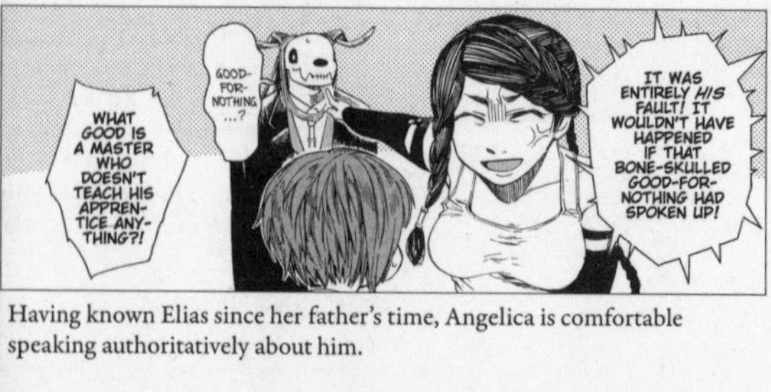
IT WAS ENTIRELY HIS FAULT! IT WOULDN'T HAVE HAPPENED IF THAT BONE-SKULLED GOOD-FOR-NOTHING HAD SPOKEN UP!
GOOD-FOR-NOTHING ...?
WHAT GOOD IS A MASTER WHO DOESN'T TEACH HIS APPRENTICE ANYTHING?!

Having known Elias since her father's time, Angelica is comfortable speaking authoritatively about him.

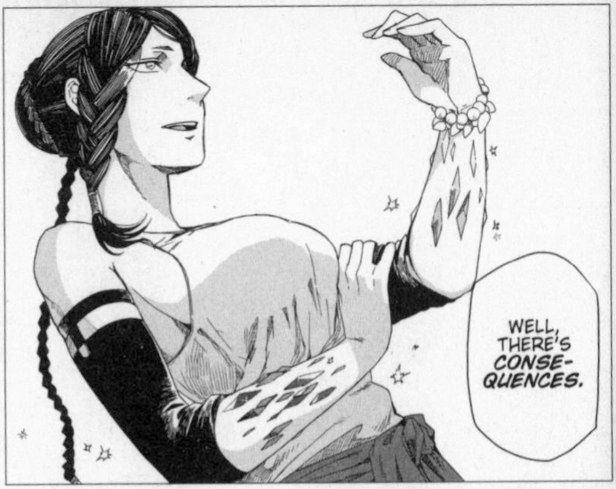
WELL, THERE'S CONSE-QUENCES.

She still carries a physical reminder of having once been careless when she studied magic as a child. She usually covers her forearms with long sleeves or bracers.

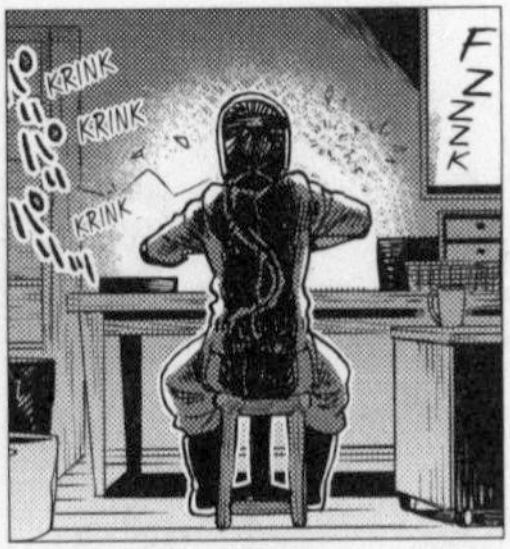
KRINK
KRINK
KRINK
FZZZK

She gets so absorbed in her work that she doesn't hear her husband speaking to her.

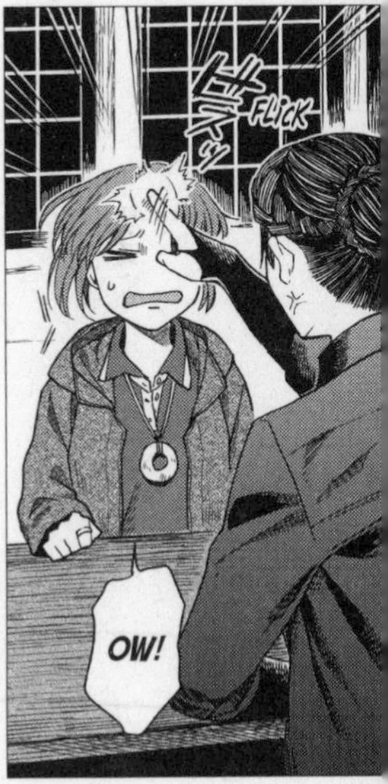
FLICK
OW!

She flicks Chise's forehead hard for hiding her poor health, but then begins to mentor her.

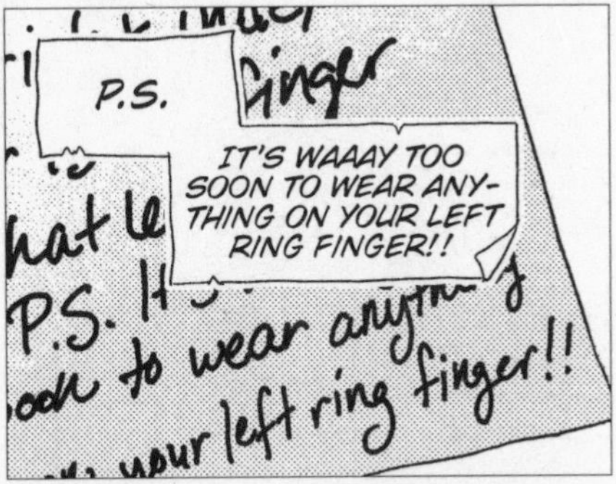
P.S.
IT'S WAAAY TOO SOON TO WEAR ANY-THING ON YOUR LEFT RING FINGER!!

Angelica includes a note with the ring Elias commissions from her. Only someone with a background like hers can truly grasp the nature of Chise and Elias' relationship.

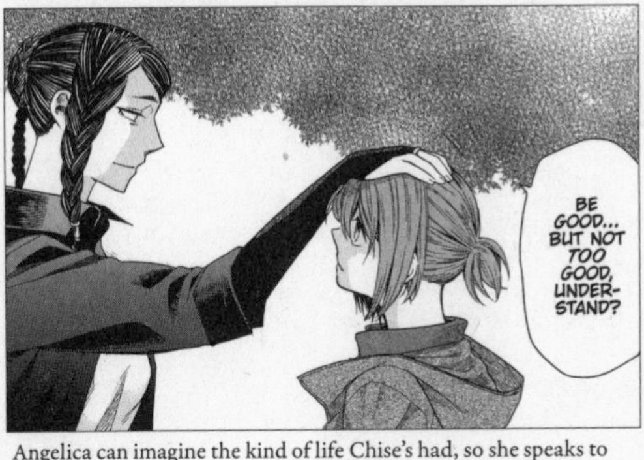
BE GOOD... BUT NOT TOO GOOD, UNDER-STAND?

Angelica can imagine the kind of life Chise's had, so she speaks to her in a motherly sort of way and tells her to be a bit more selfish.

KNOWN AS

- **ELIAS:** Gem Bee
- **DAVID, ELIAS:** Angie
- **ALTHEA:** Mama

DAVID PURLEY	
AGE:	43
ORIGIN:	England
HEIGHT:	181cm (5′11″)
WEIGHT:	79kg (174lb)
RACE:	Human
SEX:	Male

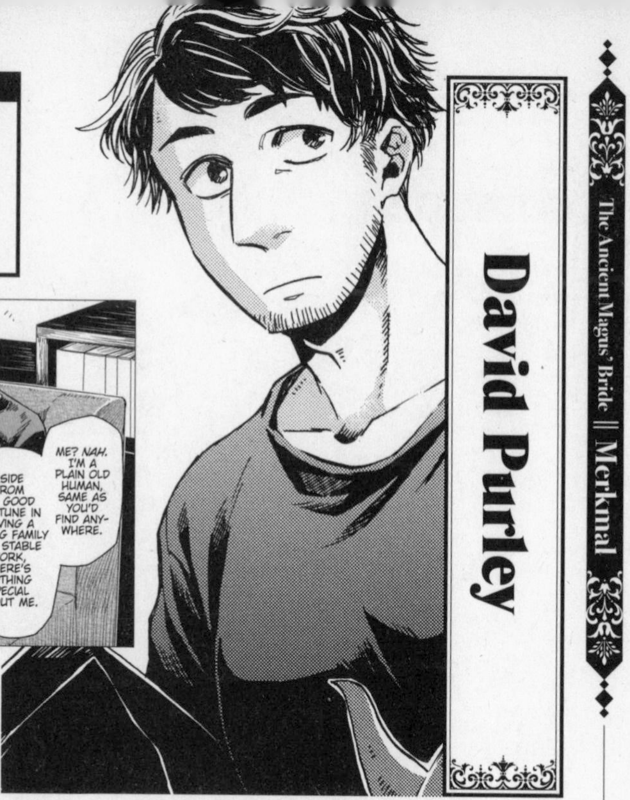

David Purley

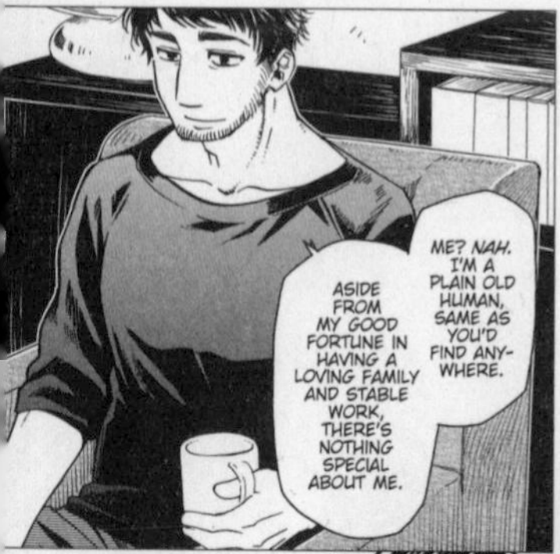
ME? *NAH.* I'M A PLAIN OLD HUMAN, SAME AS YOU'D FIND ANYWHERE.
ASIDE FROM MY GOOD FORTUNE IN HAVING A LOVING FAMILY AND STABLE WORK, THERE'S NOTHING SPECIAL ABOUT ME.

Some understandable concerns arise when an ordinary human marries a mage, but it seems to be working for them.

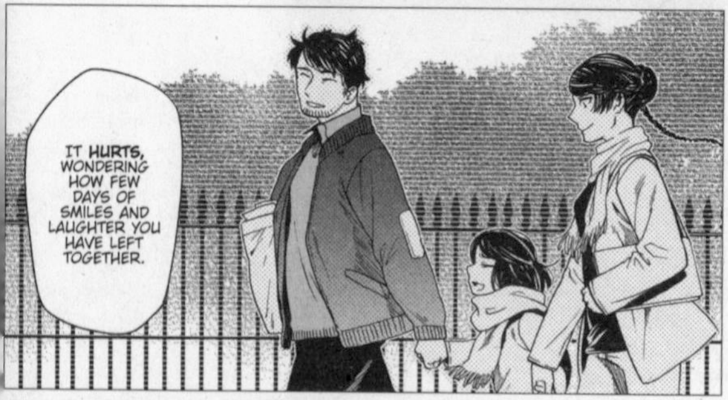
IT **HURTS**, WONDERING HOW FEW DAYS OF SMILES AND LAUGHTER YOU HAVE LEFT TOGETHER.

Their daughter has mage talent. David goes through life fully aware that he'll die long before his child does, and their happiness is bittersweet because it is fleeting.

Angelica's husband, an ordinary human—and quite the romantic! He first met Angelica over twenty years ago, and spent more than ten years wooing her. The couple has one daughter, Althea. David lives with the knowledge that they will both outlive him, but this is the family he's chosen.

KNOWN AS

+ **ANGELICA:** David
+ **ALTHEA:** Papa

Althea Purley

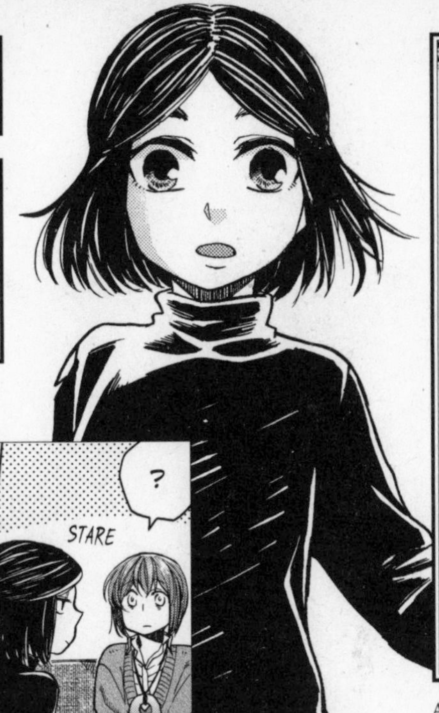

KNOWN AS	
+ ANGELICA, DAVID:	Althea

ALTHEA PURLEY	
AGE:	9
ORIGIN:	England
HEIGHT:	120cm (3′11″)
WEIGHT:	25kg (55lb)
RACE:	Human
SEX:	Female

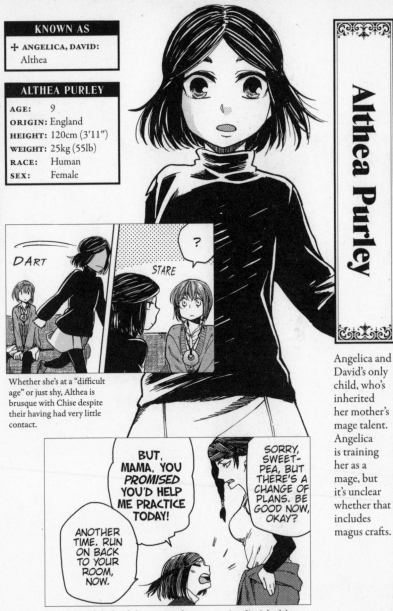

Angelica and David's only child, who's inherited her mother's mage talent. Angelica is training her as a mage, but it's unclear whether that includes magus crafts.

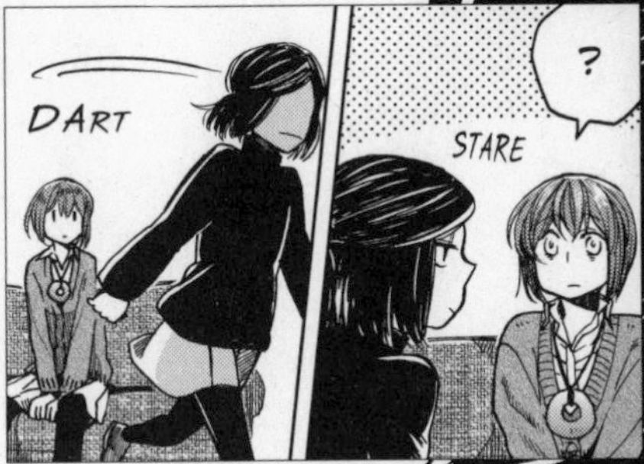
?
STARE
DART

Whether she's at a "difficult age" or just shy, Althea is brusque with Chise despite their having had very little contact.

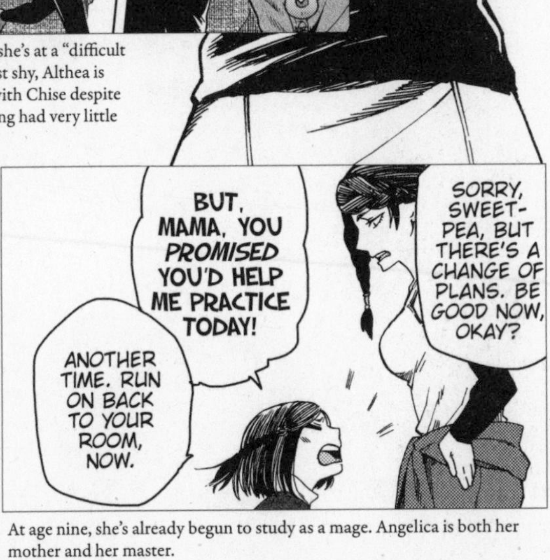
SORRY, SWEET-PEA, BUT THERE'S A CHANGE OF PLANS. BE GOOD NOW, OKAY?
BUT, MAMA, YOU PROMISED YOU'D HELP ME PRACTICE TODAY!
ANOTHER TIME. RUN ON BACK TO YOUR ROOM, NOW.

At age nine, she's already begun to study as a mage. Angelica is both her mother and her master.

Mikhail Renfred

MIKHAIL RENFRED	
AGE:	33
ORIGIN:	England
HEIGHT:	180cm (5′11″)
WEIGHT:	75kg (165lb)
RACE:	Human
SEX:	Male

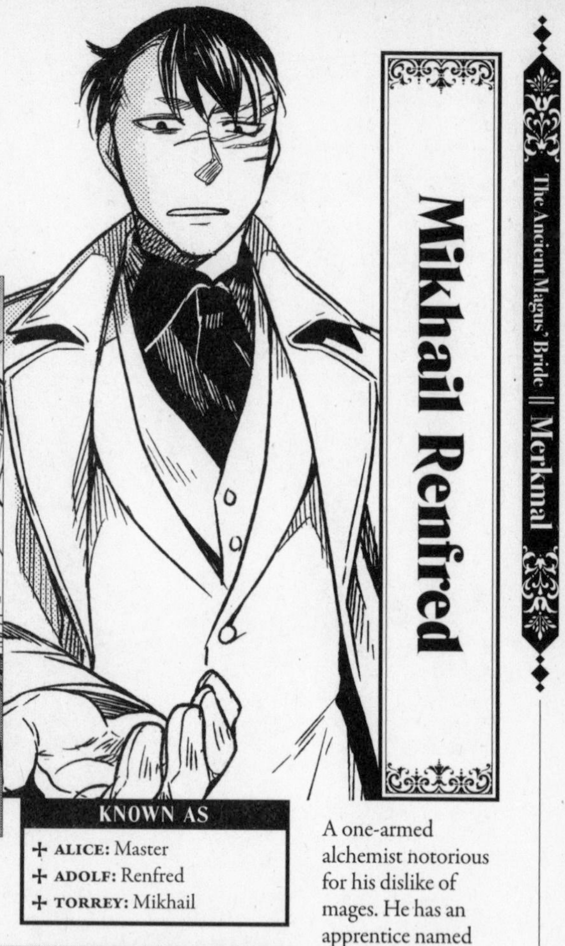

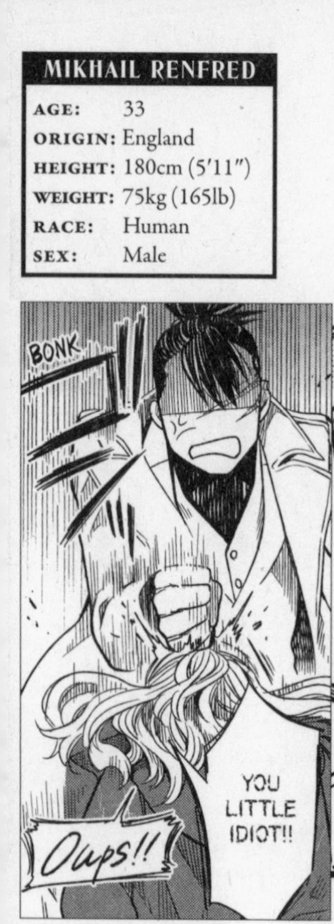
BONK
YOU LITTLE IDIOT!!
Oups!!
Alice is both his bodyguard and his apprentice. Here he can be seen rebuking her sternly for being out of line.

KNOWN AS
✝ ALICE: Master
✝ ADOLF: Renfred
✝ TORREY: Mikhail

A one-armed alchemist notorious for his dislike of mages. He has an apprentice named Alice, and has known Elias for a long time. While being coerced into assisting Cartaphilus, Renfred runs into Elias and Chise. Since Chise is human, he worries about her, and hopes that she'll wind up coming to the college. He's half Russian.

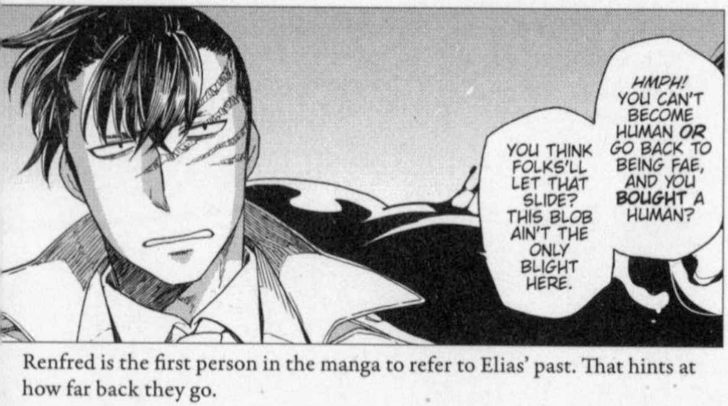
HMPH! YOU CAN'T BECOME HUMAN OR GO BACK TO BEING FAE, AND YOU BOUGHT A HUMAN?
YOU THINK FOLKS'LL LET THAT SLIDE? THIS BLOB AIN'T THE ONLY BLIGHT HERE.
Renfred is the first person in the manga to refer to Elias' past. That hints at how far back they go.

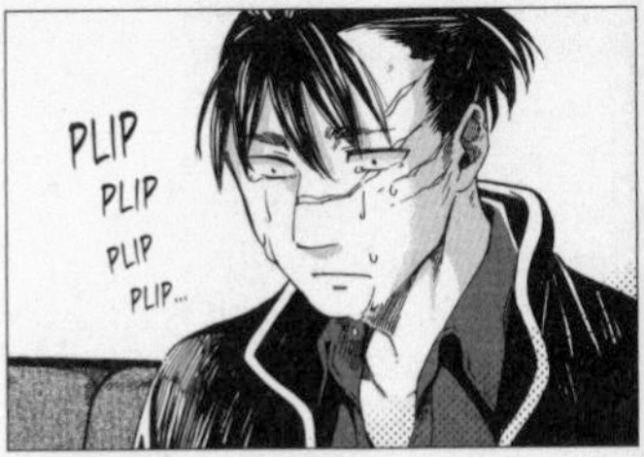
PLIP
PLIP
PLIP
PLIP...

Renfred gives the impression of being tough, but he's a weepy drunk. Once he starts complaining, he can't stop.

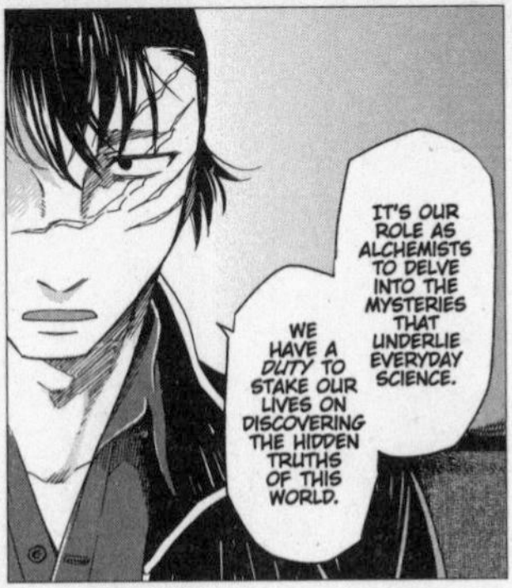
IT'S OUR ROLE AS ALCHEMISTS TO DELVE INTO THE MYSTERIES THAT UNDERLIE EVERYDAY SCIENCE.
WE HAVE A *DUTY* TO STAKE OUR LIVES ON DISCOVERING THE HIDDEN TRUTHS OF THIS WORLD.

Alchemists know a side of the world most do not. Renfred is dedicated to mapping it out.

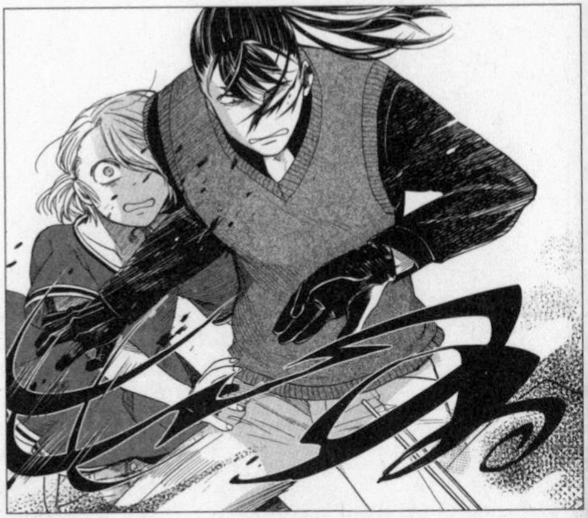

When Alice's carelessness sets off a trap in a book, Renfred physically places himself between her and the danger, and his face is scarred as a result.

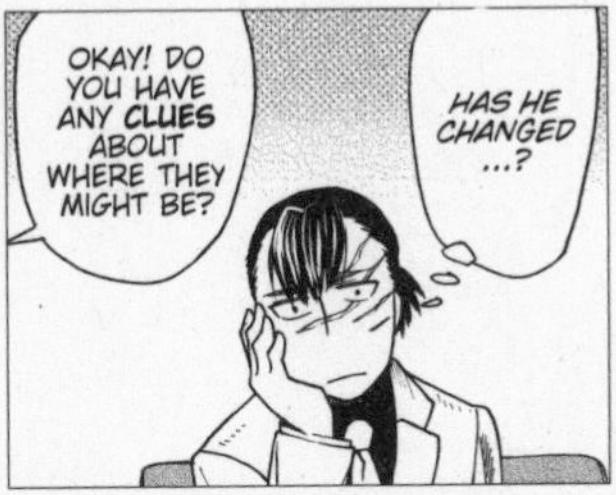
HAS HE CHANGED ...?
OKAY! DO YOU HAVE ANY **CLUES** ABOUT WHERE THEY MIGHT BE?

Having known Elias before Chise appeared on the scene, Renfred notices a change in Elias when Elias agrees to Chise's request.

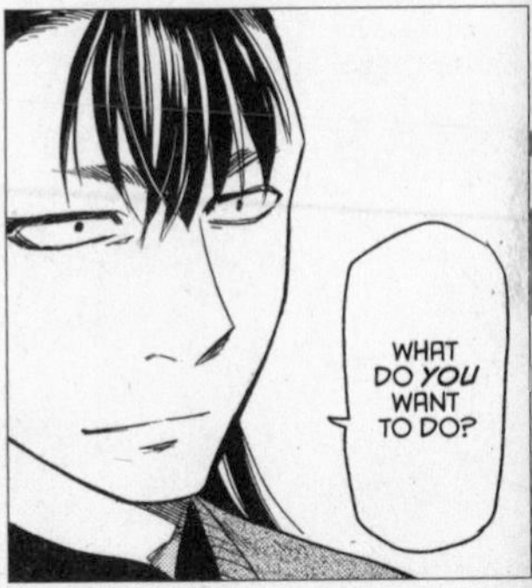
WHAT DO *YOU* WANT TO DO?

Renfred takes in the orphaned Alice and gives her a choice about what to do with her life.

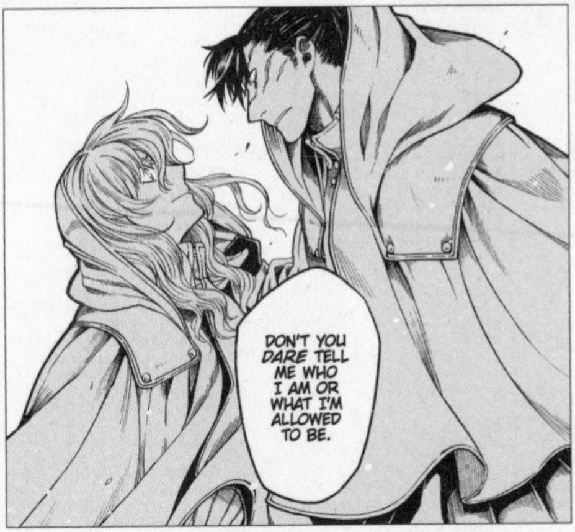
DON'T YOU *DARE* TELL ME WHO I AM OR WHAT I'M ALLOWED TO BE.

When Elias touches on his past, Renfred challenges him with a vehemence even Alice has never seen before.

Alice

ALICE	
AGE:	18
ORIGIN:	England
HEIGHT:	167cm (5′6″)
WEIGHT:	59kg (130lb)
RACE:	Human
SEX:	Female

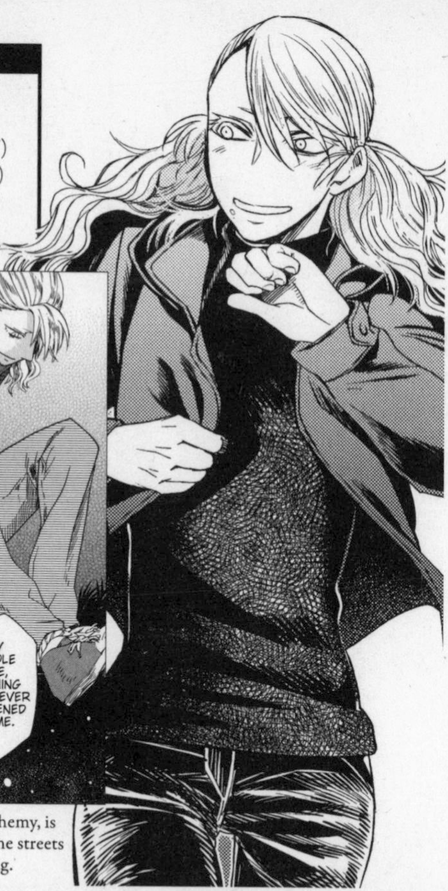

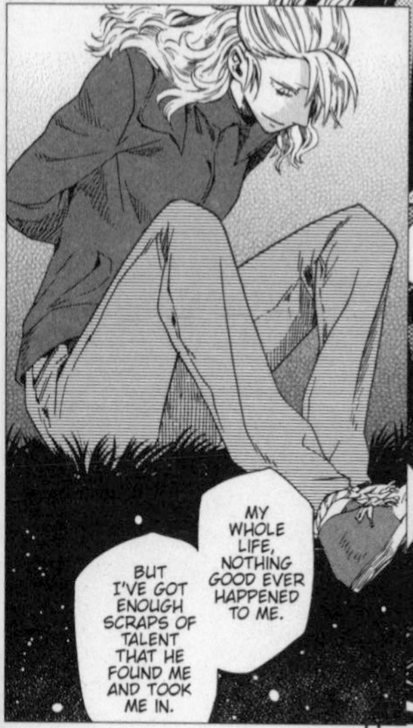
MY WHOLE LIFE, NOTHING GOOD EVER HAPPENED TO ME.
BUT I'VE GOT ENOUGH SCRAPS OF TALENT THAT HE FOUND ME AND TOOK ME IN.

Alice, with her gift for alchemy, is rescued from her life on the streets when Renfred comes along.

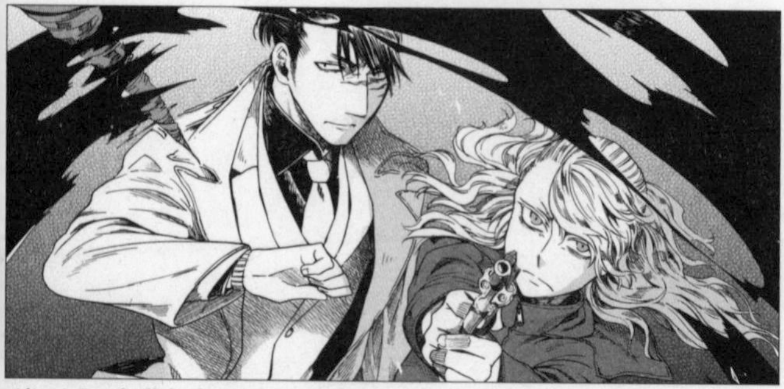

Alice is Renfred's bodyguard as well as his apprentice. They make a terrific team in the Black Dog Arc.

Alice is Renfred's apprentice in alchemy, and also his bodyguard. When she was a child, her parents forced her into drug addiction and dealing. That was her life until Renfred took her in, earning her intense devotion. While she was initially an adversary of Chise's, the two girls' similar ages and backgrounds bring them together as friends.

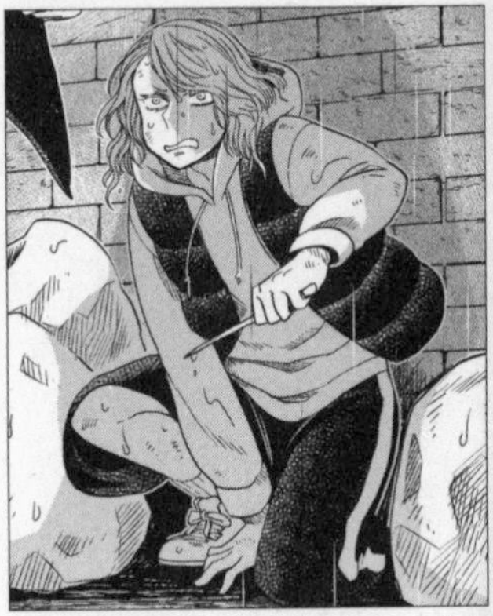

She had a much rougher look when she lived on the street.

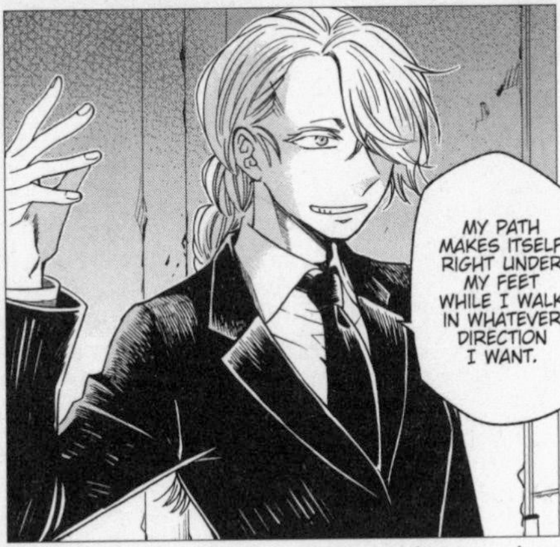
MY PATH MAKES ITSELF RIGHT UNDER MY FEET WHILE I WALK IN WHATEVER DIRECTION I WANT.

Alice takes pride in having made her own decision to be Renfred's bodyguard and apprentice. When asked about her life, she snaps back, as many young people would.

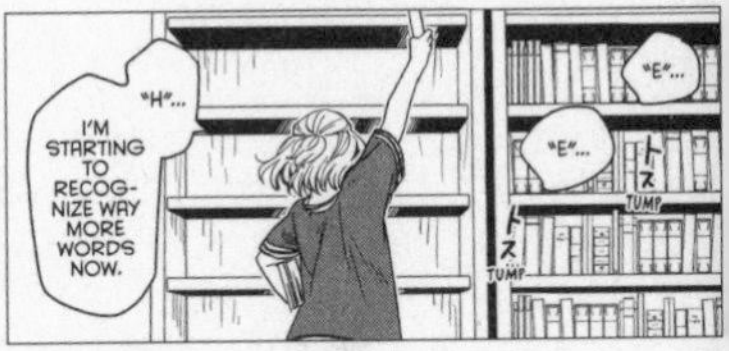
"E"...
"E"...
TUMP
"H"...
I'M STARTING TO RECOGNIZE WAY MORE WORDS NOW.
TUMP

Alice steadily builds her vocabulary in the course of her service to Renfred.

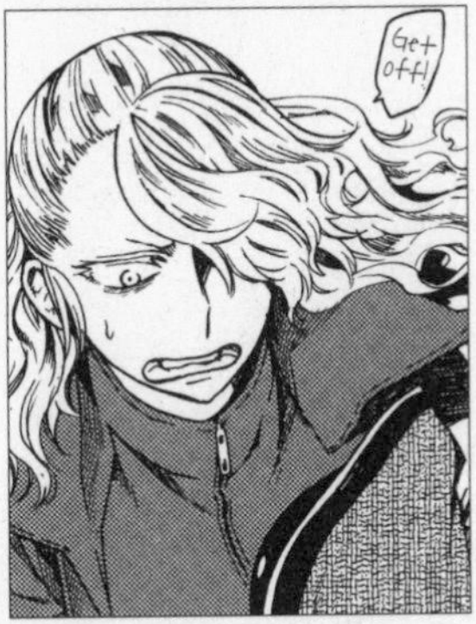
Get off!

Fairies love her blonde hair.

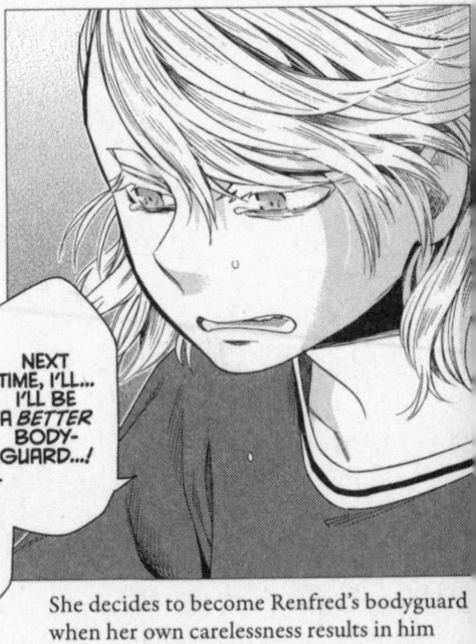
NEXT TIME, I'LL... I'LL BE A *BETTER* BODYGUARD...!
I *WON'T* LET YOU GET HURT AGAIN.

She decides to become Renfred's bodyguard when her own carelessness results in him being wounded.

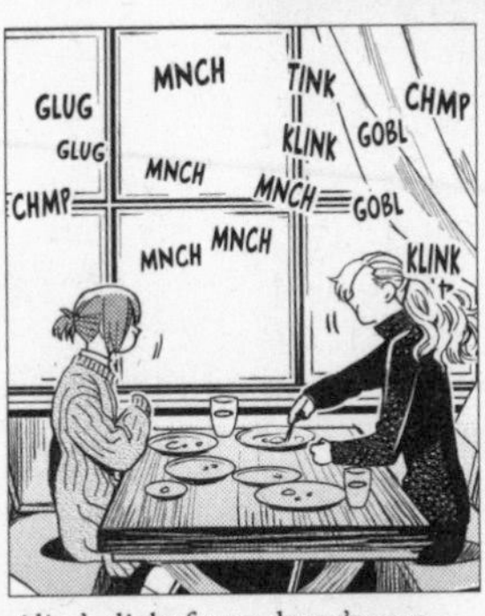
CHMP
TINK
MNCH
GOBL
KLINK
GLUG
GLUG
MNCH
MNCH
GOBL
CHMP
KLINK
MNCH
MNCH

Alice's slight frame doesn't even hint at how much she eats. Between that and Renfred's melancholy when he drinks, they're a pair full of surprises.

Adolf Stroud

Works in the administration of the college, which he joined later than Renfred. He describes Lindel as his first teacher, having studied under him in hopes of becoming a mage. This may explain why he's already acquainted with Lindel's familiar, Merituuli.

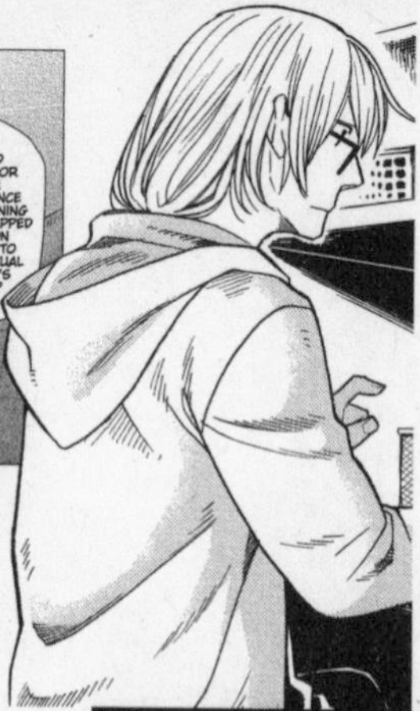

ADOLF STROUD	
AGE:	???
ORIGIN:	Germany
HEIGHT:	170cm (5′7″)
WEIGHT:	58kg (128lb)
RACE:	Human
SEX:	Male

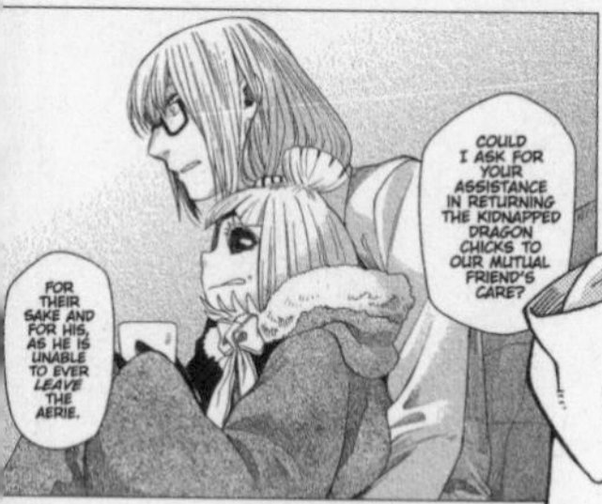
COULD I ASK FOR YOUR ASSISTANCE IN RETURNING THE KIDNAPPED DRAGON CHICKS TO OUR MUTUAL FRIEND'S CARE?
FOR THEIR SAKE AND FOR HIS, AS HE IS UNABLE TO EVER *LEAVE* THE AERIE.

Adolf's comment that Lindel, caretaker of the dragon aerie, is "unable" to leave it suggests a lingering affection, even having parted ways.

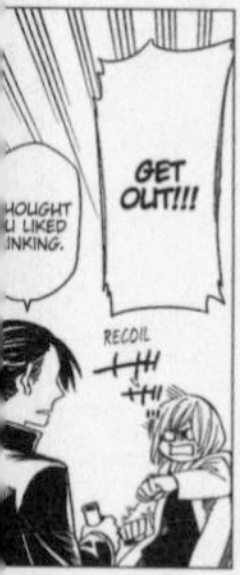
GET OUT!!!
RECOIL

Because Renfred has mentored Adolf in the past, Adolf knows what he's like when he's drunk. That's why he tries to get Renfred to go home when Renfred shows up with alcohol.

Torrey Innis

Another representative of the college, and a drinking buddy of Adolf and Renfred's. A happy-go-lucky fellow who skips past the formalities to get what he wants, such as when he grabs Chise, a sleigh beggy, by the face without so much as an introduction. He's also an outstanding alchemist who spends his days working on his own research and training his successors.

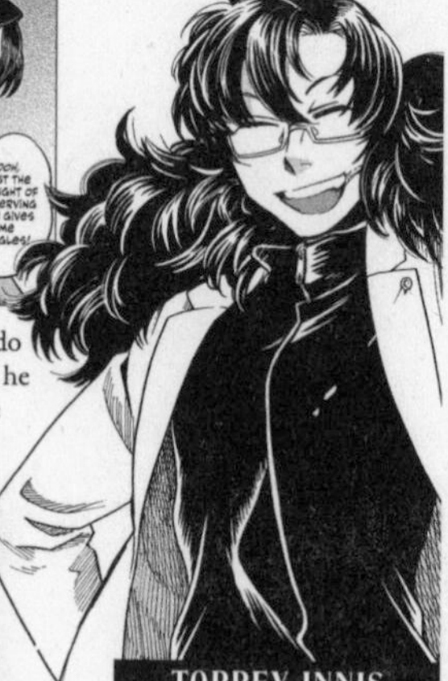

TORREY INNIS	
AGE:	29
ORIGIN:	United States
HEIGHT:	175cm (5′9″)
WEIGHT:	64kg (141lb)
RACE:	Human
SEX:	Male

'orrey's esearch ocuses on nages, so he sks Renfred o introduce im to Elias.

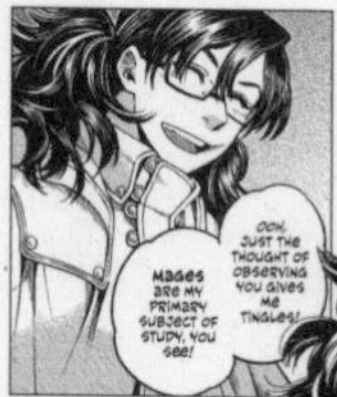
OOH, JUST THE THOUGHT OF OBSERVING YOU GIVES ME TINGLES!
MAGES ARE MY PRIMARY SUBJECT OF STUDY, YOU SEE!

'd be an exaggeration to say he'll do ings by any means necessary, but he oes tend to ignore a lot of barriers etween him and what he wants.

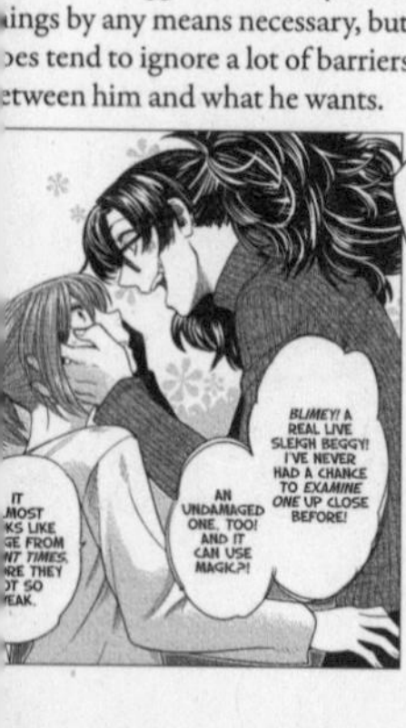
BLIMEY! A REAL LIVE SLEIGH BEGGY! I'VE NEVER HAD A CHANCE TO *EXAMINE ONE* UP CLOSE BEFORE!
AN UNDAMAGED ONE, TOO! AND IT CAN USE MAGIC?!

Joel Garland

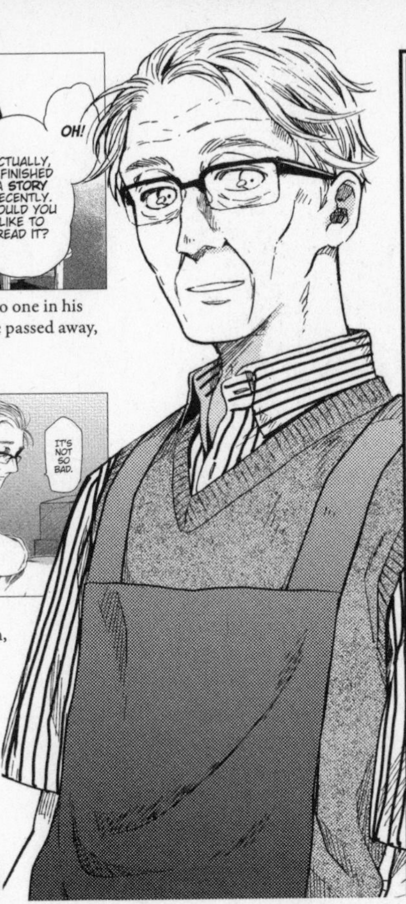

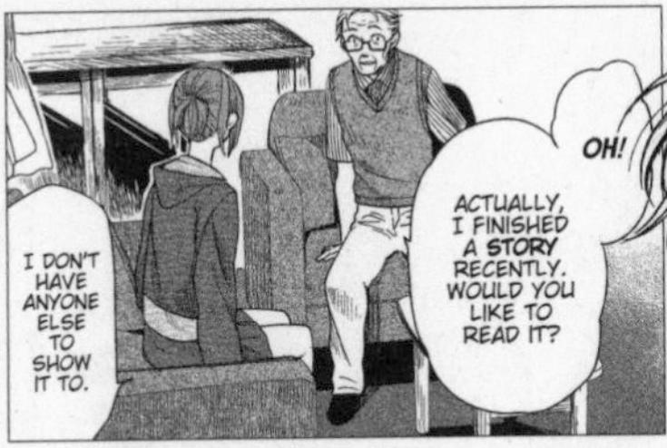
OH!
ACTUALLY, I FINISHED A STORY RECENTLY. WOULD YOU LIKE TO READ IT?
I DON'T HAVE ANYONE ELSE TO SHOW IT TO.

An earnest amateur writer. With no one in his life to read his stories once his wife passed away, he simply let them pile up.

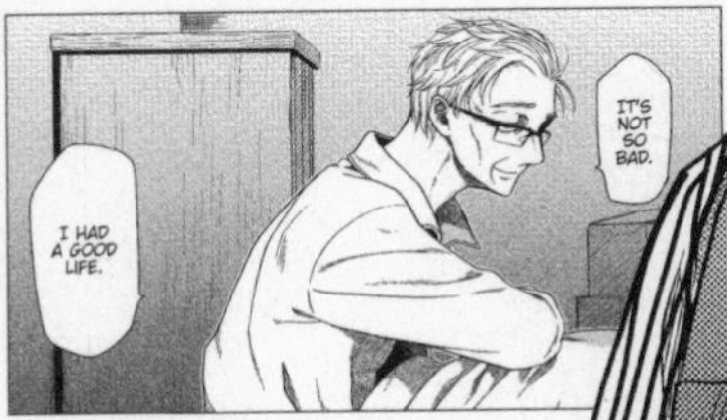
IT'S NOT SO BAD.
I HAD A GOOD LIFE.

After Elias tells him how long he has left to live, Joel still fears death, but he looks back on his life with satisfaction.

Joel thanks the leannán sídhe who indirectly drove him to death for providing his life with meaning.

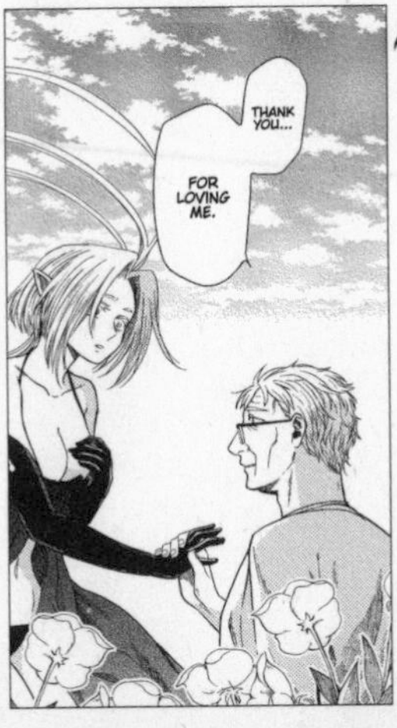
THANK YOU...
FOR LOVING ME.

An older man who resides in the same village as Chise and Elias. Alone in the world after his wife's death, he lives in a house with a rose garden. His love of books leads him to begin writing his own stories. After finally connecting with the leannán sídhe who haunts him, he grants her his life and welcomes death among the roses.

JOEL GARLAND	
AGE:	58
ORIGIN:	England
HEIGHT:	170cm (5′7″)
WEIGHT:	50kg (110lb)
RACE:	Human
SEX:	Male

Mina

In life, she was a sickly woman living in the village of Ulthar with her husband, Matthew. The two were known to be a devoted, loving couple. However, as a result of an elixir concocted by Matthew, Mina becomes the core of a devastating blight. She is eventually freed from this horrifying, unreasoning fate and her endless anguish thanks to Chise's purifying power.

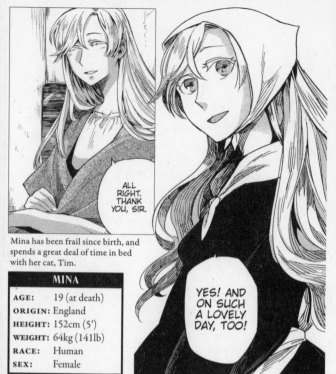

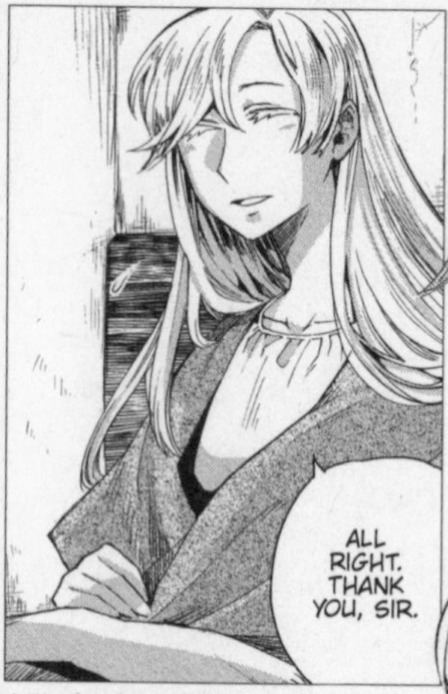
ALL RIGHT. THANK YOU, SIR.

Mina has been frail since birth, and spends a great deal of time in bed with her cat, Tim.

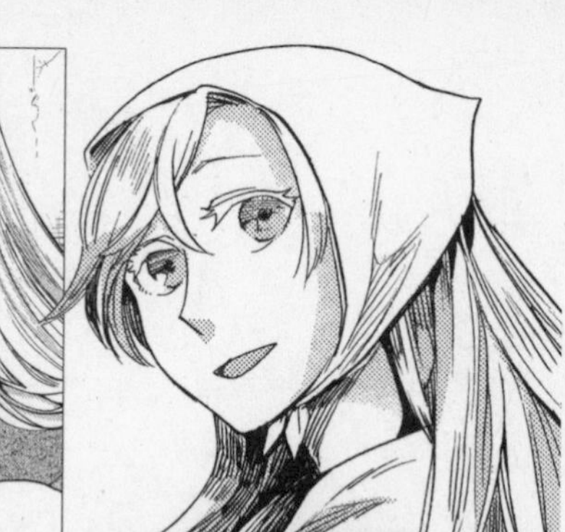
YES! AND ON SUCH A LOVELY DAY, TOO!

MINA	
AGE:	19 (at death)
ORIGIN:	England
HEIGHT:	152cm (5′)
WEIGHT:	64kg (141lb)
RACE:	Human
SEX:	Female

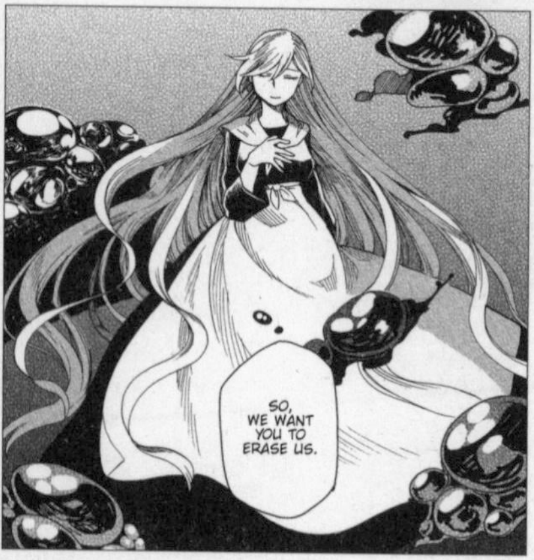
SO, WE WANT YOU TO ERASE US.

Mina's soul remains trapped at the core of the blight with Matthew for untold years.

When Matthew is tricked by Cartaphilus into forcing Mina to drink a concoction of concentrated cat blood, her body dissolves.

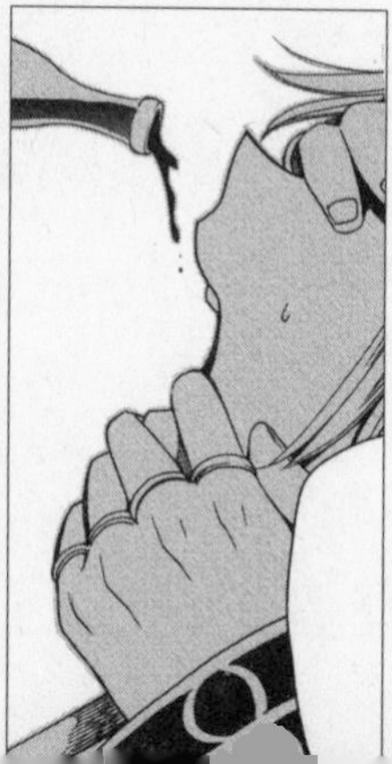

Matthew

A young man who lives in Ulthar before the blight com into existence. He is married to Mina, whom he has known since childhoo His worry over her poor health leads him to ask for help from a travelin alchemist, Cartaphilus. Tragically, Matthew is tricked into performing an experiment tha dissolves Mina' body, turning her into the co of the blight o the village.

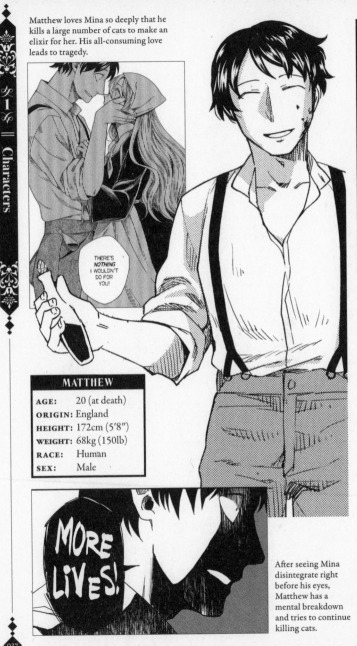

Matthew loves Mina so deeply that he kills a large number of cats to make an elixir for her. His all-consuming love leads to tragedy.

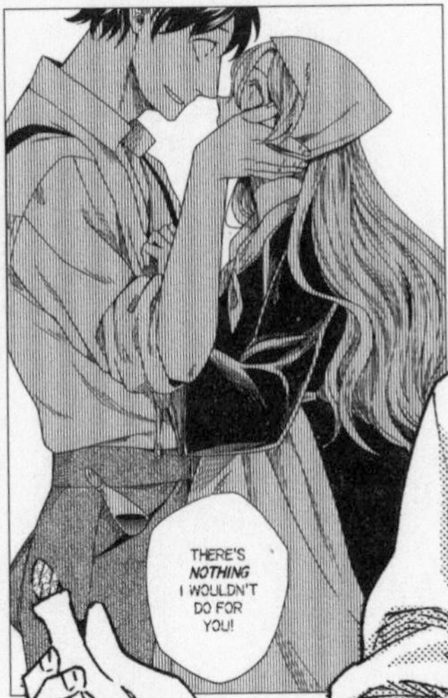
THERE'S *NOTHING* I WOULDN'T DO FOR YOU!

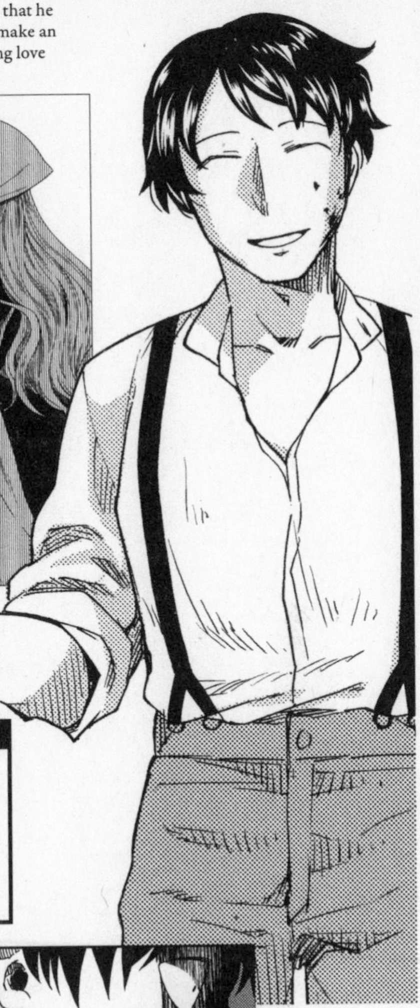

MATTHEW	
AGE:	20 (at death)
ORIGIN:	England
HEIGHT:	172cm (5′8″)
WEIGHT:	68kg (150lb)
RACE:	Human
SEX:	Male

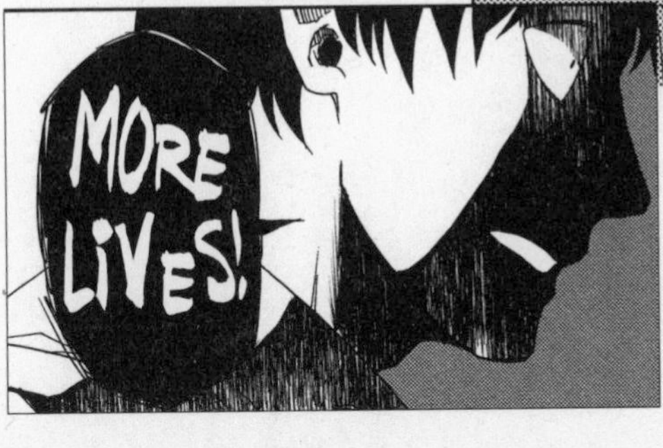
MORE LIVES!

After seeing Mina disintegrate right before his eyes, Matthew has a mental breakdown and tries to continue killing cats.

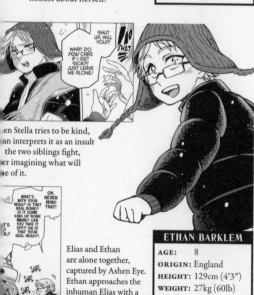

Stella Barklem

A ten-year-old with a talent for baking. While visiting Chise and Elias' village for her Christmas holiday, she has a fight with her brother, Ethan, which ultimately results in his very existence being forgotten by the world. In the course of remedying the situation, she becomes friends with Chise. Stella winds up making multiple visits to Elias' home, and seems unfazed by his skull head. She's a strong girl.

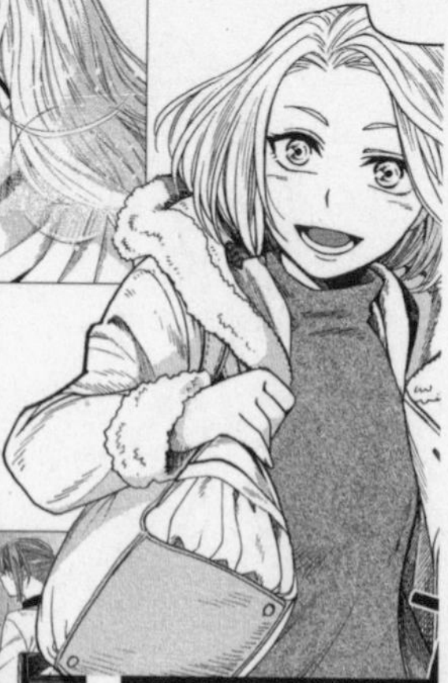

STELLA BARKLEM	
AGE:	10
ORIGIN:	England
HEIGHT:	136cm (4'6")
WEIGHT:	31kg (68lb)
RACE:	Human
SEX:	Female

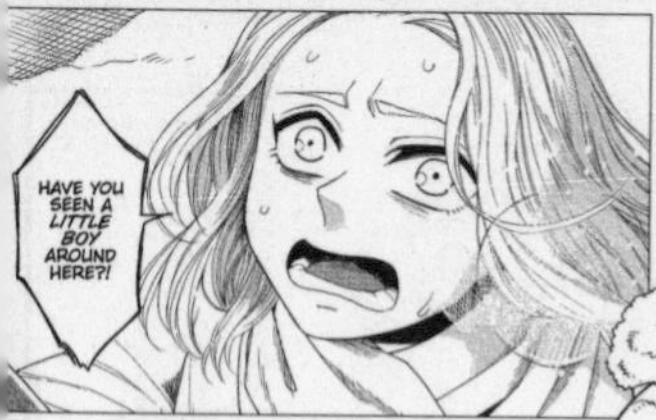
HAVE YOU SEEN A LITTLE BOY AROUND HERE?!

ɪile running around the ·age looking for Ethan, who ɪappeared after their fight, ·lla meets Chise.

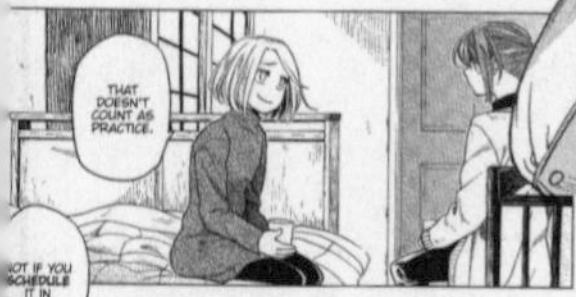
THAT DOESN'T COUNT AS PRACTICE.
OT IF YOU SCHEDULE IT IN ADVANCE.

Having befriended Chise, Stella visits Elias' home. When Chise admits to not knowing what to do with friends, Stella's advice is to simply be honest about herself.

Ethan Barklem

A curious little boy who frolics in the snow when he sees it for the first time, and later examines Elias' skull head with great interest. While Ethan, Stella, and their parents are visiting the village where his grandmother lives, he's abducted by Ashen Eye. When Elias is trapped with him, Ethan offers Elias a child's view of what "family" is.

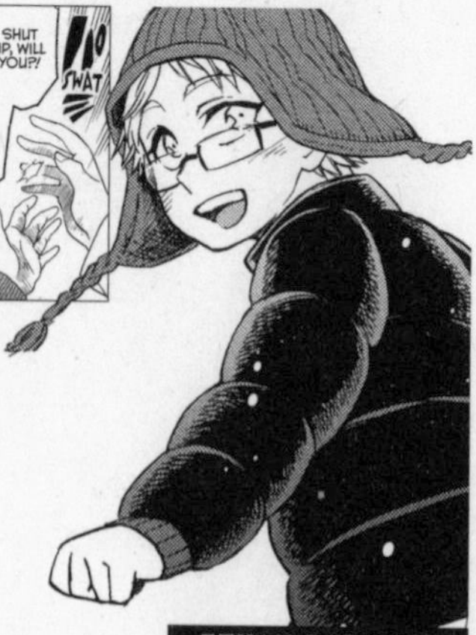

ETHAN BARKLEM	
AGE:	8
ORIGIN:	England
HEIGHT:	129cm (4'3")
WEIGHT:	27kg (60lb)
RACE:	Human
SEX:	Male

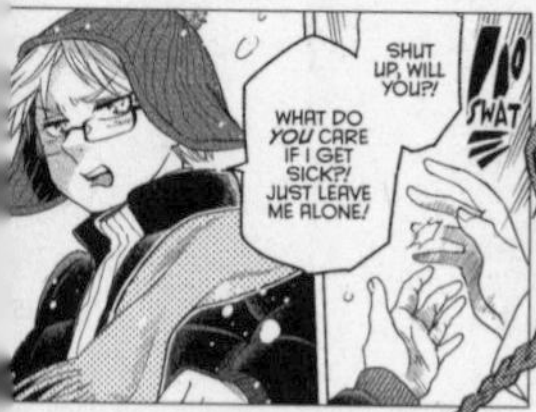
SWAT
SHUT UP, WILL YOU?!
WHAT DO YOU CARE IF I GET SICK?! JUST LEAVE ME ALONE!

ɪen Stella tries to be kind, ɪan interprets it as an insult the two siblings fight, ɪer imagining what will ɪe of it.

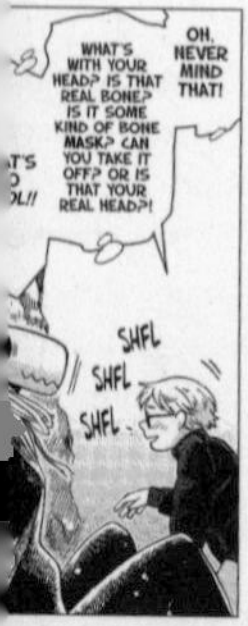
OH, NEVER MIND THAT!
WHAT'S WITH YOUR HEAD? IS THAT REAL BONE? IS IT SOME KIND OF BONE MASK? CAN YOU TAKE IT OFF? OR IS THAT YOUR REAL HEAD?!
SHFL
SHFL
SHFL

Elias and Ethan are alone together, captured by Ashen Eye. Ethan approaches the inhuman Elias with a child's curiosity.

Seth Noel

The broker who helps Chise put herself up for auction. When Chise and her allies come looking for the dragons taken by Cartaphilus Seth helps them check the listings and gain access to the auction house. He is aware of the world of mages and alchemists and has the gift to perceive things most humans can't, but otherwise has no special powers.

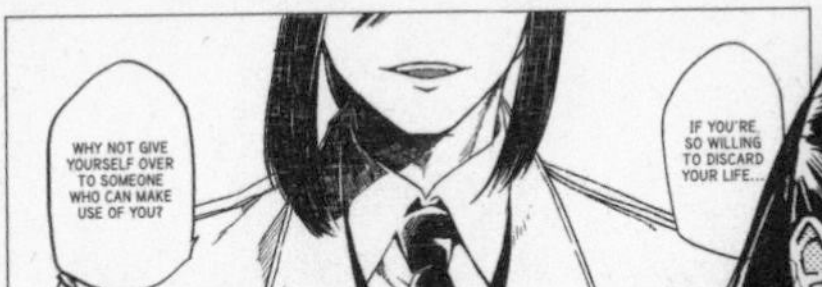
IF YOU'RE SO WILLING TO DISCARD YOUR LIFE...
WHY NOT GIVE YOURSELF OVER TO SOMEONE WHO CAN MAKE USE OF YOU?

Seth gave Chise the option of putting herself up for auction and placing her life in someone else's hands when she wanted to die. In a sense, he enabled the beginning of the story.

SETH NOEL	
AGE:	29
ORIGIN:	England
HEIGHT:	190cm (6′3″)
WEIGHT:	67kg (148lb)
RACE:	Human
SEX:	Male

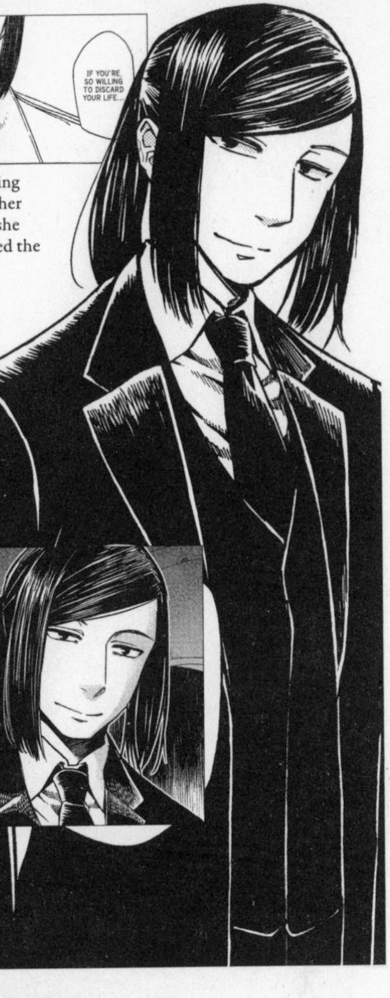

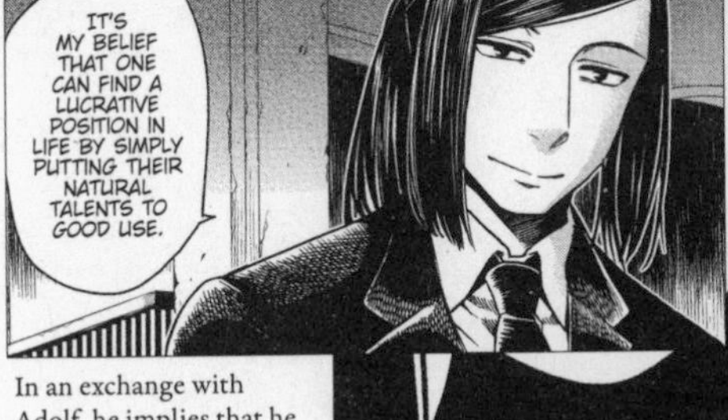
IT'S MY BELIEF THAT ONE CAN FIND A LUCRATIVE POSITION IN LIFE BY SIMPLY PUTTING THEIR NATURAL TALENTS TO GOOD USE.

In an exchange with Adolf, he implies that he has the sight. Whether he is a mage or alchemist is unknown.

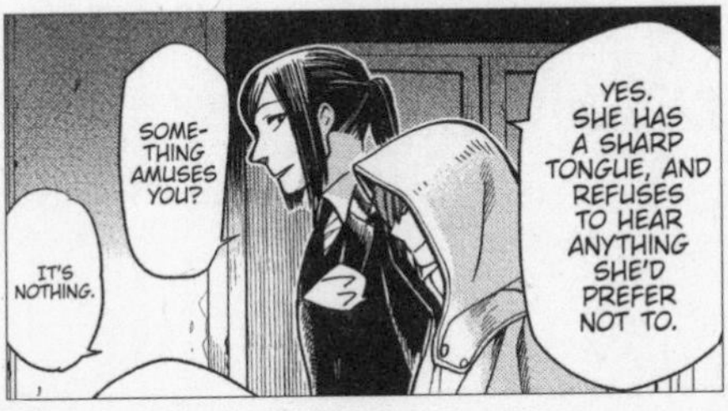
YES. SHE HAS A SHARP TONGUE, AND REFUSES TO HEAR ANYTHING SHE'D PREFER NOT TO.
SOMETHING AMUSES YOU?
IT'S NOTHING.

It's been mentioned that Seth has a sister, although she hasn't played a part in the story. Might she become involved in the future, just as Seth has reappeared? Only time will tell!

Silky

A brownie living in Elias' house. She was once a banshee who lost the house she haunted, but through the good offices of Spriggan, she became a domestic spirit. Due to her appearance, she is also known as the Silver Lady. She never speaks; instead, she communicates with Chise and others through gestures.

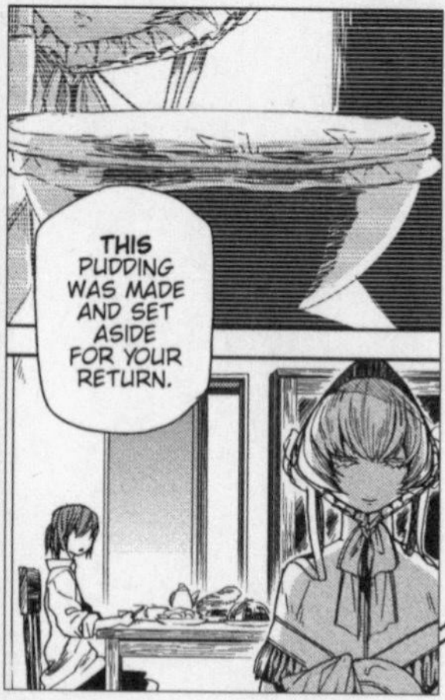
THIS PUDDING WAS MADE AND SET ASIDE FOR YOUR RETURN.

Silky does the cooking at Elias' house. While Chise is unconscious at the end of the Ulthar Arc, Silky prepares a pudding and waits for her mistress's return.

SILKY	
AGE:	???
ORIGIN:	Scotland
HEIGHT:	157cm (5′2″)
WEIGHT:	???
RACE:	Brownie
SEX:	Female

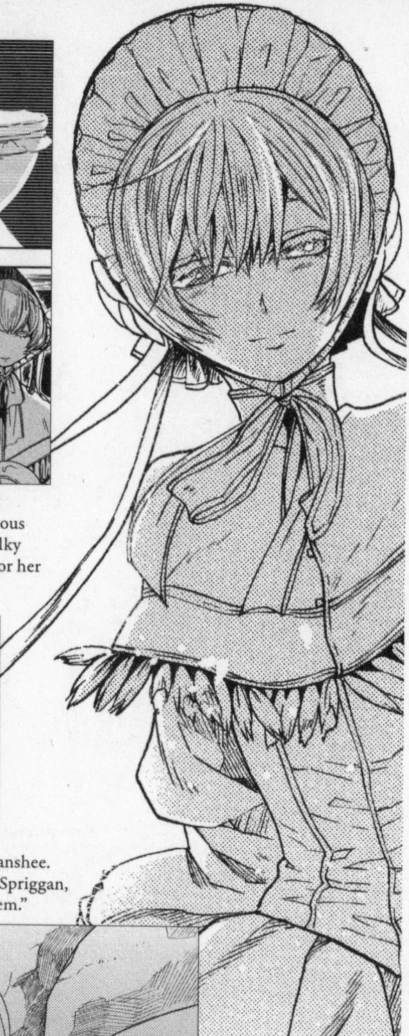

A flashback reveals Silky as a banshee. Having lost her home, she tells Spriggan, "All I wanted was to be with them."

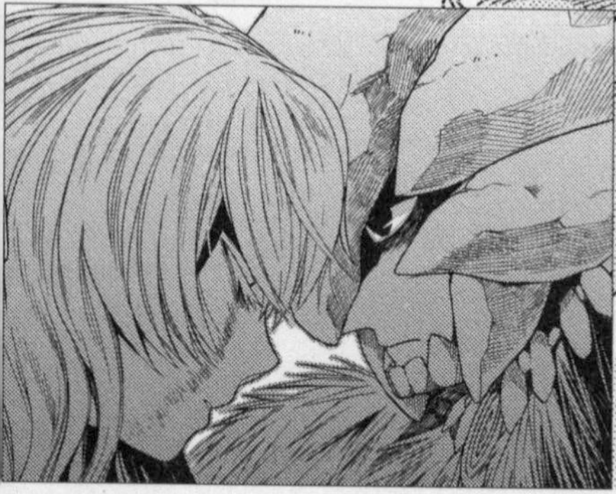

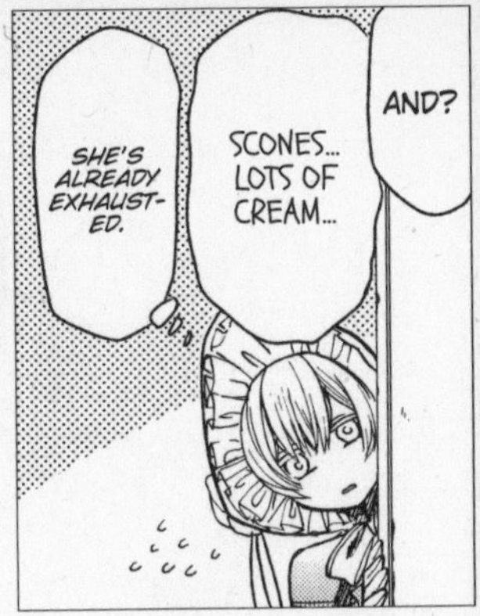
AND?
SCONES... LOTS OF CREAM...
SHE'S ALREADY EXHAUST-ED.

Silky takes care of Elias and Chise. Chise's recklessness makes Silky worry for her health.

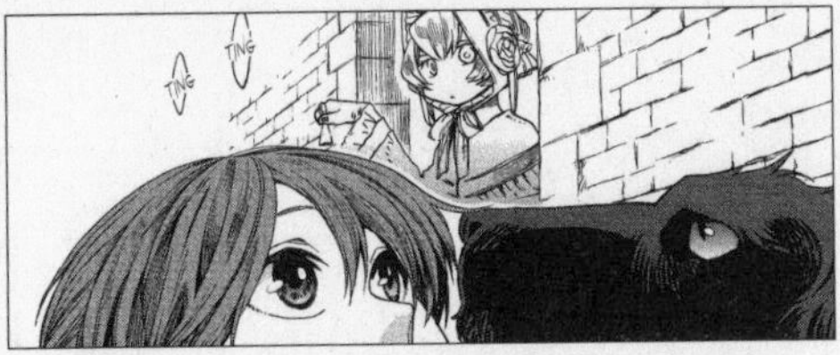
TING
TING

Silky does not speak, but rings a bell when she wishes to summon Chise and others.

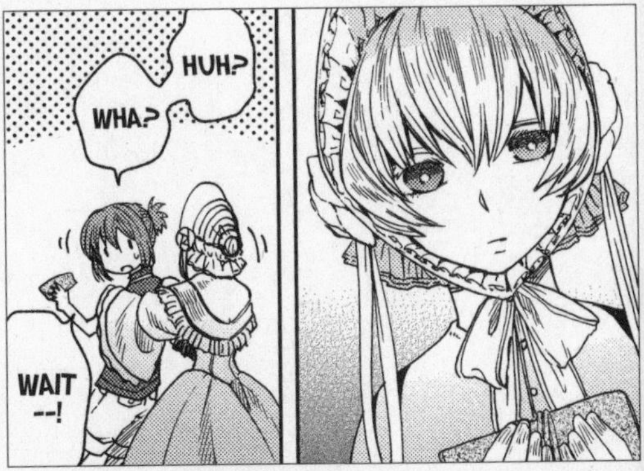
HUH?
WHA?
WAIT --!

When Elias is in poor condition, Silky gives Chise some spending money and sends her off to cheer up. She's quite considerate.

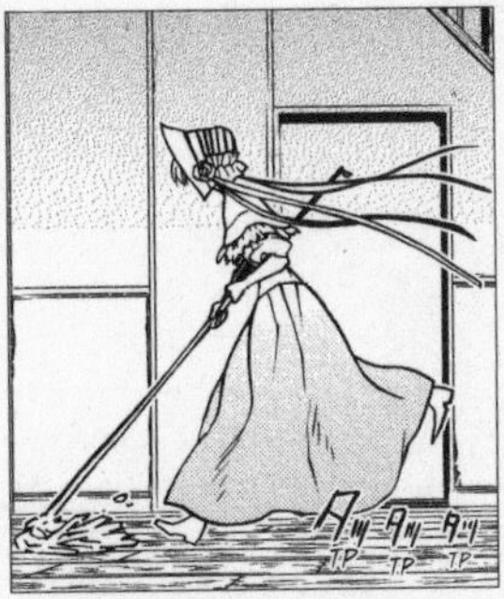

Silky lives up to her role as a domestic spirit in cleaning.

KNOWN AS

+ **CHISE, ELIAS:** Silver Lady + **SIMON:** Maid

Having lost the house she haunted, Silky herself is lost. When she tries to wail, no sound emerges.

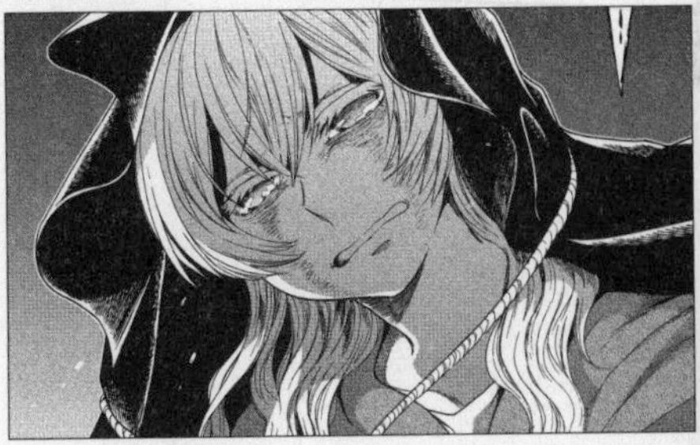

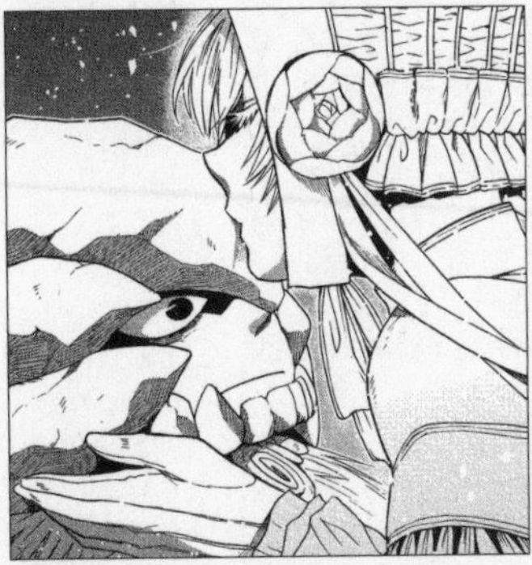

Silky kisses Spriggan when he finds her a new home and calls her "Silky" for the first time.

Ruth

Chise's familiar. Once an ordinary dog named Ulysse, he becomes a church grim after the death of his master, Isabel. He meets Chise when she is helping Elias carry out the three errands Simon charged him with, and in the course of this they form a bond. He shares everything with Chise and sometimes speaks up for her when she won't speak for herself.

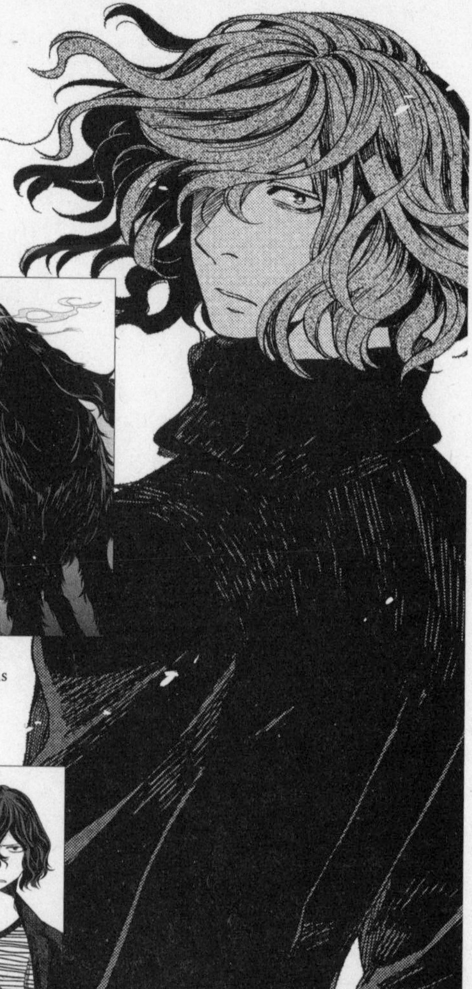

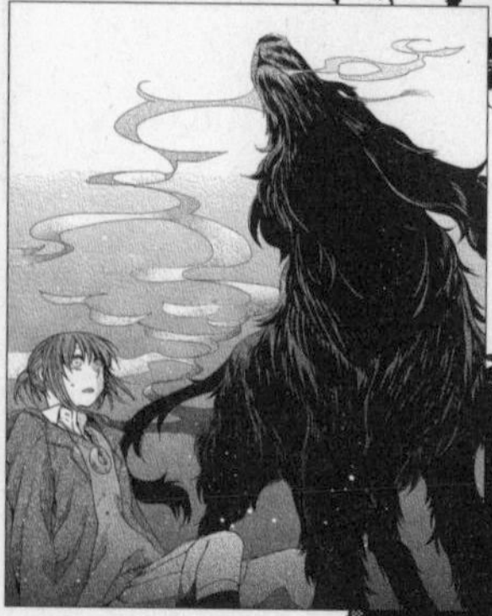

When Ruth first meets Chise, he's forgotten his duty as a church grim: to chase grave robbers to Hell.

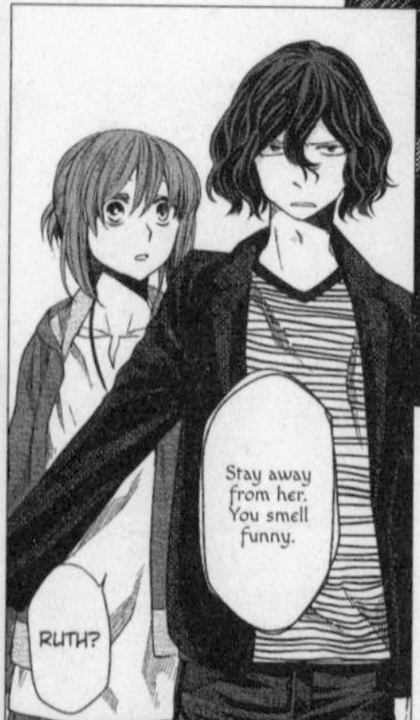
Stay away from her. You smell funny.
RUTH?

After Ruth becomes Chise's familiar, he takes on a younger appearance so that people will see him as her brother.

RUTH	
AGE:	???
ORIGIN:	Scotland
HEIGHT:	160cm (5′3″) [after shrinking from 183cm (6′)]
WEIGHT:	???
RACE:	Church grim
SEX:	Male

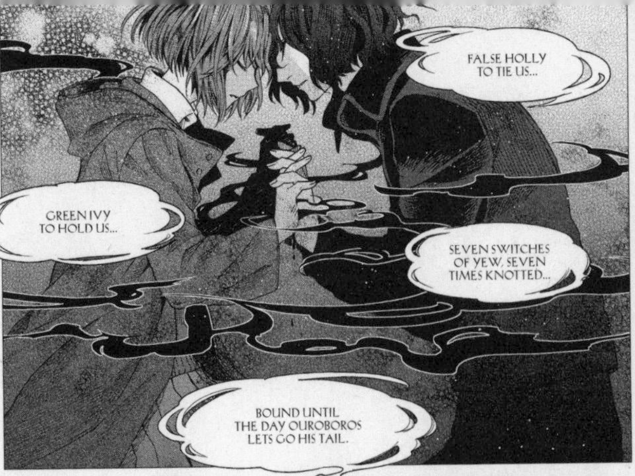
FALSE HOLLY TO TIE US...
GREEN IVY TO HOLD US...
SEVEN SWITCHES OF YEW, SEVEN TIMES KNOTTED...
BOUND UNTIL THE DAY OUROBOROS LETS GO HIS TAIL.

At the end of the Black Dog Arc, Ruth remembers who he is and asks Chise to bind him as her familiar.

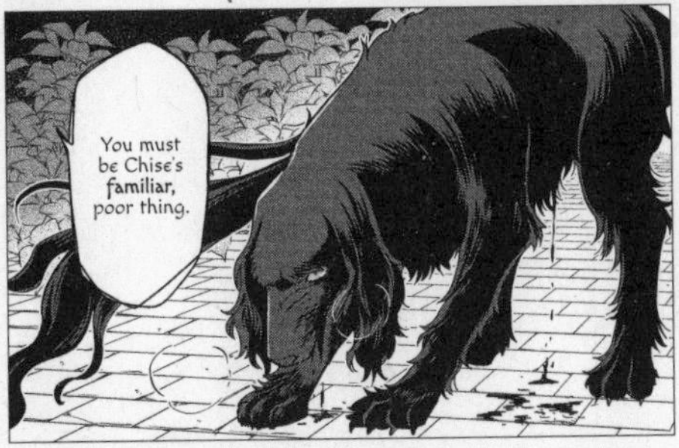
You must be Chise's familiar, poor thing.

Now that Ruth shares everything with Chise, any physical trauma she suffers affects him directly.

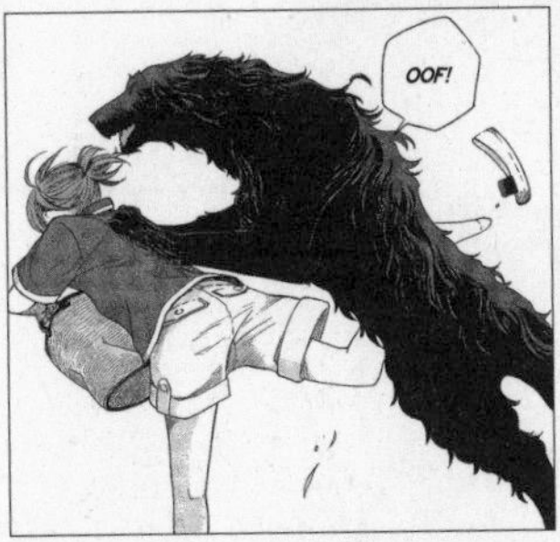
OOF!

In life, Ruth was a large dog. His instincts from that time can still be seen when he explores Elias' residence and leaps on Chise.

ULYSSE'S OWNER, ISABEL

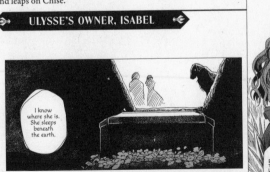

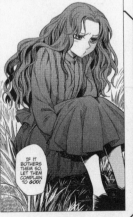

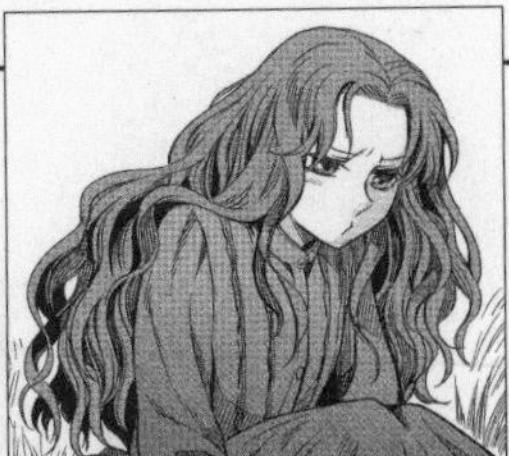
IF IT BOTHERS THEM SO, LET THEM COMPLAIN TO GOD!

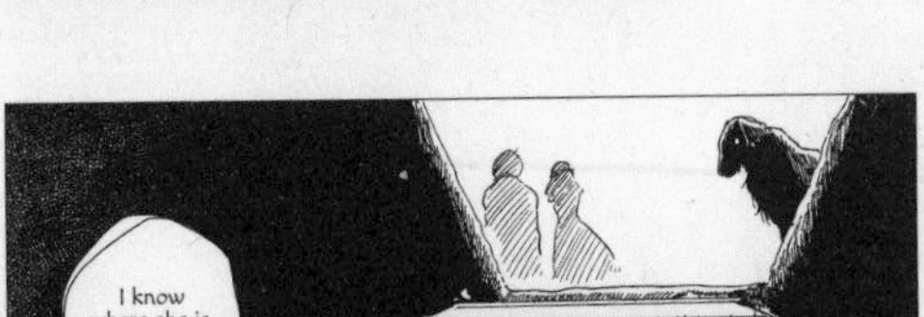
I know where she is. She sleeps beneath the earth.

When Ruth was Ulysse, his master was a red-haired, green-eyed girl named Isabel. Ulysse loved her as his sister, but she died in an accident.

Titania

Queen of the fae and wife of Oberon. She calls all fae her children, including sleigh beggy, and treats them maternally. She and Oberon both know of Elias' origins and call him kin. Titania repeatedly urges Elias to come dwell in the Faerie Kingdom.

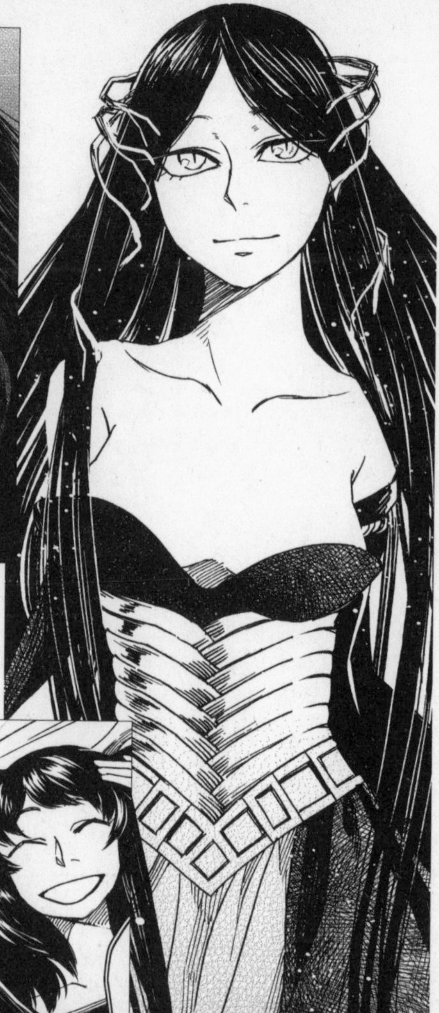

TITANIA	
AGE:	???
ORIGIN:	Britain & Ireland
HEIGHT:	164cm (5′5″)
WEIGHT:	???
RACE:	Faerie
SEX:	Female

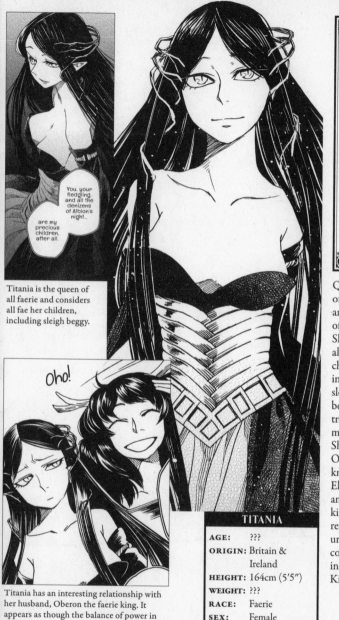

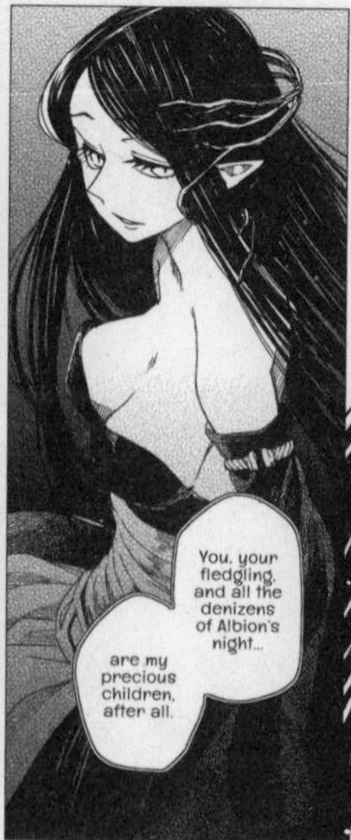
You, your fledgling, and all the denizens of Albion's night...
are my precious children, after all.

Titania is the queen of all faerie and considers all fae her children, including sleigh beggy.

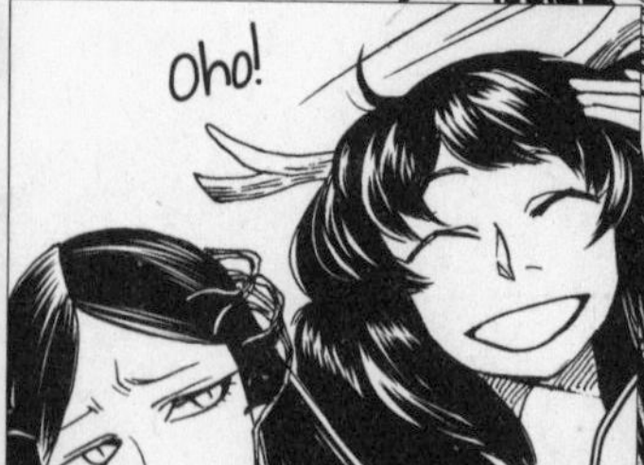
Oho!

Titania has an interesting relationship with her husband, Oberon the faerie king. It appears as though the balance of power in their marriage is weighted toward her.

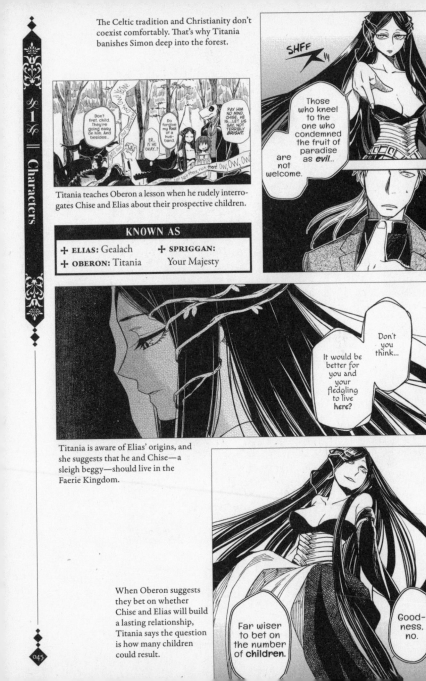

The Celtic tradition and Christianity don't coexist comfortably. That's why Titania banishes Simon deep into the forest.

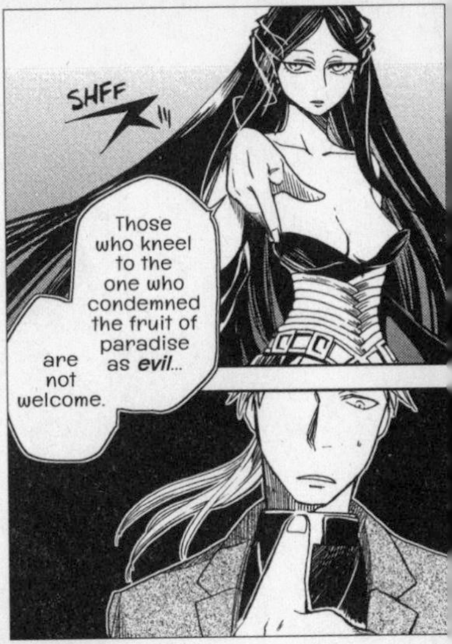
SHFF
Those who kneel to the one who condemned the fruit of paradise as *evil*...
are not welcome.

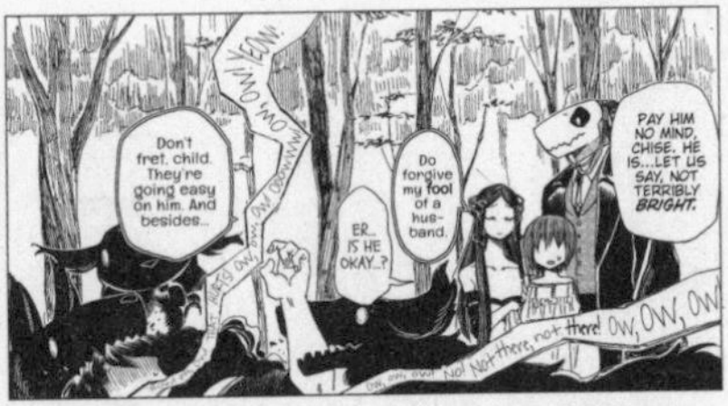
PAY HIM NO MIND, CHISE. HE IS...LET US SAY, NOT TERRIBLY *BRIGHT*.
Do forgive my fool of a husband.
ER... IS HE OKAY...?
Don't fret, child. They're going easy on him. And besides...
Not there, not there! OW, OW, OW!

Titania teaches Oberon a lesson when he rudely interrogates Chise and Elias about their prospective children.

KNOWN AS	
+ **ELIAS:** Gealach	+ **SPRIGGAN:** Your Majesty
+ **OBERON:** Titania	

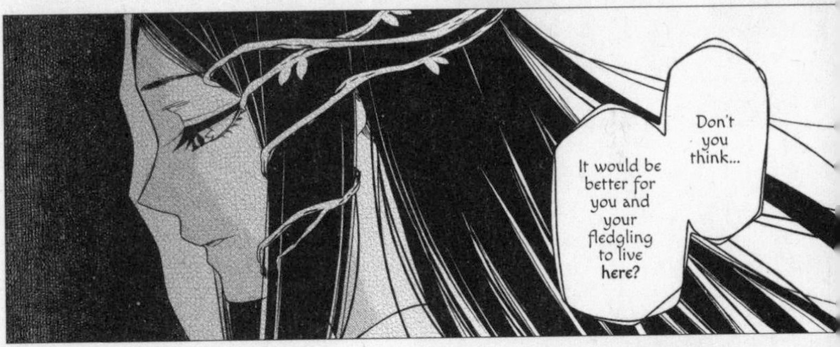
Don't you think...
It would be better for you and your fledgling to live **here?**

Titania is aware of Elias' origins, and she suggests that he and Chise—a sleigh beggy—should live in the Faerie Kingdom.

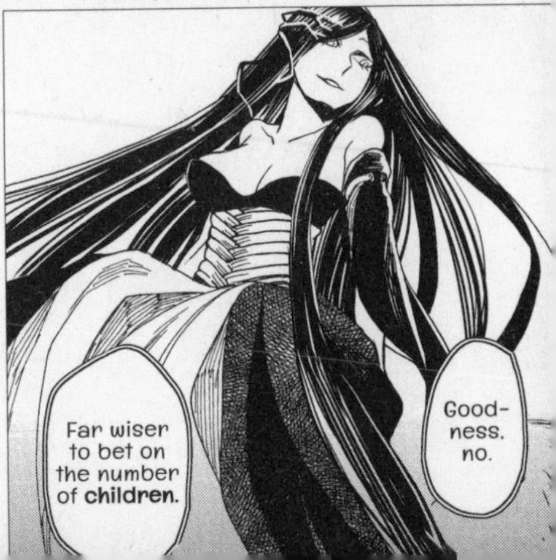
Good-ness, no.
Far wiser to bet on the number of **children.**

When Oberon suggests they bet on whether Chise and Elias will build a lasting relationship, Titania says the question is how many children could result.

Oberon

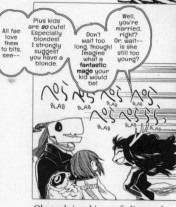

Titania's husband and king of the fae, distinguished by his antlers. A rather embarrassing individual, as evidenced by Elias' assertion that he's "not terribly bright" and by Titania referring to him as "my fool of a husband." Oberon is also a masochist. Still, there are moments when he displays kingly qualities, such as when he rebukes and guides Elias through his distress when Chise coughs up blood and loses consciousness.

OBERON	
AGE:	???
ORIGIN:	Britain & Ireland
HEIGHT:	165cm (5′5″)
WEIGHT:	???
RACE:	Faerie
SEX:	Male

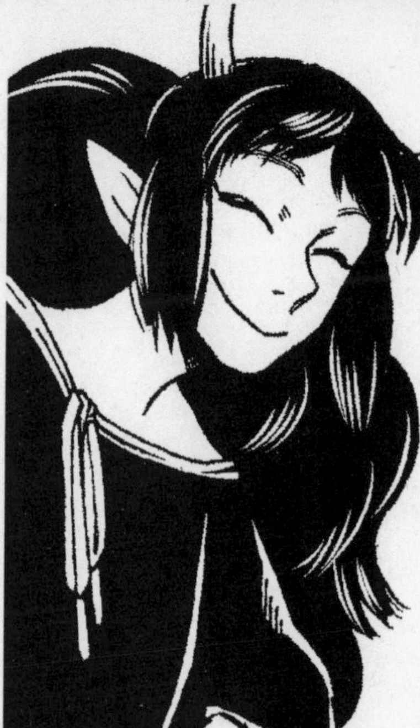

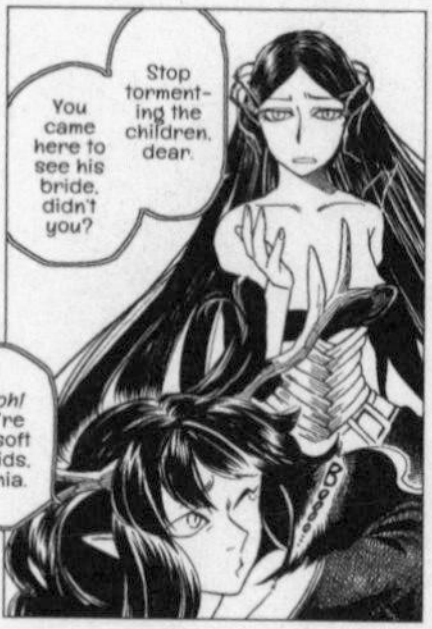
Stop torment-ing the children, dear.
You came here to see his bride, didn't you?
Hmph! You're too soft on kids, Titania.

Oberon is the husband of Titania, who regards all fae as her children. Their conversation makes them sound like any other couple arguing over how to raise their little ones.

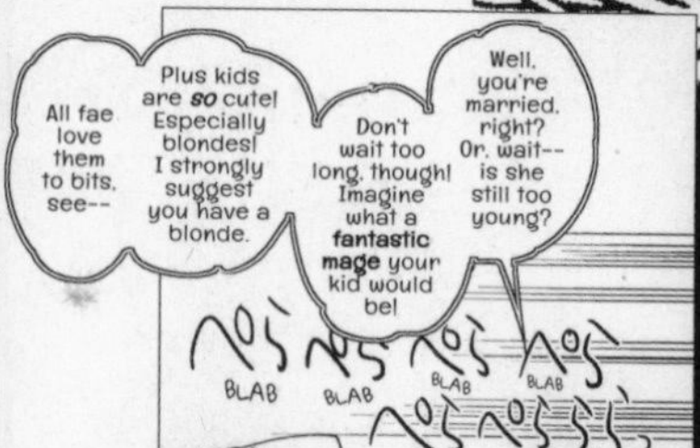
Well, you're married, right? Or, wait-- is she still too young?
Don't wait too long, though! Imagine what a fantastic mage your kid would be!
Plus kids are SO cute! Especially blondes! I strongly suggest you have a blonde.
All fae love them to bits, see--
BLAB BLAB BLAB BLAB
BLAB BLAB BLAB

Oberon brings his own feelings and preferences to the subject of Chise and Elias' children. He knows who's king.

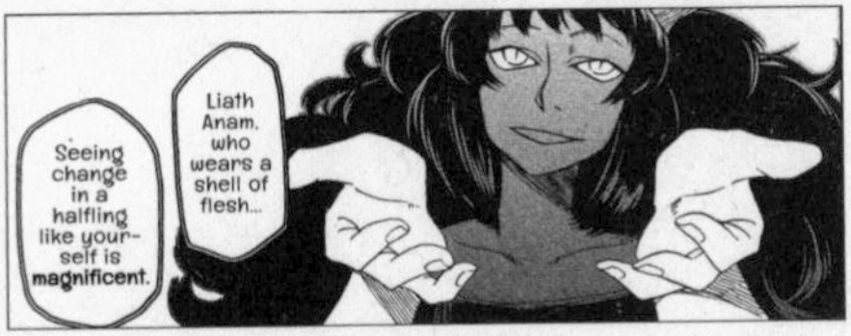
Liath Anam, who wears a shell of flesh...
Seeing change in a halfling like yourself is **magnificent**.

Oberon also knows Elias' origins. He speaks to Elias with some irony upon seeing how Elias has changed since buying Chise.

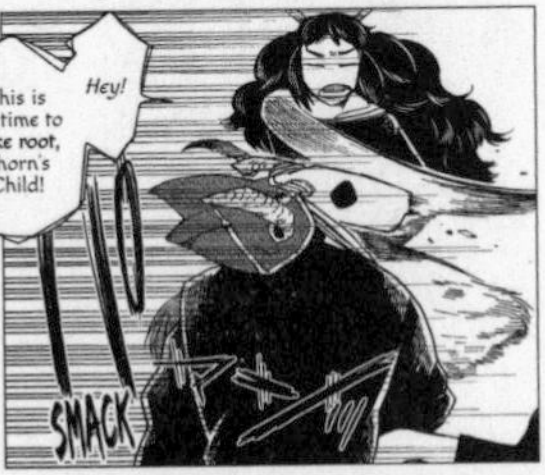
Hey!
This is no time to take root, Thorn's Child!
SMACK

When Chise's physical breakdown makes Elias freeze up, Oberon slaps some sense into him and tells him what he should do.

KNOWN AS	
+ **ELIAS:** Grian	+ **TITANIA:** Oberon, dear

Like Titania, Oberon sees fae and all such beings, including sleigh beggy, as his children.

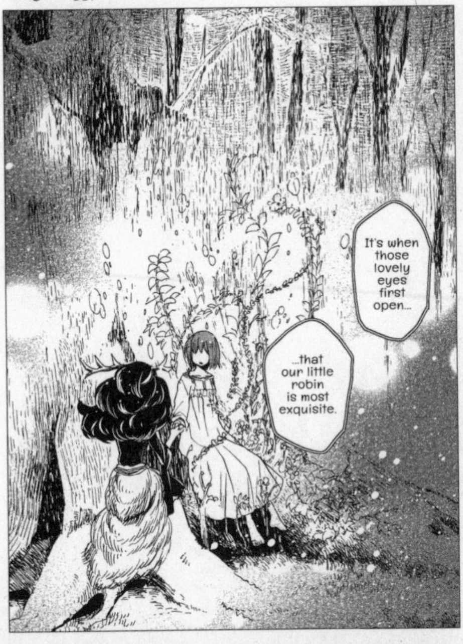
It's when those lovely eyes first open...
...that our little robin is most exquisite.

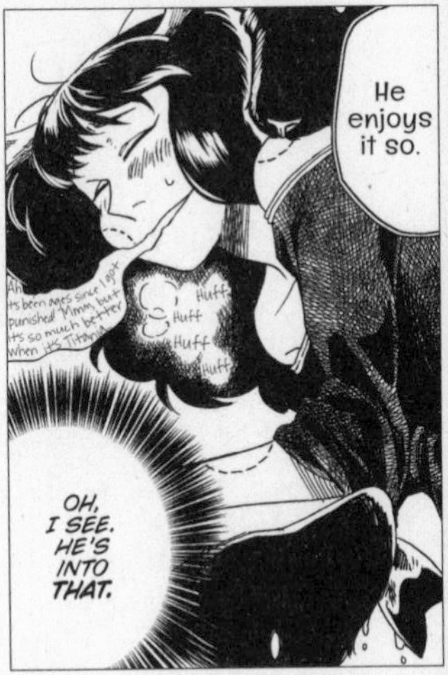
He enjoys it so.
Ah it's been ages since I got punished! Mmm, but it's so much better when it's Titania
Huff Huff Huff Huff
OH, I SEE. HE'S INTO THAT.

Oberon enjoys it when Titania sets dogs on him, but it does seem as if he'd prefer it if Titania administered his punishment personally.

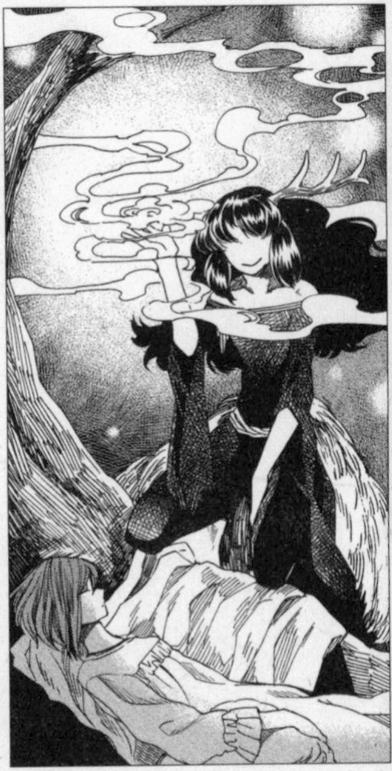

When Chise will not wake up for lack of magic, Oberon replenishes her. Surely such magic can be worked only by someone like a faerie king!

Shannon

A doctor who lives in the Faerie Kingdom, Shannon is a changeling: born fae, but swapped for a human child. She grew up among humans, who were suspicious of her because she didn't age normally. Eventually the human-born Shanahan, who took her place among the fae, came to bring her home. She's lived in the Faerie Kingdom ever since.

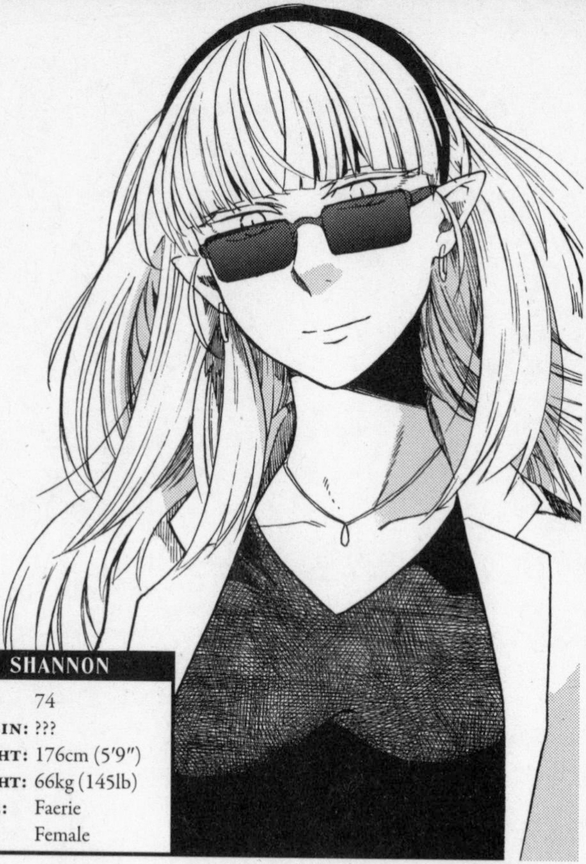

SHANNON	
AGE:	74
ORIGIN:	???
HEIGHT:	176cm (5'9")
WEIGHT:	66kg (145lb)
RACE:	Faerie
SEX:	Female

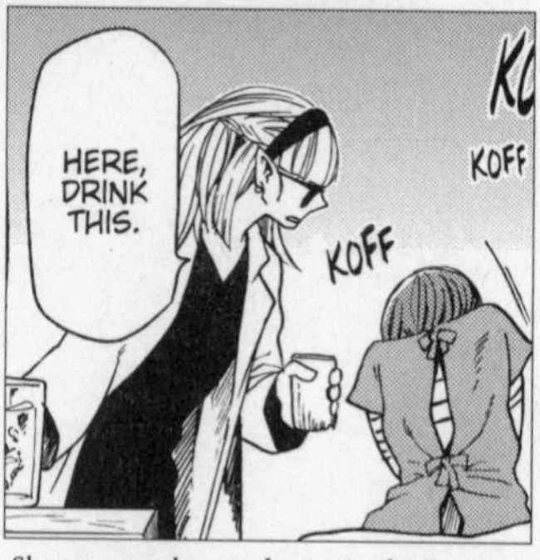
KO
KOFF
HERE, DRINK THIS.
KOFF

Shannon works as a doctor in the Faerie Kingdom using techniques she learned in the human world. When Chise is gravely ill, Shannon is able to treat her.

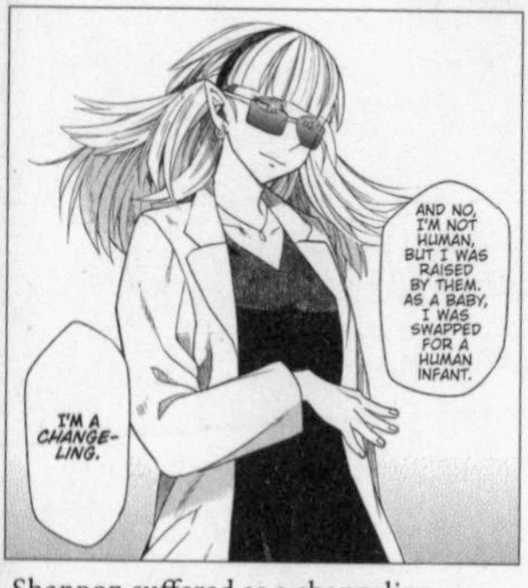
AND NO, I'M NOT HUMAN, BUT I WAS RAISED BY THEM. AS A BABY, I WAS SWAPPED FOR A HUMAN INFANT.
I'M A CHANGE-LING.

Shannon suffered as a changeling. Ordinarily changelings return to their original homes while still small.

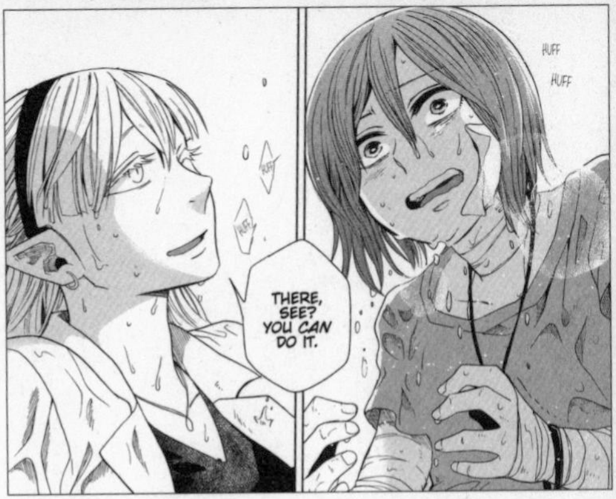
HUFF
HUFF
THERE, SEE? YOU *CAN* DO IT.

Seeing that Chise's will to live has dwindled, Shannon takes drastic measures to restore it.

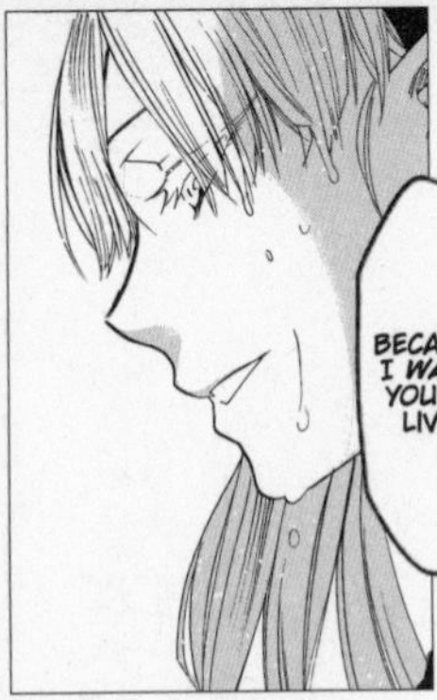
BECAUSE I *WANT* YOU TO LIVE.

She is a doctor who will never abandon a patient. When she says, "I want you to live," she's speaking from the deepest principles of her heart.

Shanahan

SHANAHAN	
AGE:	74
ORIGIN:	???
HEIGHT:	157cm (5′2″)
WEIGHT:	???
RACE:	Centaur
SEX:	Male

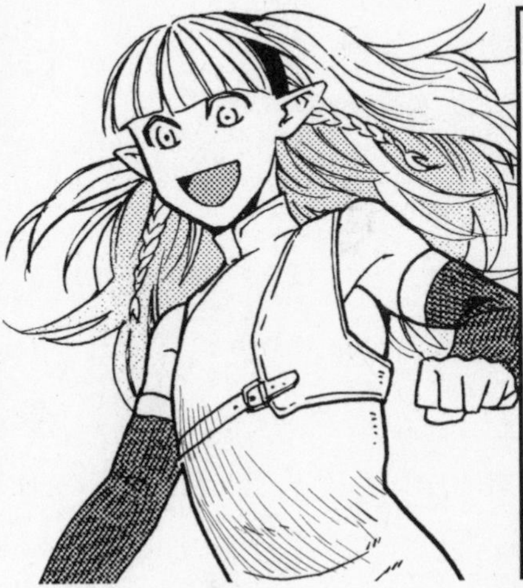

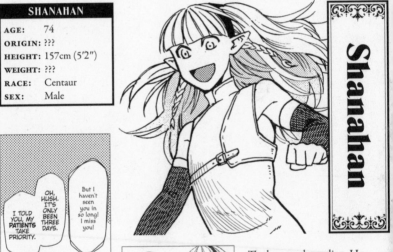

The human changeling. He lived in the Faerie Kingdom for half a century after the switch was made, and as a result, he now has the inhuman form of a centaur. He still lives in the Faerie Kingdom and is married to Shannon.

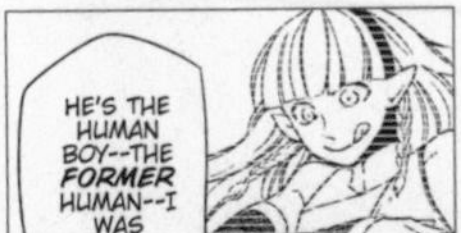
HE'S THE HUMAN BOY--THE *FORMER* HUMAN--I WAS TRADED AWAY FOR.

Shanahan was human when he was taken, but after living in the Faerie Kingdom for so long, he has become something else.

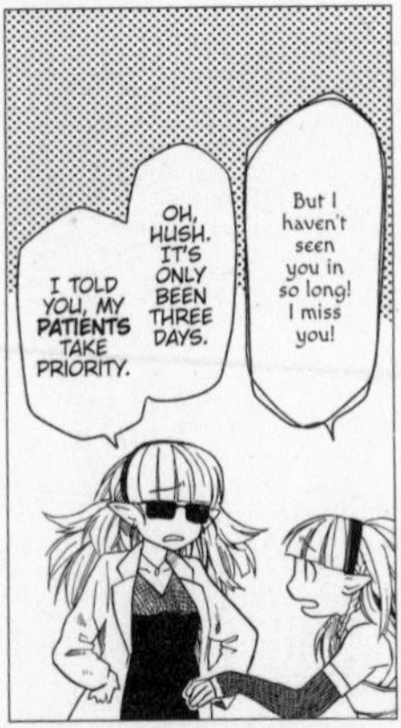
But I haven't seen you in so long! I miss you!
OH, HUSH. IT'S ONLY BEEN THREE DAYS.
I TOLD YOU, MY **PATIENTS** TAKE PRIORITY.

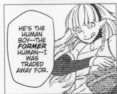

Long after being switched at birth, Shannon and Shanahan reunite, marry, and live together in the Faerie Kingdom.

Ariel

A wind faerie. Upon first meeting Chise, she tries to lure the sleigh beggy into the Faerie Kingdom. Later, she comes to help Chise purify the blight in the Ulthar Arc by lending Chise her power, in order to manifest the magic Chise chooses after talking to Mina, the entity at the blight's core. The blight is transformed into flowers and blows away on the wind.

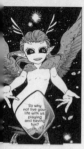

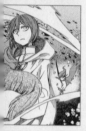

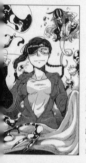

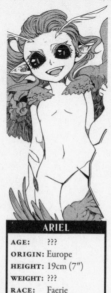

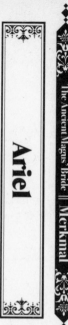

ARIEL	
AGE:	???
ORIGIN:	Europe
HEIGHT:	19cm (7″)
WEIGHT:	???
RACE:	Faerie
SEX:	Androgynous

So why not live your life with us playing and having fun?

Ariel invites Chise into the Faerie Kingdom, in hopes of having a sleigh beggy living among them. The scene offers a glimpse into the terrors of the fae world.

Chise purifies the blight and sends Mina and Matthew's souls back where they belong. She's assisted in this endeavor by Ariel's power as a wind faerie.

KNOWN AS
+ **CHISE:** Neighbor

Hugo

Angelica's familiar, a type of water spirit called a vodyanoi. As Angelica explains, "He's a bit of a prankster, but he does his part when there's work." Hugo is able to assist in the creation of magical tools with ease—as one might expect from the familiar of a Magus Craft Artificer. He's also involved in customizing the provisional items Angelica provides Chise with.

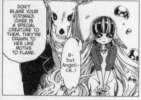

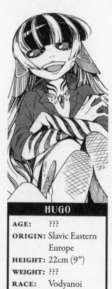

HUGO	
AGE:	???
ORIGIN:	Slavic Eastern Europe
HEIGHT:	22cm (9″)
WEIGHT:	???
RACE:	Vodyanoi
SEX:	Male

Angelica's familiar, Hugo, helps with her work, including getting important items ready for Chise.

DON'T BLAME YOUR VODYANOI. CHISE IS A SPECIAL CREATURE TO THEM. THEY'RE DRAWN TO HER LIKE MOTHS TO FLAME.
B-but, Angelica...!

Familiar or not, a fae is still fae, and Hugo is drawn to a sleigh beggy just as instinctively as any other faerie creature would be.

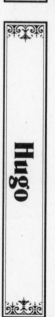

Nevin

An uir dragon Chise meets while visiting the dragons' aerie on an errand from Simon. Nevin is nearly five hundred years old and about to return to the earth. As he makes that transition, he and Chise dream of soaring through the sky. Later, Chise crafts her wand fror the linden tha grows from hi body.

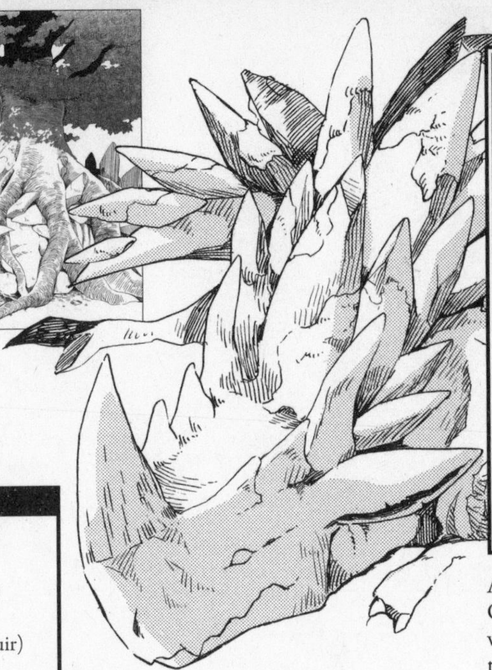

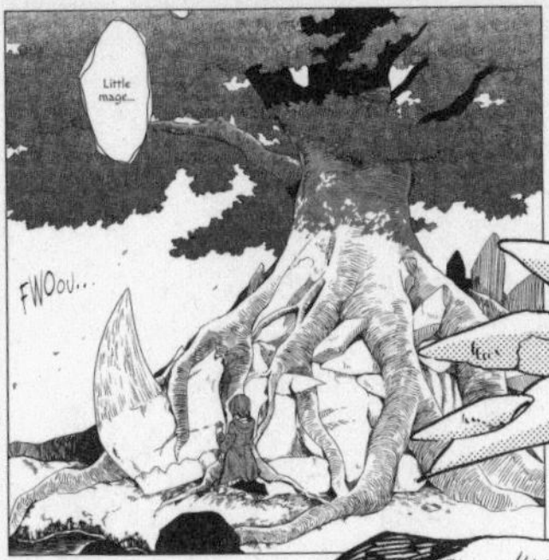
Little mage...
FWOOU...

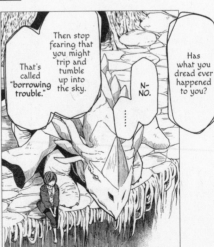

Before he returns, Nevin borrows Chise's power to fly through the sky once more. It marks the end of his long life.

NEVIN	
AGE:	Over 400
ORIGIN:	???
HEIGHT:	10m (33′)
WEIGHT:	???
RACE:	Dragon (uir)
SEX:	Male

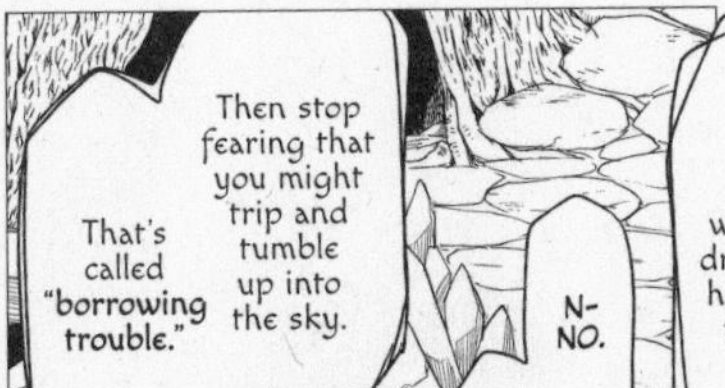
Has what you dread ever happened to you?
N-NO.
......
Then stop fearing that you might trip and tumble up into the sky.
That's called "borrowing trouble."

Chise fashions her wand from a branch of the linden that grew from Nevin. Lindel adds the finishing touches.

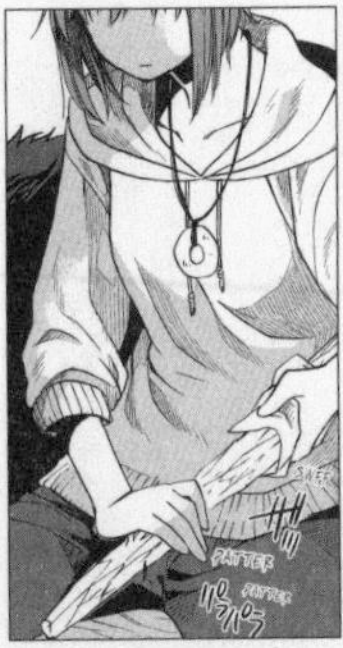
PATTER
PATTER

When Chise meets Nevin again in a dream, he offers her counsel on the changes taking place in her heart, and his wisdom gives her determination.

Spriggan

A faerie who serves Titania. He shuns Elias as a "halfling" and never speaks kindly of him. However, Spriggan is very warm toward other fae. When Silky, as a banshee, lost the home she'd been connected to, it was Spriggan who helped her find a new place for herself. Spriggan often has a black dog at his side.

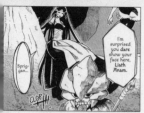

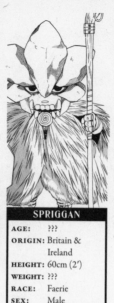

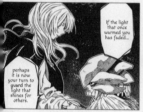

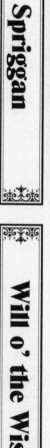

SPRIGGAN	
AGE:	???
ORIGIN:	Britain & Ireland
HEIGHT:	60cm (2′)
WEIGHT:	???
RACE:	Faerie
SEX:	Male

I'm surprised you dare show your face here, Liath Anam.
Sprig-gan...
CLOP

Spriggan regards Elias as a black sheep of Faerie, calling him a "flesh-clad halfling." Spriggan is also harsh to humans, as they belong to a different world.

If the light that once warmed you has faded...
perhaps it is now your turn to guard the light that shines for others.

He is, however, very warm to fae. Silky would not be who she is now without Spriggan's kindness.

Will o' the Wisp

A fae that haunts graves and forests, also known as Blue Flame. In the Black Dog Arc, this fae helps Chise and her friends evade Cartaphilus when Chise gets carried away and overexerts herself. He also helps Ruth recall his duty as a church grim. Finally, he gives the souls of Isabel and those with her a proper sendoff.

WILL O' THE WISP	
AGE:	???
ORIGIN:	Britain & Ireland
HEIGHT:	40cm (1′4″)
WEIGHT:	???
RACE:	Faerie
SEX:	Male

See you later.

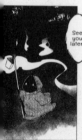

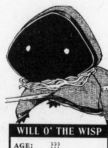

His duty is to guide the souls of the dead to the other side. He is the boatman to the afterlife.

Stop spouting that nonsense, you foolish mutt!

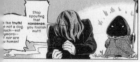

He only appears in the Black Dog Arc, but he performs many critical tasks, such as helping the party retreat and waking the black dog.

KNOWN AS
✛ **ELIAS:** Blue Flame

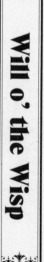

Leannán Sídhe

A type of faerie that possesses young men and grants them literary genius in exchange for their life. She is attracted by the beauty of Joel's roses and is drawn to him, but struggles with her nature. After Joel's death, she decides to remain in his house.

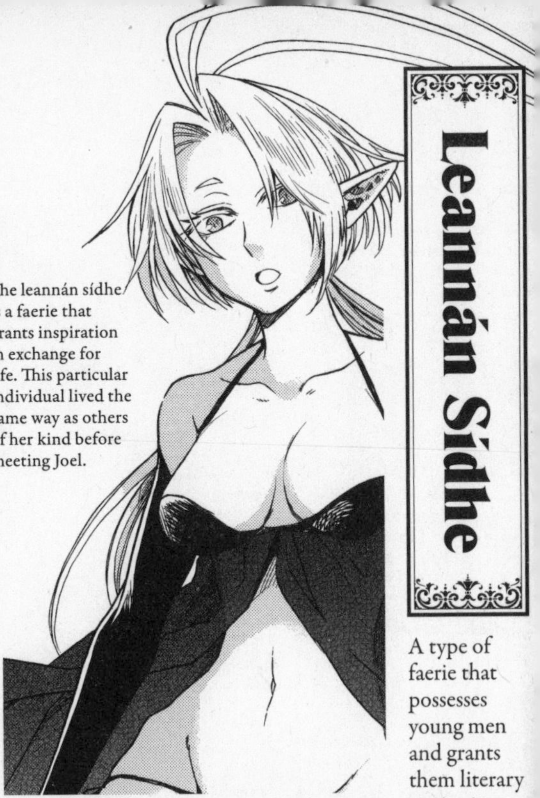

The leannán sídhe is a faerie that grants inspiration in exchange for life. This particular individual lived the same way as others of her kind before meeting Joel.

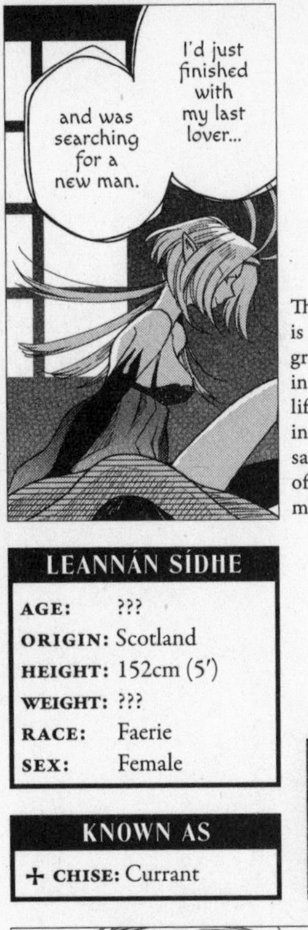
I'd just finished with my last lover...
and was searching for a new man.

LEANNÁN SÍDHE	
AGE:	???
ORIGIN:	Scotland
HEIGHT:	152cm (5′)
WEIGHT:	???
RACE:	Faerie
SEX:	Female

KNOWN AS
+ **CHISE:** Currant

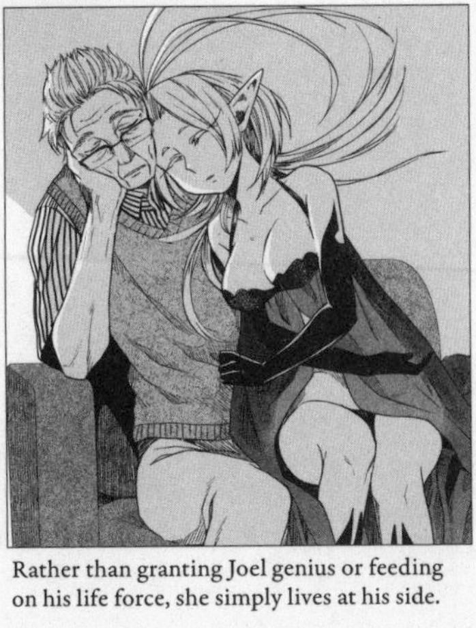

Rather than granting Joel genius or feeding on his life force, she simply lives at his side.

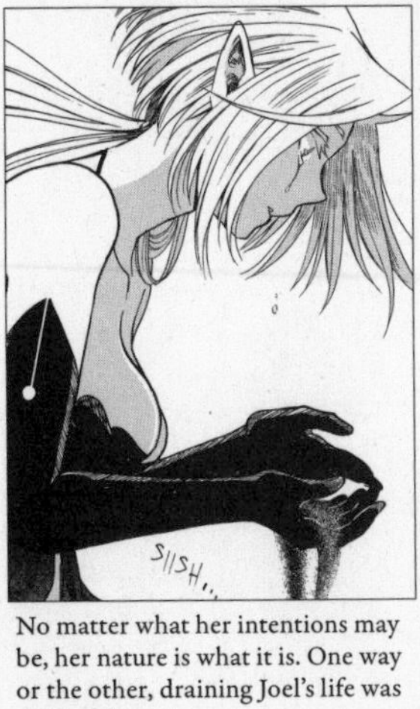
SIISH...

No matter what her intentions may be, her nature is what it is. One way or the other, draining Joel's life was inevitable.

Merituuli

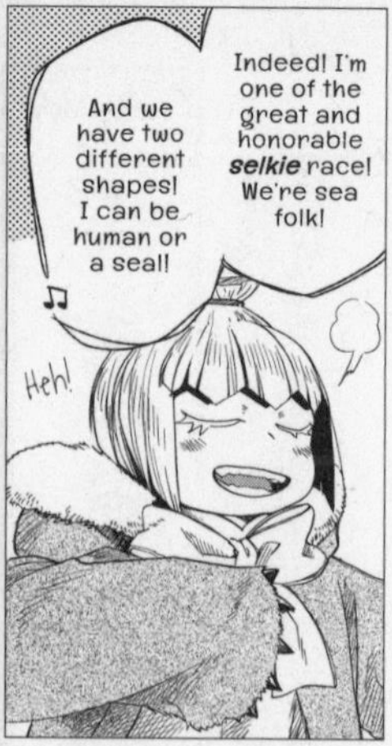
Indeed! I'm one of the great and honorable *selkie* race! We're sea folk!
And we have two different shapes! I can be human or a seal! ♫
Heh!

Merituuli is Lindel's familiar and can take the shape of a seal or a human. The shape of his hands reflects his nature.

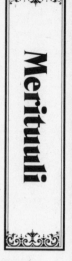

MERITUULI	
AGE:	87
ORIGIN:	Scotland
HEIGHT:	120cm (3′11″)
WEIGHT:	???
RACE:	Selkie
SEX:	Male

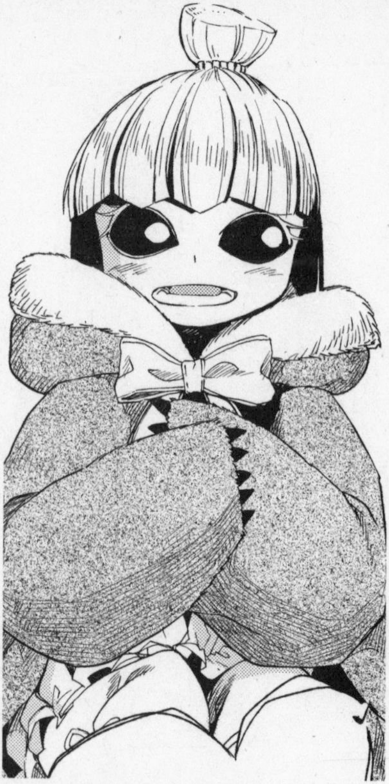

Lindel's familiar, a selkie. His usual appearance is somewhat like that of a human child, but he can also turn into a seal. He often brings Chise and Adolf messages on Lindel's behalf, as Lindel cannot leave the dragons' aerie. Merituuli is quite friendly and often climbs onto Chise's head or Adolf's lap.

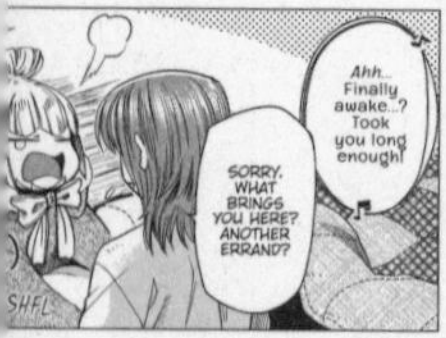
Ahh... Finally awake...? Took you long enough!
SORRY. WHAT BRINGS YOU HERE? ANOTHER ERRAND?
SHFL

Merituuli is very friendly and is readily affectionate even with humans, as we see with Adolf—who was once Lindel's apprentice—and Chise.

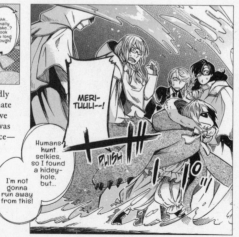

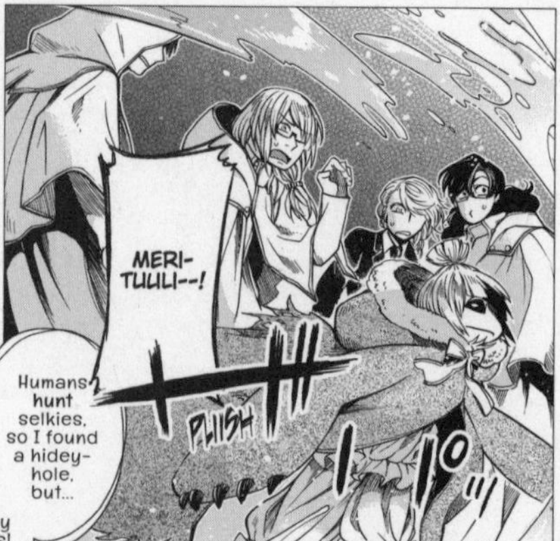
MERI-TUULI--!
Humans hunt selkies, so I found a hidey-hole, but...
I'm not gonna run away from this!
PLIISH

Merituuli is able to stand against the fire breathed by a dragon gone berserk at the auction house. Sea folk are perfectly suited for such a situation.

HAZEL	
AGE:	35
ORIGIN:	Scotland
HEIGHT:	205cm (6′9″)
WEIGHT:	???
RACE:	Centaur
SEX:	Male

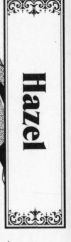

Hazel

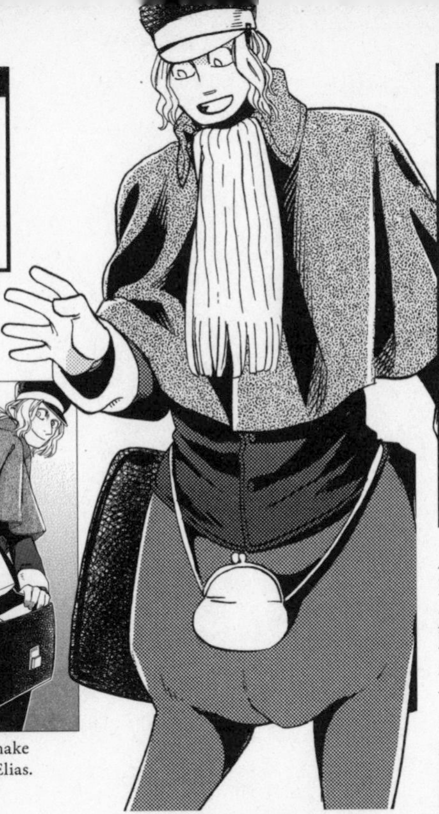

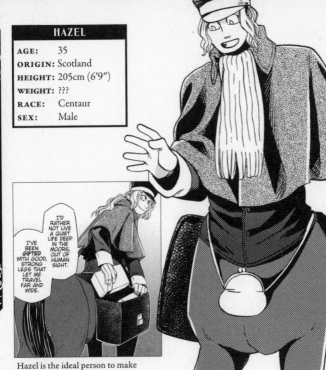

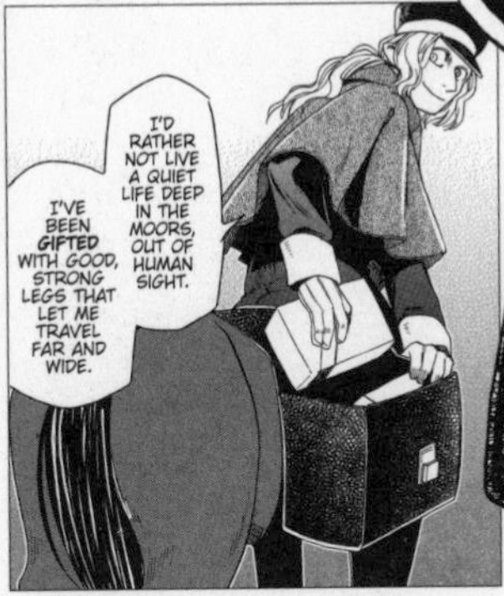
I'D RATHER NOT LIVE A QUIET LIFE DEEP IN THE MOORS, OUT OF HUMAN SIGHT.
I'VE BEEN GIFTED WITH GOOD, STRONG LEGS THAT LET ME TRAVEL FAR AND WIDE.

Hazel is the ideal person to make deliveries for mages such as Elias.

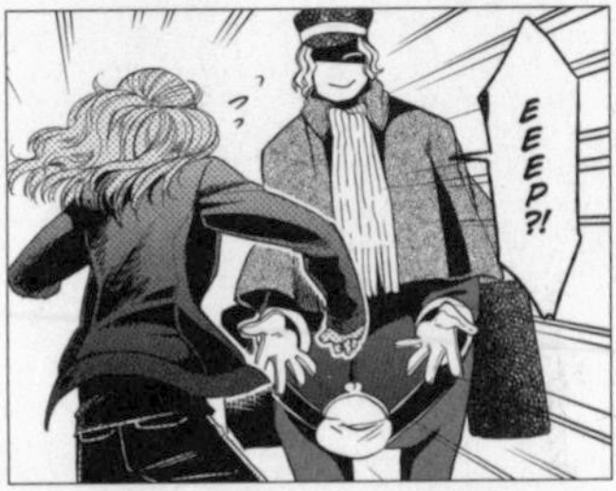
EEEP?!

Hazel usually wears a glamour so that only mages notice him. Even Alice couldn't detect his presence.

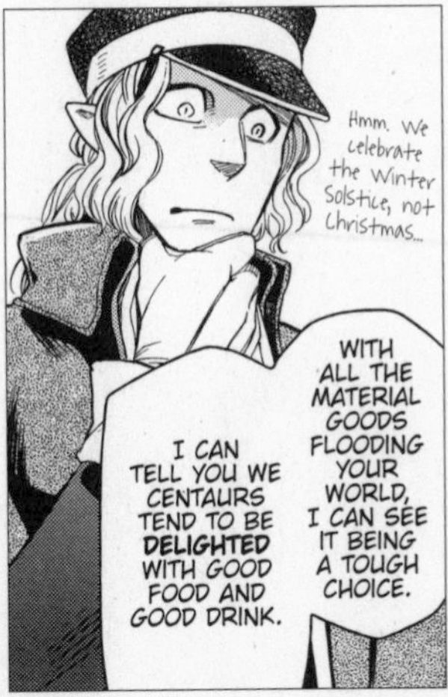
Hmm. We celebrate the Winter Solstice, not Christmas...
WITH ALL THE MATERIAL GOODS FLOODING YOUR WORLD, I CAN SEE IT BEING A TOUGH CHOICE.
I CAN TELL YOU WE CENTAURS TEND TO BE DELIGHTED WITH GOOD FOOD AND GOOD DRINK.

As Chise and Alice are struggling to choose what Christmas gifts to buy, Hazel suggests purchasing something they can easily imagine the recipient using.

As a centaur, Hazel has a powerful equin lower body, meaning he's well equipped t make deliveries far and wide. He can be summoned by tapping an old stone on a hazel branch twelve times. H usually wears a glamour so that only mage can perceive him. When Chise and Alic are struggling to choose Christmas presents, he offers his assistance.

Marielle

A witch who belongs to a coven. She reaches out to Chise at the auction house where the dragon chicks are being sold, and offers help in hopes of being able to free her coven's priestess, Phyllis. It appears that witches are extremely long-lived. Marielle's reference to Marie Antoinette's execution implies that she's been around since at least the 18th century.

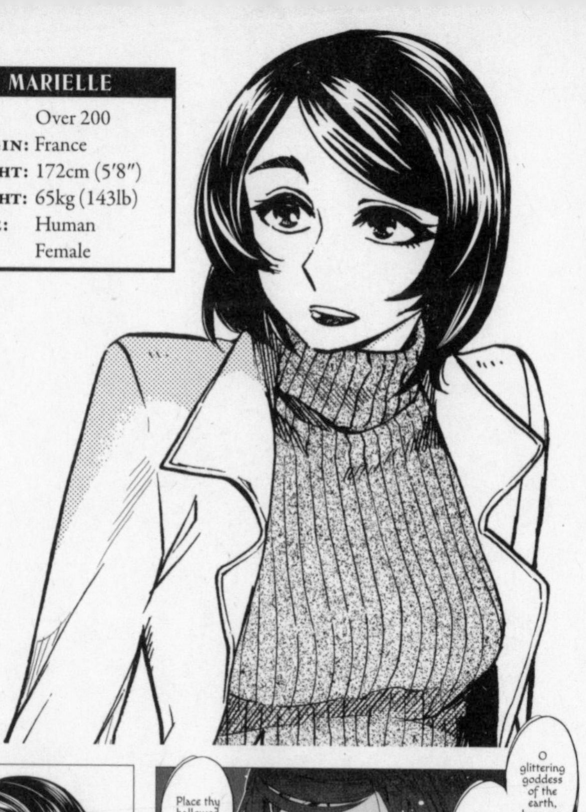

MARIELLE

AGE:	Over 200
ORIGIN:	France
HEIGHT:	172cm (5′8″)
WEIGHT:	65kg (143lb)
RACE:	Human
SEX:	Female

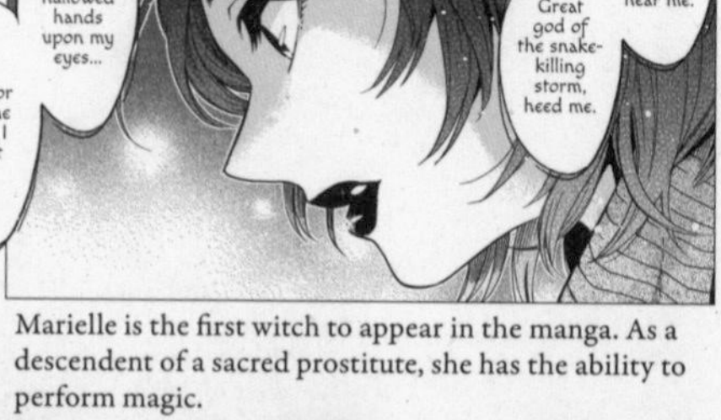
O glittering goddess of the earth, hear me.
Great god of the snake-killing storm, heed me.
Place thy hallowed hands upon my eyes...
That for but one blink, I might see.

Marielle is the first witch to appear in the manga. As a descendent of a sacred prostitute, she has the ability to perform magic.

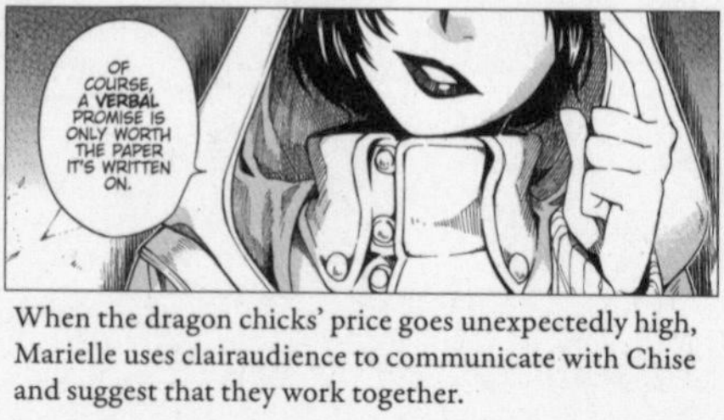
OF COURSE, A VERBAL PROMISE IS ONLY WORTH THE PAPER IT'S WRITTEN ON.

When the dragon chicks' price goes unexpectedly high, Marielle uses clairaudience to communicate with Chise and suggest that they work together.

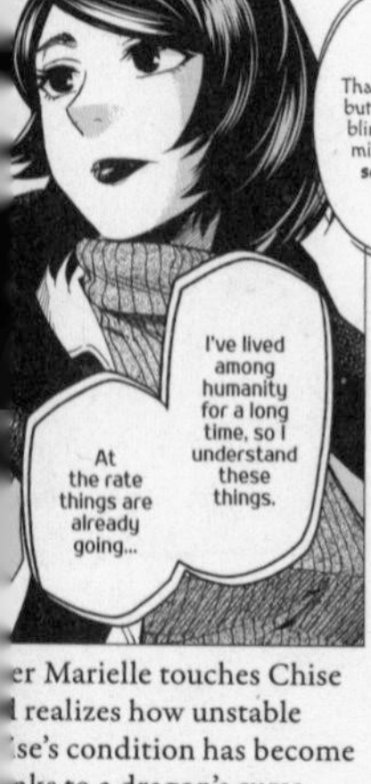
I've lived among humanity for a long time, so I understand these things.
At the rate things are already going...

er Marielle touches Chise
l realizes how unstable
ise's condition has become
nks to a dragon's curse,
shares with Elias that
ise is unlikely to last long.

Ashen Eye

An inhuman being, thousa of years old, w occasionally has dealings with Elias; als a trickster wh innocently wreaks havoc in Elias and Chise's lives. I was Ashen Ey who gave Chi the pelt that turns her into werebeast, an who carried Ethan off afte his fight with Stella. Judgin by some thing Ashen Eye an Elias have sai this entity ma know someth about Elias' origins.

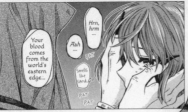

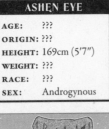

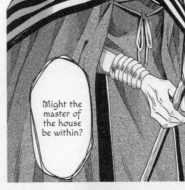

Might the master of the house be within?

Hrn, hrm ...
Aah ...
Your blood comes from the world's eastern edge...
PAT
Smells like sand.
PAT
PAT

Ashen Eye sees Elias from time to time, and arrives on his doorstep to celebrate the news that Chise, a new mage, has arrived.

ASHEN EYE	
AGE:	???
ORIGIN:	???
HEIGHT:	169cm (5′7″)
WEIGHT:	???
RACE:	???
SEX:	Androgynous

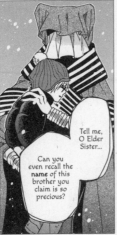

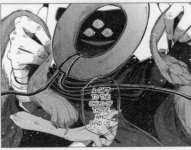

A GIFT TO THE CHILD OF THOSE WHO BIND US.

Seen through the magical stone, Ashen Eye's inhuman nature is even more evident, as three unfocused eyes and a broad mouth become visible. Is this a glimpse of Ashen Eye's true form, or is the reality stranger still?

Tell me, O Elder Sister...
Can you even recall the name of this brother you claim is so precious?

In a heated moment, Stella says that she does not want Ethan—at which Ashen Eye takes him away, telling Stella that words cannot be taken back once they've been spoken.

Cartaphilus

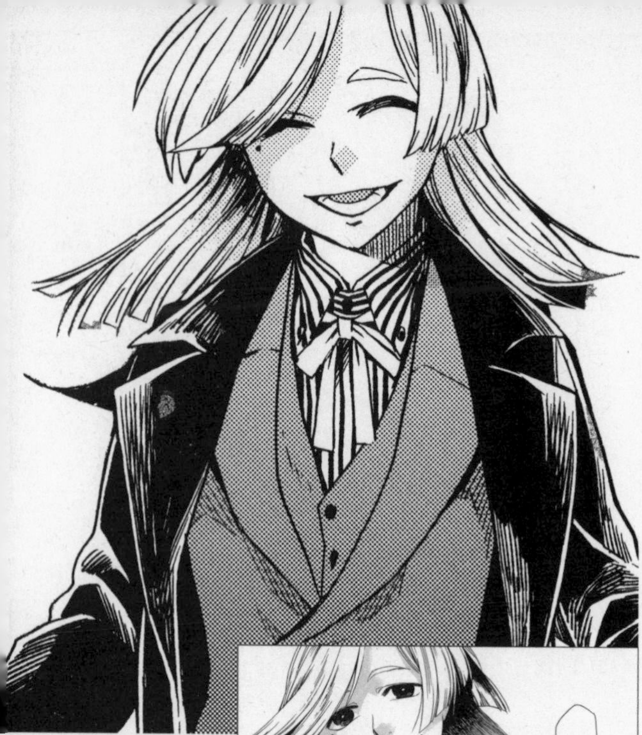

An alchemist with the appearance of a young boy. Other alchemists, including Renfred, refer to him as the Wandering Jew. Cartaphilus collects creatures such as the blight of Ulthar, the church grim, and the dragon chicks, but his ultimate goal has not yet been made clear.

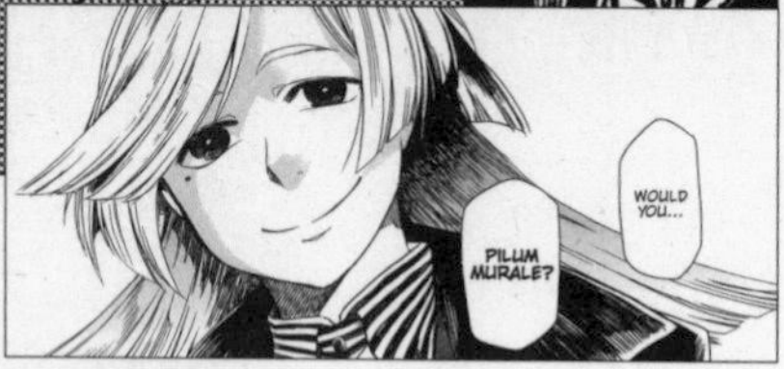
WOULD YOU...
PILUM MURALE?

He calls Elias "Pilum Murale," and Elias knows his name. They seem to have some sort of history.

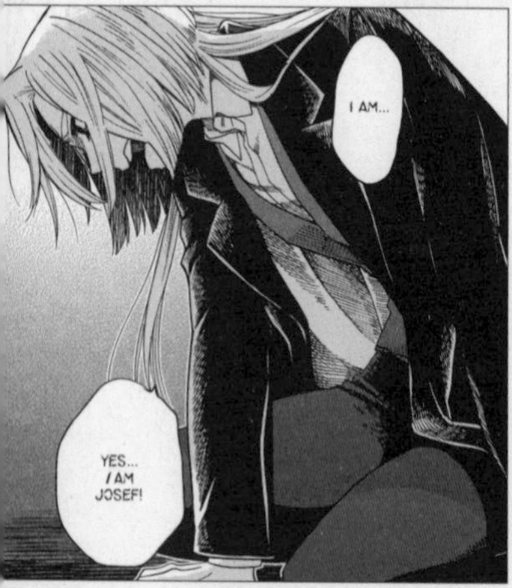
I AM...
YES... I AM JOSEF!

Sometimes he calls himself Josef or seems to argue with himself about who he is, as if he has a split personality.

CARTAPHILUS	
AGE:	???
ORIGIN:	Eastern Europe
HEIGHT:	148cm (4'10")
WEIGHT:	48kg (106lb)
RACE:	Human
SEX:	Male

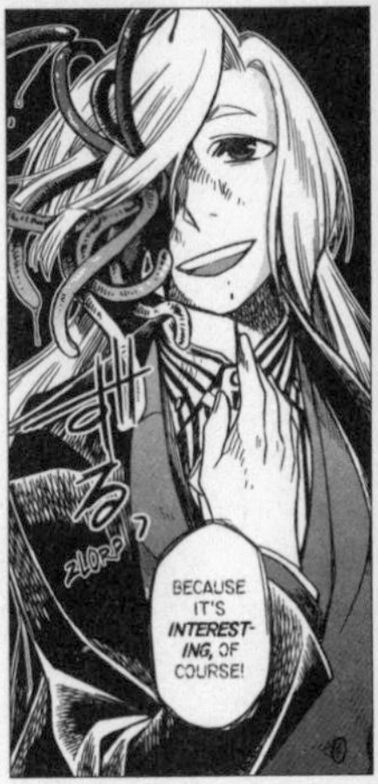
BECAUSE IT'S INTERESTING, OF COURSE!

He appears human, but he does not react as if in pain even when shot in the head or when his arm is blown off. In fact, he repairs his brain on the spot.

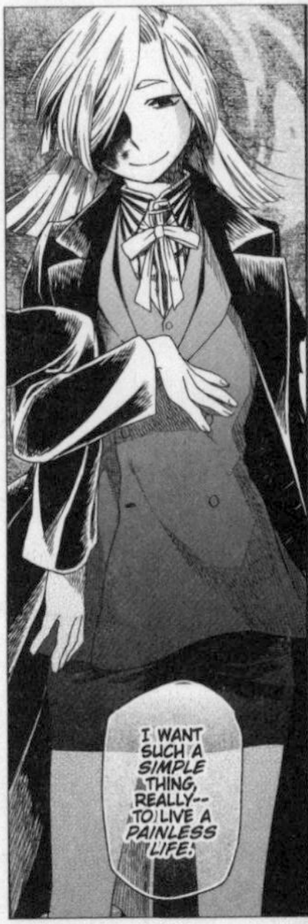
I WANT SUCH A SIMPLE THING, REALLY-- TO LIVE A PAINLESS LIFE.

The precise means by which he plans to attain a life free of pain have not yet been revealed.

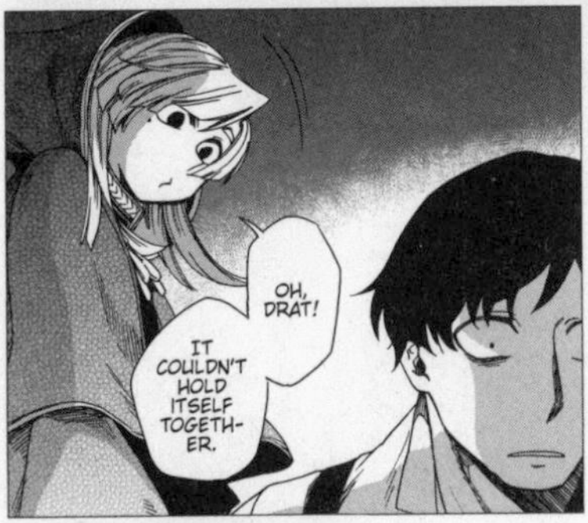
OH, DRAT!
IT COULDN'T HOLD ITSELF TOGETH-ER.

The gruesome events of the Ulthar Arc are set in motion by an experiment Cartaphilus once conducted.

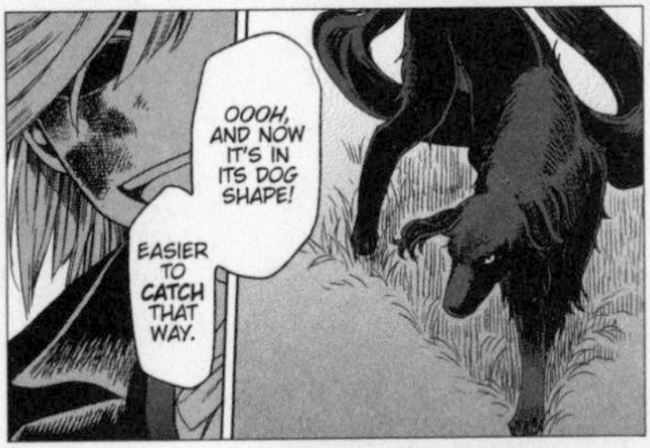
OOOH, AND NOW IT'S IN ITS DOG SHAPE!
EASIER TO CATCH THAT WAY.

In the Black Dog Arc, Cartaphilus tries to capture a fae that is oblivious to its own nature, and keeps on fighting even after he is barred from his goal.

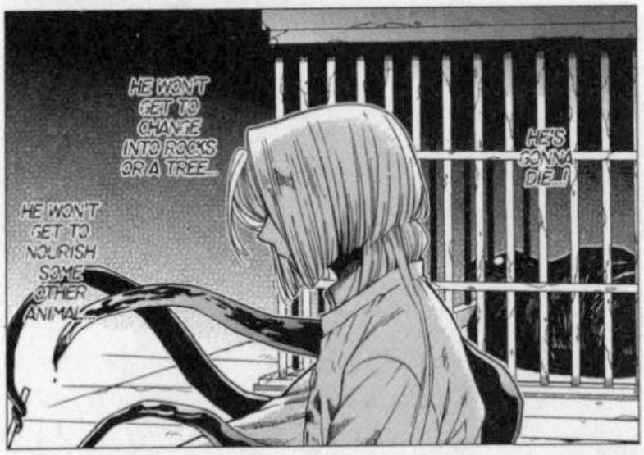
HE'S GONNA DIE...!
HE WON'T GET TO CHANGE INTO ROCKS OR A TREE...
HE WON'T GET TO NOURISH SOME OTHER ANIMAL.

Chise and friends keep him from acquiring his targets until he goes after the dragon chicks, with much better results.

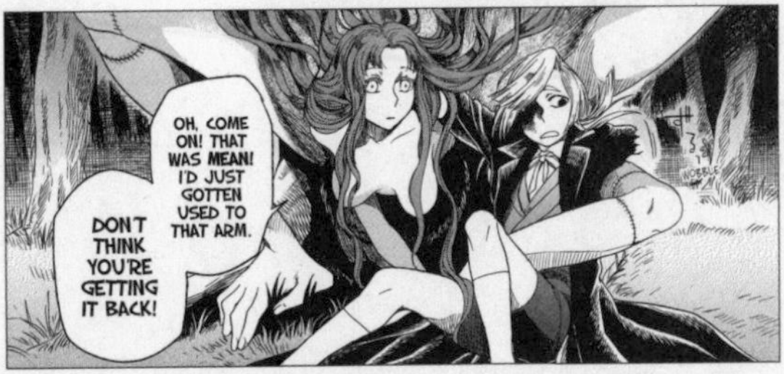
WOBBLE
OH, COME ON! THAT WAS MEAN! I'D JUST GOTTEN USED TO THAT ARM.
DON'T THINK YOU'RE GETTING IT BACK!

We've yet to see Cartaphilus actually performing alchemy, but his chimera is ferocious in combat.

KNOWN AS

+ **ALCHEMISTS:** Wandering Jew

Other Characters

MOLLY'S OWNER

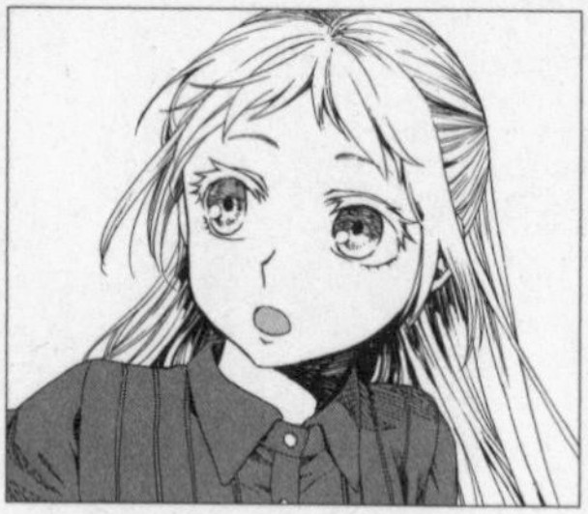

A girl in Ulthar whom Molly regards as her daughter.

MOLLY

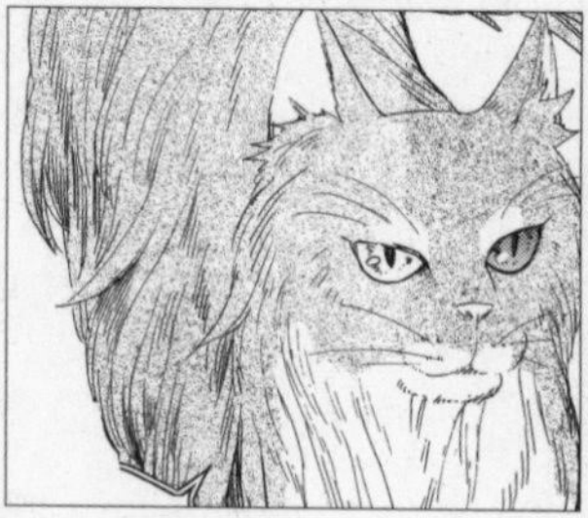

The odd-eyed "King of Cats" in Ulthar, on the last of her nine lives.

DARK LADY

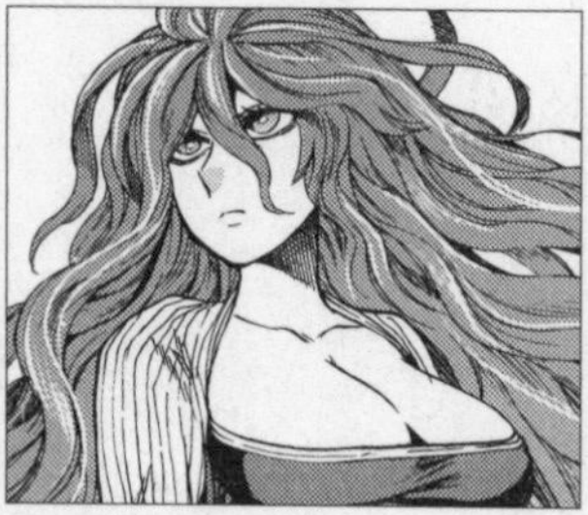

She and the Horned God are said to be winter gods—gods of death.

HERALDS OF YULE

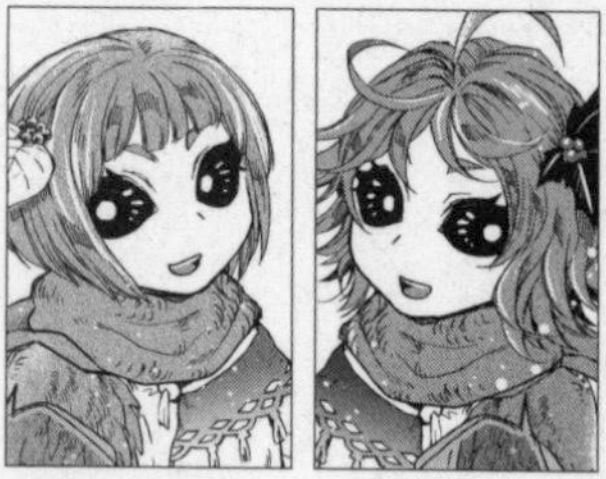

Twins who appear on the winter solstice and encourage all to prepare for Yule. Not even Elias knows much about them.

PHYLLIS

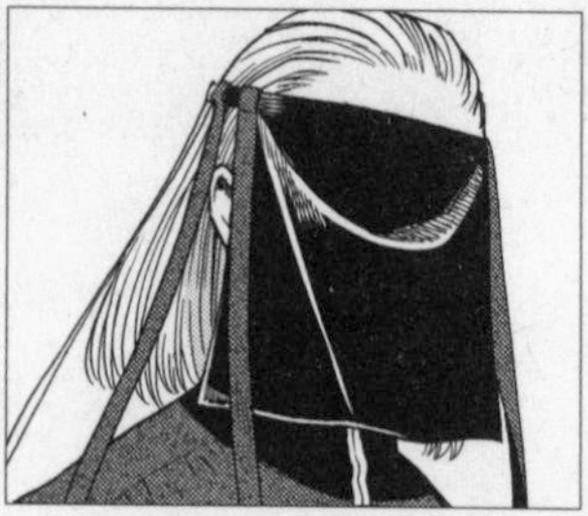

High priestess and leader of Marielle's coven, bound within a tree.

YOUNG WINTER GODDESS

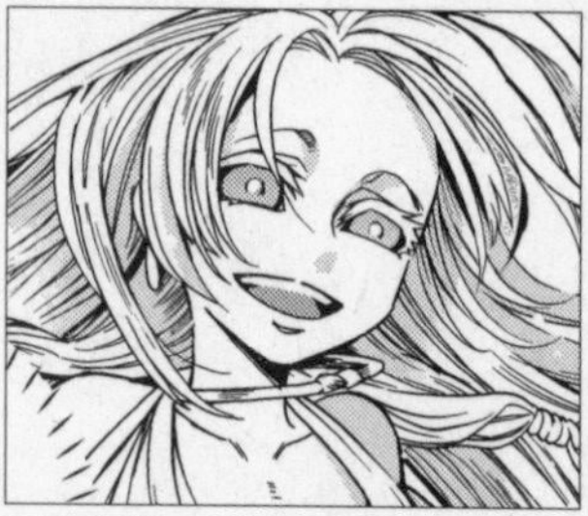

The childhood form of the Dark Lady. In turn, she will be the next winter's Dark Lady.

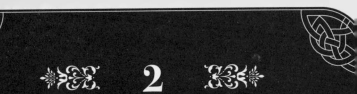

2

View of the World

This chapter introduces the characters' homes
and communities. Relish the attention to detail
for which *The Ancient Magus' Bride* and its British
setting are known.

Chise and Elias' House

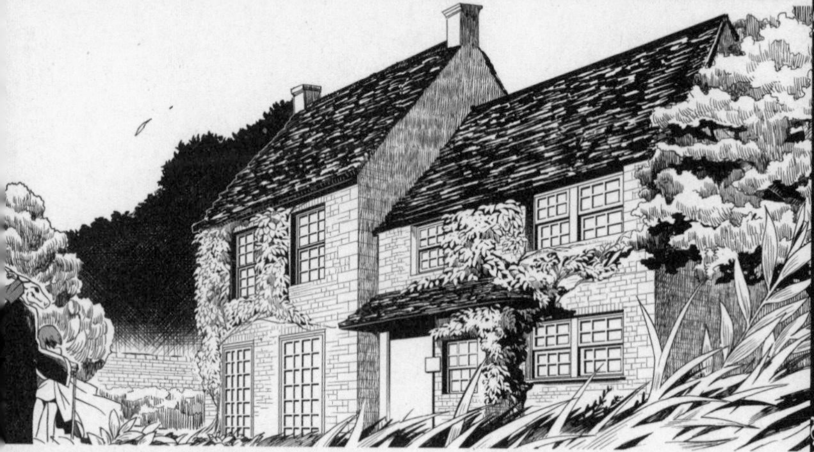

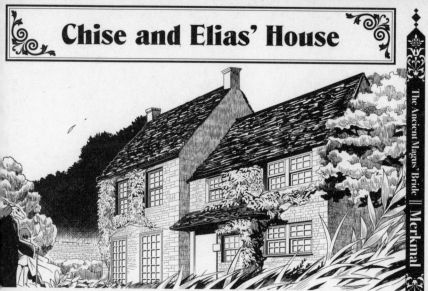

Most of the rooms in Elias' residence relate to Elias himself, as the house's master. Elias' and Chise's private rooms face each other.

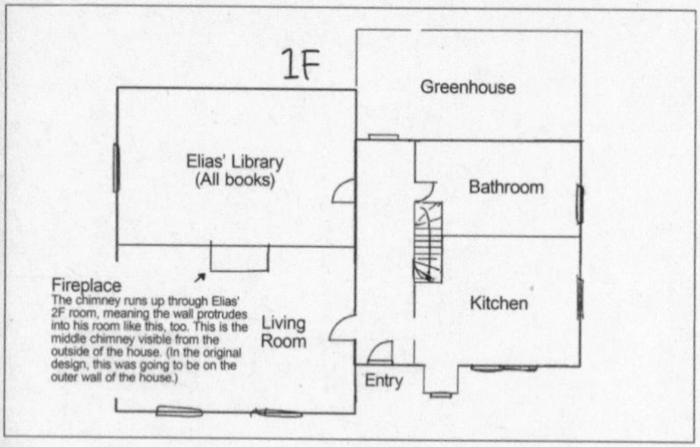
1F
Greenhouse
Elias' Library
(All books)
Bathroom
Fireplace
The chimney runs up through Elias' 2F room, meaning the wall protrudes into his room like this, too. This is the middle chimney visible from the outside of the house. (In the original design, this was going to be on the outer wall of the house.)
Kitchen
Living Room
Entry

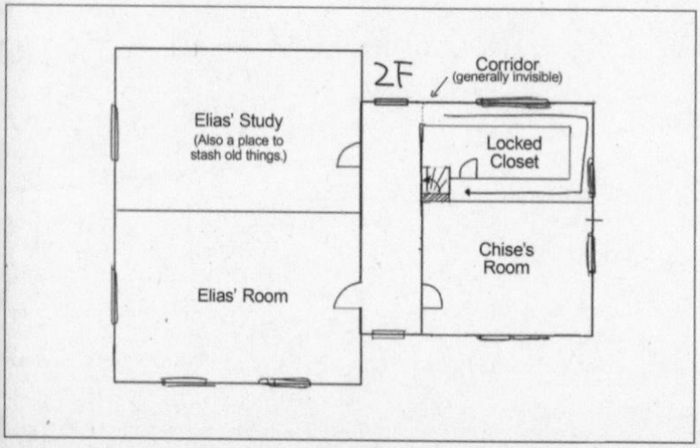
2F
Corridor
(generally invisible)
Elias' Study
(Also a place to stash old things.)
Locked Closet
Chise's Room
Elias' Room

Chise and Elias live in a house situated, as Elias describes it, in "the countryside west of London, on the shores of England." Given that Chise transfers from a bus to a train to travel, one can extrapolate that the village is a good distance into the countryside.

The house has two floors and seven rooms. There is a greenhouse on the first floor for nurturing seedlings. The second floor also has a locked closet that can only be reached by circling through a corridor.

BATHROOM

Bathroom
Laundry Basket

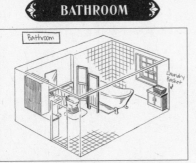

Contains a tub, a toilet, and a sink. Unlike an equivalent space in Japan, it's truly large enough to be called a "room."

LIVING ROOM

Elias' House Living Room

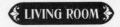

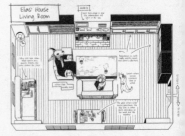

As it's often chilly in the U.K., the room centers around the hearth. There is a sofa for Silky.

ELIAS' ROOM

Elias' Room
Fairly Simple overall

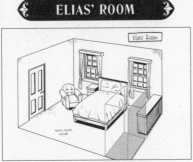

Elias' room is very simple. One must notice, however, the size of the bed required for someone of his stature.

KITCHEN

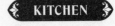

The British put the washing machine in the kitchen. The machine itself opera differently from thos found in Japan.

Kitchen

CLOSET

UP ON THE SECOND FLOOR, THERE'S A LOCKED CLOSET.

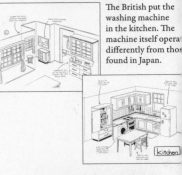

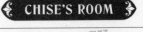

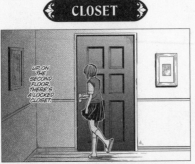

Down a normally invisible corridor lies a locked closet. It opens only when Elias needs something.

CHISE'S ROOM

Chise's Room

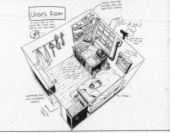

Compared to Elias' room, Chise's is quite busy. Note that she has her own mini stove and chimne

Chise and Elias' Village

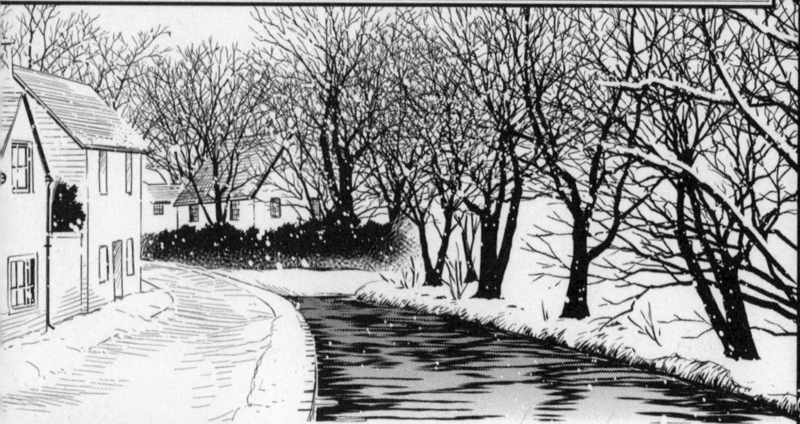

Chise and Elias live in a small country village in which almost everyone knows each other. Naturally, it has few tall buildings such as you would see in London. Instead, it is rich in natural features such as woods and streams.

In the story, we see Simon's church, and also Joel's house with its rose garden.

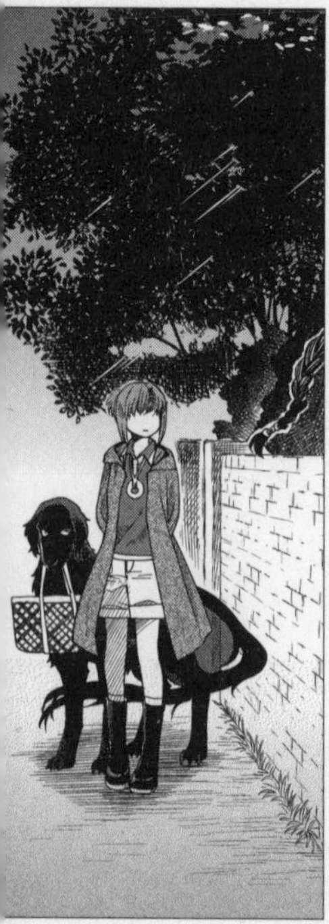

Brick walls demarcate lots from the road. This sort of detail brings out the country atmosphere.

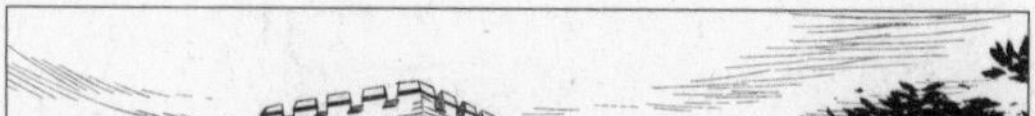

There is a church in the village, where Simon lives. There is a garden on the property. Simon does his share of gardening.

TOWN

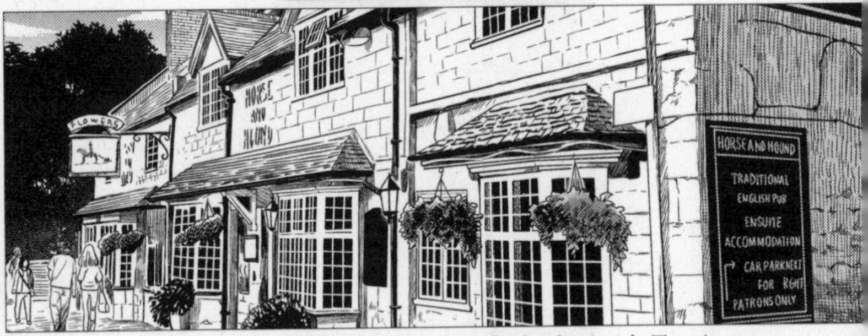
FLOWERS
HORSE AND HOUND
TRADITIONAL
ENGLISH PUB
ENSUITE
ACCOMMODATION
CAR PARK NEXT
PATRONS ONLY

A commercial road offers places for people to buy everyday food and essentials. There is an open-air terrace where residents can relax.

BUS STOP

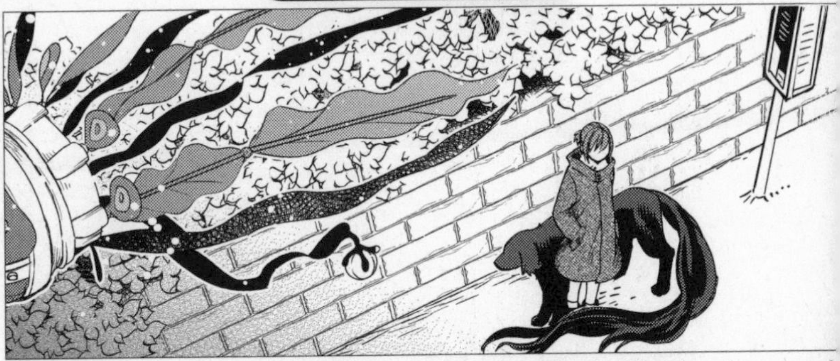

Although this hasn't been clearly shown in the story, we can presume that the village depends on cars and other motor vehicles. Since Chise doesn't have a car, she's seen waiting at the bus stop.

NIGHT FOREST

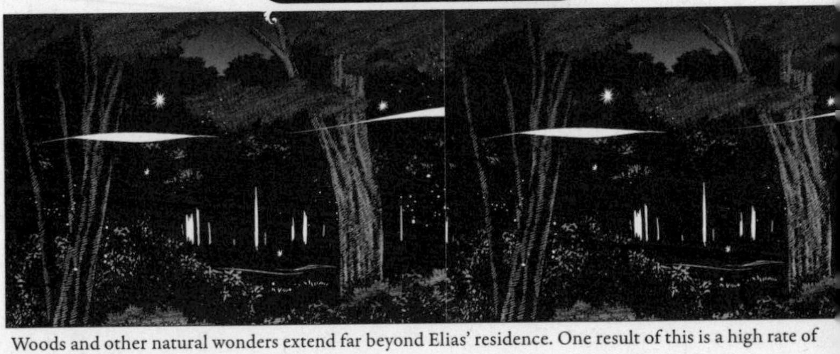

Woods and other natural wonders extend far beyond Elias' residence. One result of this is a high rate of encounters with neighbors of the fae variety.

Angelica's Workshop

FLOOR PLAN

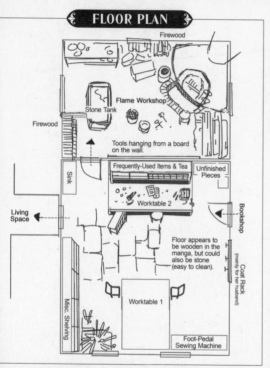

Firewood

Flame Workshop

Stone Tank

Firewood

Tools hanging from a board on the wall.

Sink

Living Space

Frequently-Used Items & Tea

Unfinished Pieces

Worktable 2

Bookshop

Floor appears to be wooden in the manga, but could also be stone (easy to clean).

Coat Rack (mainly for her husband)

Misc. Shelving

Worktable 1

Foot-Pedal Sewing Machine

Angelica's workshop is in London. The space at the front of the building is occupied by what appears to be an old bookshop, providing cover for her work. The door connecting the storefront to her workshop can only be opened by magic.

SINK

SO THAT OLD HERMIT AINSWORTH DECIDED TO GET HIMSELF AN APPRENTICE, EH?

There's a sink by the door to the living quarters.

WORKTABLE

Various things used for creating magus crafts lie on the worktable, including machinery, jewels, puppets, and other devices.

DOOR TO LIVING QUARTERS

ARE THERE CUSTOMERS?

ALTHEA!

The living quarters are someplace else entirely, connected by magic.

STOREFRONT FLOOR PLAN

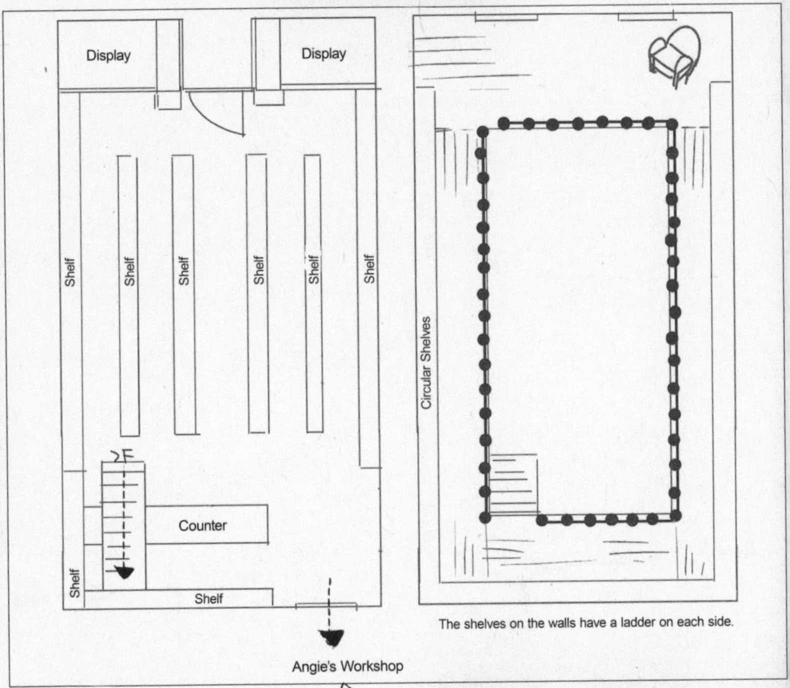
Display
Display
Shelf
Shelf
Shelf
Shelf
Shelf
Shelf
2F
Counter
Shelf
Shelf
Angie's Workshop
Circular Shelves
The shelves on the walls have a ladder on each side.

ENTRY

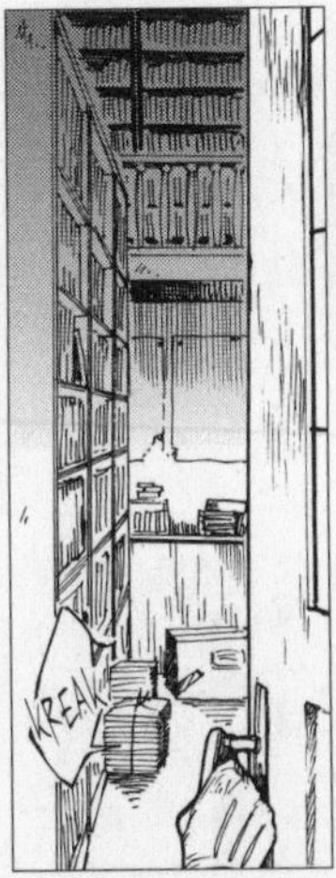
KREAK

The place looks dingy and uninviting.

SHELVES

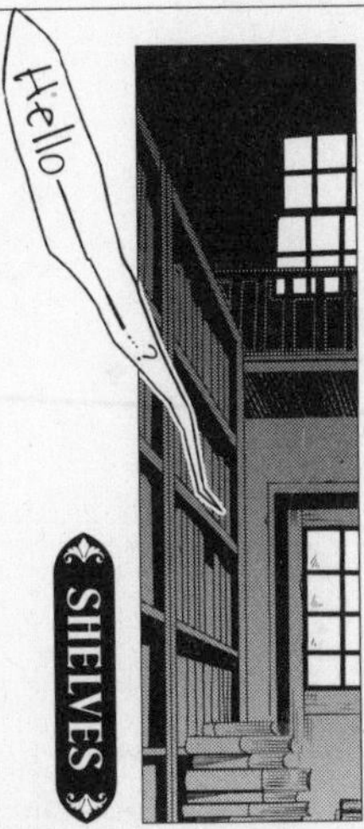
Hello—...?

The storefront is full of shelves, as it's meant to be a bookshop.

2ND FLOOR CHAIR

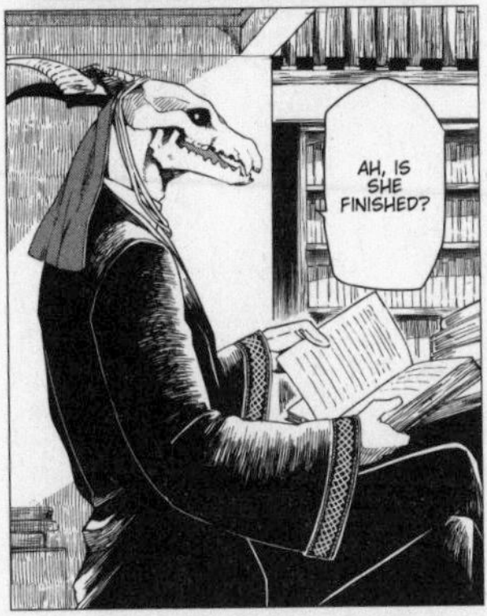
AH, IS SHE FINISHED?

The second floor of the shop offers seating where one can relax and peruse the contents of the books.

Ulthar

Chise and Elias visit Ulthar on an "errand" from Simon. The town is as full of cats as one might expect from a place known as "the town where cats congregate." With its woods and lake, Ulthar's natural beauty gives it some resemblance to the village where Chise and Elias live.

The town appears to be readily accessible by train, so presumably it has its own station.

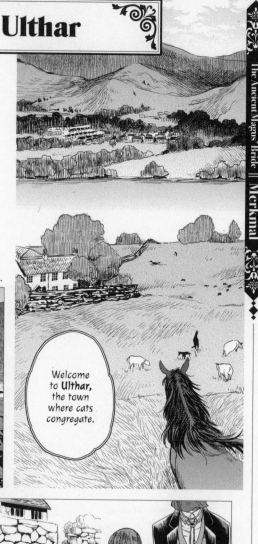

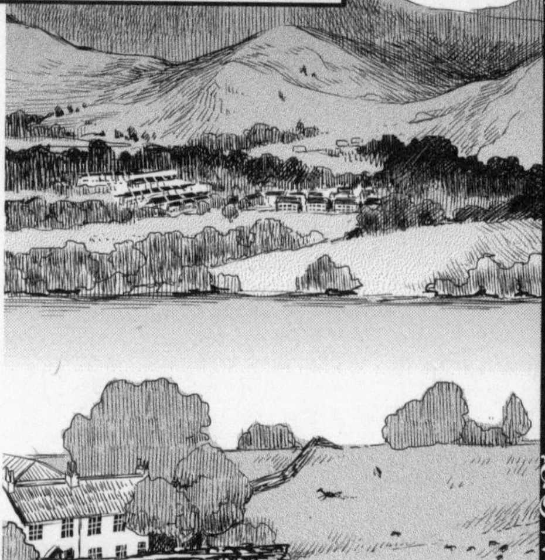
Welcome to **Ulthar,** the town where cats congregate.

Because Chise and Elias arrive by train, it seems to have a conveniently located station.

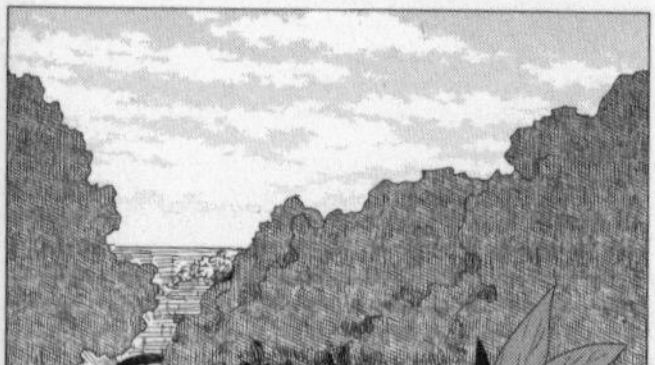

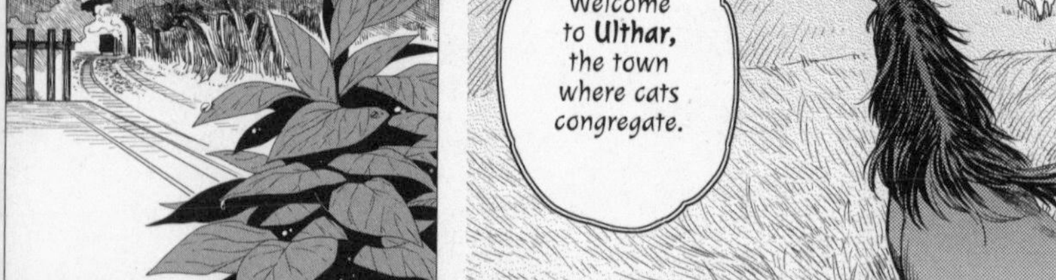

Like the natural soundings, Ulthar's manmade buildings are somewhat similar to those in Chise and Elias' village, such as the stone walls marking the boundaries of each lot.

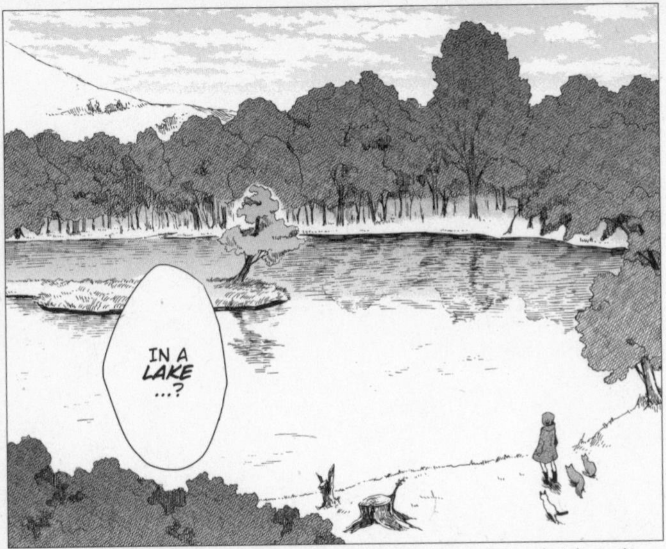
IN A LAKE ...?

There is a substantial lake at the town's edge, and the blight is sealed on the islet in the center. At the cats' request, Chise sets out to purify it.

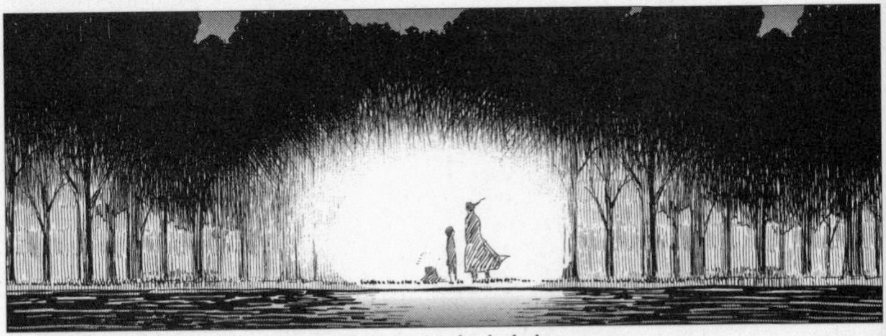

The lake is surrounded by forest, so at night, it is completely dark.

ULTHAR IN THE PAST

The shed is a typical brick building. The chimney indicates that it contains a fireplace.

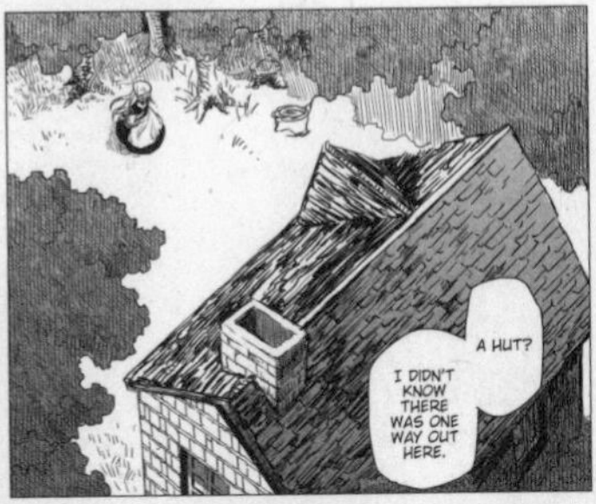
A HUT?
I DIDN'T KNOW THERE WAS ONE WAY OUT HERE.

In both the past and present, we can see the forest's lushness. Ulthar's residents seem to have lived in harmony with it, even while harvesting firewood.

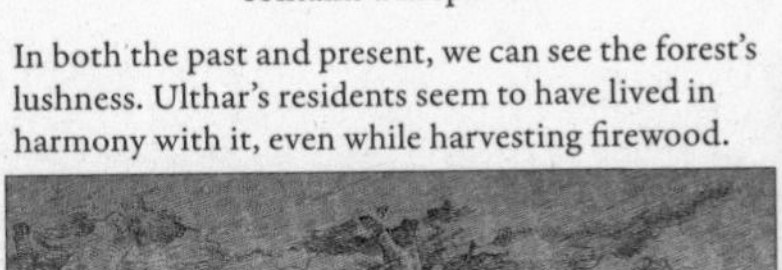

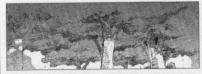

Dragons' Aerie

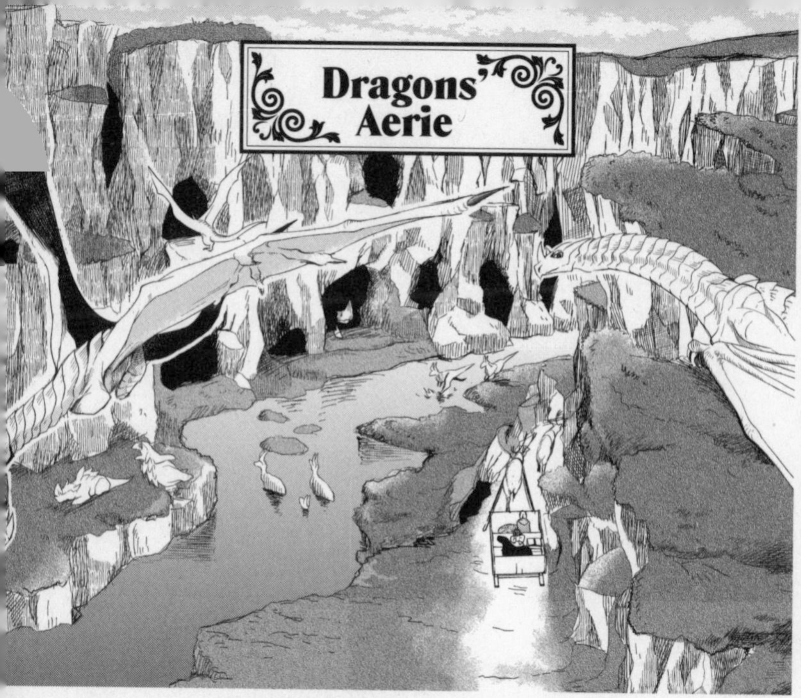

Lindel, the aerie's only human occupant, sleeps in a cave. It's furnished to accommodate potential overnight guests.

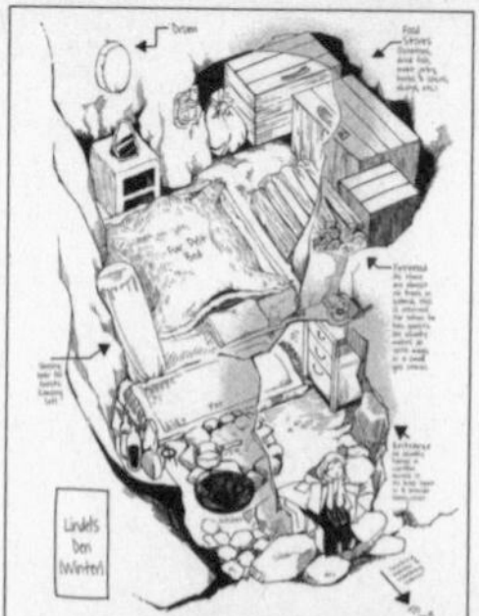

Drum
Food Stores
Lindel's Den (Winter)

The dragons' aerie is built on one of the rifts characteristic of Iceland. Its first caretaker gathered dragons from all over the world. Lindel, the current caretaker, lives there with the dragons and reindeer.

Chise and Elias first visit the aerie on an "errand" from Simon. Later, Chise returns alone to fashion her wand.

In the summer, he puts up a tent in case of rain, just as if he were camping. When it's sunny, he even eats outdoors.

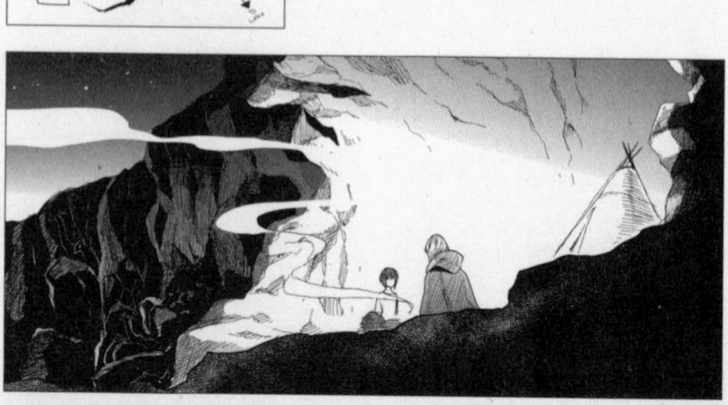

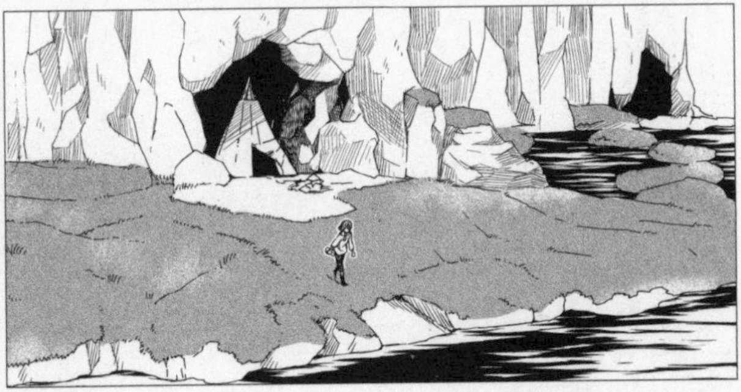

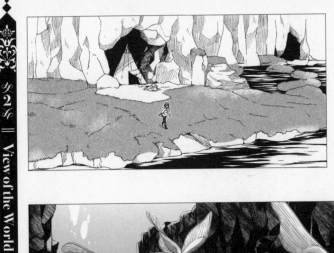

A river runs in front of Lindel's den, providing drinking water and making it easier to clean and do laundry.

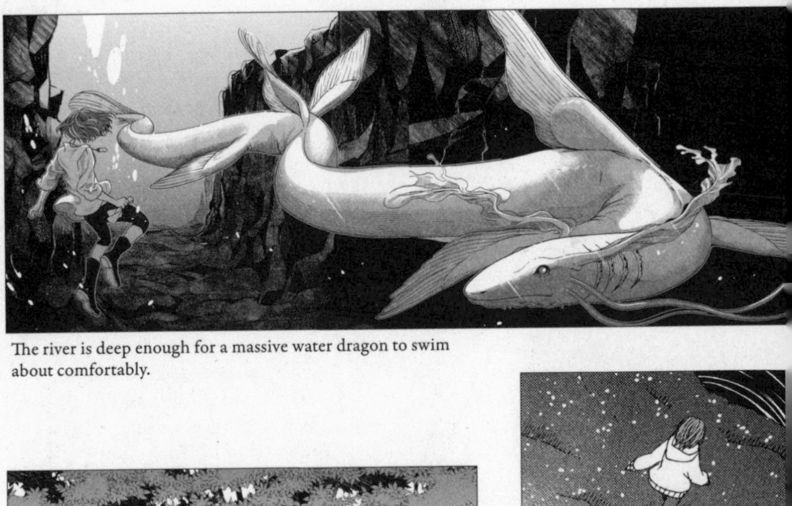

The river is deep enough for a massive water dragon to swim about comfortably.

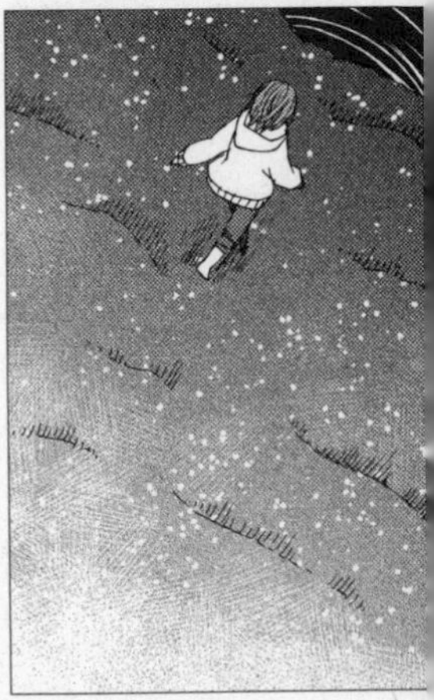

The moss growing on the rocks provides sustenance for the reindeer and dragons.

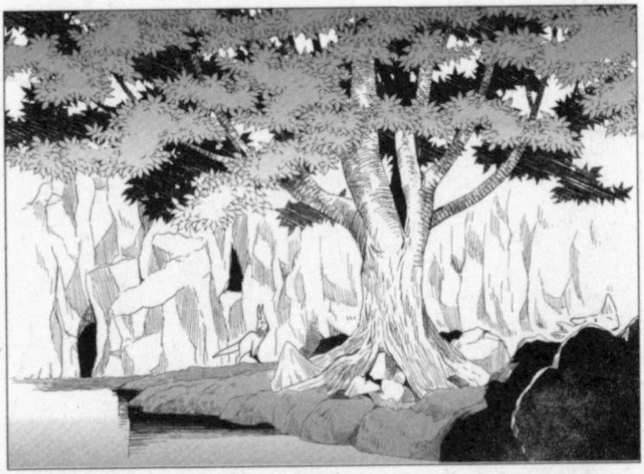

Iceland isn't conducive to the growth of tall trees, but when Nevin returns to the earth and becomes a seedbed, a majestic linden grows there.

Joel's House

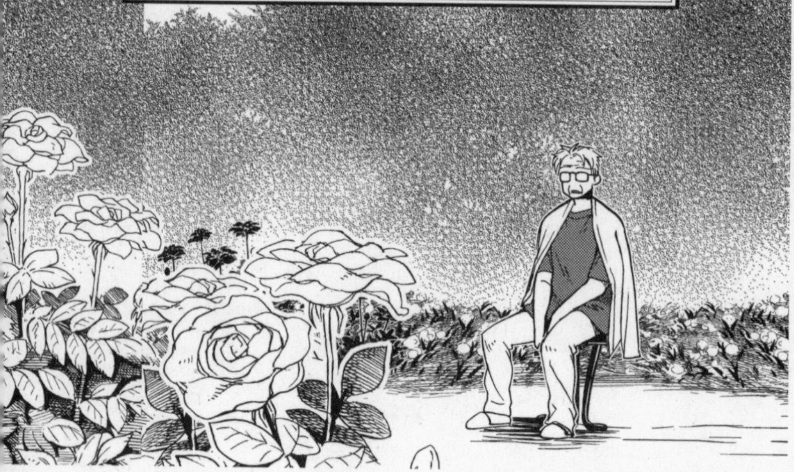

Joel lives in the same village as Elias and Chise, in the house he shared with his wife until her death. The rose garden was originally tended by his wife, and after she passes away, Joel takes over its care.

After Joel's death, the house goes up for sale, but it's also possible that relatives might come to live there.

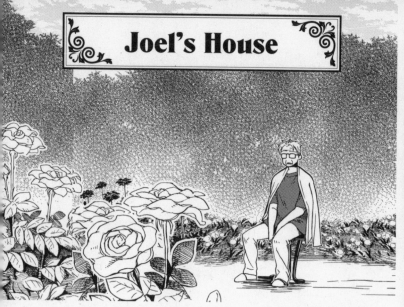

After his wife passes away, Joel carefully tends the garden, cultivating exquisite roses.

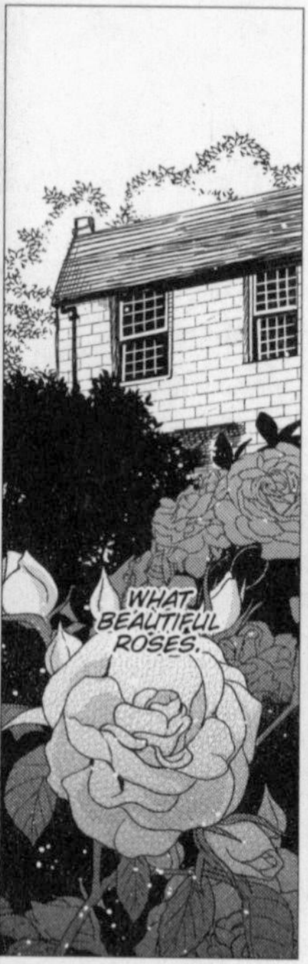
WHAT BEAUTIFUL ROSES.

Joel's house is brick, as is so common in the village. It also appears to be surrounded by a brick wall.

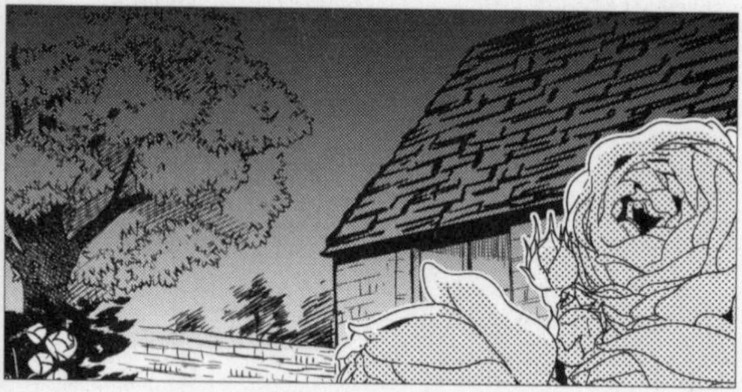

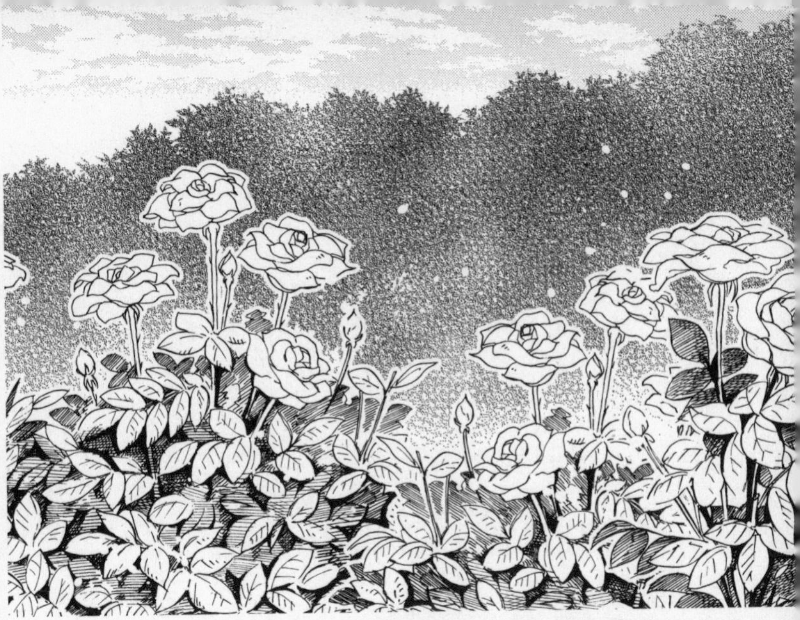

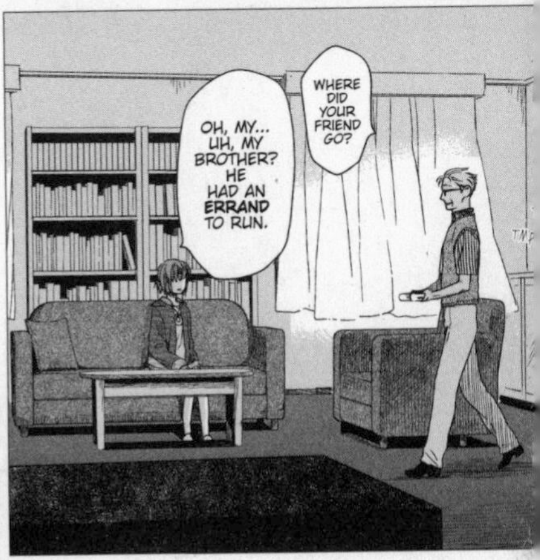
WHERE DID YOUR FRIEND GO?
OH, MY... UH, MY BROTHER? HE HAD AN ERRAND TO RUN.

Joel's home has many bookcases, all of them bursting with books. His passion for reading leads him to start writing.

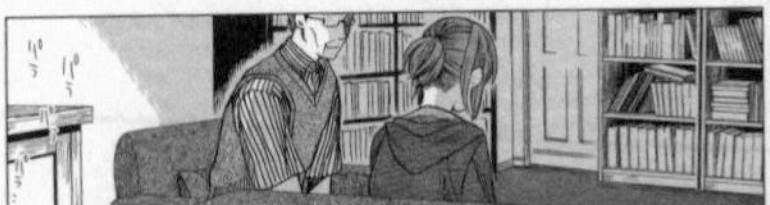

After Joel's death, his house is left empty, and his relatives put it up for sale.

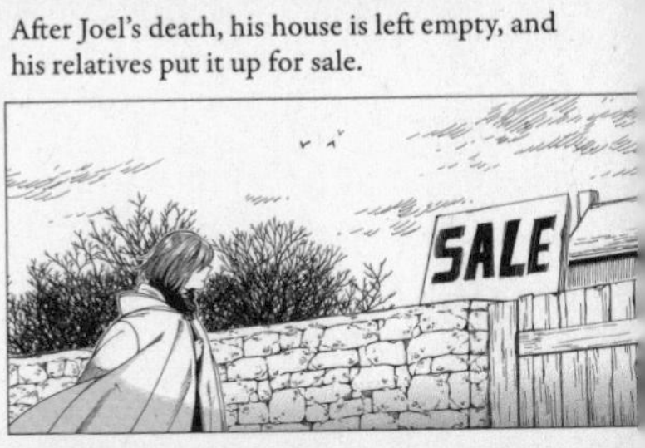
SALE

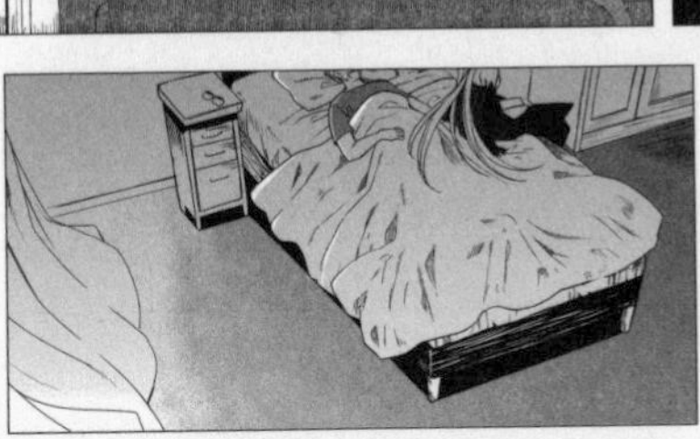

Joel's room is simply furnished, with a bed, a nightstand, and a cabinet.

The Faerie Kingdom

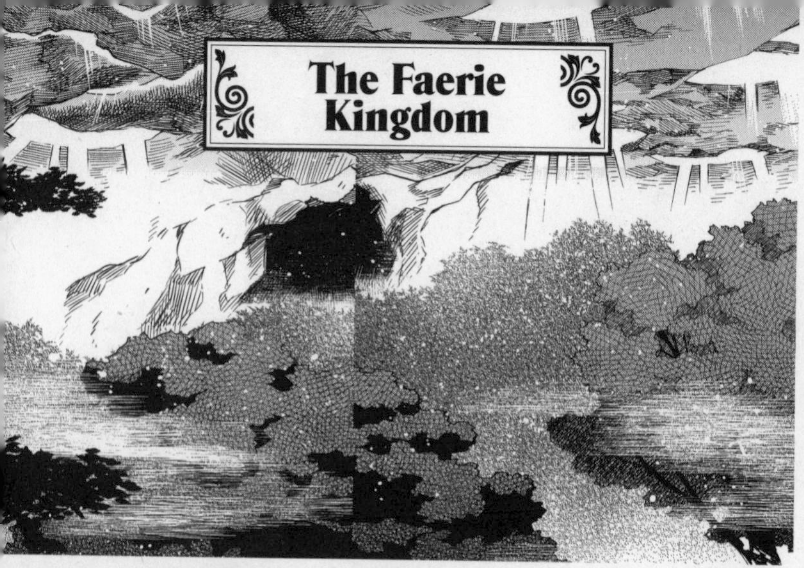

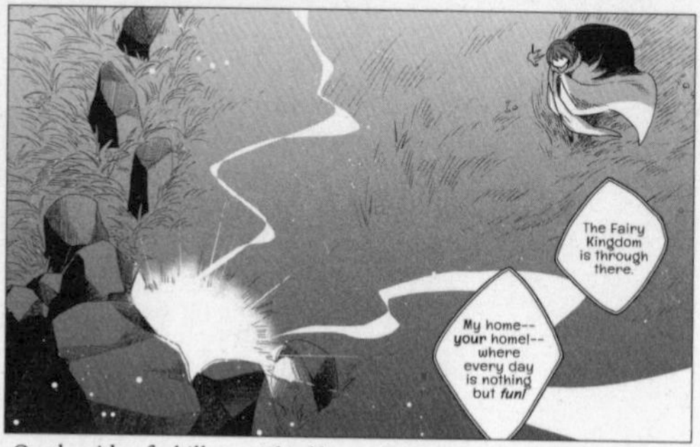
The Fairy Kingdom is through there.
My home-- your home!-- where every day is nothing but *fun!*

On the side of a hill near Elias' house lies a spot connected to the Faerie Kingdom. Ariel lures Chise there and tries to draw her in.

The faeries live in a place called the Faerie Kingdom. It seems to encompass a number of regions; the area Chise and Elias go to from the hill near their house is called the Ant Hill. The entrance to the Faerie Kingdom is not always open, so it's not possible for someone to come and go as they please.

If an ordinary human stays too long in the Faerie Kingdom, their body and appearance may be permanently altered. For example, the changeling Shanahan was once human, but over the course of his time there he took the shape of a centaur.

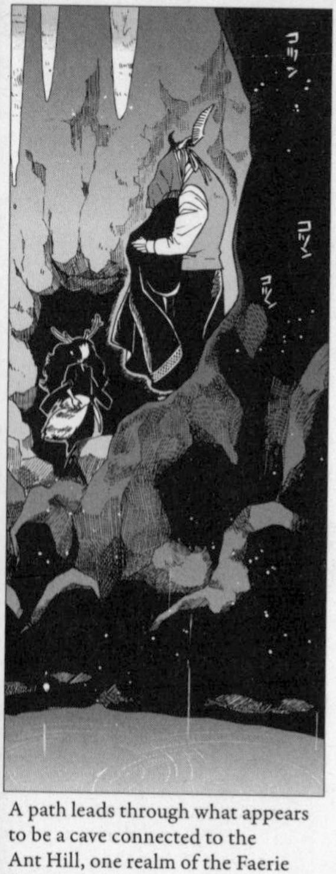

A path leads through what appears to be a cave connected to the Ant Hill, one realm of the Faerie Kingdom.

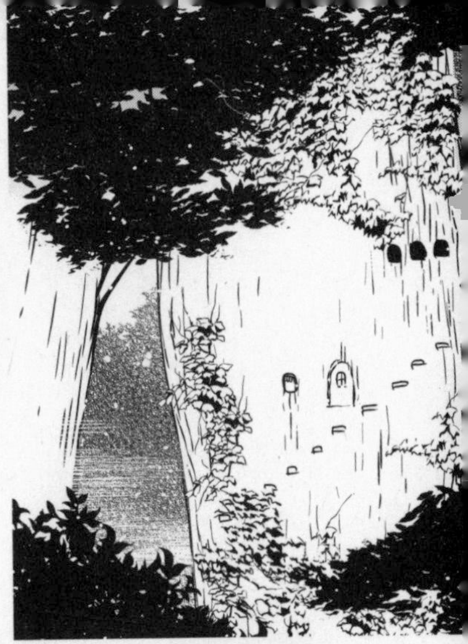

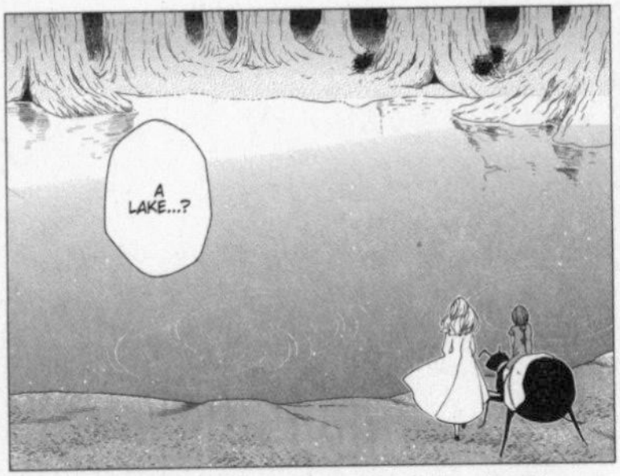
A LAKE...?

The Ant Hill has a lake whose water has healing properties. Shannon tries to heal Chise with it.

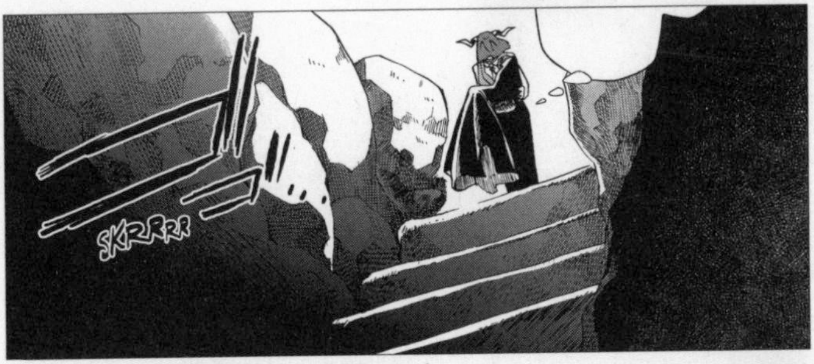
SKRRRR

Beyond the rock opening, stairs lead down to the subterranean Faerie Kingdom.

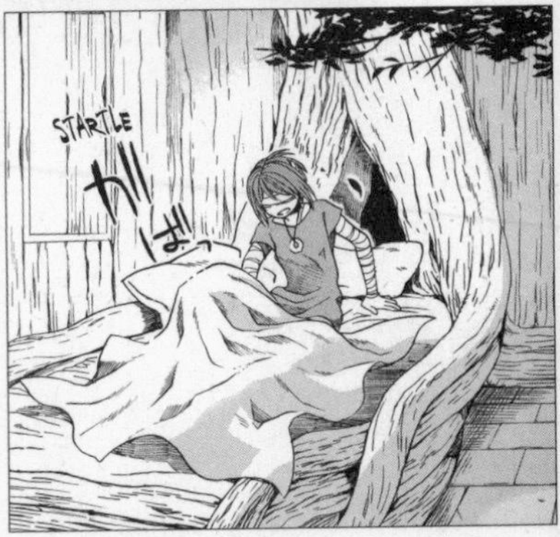
STARTLE

Shannon's hospital has rooms and stairs built into the center of a tree. The Faerie Kingdom seems to live symbiotically with the forest.

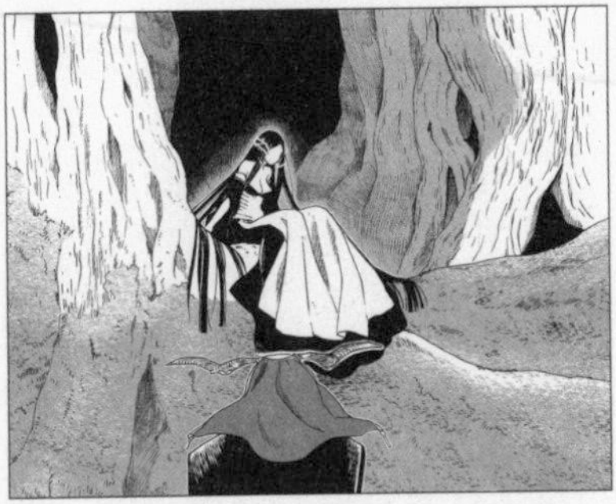

When Elias visits the Faerie Kingdom, Titania converses with him within a circle inside a grove.

Renfred's House

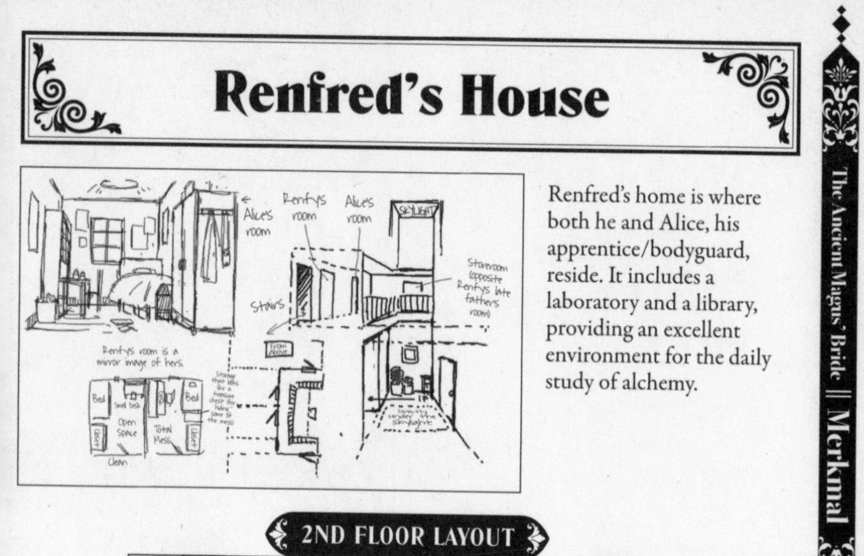

Alice's room
Renfys room
Alice's room
SKYLIGHT
Storeroom (opposite Renfys late fathers room)
Stairs
From above
Renfys room is a mirror image of hers.
Bed
Small Desk
Open Space
Closet
Clean
Bed
Total Mess
Closet
Storage that looks like a treasure chest (for hiding some of the mess)
Directly under the skylight

Renfred's home is where both he and Alice, his apprentice/bodyguard, reside. It includes a laboratory and a library, providing an excellent environment for the daily study of alchemy.

2ND FLOOR LAYOUT

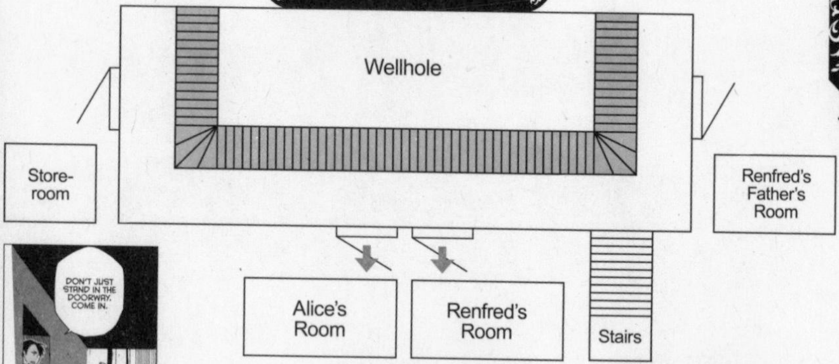

Wellhole
Store-room
Renfred's Father's Room
Alice's Room
Renfred's Room
Stairs

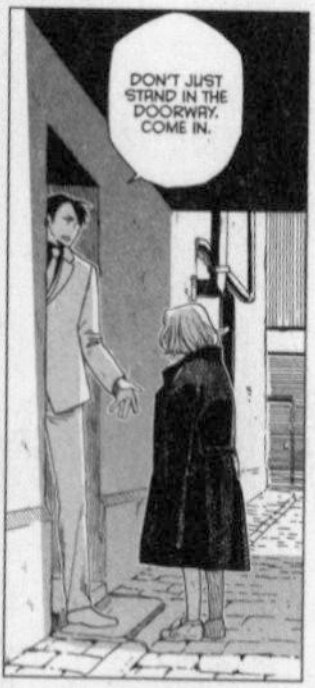

DON'T JUST STAND IN THE DOORWAY. COME IN.

The underground part of Renfred's house, accessible via a staircase from the second floor, is the most-used area. Renfred and Alice have adjacent private rooms on the second floor.

ALICE'S ROOM

RENFRED'S ROOM

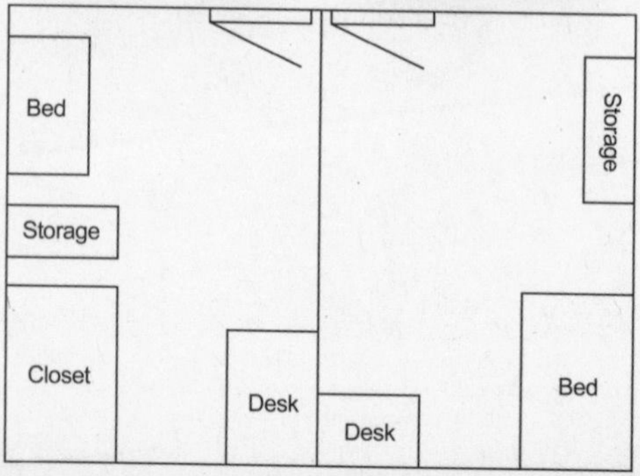

Bed
Storage
Closet
Desk
Desk
Storage
Bed

COURTYARD

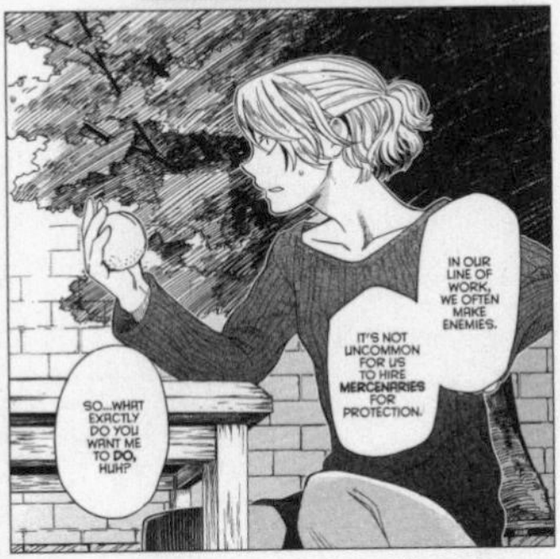
IN OUR LINE OF WORK, WE OFTEN MAKE ENEMIES.
IT'S NOT UNCOMMON FOR US TO HIRE MERCENARIES FOR PROTECTION.
SO...WHAT EXACTLY DO YOU WANT ME TO DO, HUH?

The courtyard has a wooden table and chairs, offering a relaxing spot to sit and discuss things.

ENTRY

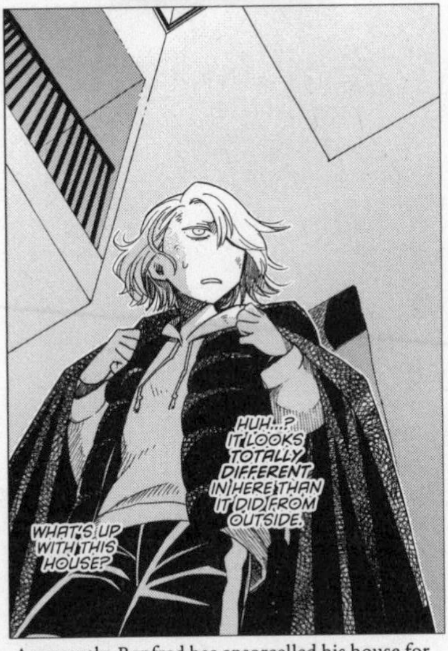
HUH...? IT LOOKS TOTALLY DIFFERENT IN HERE THAN IT DID FROM OUTSIDE.
WHAT'S UP WITH THIS HOUSE?

Apparently, Renfred has ensorcelled his house for security reasons, rendering it impossible to discern the building's layout from outside.

UNDERGROUND LAYOUT

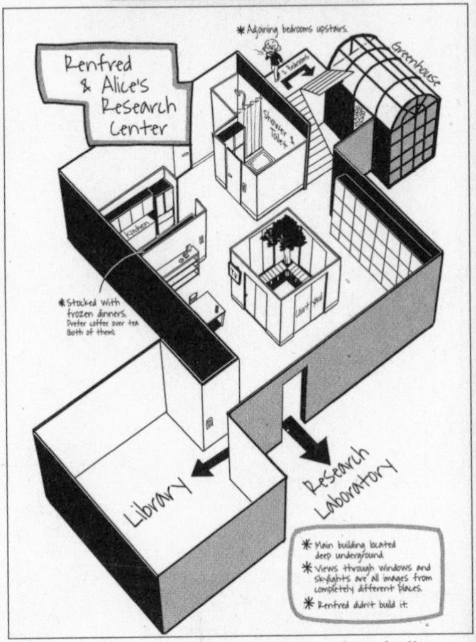
Renfred & Alice's Research Center
* Adjoining bedrooms upstairs.
Greenhouse
Shower Toilet
Kitchen
TV
* Stocked with frozen dinners. Prefer coffee over tea (Both of them)
Library
Research Laboratory
* Main building located deep underground.
* Views through windows and skylights are all images from completely different places.
* Renfred didn't build it.

This is the layout of Renfred's underground research center. The courtyard is a unique touch. There's a greenhouse (over by the stairs) because alchemists use herbs and other plants in their work.

LIBRARY

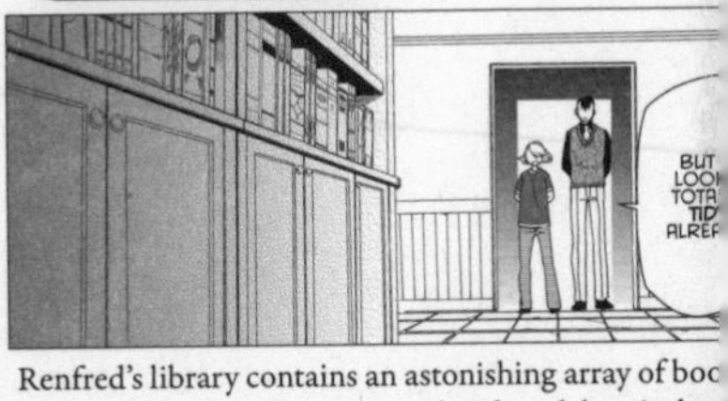

Renfred's library contains an astonishing array of boc
Presumably most of them are related to alchemical st

London

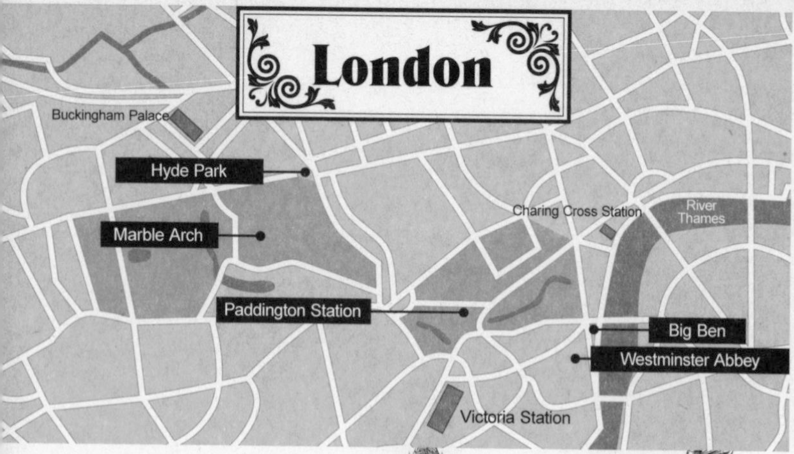
Buckingham Palace
Hyde Park
Marble Arch
Charing Cross Station
River Thames
Paddington Station
Big Ben
Westminster Abbey
Victoria Station

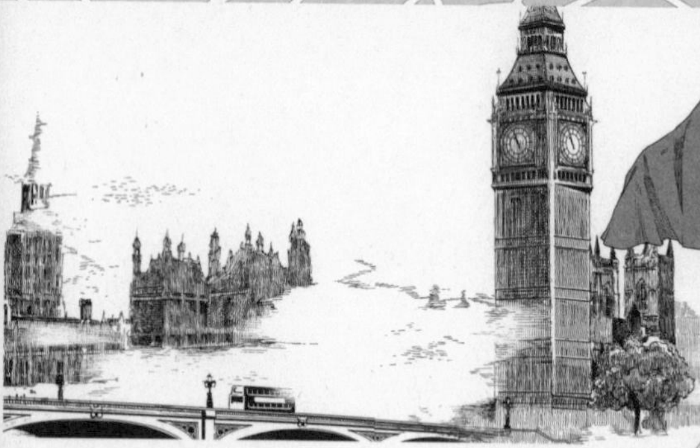

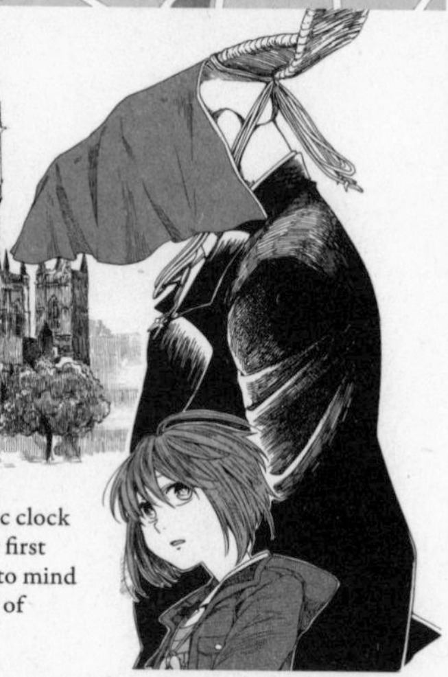

Big Ben, the iconic clock tower, may be the first thing that comes to mind when many think of London.

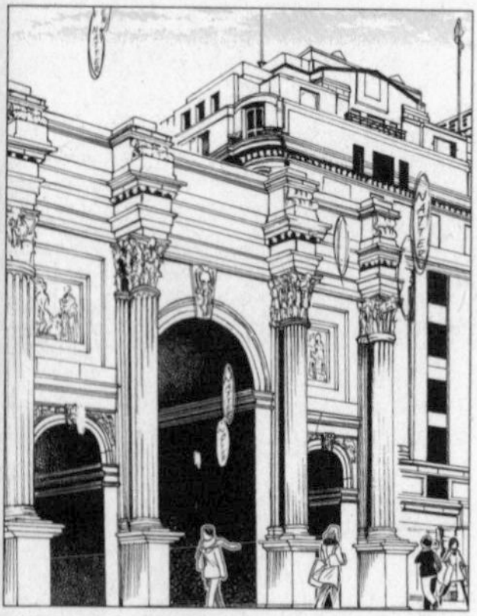

Chise and Alice meet under the Marble Arch. Later they sit on a bench in Hyde Park, by the Serpentine Lake, and talk about Alice's past.

As *The Ancient Magus' Bride* is set in the United Kingdom, it's no surprise that the manga takes us to London! Chise's first trip there is to visit Angie's workshop, and she also goes with Alice to do some Christmas shopping, which takes them all over the city.

London is one of the world's most famous cities and one of the most popular tourist destinations. Its many renowned attractions include Big Ben and the British Museum.

3

Items

Learn more about an array of objects used by mages and alchemists, as well as the clothing the characters wear and the food and drink they consume.

Items Used by Mages and Alchemists

This chapter takes a look at the items mages and alchemists utilize in *The Ancient Magus' Bride.* In the course of the story we sometimes see magic being worked in ways that are familiar from different anime and video games, but there are also many objects that have been endowed with magical properties by mages, or that alchemists have manipulated with their arts.

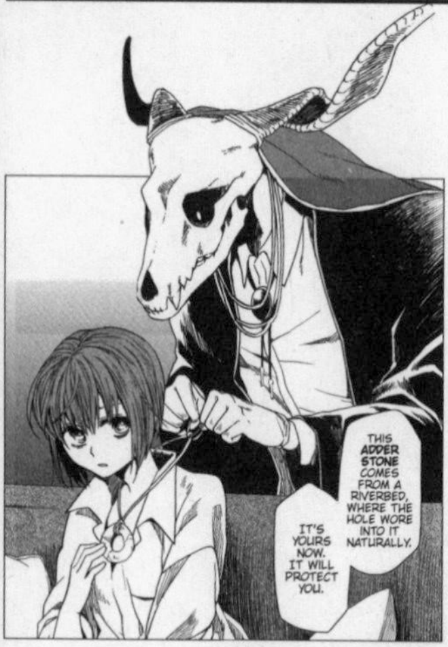
THIS ADDER STONE COMES FROM A RIVERBED, WHERE THE HOLE WORE INTO IT NATURALLY.
IT'S YOURS NOW. IT WILL PROTECT YOU.

The first thing Elias gives Chise is an adder stone. If she looks through the hole in the stone's center, she can perceive the true nature of what she's looking at.

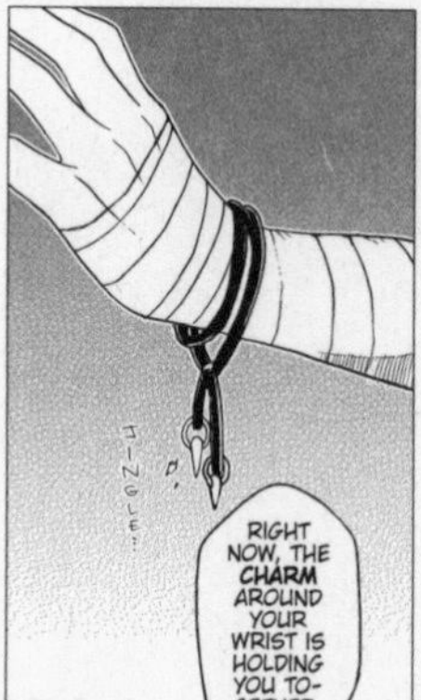
JINGLE
RIGHT NOW, THE CHARM AROUND YOUR WRIST IS HOLDING YOU TO-GETHER.

Shannon, a doctor in the Faerie Kingdom, gives Chise a charm that helps keep her from generating so much magic.

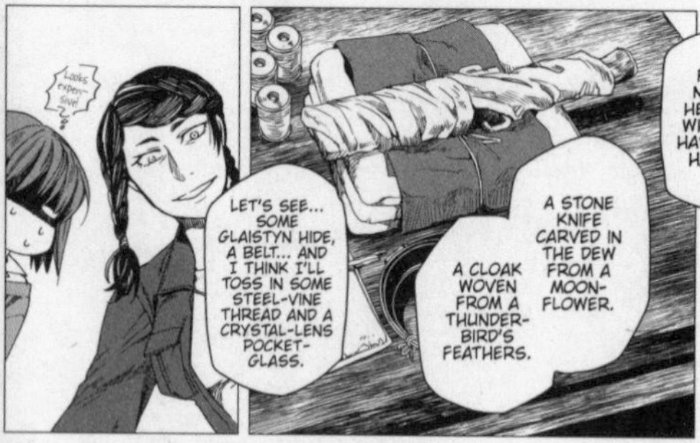
FOR NOW, HERE'S WHAT I HAVE ON HAND.
A STONE KNIFE CARVED IN THE DEW FROM A MOON-FLOWER.
A CLOAK WOVEN FROM A THUNDER-BIRD'S FEATHERS.
Looks expen-sive!
LET'S SEE... SOME GLAISTYN HIDE, A BELT... AND I THINK I'LL TOSS IN SOME STEEL-VINE THREAD AND A CRYSTAL-LENS POCKET-GLASS.

Since Chise will need a variety of items as a mage, Angelica gathers up what she has on hand in her workshop.

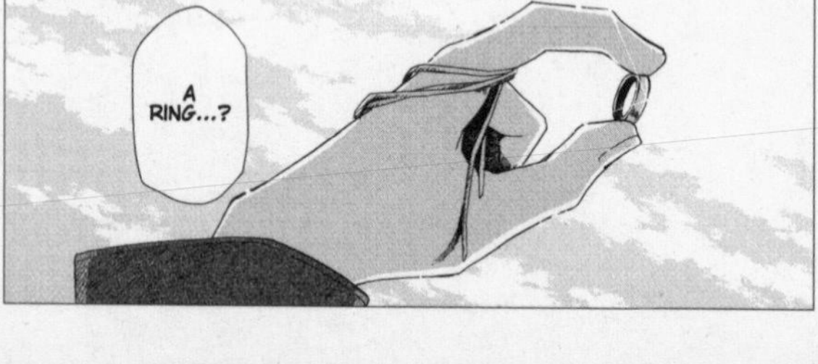
A RING...?

Sleigh beggys' bodies generate excess magic. Chise wears a magic ring to help minimize it.

FWUF

Chise's pouch can hold far more than its apparent size allows for. She keeps many things in it, including her wand and werebeast pelt.

When Chise goes to purify the blight in Ulthar, lack of preparation time means she makes do with things she can easily lay hands on.

WANDS

CHISE

As we see in the story, Chise uses a branch of Nevin's tree to make her wand. Lindel puts on the finishing touches.

ELIAS

Elias rarely uses a wand, but he does so in the scene where he tries to erase Chise's memory upon returning from the auction house.

AH, HERE WE ARE.

SPTOO!

LINDEL

Lindel seems to use a wand even less often than Elias. The only time we see him holding one is when he calls on his master at her home.

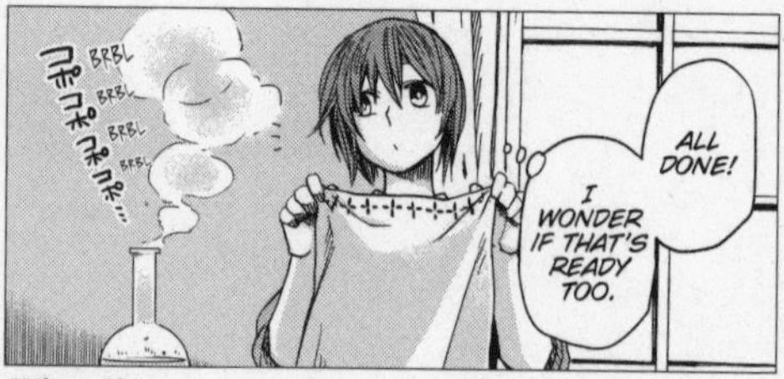
BRBL
BRBL
BRBL
BRBL
ALL DONE!
I WONDER IF THAT'S READY TOO.

When Chise tries to enchant a flask of water to ward off Helena's nightmares, she accidentally uses too much magic and makes a sleeping potion.

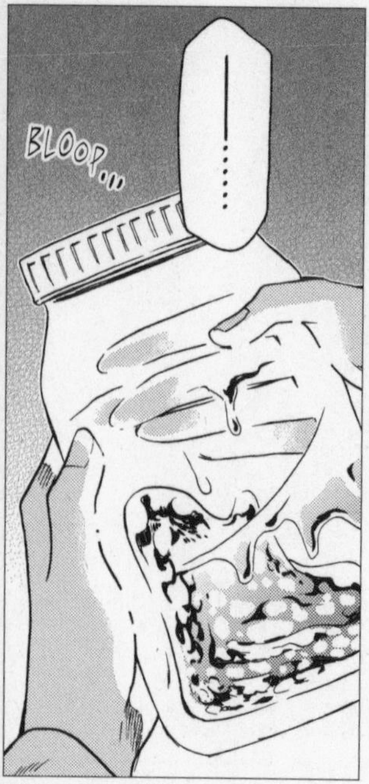
......
BLOOP...

Chise prepares fairy ointment for Joel, who lacks the sight, so that he can see the leannán sídhe.

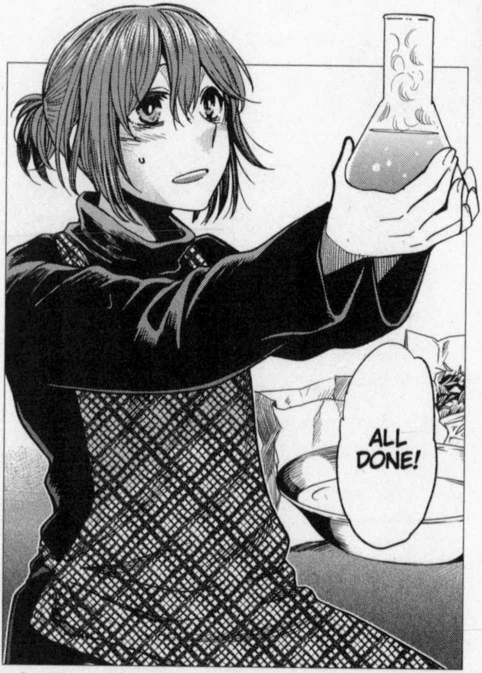
ALL DONE!

After Chise accidentally sings Elias to sleep, she has to mix a potion—following Angelica's instructions—to wake him up again.

While the church grim is asleep, Chise lights warding incense for protection.

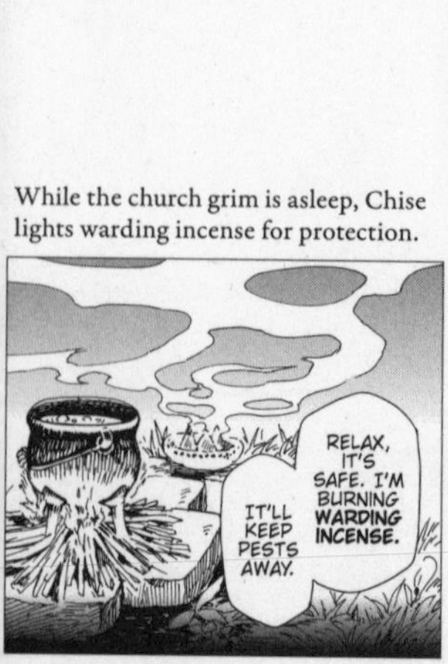
RELAX, IT'S SAFE. I'M BURNING WARDING INCENSE.
IT'LL KEEP PESTS AWAY.

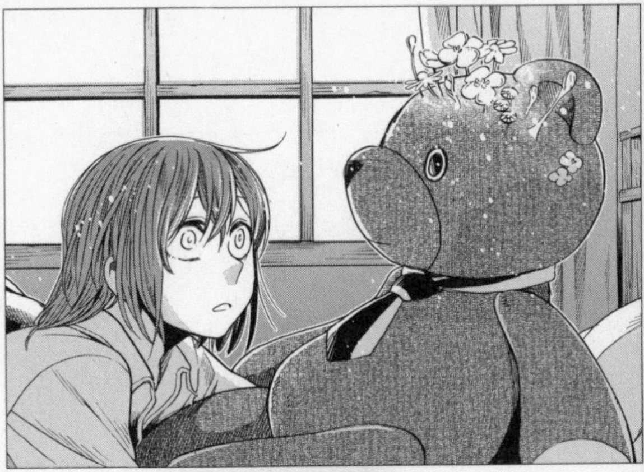

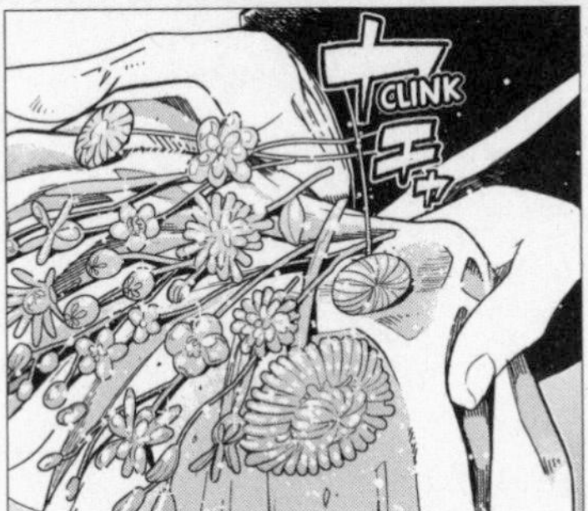
CLINK

The teddy bear Elias gives Chise for Christmas soaks up her excess magic and transforms it into flowers, which prove useful in finding Ethan.

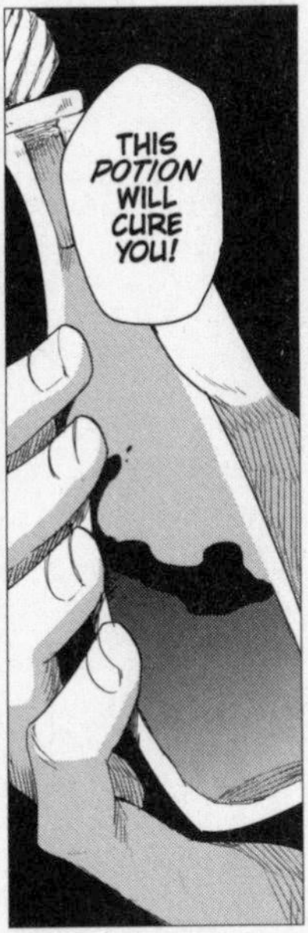
THIS POTION WILL CURE YOU!

Matthew distills the souls of cats into a potion to heal Mina's lifelong fragility, but instead, it dissolves her body.

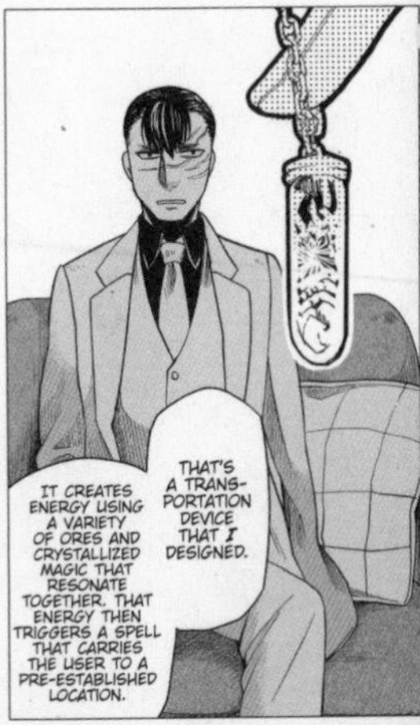
THAT'S A TRANS-PORTATION DEVICE THAT *I* DESIGNED.
IT CREATES ENERGY USING A VARIETY OF ORES AND CRYSTALLIZED MAGIC THAT RESONATE TOGETHER. THAT ENERGY THEN TRIGGERS A SPELL THAT CARRIES THE USER TO A PRE-ESTABLISHED LOCATION.

A creation of Renfred's that enables transportation. It can only be made use of with magic.

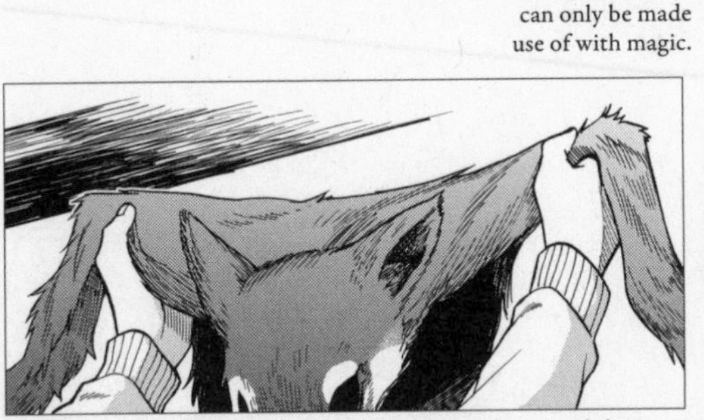

Ashen Eye gives Chise a pelt that allows her to take animal shape. The pelt resonates with the user's inner voice to determine which animal they will become.

Clothing

Let's take a look at the various characters' clothing. Unsurprisingly, being our protagonist and a young girl, Chise wears a wide variety of outfits. However, we can see that Lindel also has an extensive wardrobe and has a perhaps-unexpected knack for dressing smartly in modern clothing. We should also note that Alice displays a feminine savvy when it comes to selecting appropriate clothes for whatever occasion arises.

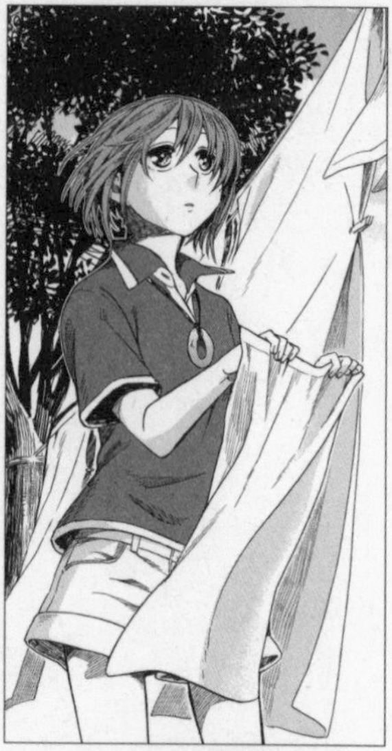

When summer arrives, Chise wears a short-sleeved polo shirt, which gives her a nice healthy look.

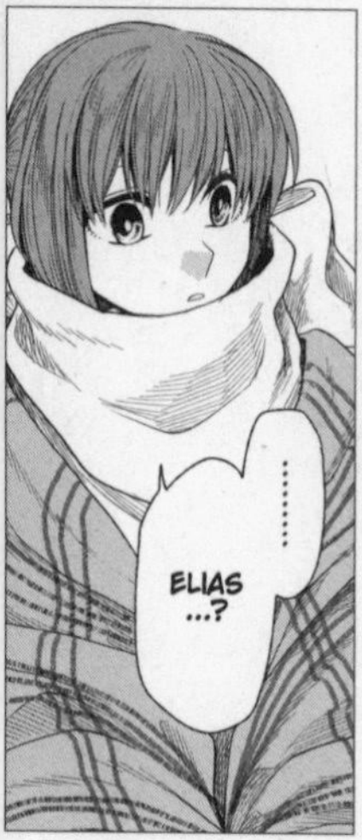
......
ELIAS
...?

When visiting the dragons' aerie, Chise bundles up.

Elias' style of dress doesn't change when he takes on human form.

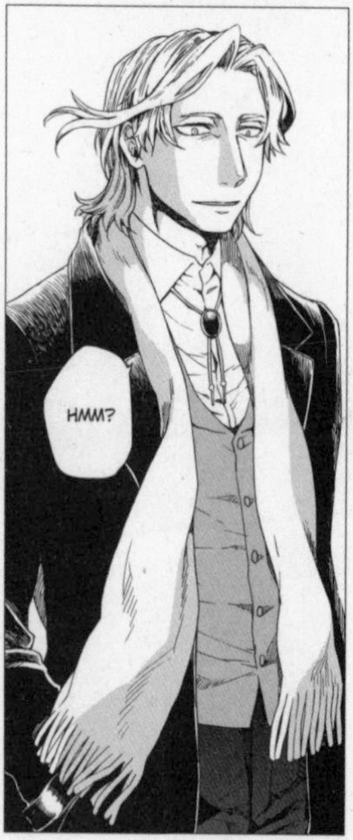
HMM?

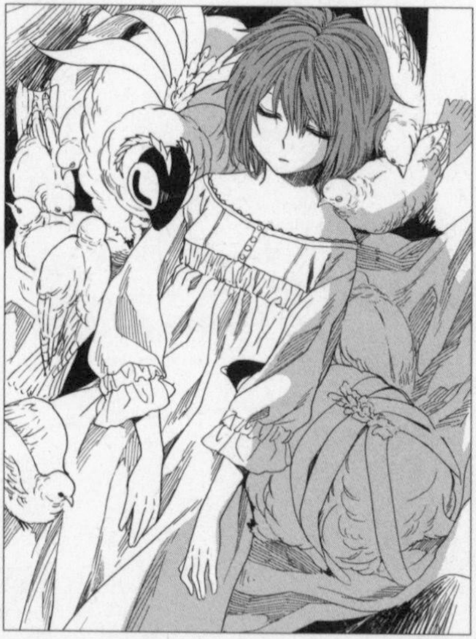

.ring her
.longed
consciousness
.m magic
.austion,
.ise wears a
.htgown.

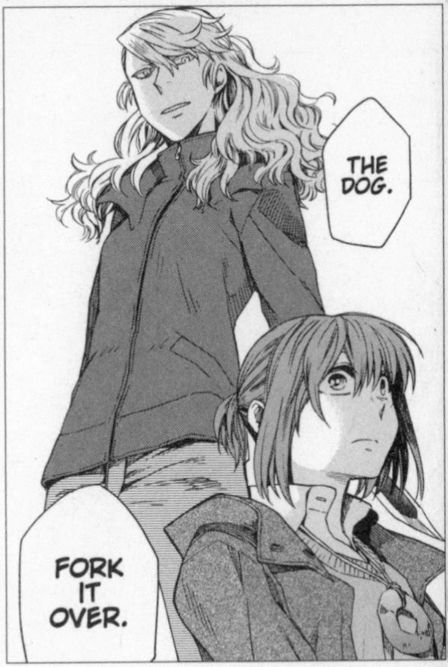
THE DOG.
FORK IT OVER.

In the Ulthar Arc and the Black Dog Arc, Alice is dressed for ease of motion.

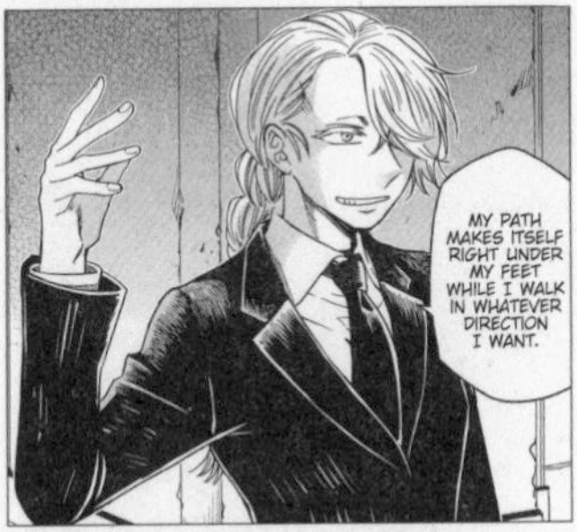
MY PATH MAKES ITSELF RIGHT UNDER MY FEET WHILE I WALK IN WHATEVER DIRECTION I WANT.

At the auction house, Alice displays an androgynous beauty in a black pantsuit.

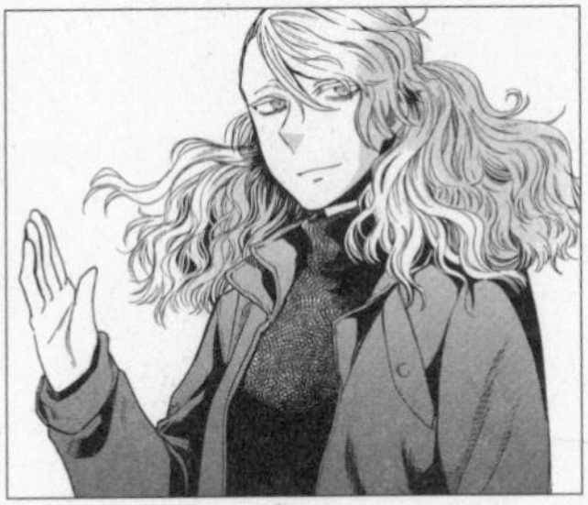

Alice tends to wear pants. Here we see her in leather pants and a jacket.

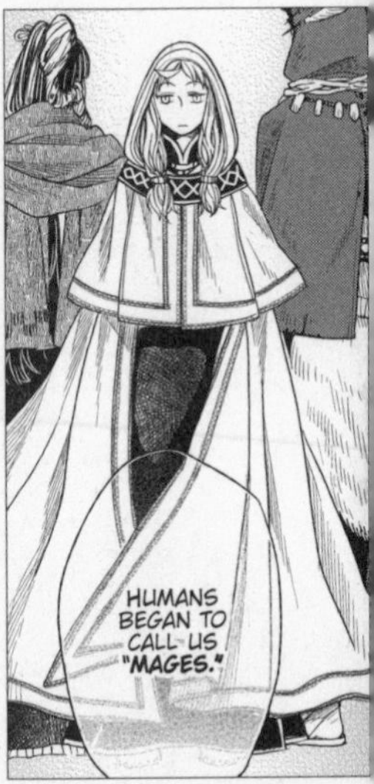
HUMANS BEGAN TO CALL US "MAGES."

Lindel usually wears a robe, as one might imagine on a druid.

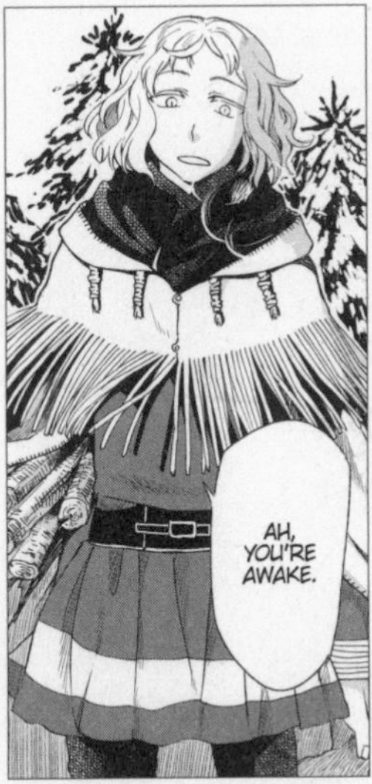
AH, YOU'RE AWAKE.

Before Lindel became the aerie's caretaker, he dressed in a more pastoral manner.

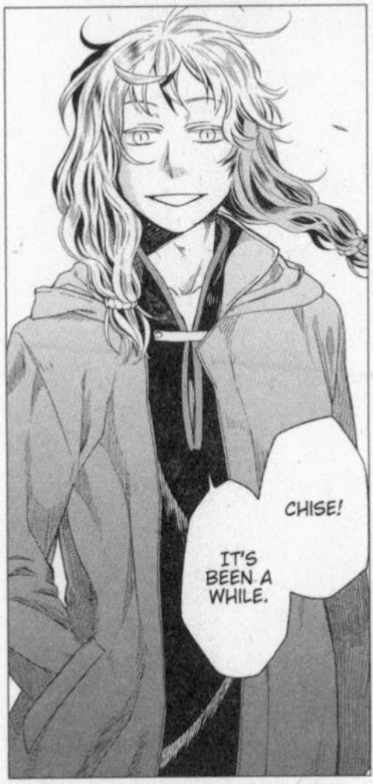
CHISE!
IT'S BEEN A WHILE.

Here Lindel wears modern clothes, which he says he purchased in town.

Food and Drink

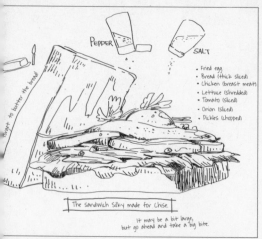

As *The Ancient Magus' Bride* is set in the United Kingdom, most of the foods that appear in it are traditional British fare. While British cuisine is not terribly well known in Japan, there are a few foods the Japanese are familiar with, such as fish and chips or roast beef.

PEPPER
SALT
forget to butter the bread
• Fried egg
• Bread (thick sliced)
• Chicken (breast meat)
• Lettuce (shredded)
• Tomato (sliced)
• Onion (sliced)
• Pickles (chopped)
The sandwich Silky made for Chise.
It may be a bit large, but go ahead and take a big bite.

Volume 1 includes a recipe for the sandwich Silky makes Chise in chapter 3. It's impressive both in sheer size and the variety of fillings.

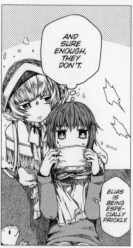

AND SURE ENOUGH, THEY DON'T.
MNCH
ELIAS IS BEING ESPE-CIALLY PRICKLY.

Silky's sandwiches tend to be gigantic.

When Chise first arrives at Elias' house, she is greeted by a British spread, including a meat pie.

ずらっ
VOILA
......!

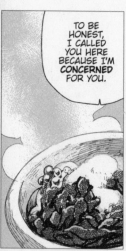

TO BE HONEST, I CALLED YOU HERE BECAUSE I'M CONCERNED FOR YOU.

Lindel serves both Chise and Elias reindeer curry.

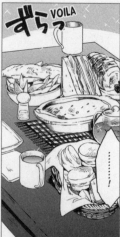

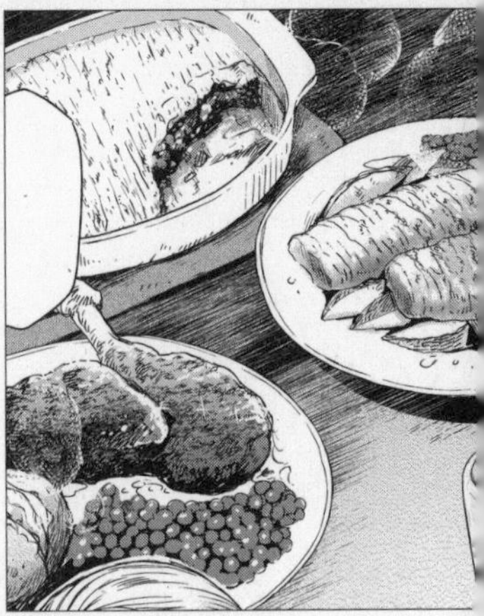

In London, Chise and Alice eat traditional fish and chips and m pie.

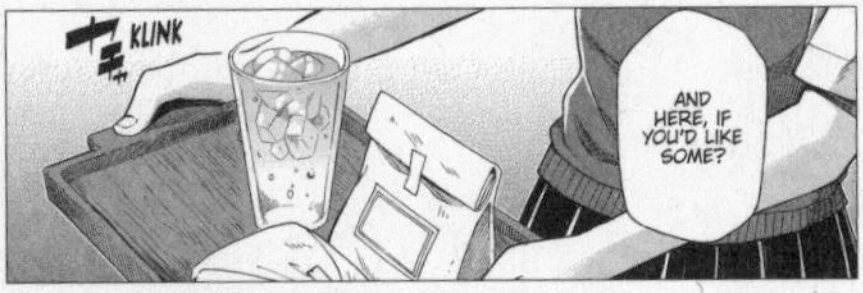
KLINK
AND HERE, IF YOU'D LIKE SOME?

Simon routinely stops by to get medicine for his cough. Chise gives him elderflower cordial, which is good for the throat.

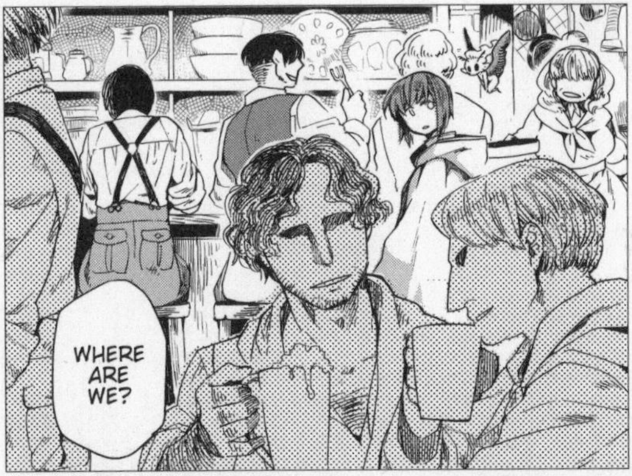
WHERE ARE WE?

When Chise experiences the past c Ulthar, she finds herself in a tavern Taverns were like modern pubs an also provided lodging. The patrons of this establishment appear to be drinking beer.

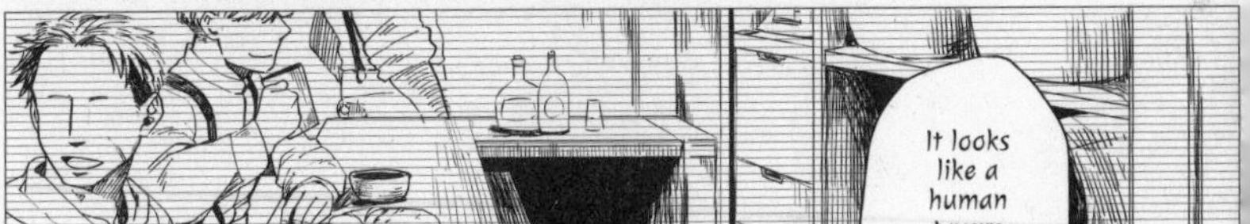
It looks like a human tavern of old.

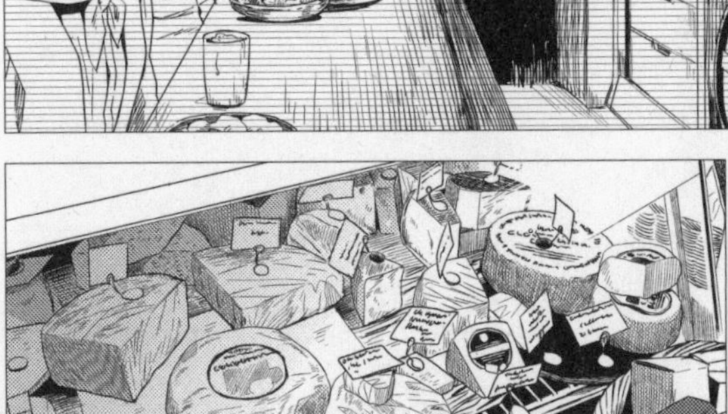

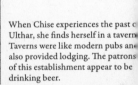

The United Kingdom produces a remarkable variety of cheeses. Cheddar cheese is British in origin.

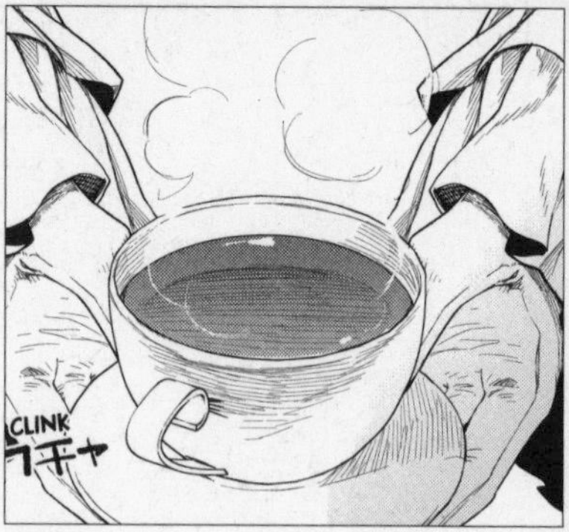
CLINK

Black tea is very British, a famous part of the meal called "afternoon tea."

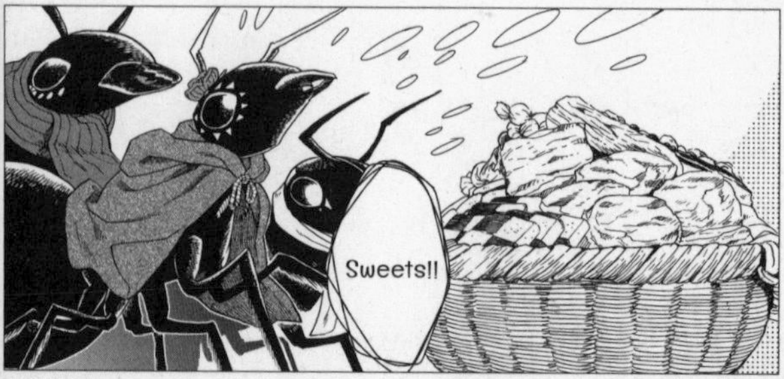
Sweets!!

When the muryans visit in Elias' absence, Silky gives them a heap of cookies.

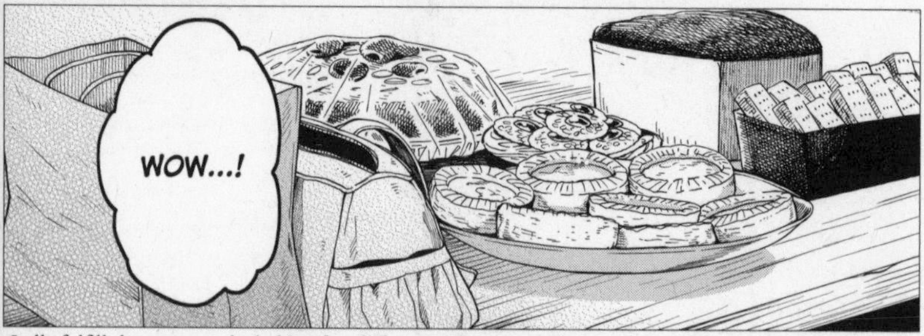
WOW...!

Stella fulfills her contract by baking five different pastries, including pound cake and shortbread.

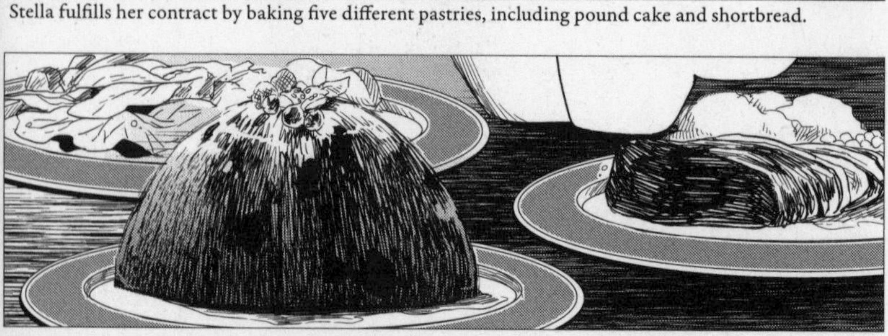

The Christmas pudding Chise eats after waking from her slumber is also a traditional British recipe.

4

Events

This chapter revisits the events that have unfolded in the first eight volumes, illustrated with some of their most memorable panels. This is the perfect way to refresh our memory of the story's highlights.

The Ancient Magus' Bride 1

魔法使いの嫁

Chise Hatori puts herself up for auction. The winning bidder is Elias Ainsworth, an inhuman mage. He informs her that she is to be his apprentice and his bride.

After coming to live with Elias, Chise meets mages Angelica Purley and Lindel, as well as Father Simon Cullum, who keeps an eye on Elias.

To begin the "errands" Simon asks them to do, Elias and Chise visit Ulthar, town of cats. There they find the alchemist Mikhail Renfred and his apprentice, Alice, standing in their way.

AS OF NOW, YOU ARE AN APPRENTICE MAGE.

Elias buys Chise at an auction in the United Kingdom for five million pounds and tells her that she is now his apprentice.

KREEE
キィ

Silky, a domestic spirit, resides in and cares for Elias' house.

BUT ALSO ...
TO MAKE YOU MY BRIDE.

Elias declares that Chise is to be not only his apprentice but his bride.

The Ancient Magus' Bride
1
Story & Art by
KORE YAMAZAKI

RELEASED: April 10, 2014
ENGLISH EDITION: May 12, 2015

Angelica is a mage and an artificer who makes magus crafts. Chise picks up the equipment she needs as a mage at Angelica's shop.

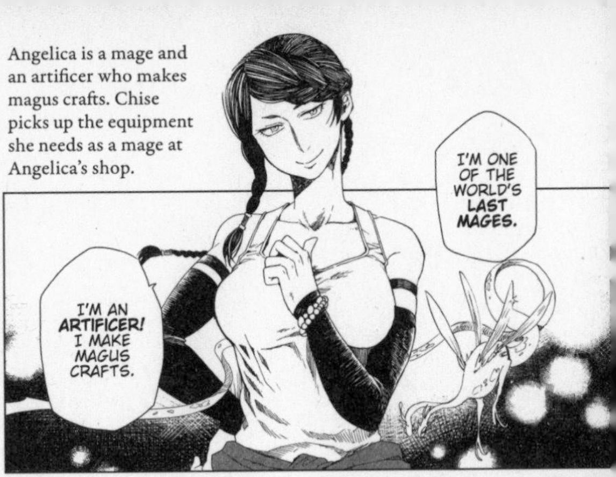
I'M ONE OF THE WORLD'S **LAST MAGES.**
I'M AN **ARTIFICER!** I MAKE MAGUS CRAFTS.

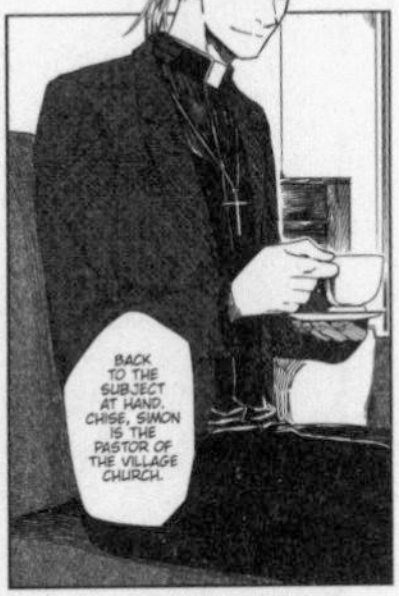
BACK TO THE SUBJECT AT HAND. CHISE, SIMON IS THE PASTOR OF THE VILLAGE CHURCH.

Simon is the priest of Elias' village. Having been charged with keeping an eye on Elias, he has known him for a long time.

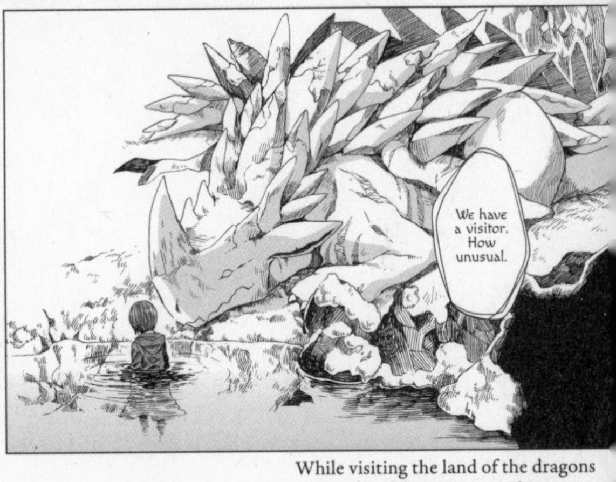
We have a visitor. How unusual.

While visiting the land of the dragons on an errand from Simon, Chise meets a dragon named Nevin. She shares in his dream of flying through the sky.

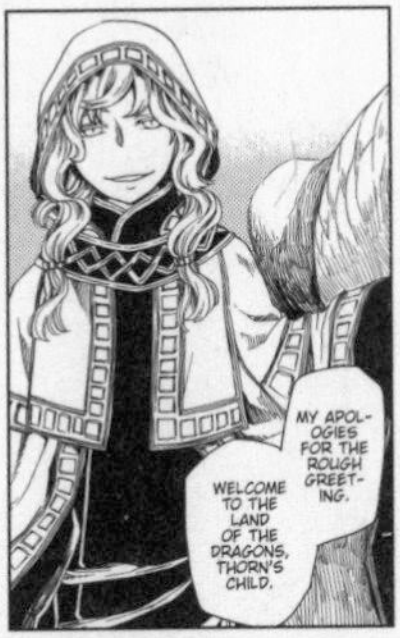
MY APOLOGIES FOR THE ROUGH GREETING.
WELCOME TO THE LAND OF THE DRAGONS, THORN'S CHILD.

The mage Lindel is the caretaker of the dragons' aerie. The task of checking in on the dragons naturally means meeting with Lindel and asking how the dragons have been.

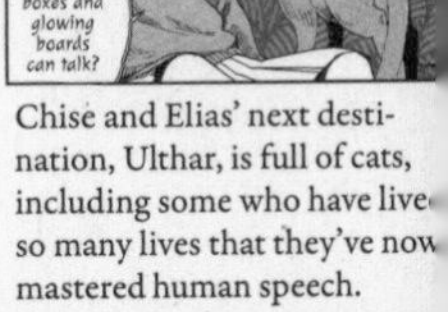
HUH?! TH-THE **CAT** JUST **SPOKE?!**
You find that odd in an age where metal boxes and glowing boards can talk?

Chise and Elias' next destination, Ulthar, is full of cats, including some who have lived so many lives that they've now mastered human speech.

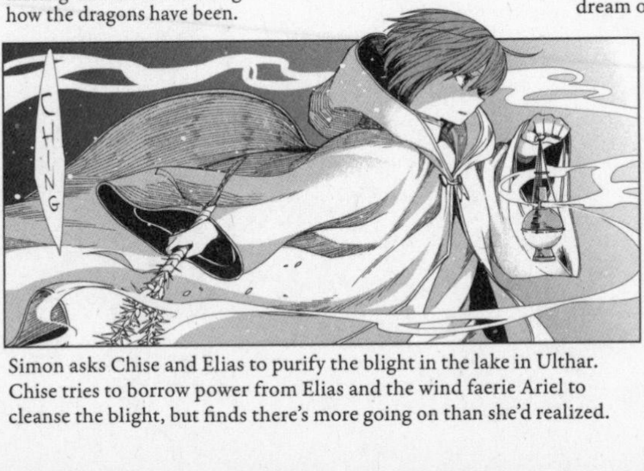
CHING

Simon asks Chise and Elias to purify the blight in the lake in Ulthar. Chise tries to borrow power from Elias and the wind faerie Ariel to cleanse the blight, but finds there's more going on than she'd realized.

Despite Renfred's interference, Chise plunges into the blight with the King of Cats and Ariel in order to purify it. Once inside, she's able to communicate with the blight's core and learn what led to its creation. Rather than obliterating it, she decides to transform it into flowers. After the purification is finished, Chise loses consciousness until Titania and Oberon, queen and king of the fae, pay a visit. The magical energy Oberon pours into Chise wakes her up.

Finally, Elias and Chise go to a particular church to carry out their last errand. There, Chise meets a church grim who believes himself to be human...and then Alice and a young male alchemist arrive to seize the grim.

The Ancient Magus' Bride

2

魔法使いの嫁

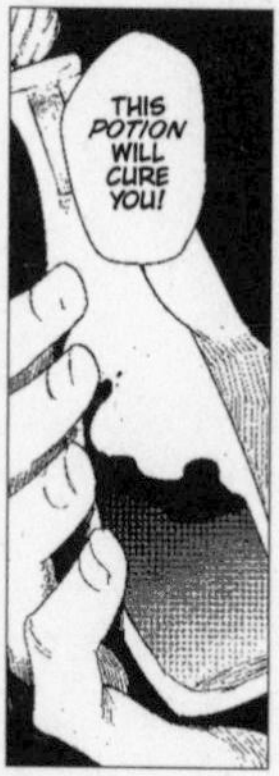
THIS POTION WILL CURE YOU!

A young man named Matthew who lives in Ulthar is tricked by a traveling alchemist, who convinces him to distill the lives of cats into a potion.

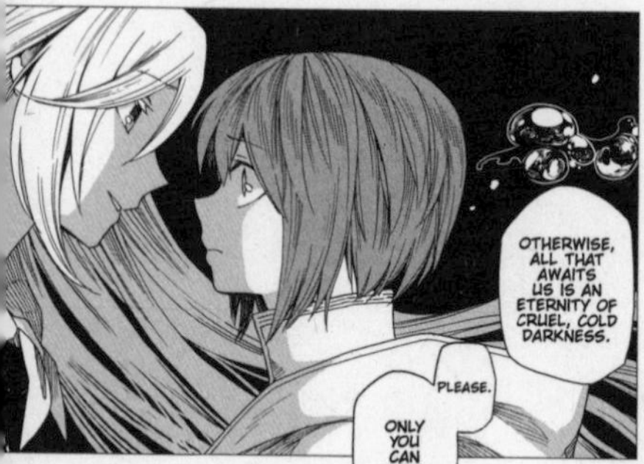
OTHERWISE, ALL THAT AWAITS US IS AN ETERNITY OF CRUEL, COLD DARKNESS.
PLEASE.
ONLY YOU CAN HELP US.

Matthew's wife, Mina, says that she caused the blight, and she has been trapped in its core for ages as a result.

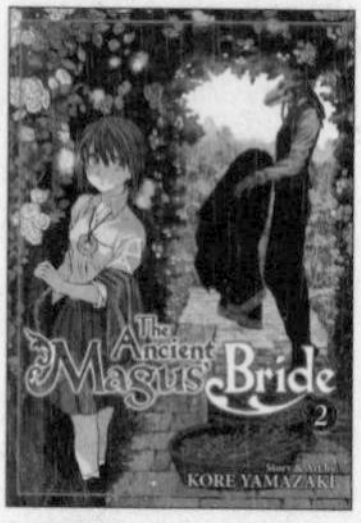
The Ancient Magus' Bride
2
KORE YAMAZAKI

RELEASED: Sept. 10, 2014
ENGLISH EDITION: Sept. 1, 2015

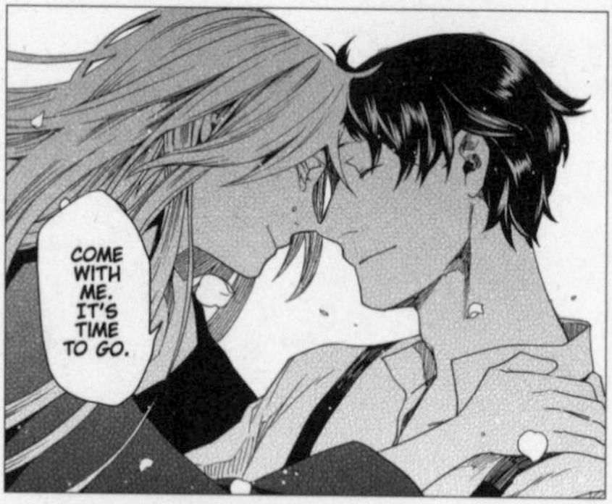
COME WITH ME. IT'S TIME TO GO.

Thanks to Chise and Ariel's power, Mina and Matthew are purified and finally delivered from their horrific suffering.

Having exhausted her magic, Chise collapses. As she lies unconscious, Titania and Oberon stop by to see Elias' new apprentice and bride. The two of them, a married couple, are queen and king of the fae.

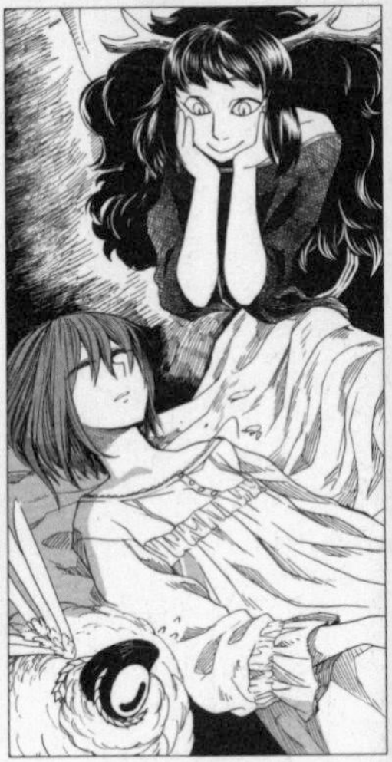

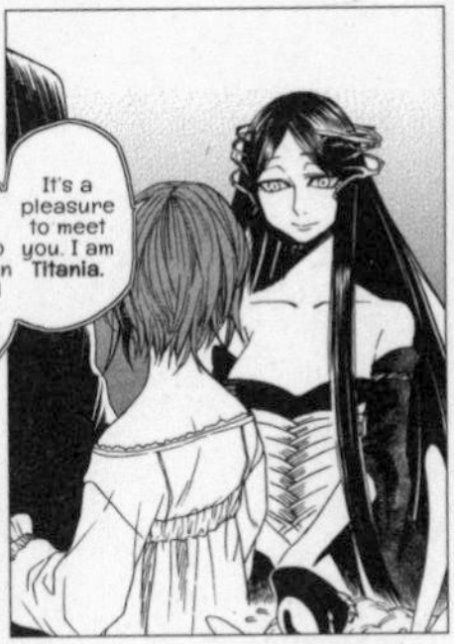
It's a pleasure to meet you. I am **Titania.**
I am queen of the fae who reside within Albion, and thus all of Tír na nÓg.

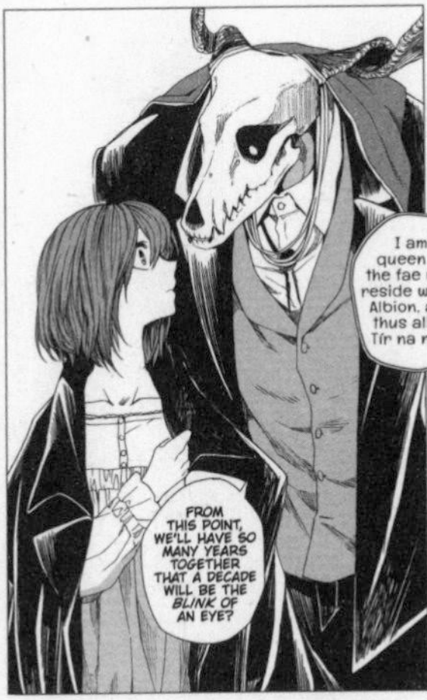
FROM THIS POINT, WE'LL HAVE SO MANY YEARS TOGETHER THAT A DECADE WILL BE THE *BLINK* OF AN EYE?

Chise looks to the past when she wishes Elias had bought her ten years earlier. Elias looks to the future with his reply.

At the church, Chise finds the church grim, who soon passes out.

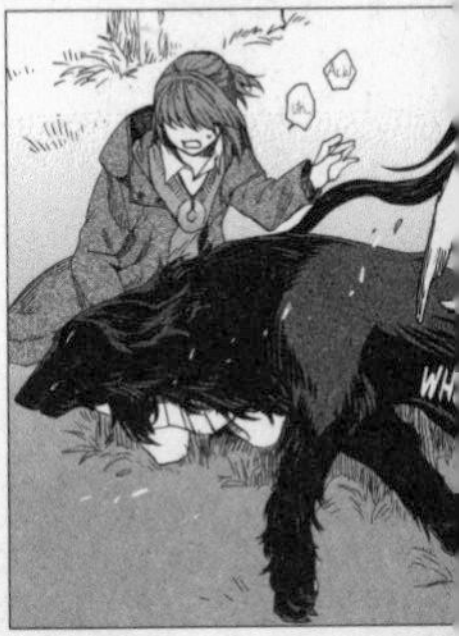

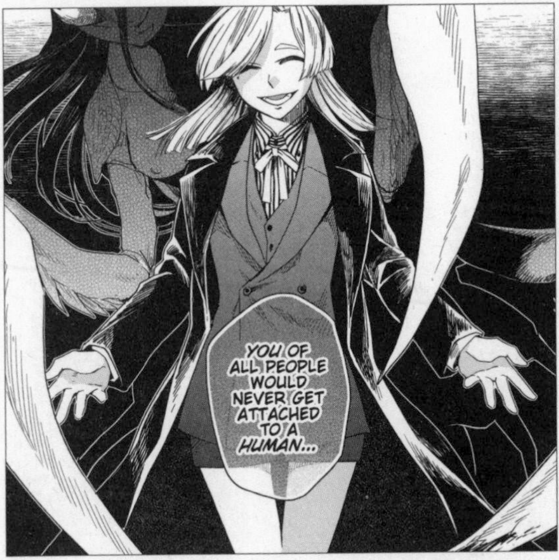
YOU OF ALL PEOPLE WOULD NEVER GET ATTACHED TO A HUMAN...

The boy arrives with a chimera and attacks Alice for sharing information, but it's Chise who takes the blow. Gathering Chise into his arms, Elias allows his rage to boil over.

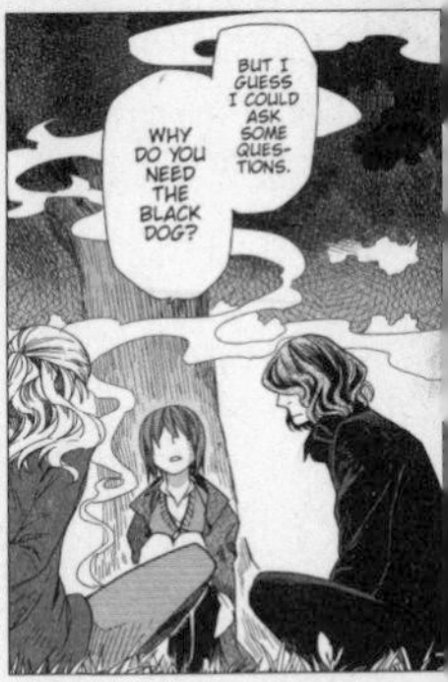
BUT I GUESS I COULD ASK SOME QUESTIONS.
WHY DO YOU NEED THE BLACK DOG?

Alice orders Chise to hand the dog over. When Chise asks why, Alice tells her about a strange boy and his chimeras.

Seeing Chise collapse, Elias erupts into a monstrous form and addresses the boy as "Cartaphilus." Renfred catches up with Alice and joins the fight, but the group are forced to withdraw temporarily with the help of Will o' the Wisp. Chise soon makes a bond with the church grim, and he becomes her familiar. Chise gives him a new name: Ruth. Cartaphilus, now unable to achieve his goal, retreats.

Once home, Elias shuts himself up in his room and refuses to come out, possibly due to lingering effects from his transformation. Chise is worried about him, all the more so when he vanishes, leaving only a note behind. She eventually tracks him down, but doesn't find his explanation all that convincing. Then she receives an invitation from Lindel, asking her to come to the dragons' aerie to fashion her own wand.

IS IT?

Having undergone a drastic physical transformation, Elias pounces at Cartaphilus, who hurt Chise.

I'll be at your side forever now, Chise.
Give me a new name for the new *me*.

The church grim begs Chise to form a bond with him. Chise agrees, and renames him Ruth.

THAT STRIKES ME AS **OVER-DEPENDENCE**, PLAIN AND SIMPLE.

While Angelica checks to be sure that the ring she gave Elias for Chise is working properly, she also has some stern words for Chise about her dependence on Elias.

The Ancient Magus' Bride 3

魔法使いの嫁

The Ancient Magus' Bride
3
KORE YAMAZAKI

RELEASE: March 10, 2015
ENGLISH EDITION: Dec. 1, 2015

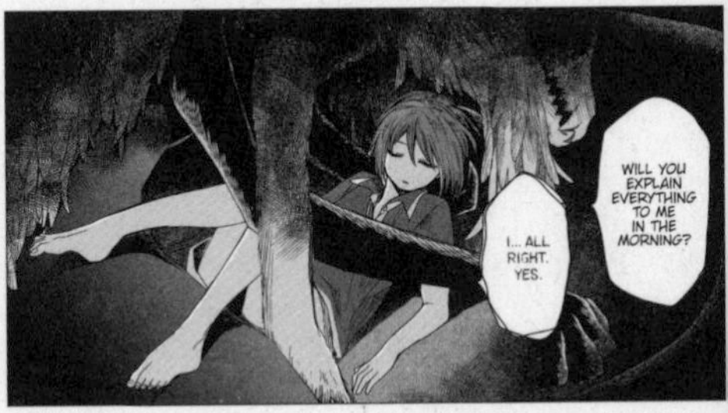
WILL YOU EXPLAIN EVERYTHING TO ME IN THE MORNING?
I... ALL RIGHT. YES.

As a result of his transformation during the battle, Elias' form has become unstable. Worried, Chise visits his room and spends the night there with him.

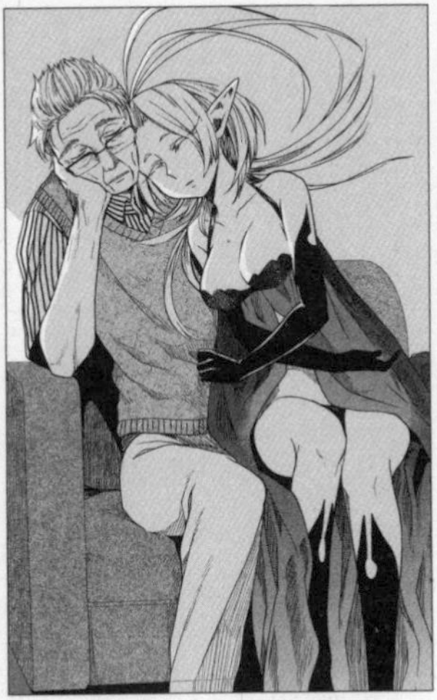

When morning comes, Elias is gone, leaving only a note behind. Chise and Ruth go through the village, searching high and low for him. During the search, Chise meets a leannán sídhe who is attached to an aging man.

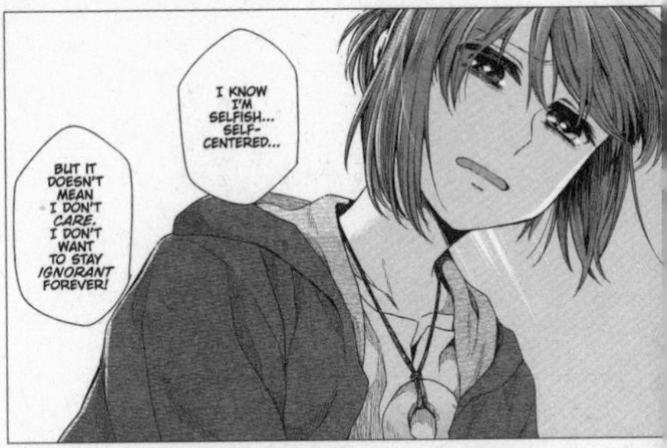
I KNOW I'M SELFISH... SELF-CENTERED...
BUT IT DOESN'T MEAN I DON'T *CARE*. I DON'T WANT TO STAY *IGNORANT* FOREVER!

At last Chise finds Elias, who is resting in a pond. The look on her face as she speaks to him is one he's never seen before.

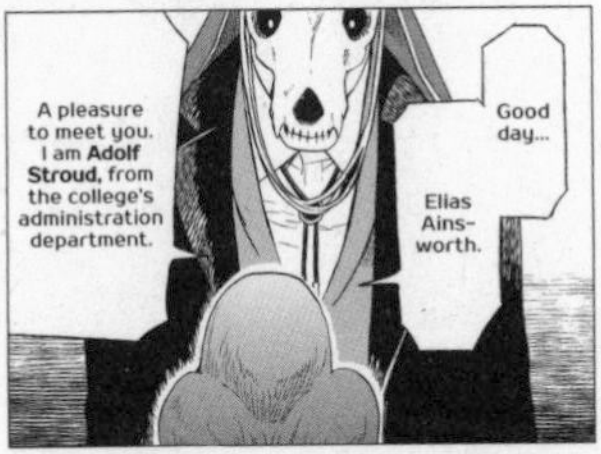
Good day...
Elias Ainsworth.
A pleasure to meet you. I am **Adolf Stroud**, from the college's administration department.

After Elias sends Chise off to the dragons' aerie, a bird arrives with a message for him from the college.

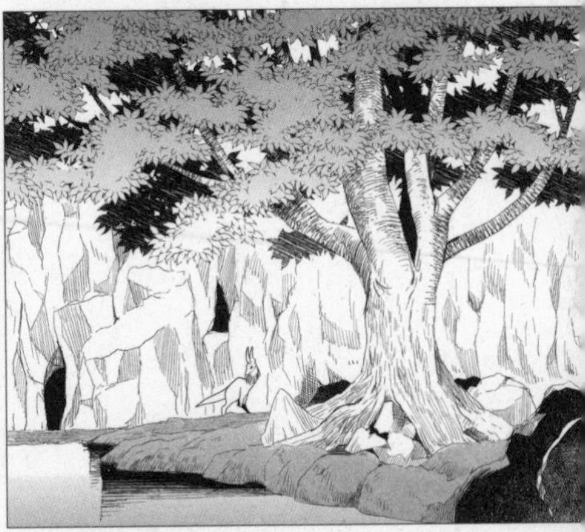

A majestic linden tree has risen from the seed Lindel planted i Nevin's body as he returned to the earth. Chise uses a branch f the tree to make her wand.

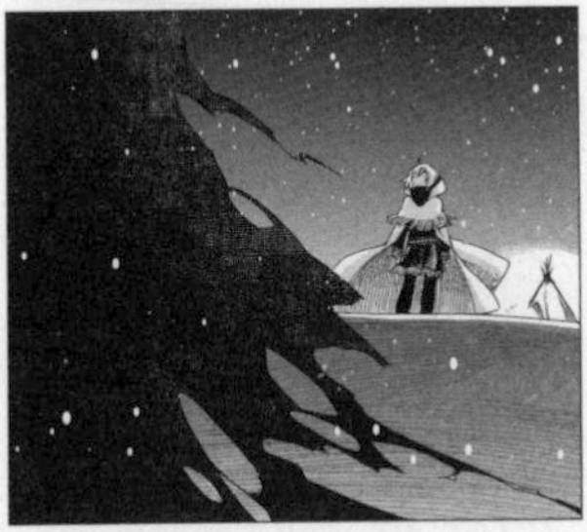

As Chise eats with Lindel, he tells her how he and Elias first met.

The Ancient Magus' Bride 4

魔法使いの嫁

The Ancient Magus Bride
4
KORE YAMAZAKI

RELEASE: Sept. 10, 2015
ENGLISH EDITION: April 12, 2016

At the dragons' aerie, Chise crafts her very own wand from a linden branch grown from Nevin. In the evening, Lindel tells her the story of how he and Elias met, and advises her to talk more with Elias. Back at home, Elias experiences an unfamiliar emotion in Chise's absence.

Once Chise's wand is finished, she hurries home to talk to Elias, who tells her that he only understands human feelings in the abstract. He asks Chise to identify the emotion he felt when she was gone. When she tells him it was loneliness, Elias accepts her answer and respectfully calls her his "teacher of human ways."

HMM? NOT GOING TO EAT?

Before Lindel came to live at the dragons' aerie, he took care of Elias, who had collapsed from hunger.

IT'S DONE...?

Chise whittles the branch to make her wand. In the quiet of the aerie, she talks to herself as she works.

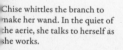

Lindel asks his master, Rahab, about Elias, but she's unable to tell him much.

HELLO, LINDEL.

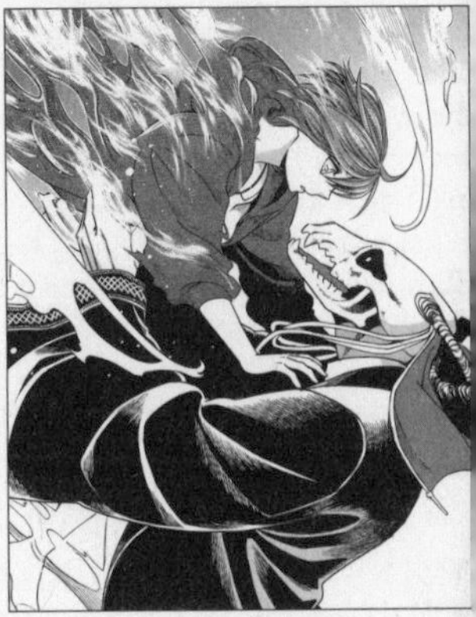

As soon as her wand is finished, Chise rushes back to Elias, borrowing the faeries' power to return like a phoenix.

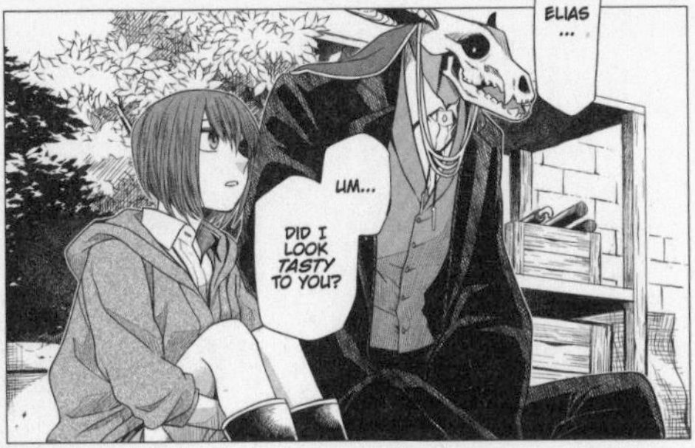
ELIAS ...
UM...
DID I LOOK TASTY TO YOU?

Having learned about Elias' history from talking to Lindel, Chise asks Elias about a time when he'd seemed to be on the verge of eating her.

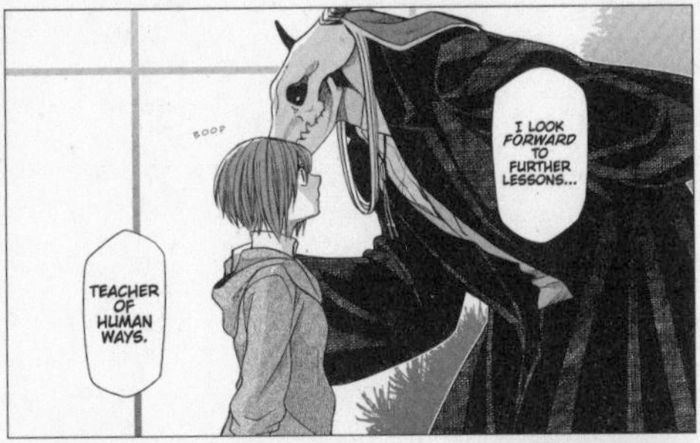
I LOOK FORWARD TO FURTHER LESSONS...
BOOP
TEACHER OF HUMAN WAYS.

Elias is able to understand human emotions in an intellectual way, but doesn't understand how to empathize with those feelings. As he takes a step toward improvement on that front, he calls Chise his "teacher of human ways."

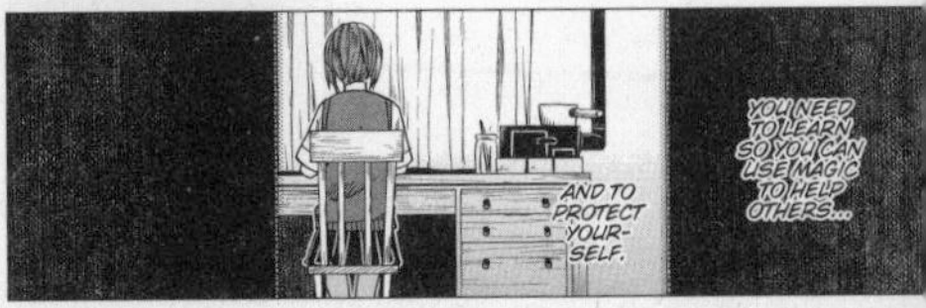
YOU NEED TO LEARN SO YOU CAN USE MAGIC TO HELP OTHERS...
AND TO PROTECT YOUR-SELF.

After her experiences in Ulthar and at the church, Chise starts studying even harder. She hopes that having a better understanding of magic and the natural laws of the world will allow her to protect herself and others better.

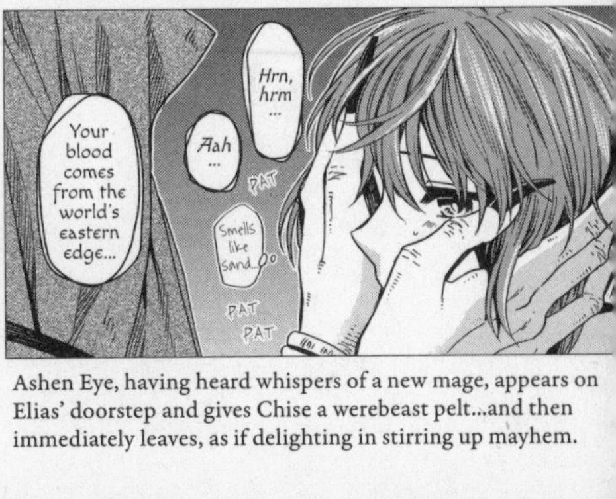
Hrn, hrm ...
Aah ...
Your blood comes from the world's eastern edge...
PAT
Smells like sand...
PAT
PAT

Ashen Eye, having heard whispers of a new mage, appears on Elias' doorstep and gives Chise a werebeast pelt...and then immediately leaves, as if delighting in stirring up mayhem.

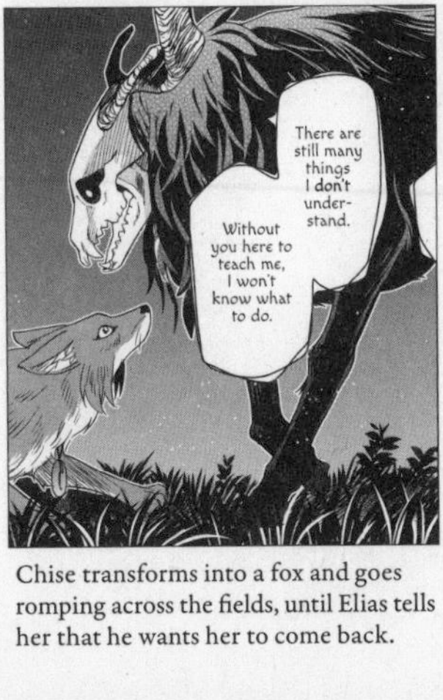
There are still many things I don't under-stand.
Without you here to teach me, I won't know what to do.

Chise transforms into a fox and goes romping across the fields, until Elias tells her that he wants her to come back.

Chise has another encounter with the leannán sídhe she first met while searching for Elias. A leannán sídhe is meant to be a fatal muse and lover to poets, but instead, this one is simply spending her time at the side of Joel Garland, an aging—and utterly ordinary—human man. The leannán sídhe, distraught at Joel's physical deterioration, begs Chise for help. Chise makes fairy ointment that enables Joel, at the end of his life, to finally see and thank the leannán sídhe who's been with him for so long.

Having pushed herself much too hard, Chise herself is in grave condition. Elias takes her to the Faerie Kingdom, where Shannon, a doctor, is able to treat her. Chise and Elias finally return home.

HE'S AT DEATH'S DOOR.

At the leannán sídhe's request, Chise checks in on Joel, who lies unconscious in bed.

FAIRY OINT-MENT!
IS IT OKAY IF I MAKE SOME?!

Upon learning that Joel is close to death, Chise makes fairy ointment for him so that he can speak with the leannán sídhe.

HUH ...?

Working on the fairy ointment for five days without sleeping takes its toll on Chise, who begins coughing up blood.

The Ancient Magus' Bride 5

魔法使いの嫁

5
The Ancient Magus' Bride

RELEASE: March 10, 2016
ENGLISH EDITION: July 5, 2016

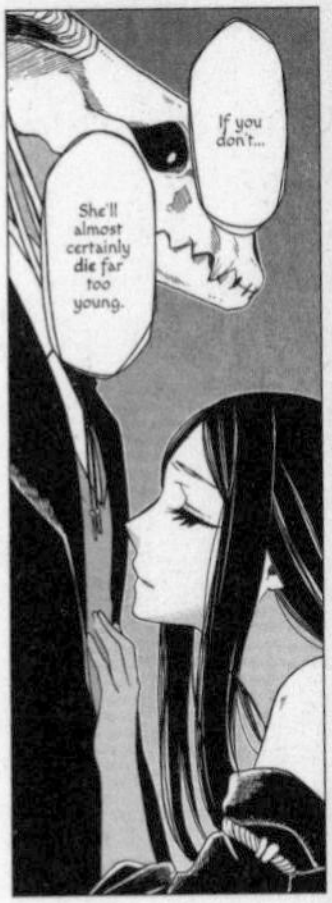
If you don't...
She'll almost certainly die far too young.

Titania once again tells Elias that he and Chise should come live in the Faerie Kingdom.

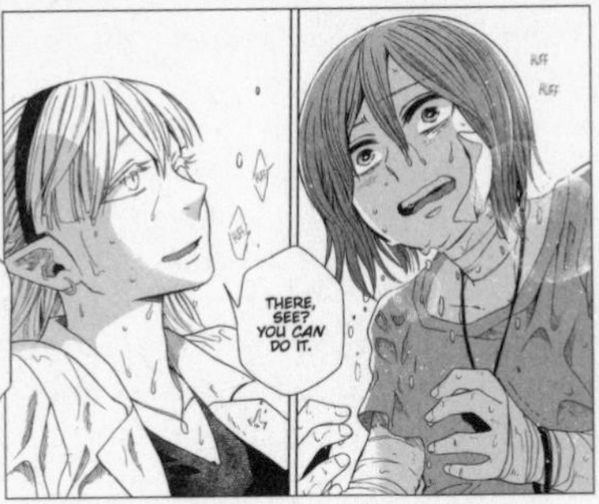
HUFF
HUFF
THERE, SEE? YOU CAN DO IT.

Shannon senses that Chise lacks a strong will to live, and takes the harsh step of dunking her in the lake.

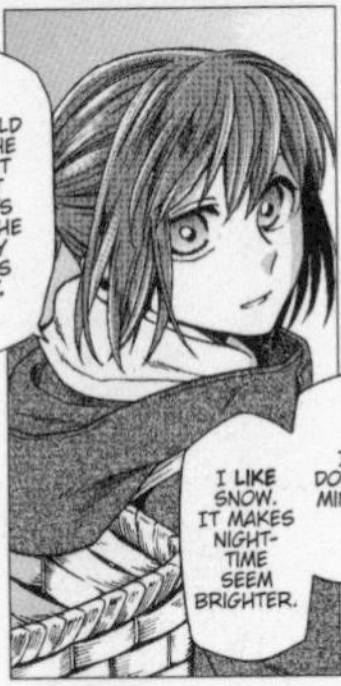
THE COLD AND THE BRIGHT NIGHT ALWAYS KEPT THE SCARY THINGS AWAY.
I DON'T MIND.
I LIKE SNOW. IT MAKES NIGHT-TIME SEEM BRIGHTER.

Chise and Elias venture into the snowy forest to gather holly and ivy.

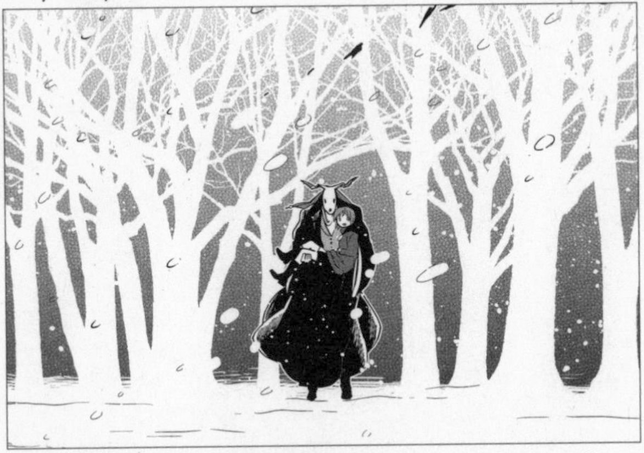

After Chise recovers, Elias takes her back to our world. It was summer when they left, but winter arrived while they were gone.

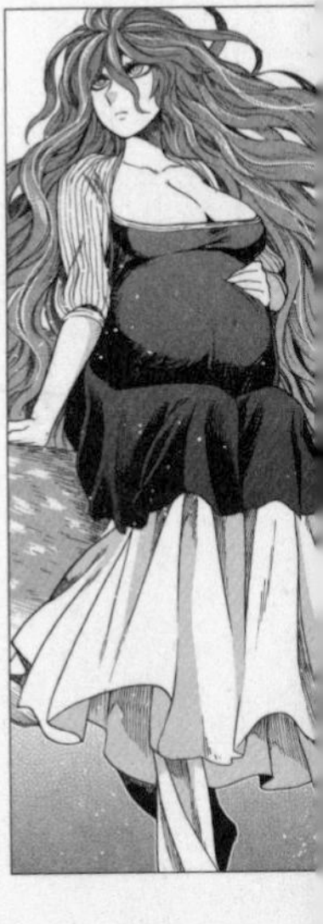

As Chise and Elias prepare for Yule, the Dark Lady and the Horned God pass before them.

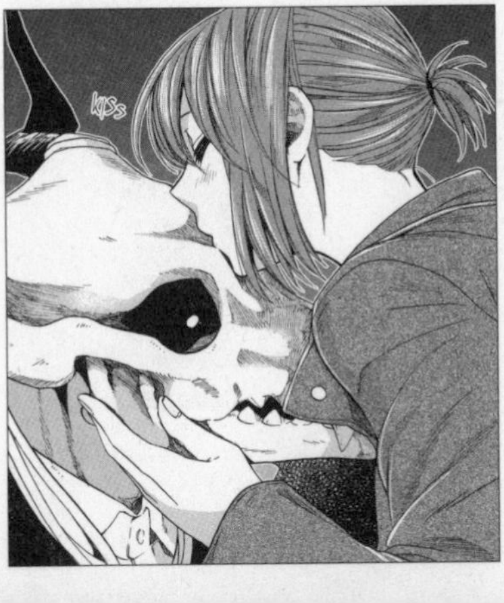
KISS

Chise and Elias follow the custom that suggests people may kiss beneath mistletoe. It's the first time she kisses him.

At Alice's invitation, Chise visits London so the two of them can go Christmas shopping. While there, they cross paths with someone from Alice's past, and Alice winds up telling Chise about her history. The two bond as they search for the right gifts, and fall back on the advice they were given by Hazel, the centaur.

The next day, Chise and Elias meet Stella Barklem, a young girl searching for her little brother, Ethan. As they help her look, they discover that Ashen Eye is behind the boy's disappearance. Ashen Eye, an inhuman being who knows Elias, winds up capturing him as well as Ethan. After saving both Elias and Ethan, Chise becomes friends with Stella.

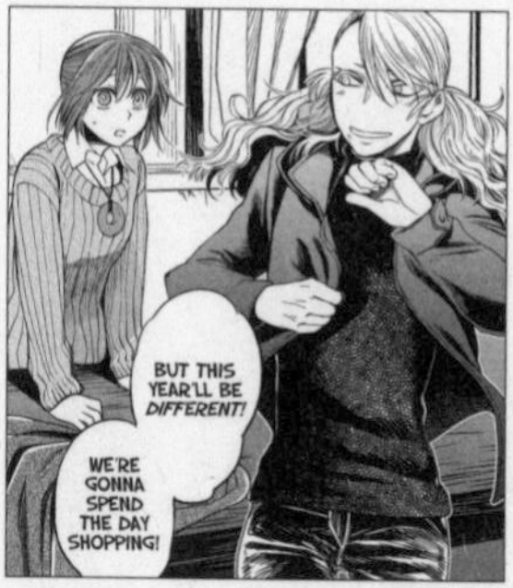
BUT THIS YEAR'LL BE *DIFFERENT!*
WE'RE GONNA SPEND THE DAY SHOPPING!

Chise and Alice wander through London to find the perfect Christmas gifts for their respective masters.

Alice, a former drug addict, runs into someone from her former life and firmly pushes him away.

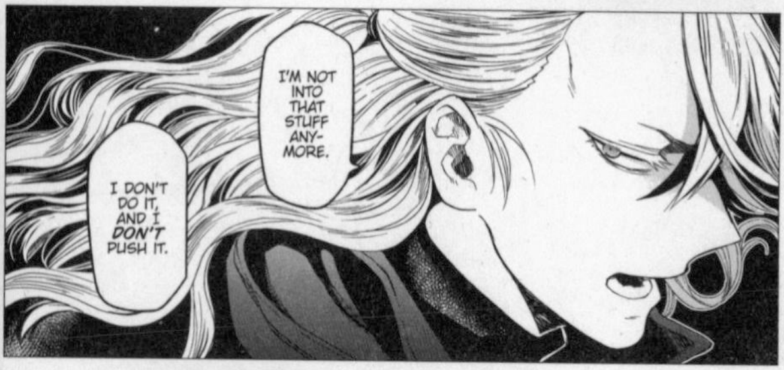
I'M NOT INTO THAT STUFF ANY-MORE.
I DON'T DO IT, AND I *DON'T* PUSH IT.

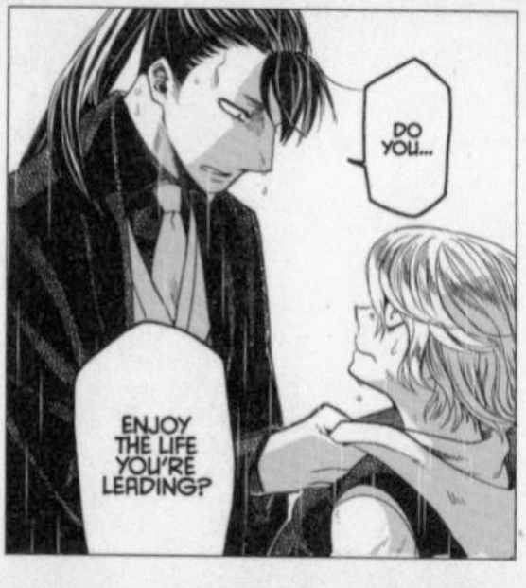
DO YOU...
ENJOY THE LIFE YOU'RE LEADING?

In a flashback, Renfred recognizes Alice's talent and takes her in off the street to be his apprentice and bodyguard.

The Ancient Magus' Bride

6

魔法使いの嫁

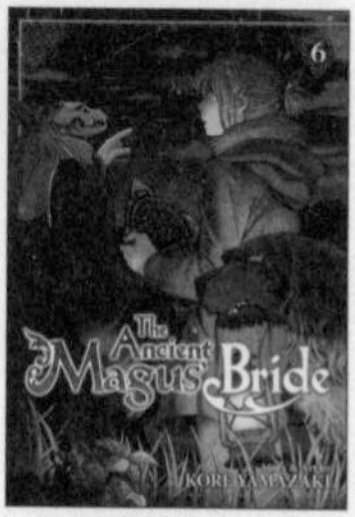
6
The Ancient Magus' Bride
KORE YAMAZAKI

RELEASE: Sept. 10, 2016
ENGLISH EDITION: Jan. 3, 2017

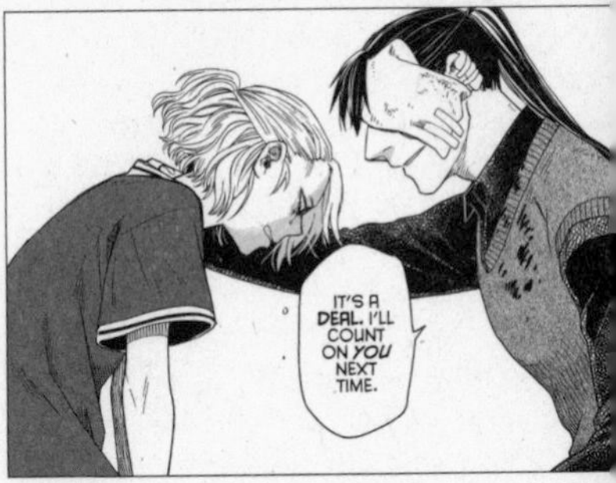
IT'S A DEAL. I'LL COUNT ON YOU NEXT TIME.

Alice slips up and Renfred is badly injured as a result. Ever since, she's been determined to serve as his bodyguard.

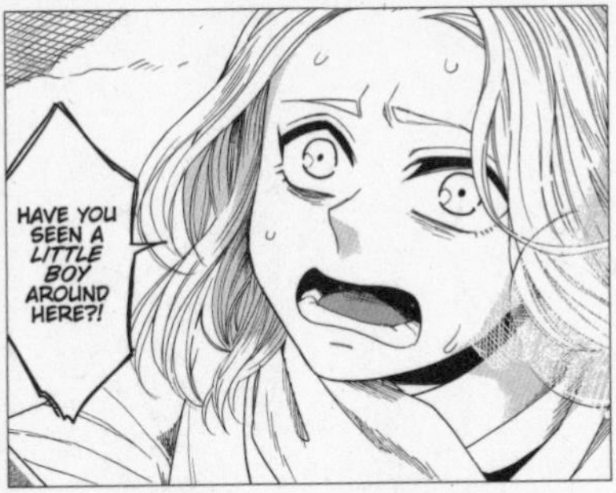
HAVE YOU SEEN A LITTLE BOY AROUND HERE?!

On a snowy Christmas Day, Chise and Elias meet Stella, a girl desperately searching for her little brother, Ethan.

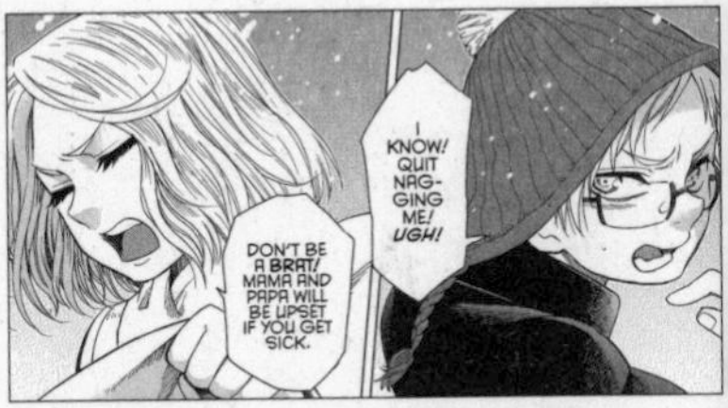
I KNOW! QUIT NAG-GING ME! UGH!
DON'T BE A BRAT! MAMA AND PAPA WILL BE UPSET IF YOU GET SICK.

While Ethan plays in the snow, he and Stella get on each other's nerves and have a fight.

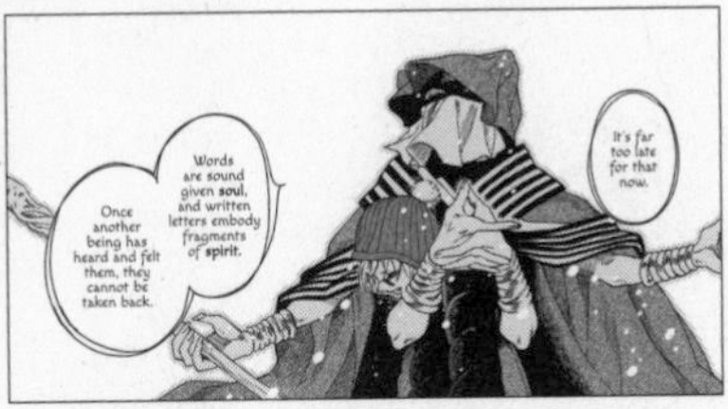
It's far too late for that now.
Words are sound given soul, and written letters embody fragments of spirit.
Once another being has heard and felt them, they cannot be taken back.

Ashen Eye takes Ethan and points out that words have enough power to form curses. The siblings find that their bond has become frayed.

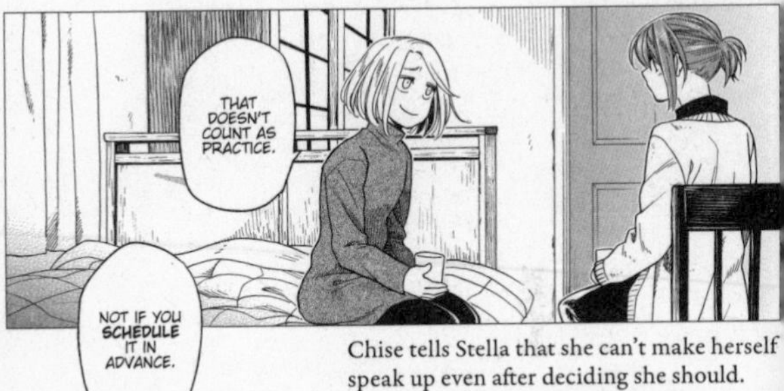
THAT DOESN'T COUNT AS PRACTICE.
NOT IF YOU SCHEDULE IT IN ADVANCE.

Chise tells Stella that she can't make herself speak up even after deciding she should. Stella says Chise just needs practice.

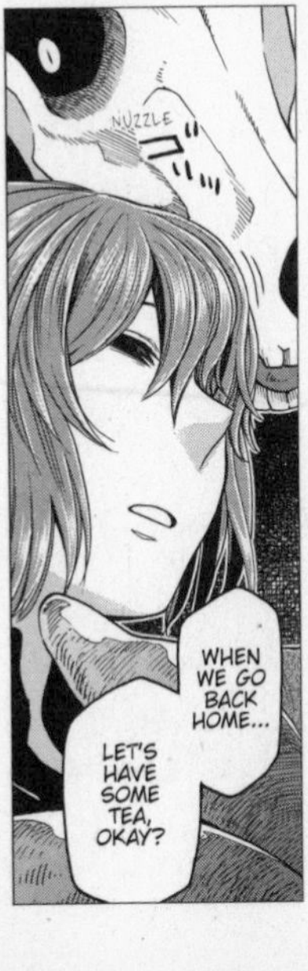
NUZZLE
WHEN WE GO BACK HOME...
LET'S HAVE SOME TEA, OKAY?

When Elias leaves the house without a word, Chise chases after him...and finds herself engulfed in his body.

After Chise's friend Stella stops by for a visit, Elias leaves the house without a word to anyone. Chise chases after him and is engulfed in his body. Sternly, she tells him that he's experiencing jealousy.

Soon after, poachers capture two dragon chicks from the aerie. Adolf Stroud, a representative of the college—a mutual aid organization for alchemists—answers the call of his former master, Lindel, and searches for the chicks. Renfred deduces that Cartaphilus is involved, and he, Adolf, and Torrey call on Elias. Chise is able to piece together where one of the chicks is, but while they're attempting a rescue mission, the young dragon goes berserk.

The Ancient Magus' Bride 7

魔法使いの嫁

ELIAS! IF YOU DON'T STOP HAVING THIS TANTRUM, I'LL HAVE TO DO SOMETHING ABOUT IT!

In the throes of jealousy over Chise and Stella's relationship, Elias is unable to release Chise. Chise lectures him like a mother talking to a sulky child.

WELL, LOOK AT THAT--TWO OF THEM! IT'S OUR LUCKY DAY.
MMMPH!

Poachers come to the aerie and abduct two dragon chicks. Lindel, as their caretaker, rushes to find them.

7
The Ancient Magus' Bride
KORE YAMAZAKI

RELEASE: March 10, 2017
ENGLISH EDITION: July 3, 2017

YOU HUMMED A LULLABY FOR HIM AND HE FELL ASLEEP...?

Chise visits Angelica in London to figure out how to wake Elias.

At the college, Renfred and Torrey Innis gather in Adolf's lab, where they have a lively debate about alchemical research.

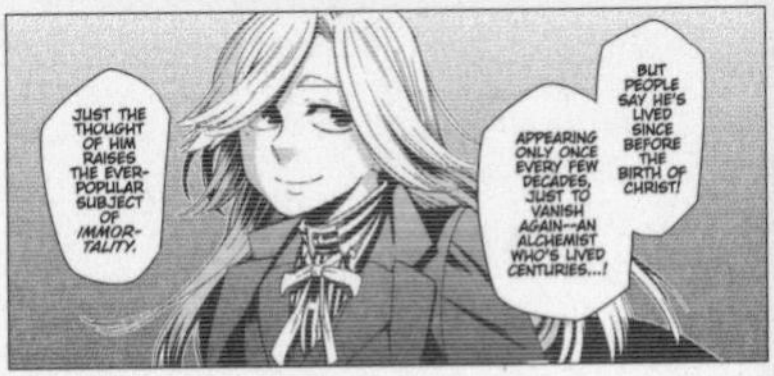
BUT PEOPLE SAY HE'S LIVED SINCE BEFORE THE BIRTH OF CHRIST!
APPEARING ONLY ONCE EVERY FEW DECADES, JUST TO VANISH AGAIN--AN ALCHEMIST WHO'S LIVED CENTURIES...!
JUST THE THOUGHT OF HIM RAISES THE EVER-POPULAR SUBJECT OF IMMORTALITY.

Chise talks to Cartaphilus in a dream, but much of what he says is too incoherent for her to follow.

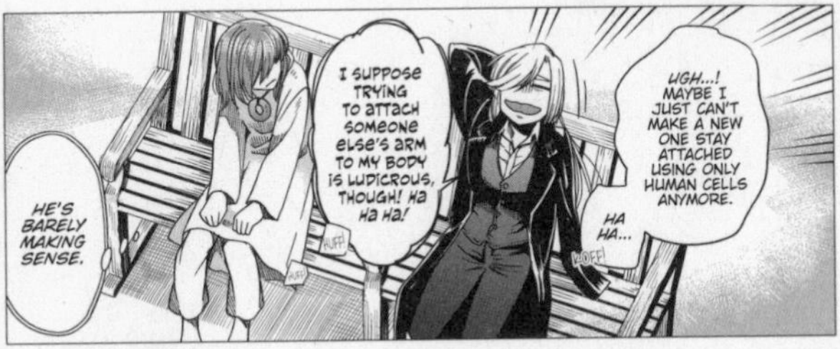
UGH...! MAYBE I JUST CAN'T MAKE A NEW ONE STAY ATTACHED USING ONLY HUMAN CELLS ANYMORE.
HA HA...
KOFF!
I SUPPOSE TRYING TO ATTACH SOMEONE ELSE'S ARM TO MY BODY IS LUDICROUS, THOUGH! HA HA HA!
HUFF!
HUFF!
HE'S BARELY MAKING SENSE.

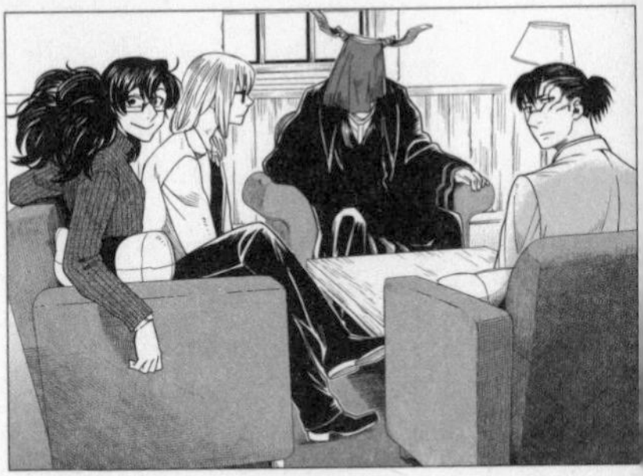

Renfred, Adolf, and Torrey come looking for help with finding the stolen dragon chicks. At first, Elias refuses, on the grounds that it is dangerous.

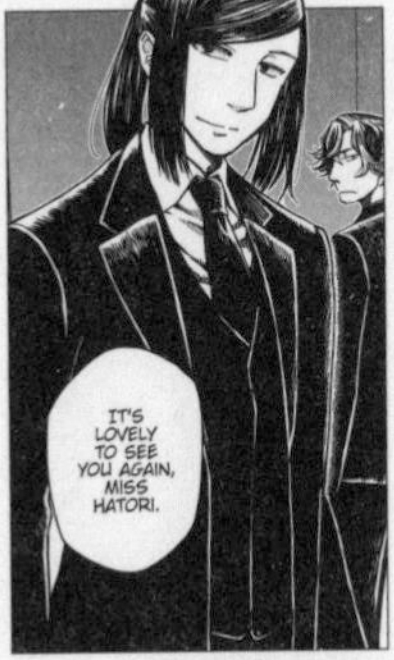
IT'S LOVELY TO SEE YOU AGAIN, MISS HATORI.

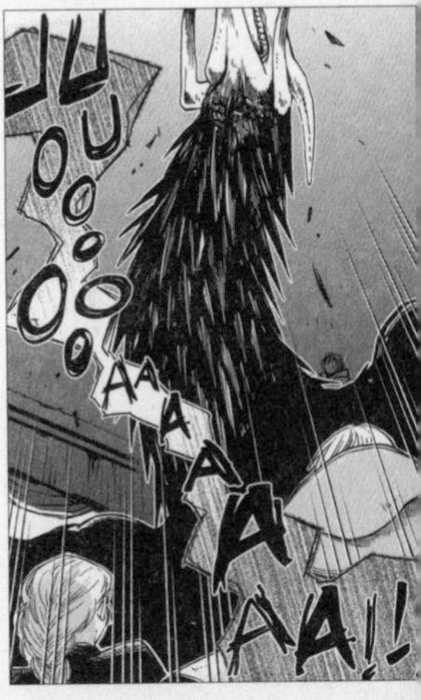
JUUOOOOOOAAAAAAA!!

They find a dragon chick at the auction house, but the dragon, terrified at what could happen to her, spirals out of control.

Hearing that the dragon chicks are extremely valuable, Chise realizes that there's a high chance they'll be auctioned off. She contacts Seth at the auction house.

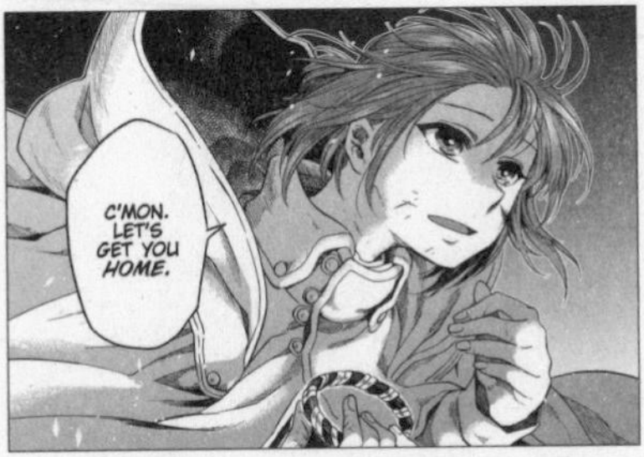
C'MON. LET'S GET YOU HOME.

The dragon chick, wild with alarm, takes to the London sky. Without stopping to think of the price she might pay, Chise removes her bracelet and absorbs the dragon's magical energy.

Timeline of *The Ancient Magus' Bride*

Season	Event	Publication
	Chise's mother commits suicide.	Vol. 1, etc.
	Chise meets Riichi Miura.	OVA
Spring	Elias purchases Chise.	Vol. 1
	▼ **Three days later:**	
	Chise meets Angelica in London.	
	▼ **The next day:**	
	Chise meets Simon in the village and Lindel in the dragons' aerie.	
	▼ **The next day:**	
	Chise meets Renfred and Alice in Ulthar.	
	▼ **Two weeks later:**	Vol. 2
	Chise wakes from a coma and meets Titania and Oberon.	
	▼ **Then:**	
	Chise meets Cartaphilus at the church.	
	Chise forms a contract with a church grim, who becomes her familiar. She names him Ruth.	
	▼ **Three days later:**	
Summer	Elias, in poor physical condition, shuts himself up in his room.	Vol. 3
	▼ **The next day:**	
	Chise meets Joel and the leannán sídhe in the village.	
	A bird arrives to give Elias a message from Adolf.	Vol. 4
	▼ **Two days later:**	
	Chise makes her wand in the dragons' aerie.	
	▼ **Then:**	
	At home, Chise meets Ashen Eye.	
	▼ **One week later:**	
	Joel passes away.	
	Chise visits the Faerie Kingdom.	Vol. 5
Autumn	▼ **Autumn having passed while she was in the Faerie Kingdom:**	
	Chise meets the Heralds of Yule and the Dark Lady.	
	▼ **Then:**	
	Chise and Alice go shopping in London.	Vol. 6
	▼ **The next day:**	
	Chise meets Stella and Ethan.	
	▼ **The next day:**	
	Stella visits Elias' house.	Vol. 7
	Two chicks are poached from the dragons' aerie.	
	▼ **The next day:**	
	Elias falls asleep and doesn't wake up.	
	▼ **Three days later:**	
	Chise meets David.	
	▼ **The next day:**	
	Elias wakes.	
	Merituuli relays a message to Adolf.	
Winter	▼ **Two days later:**	
	Renfred and the other alchemists visit Elias' house.	
	▼ **Then:**	
	Chise meets Seth at the auction house for the first time since her own sale.	
	▼ **The next day:**	
	The dragon's curse affects Chise's hand and arm.	Chap. 36
	▼ **The next day:**	
	Marielle visits Elias' house.	Chap. 37
	▼ **Then:**	
	Chise and Elias visit the coven.	Chap. 38

5

Early Designs & Storyboards

For the first time ever, see early designs from before the serialization, as well as an unused pitch for the first Don't miss this glimpse into what could have b

※ The notes on the early designs do not necessarily apply to the series as published. Likewise, the unused Chapter 1 is included as-is.

Early Designs
Chise Hatori

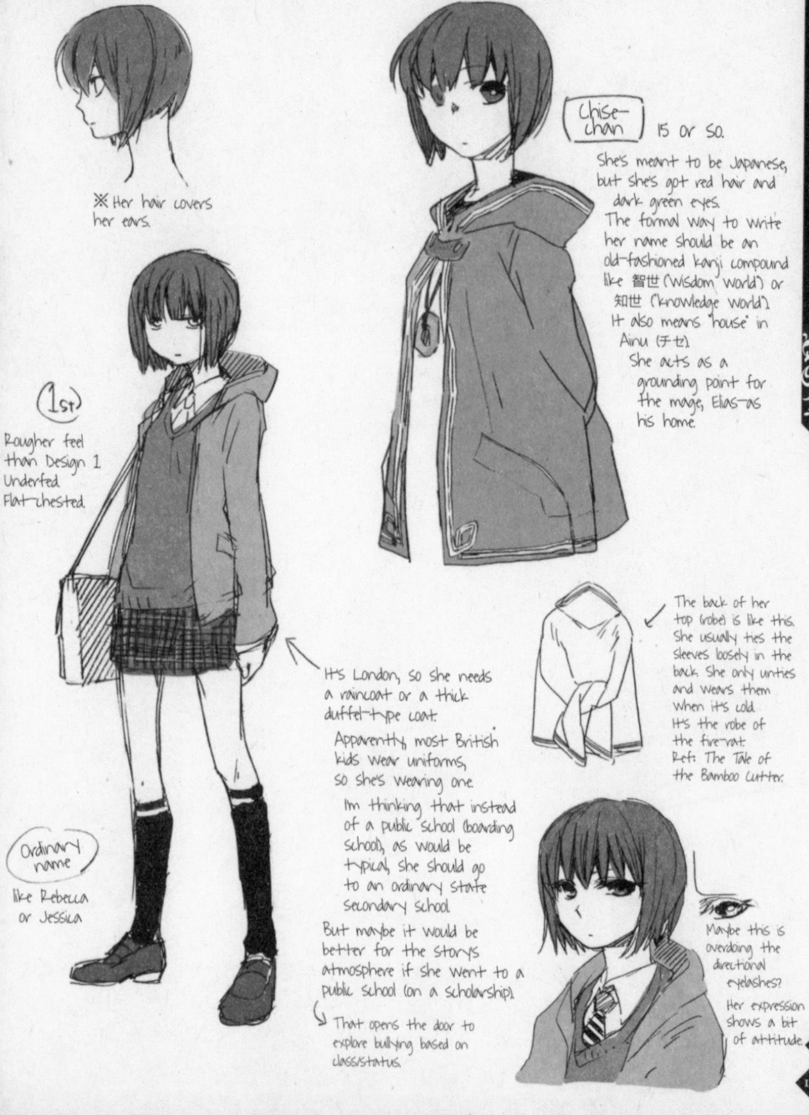
※ Her hair covers her ears.
Chise-chan
15 or so.
She's meant to be Japanese, but she's got red hair and dark green eyes.
The formal way to write her name should be an old-fashioned kanji compound like 智世 ("wisdom world") or 知世 ("knowledge world").
It also means "house" in Ainu (チセ).
She acts as a grounding point for the mage, Elias—as his home.
1st
Rougher feel than Design 1
Underfed.
Flat-chested.
The back of her top (robe) is like this. She usually ties the sleeves loosely in the back. She only unties and wears them when it's cold.
It's the robe of the fire-rat.
Ref: The Tale of the Bamboo Cutter.
It's London, so she needs a raincoat or a thick duffel-type coat.
Apparently, most British kids wear uniforms, so she's wearing one.
I'm thinking that instead of a public school (boarding school), as would be typical, she should go to an ordinary state secondary school.
But maybe it would be better for the story's atmosphere if she went to a public school (on a scholarship).
→ That opens the door to explore bullying based on class/status.
Ordinary name
like Rebecca or Jessica
Maybe this is overdoing the directional eyelashes?
Her expression shows a bit of attitude.

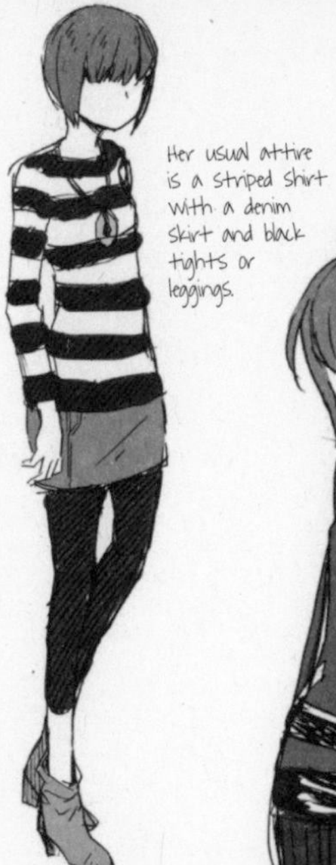
Her usual attire is a striped shirt with a denim skirt and black tights or leggings.

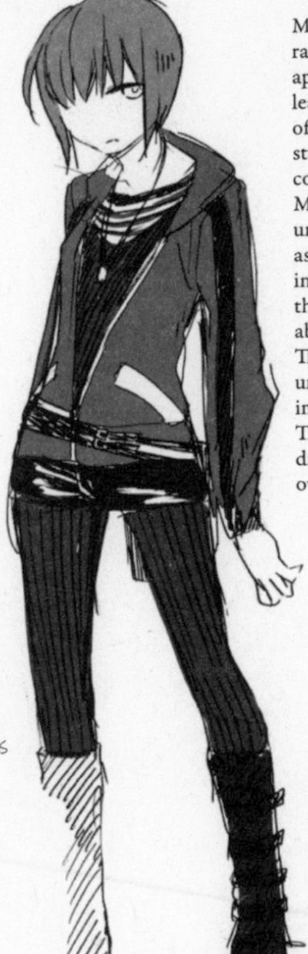

Bomber Jacket

The uniform of the "college" includes a shirt, a necktie, a cardigan, and a skirt or slacks.

Mages have a massive range of ages and appearances, so at least a very basic way of IDing them as students of the college is required. Modifying the uniform is allowed as long as it still includes the things listed above.
There's no uniform for instructors. They each dress in their own way.

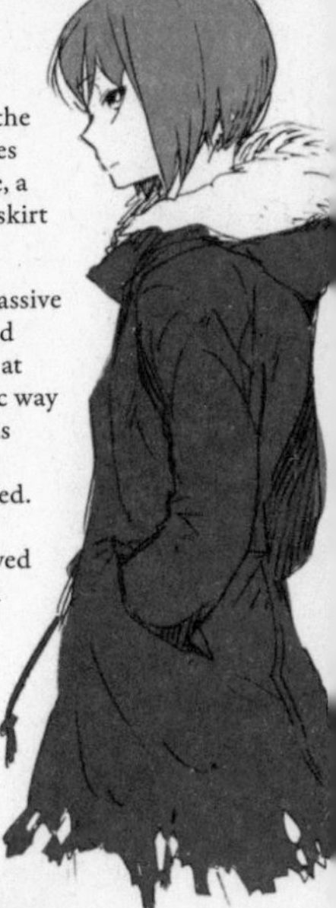

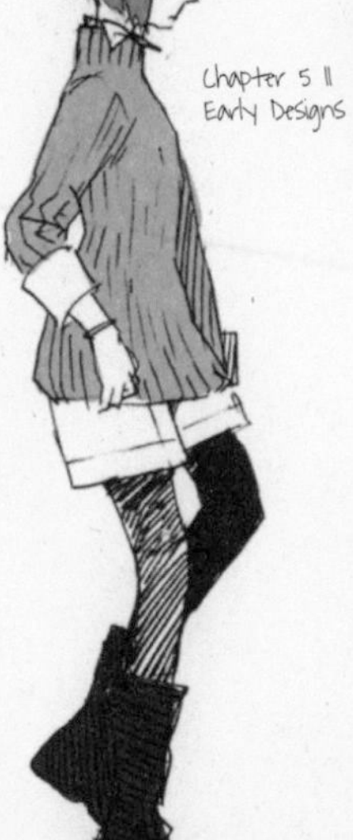
Chapter 5 ll Early Designs

Punk Look

Punk, but simple. She wears leggings or tights with skirts, except in summer.

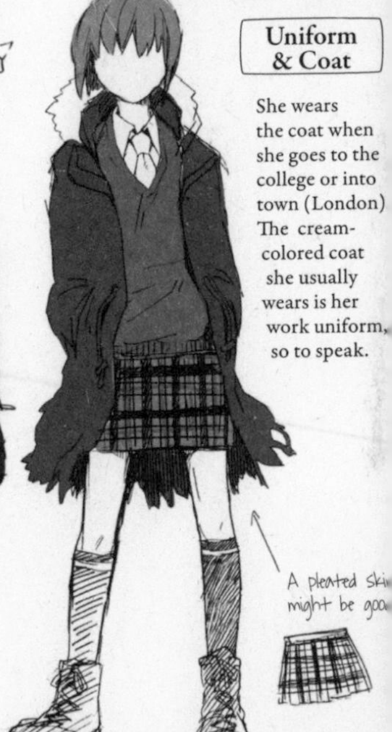
A pleated ski
might be goo

Uniform & Coat

She wears the coat when she goes to the college or into town (London)
The cream-colored coat she usually wears is her work uniform, so to speak.

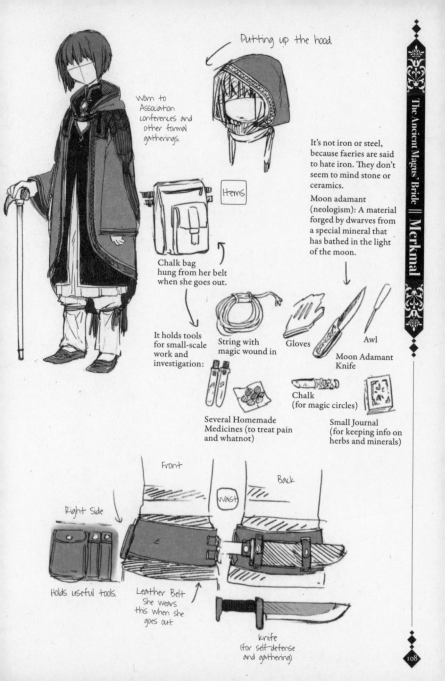

Putting up the hood.

Worn to Association conferences and other formal gatherings.

Hems

It's not iron or steel, because faeries are said to hate iron. They don't seem to mind stone or ceramics.

Moon adamant (neologism): A material forged by dwarves from a special mineral that has bathed in the light of the moon.

Chalk bag hung from her belt when she goes out.

It holds tools for small-scale work and investigation:

String with magic wound in

Gloves

Awl

Moon Adamant Knife

Chalk (for magic circles)

Several Homemade Medicines (to treat pain and whatnot)

Small Journal (for keeping info on herbs and minerals)

Front

Waist

Back

Right Side

Holds useful tools.

Leather Belt She wears this when she goes out.

Knife (for self-defense and gathering)

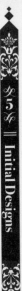

Rev. design for the knife Chise wears at her waist.

Because she uses it as a gathering knife, it has runes that help spare the plants as much damage as possible.

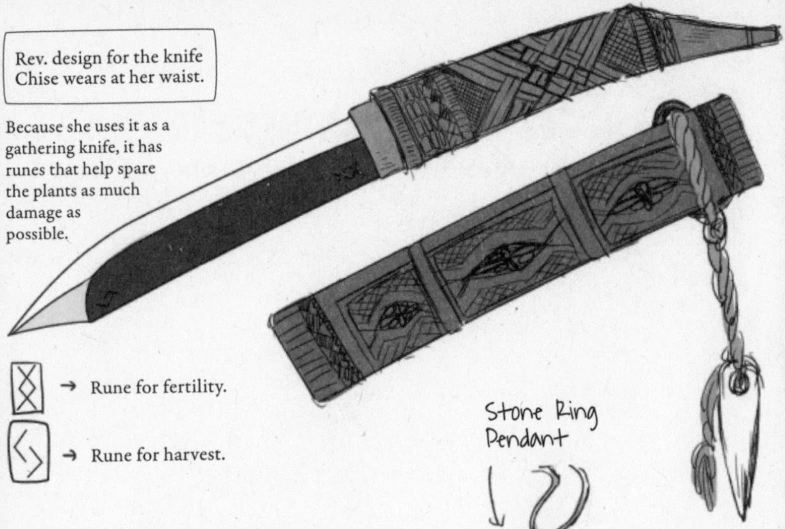

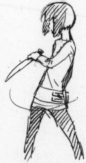

ᛝ → Rune for fertility.

ᚲ → Rune for harvest.

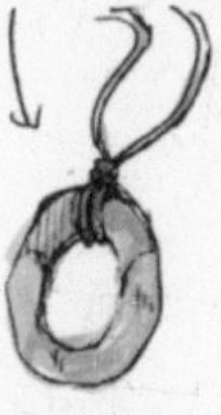
Stone Ring Pendant
Color and texture similar to jade.
The hole in the stone formed naturally underwater. Looking through it reveals the fae world.

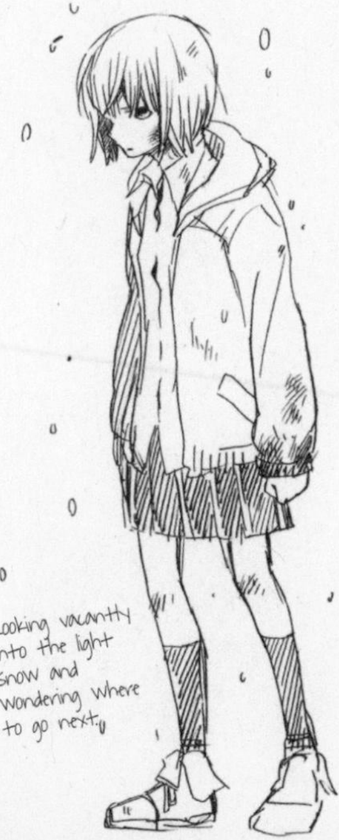
Looking vacantly into the light snow and wondering where to go next.

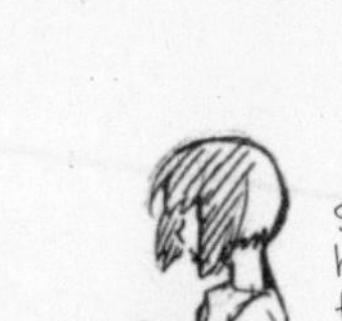
She draws it with her left hand and flips it in her hand.
Or:
She draws it backhand to begin with.
The plan is for her to team up with a black dog familiar later on. It might be useful for action.

Early Designs
Elias Ainsworth

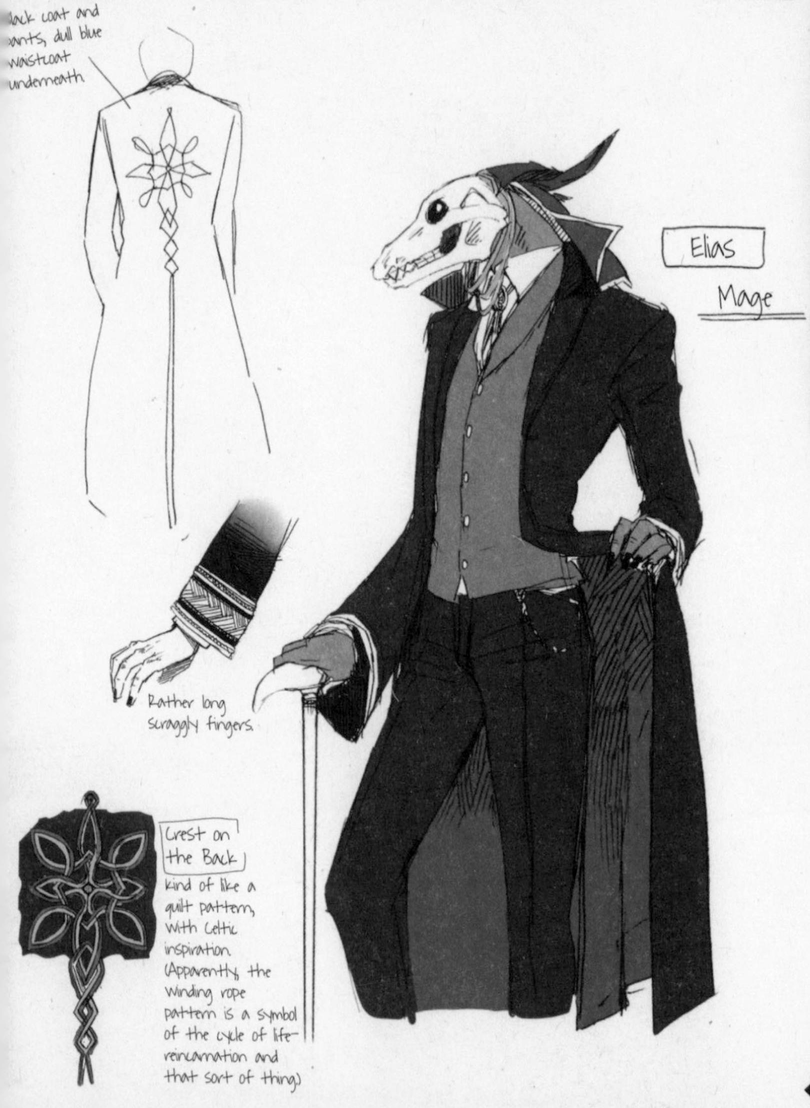

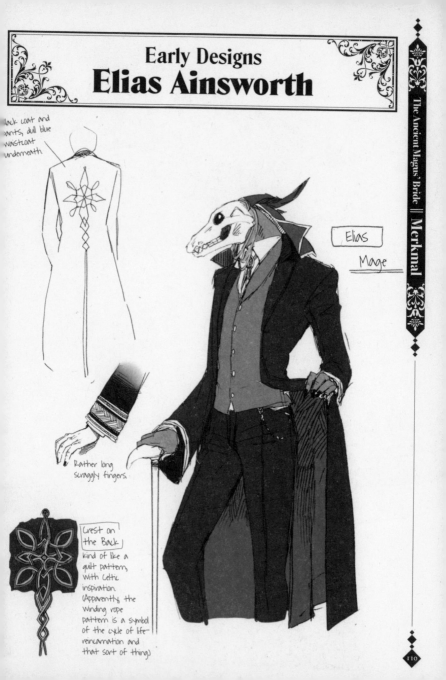

lack coat and ants, dull blue waistcoat underneath.
Elias
Mage
Rather long scraggly fingers.
Crest on the Back
kind of like a quilt pattern, with Celtic inspiration. (Apparently, the winding rope pattern is a symbol of the cycle of life-reincarnation and that sort of thing.)

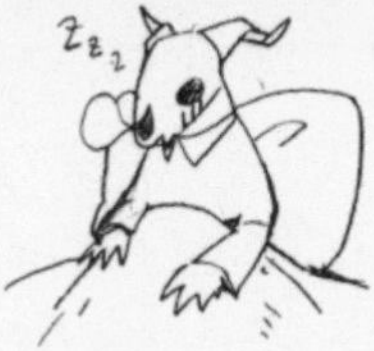

He sleeps normally (except he can't lie down because of his horns).

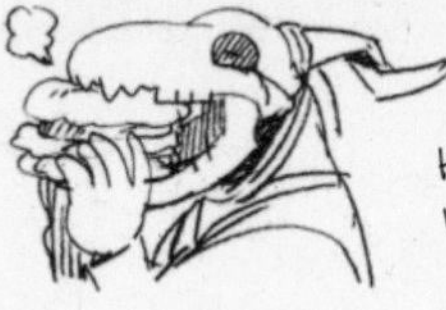

He eats normally.

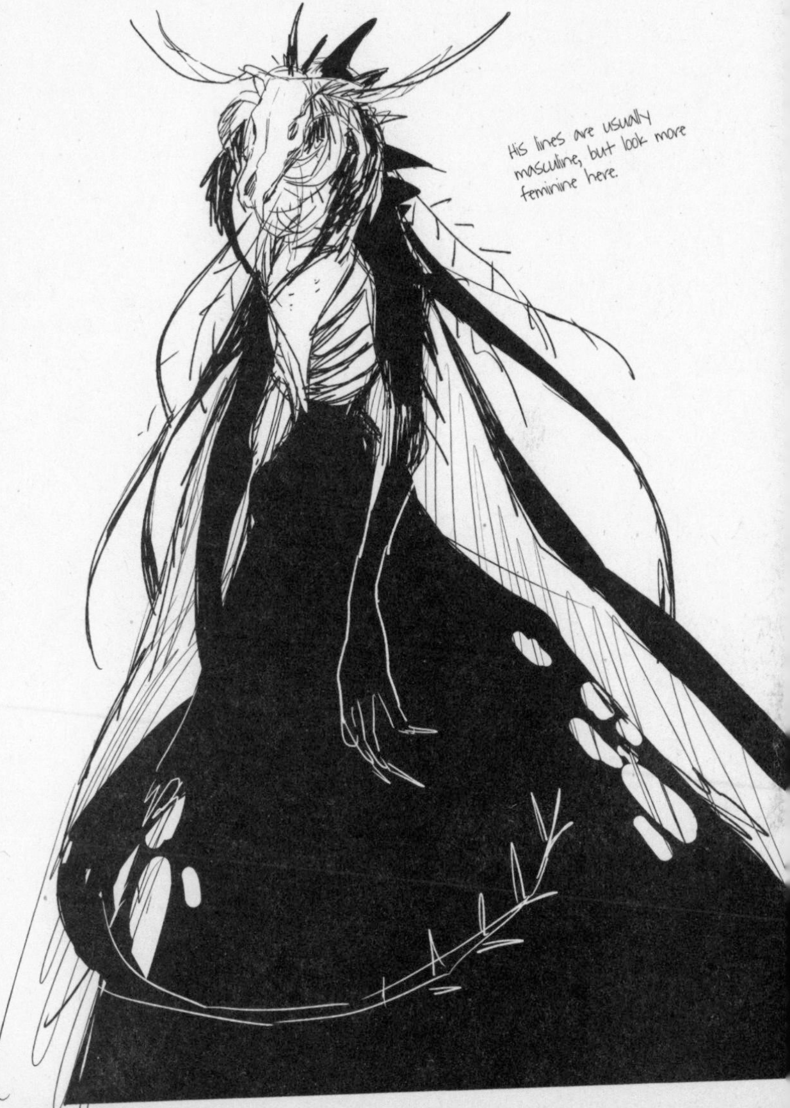

His lines are usually masculine, but look more feminine here.

Early Designs
Ruth

Original name: Lester
Name given by Chise: Makiri (Ainu for "knife")

Chise's familiar. A black Irish wolfhound who lost his master in war and stayed by his grave for decades. He still appears as a black dog, and acquires the corresponding fae power.

Chise notices him and visits the grave over the course of a month or so as she slowly wins his trust. Eventually they form a contract. Along the way, they run into some trouble owing to rumors about the black dog, such as a priest who tells her she's under the influence of the devil.

Their contract stipulates that he will treat her as his substitute master until his master returns. It's not a full familiar contract, and it gives him a long leash, but while he does take advantage of that, he generally stays at Chise's side. He likes meat and berries and is happy to beg for them. His appearance and traits are suited to nighttime activity. He can hide in Chise's shadow. Because his contract with Chise lets him manifest physically, he's able to enjoy eating (he can eat what humans eat), and he can sleep when he wants to. Normal people can see and touch him.

As a black dog (a fae dog that appears at a church as an omen of death), he can identify humans who are nearing the end of their lives.

Familiar

A being that serves a mage, intuiting and carrying out their will. Most familiars use magical energy to assume a form they come up with, or else possess the corpse of an animal. The latter is easier, since they can then make use of the animal's physical nerves and flesh. Either way, a familiar can be touched, but they lack free will. For example, it's possible for a mage to bind them to automatically shield the mage in case of danger.

He initially appears human, because that's what he believes himself to be. But Chise sees him as a dog right from the start, so there are some strange discrepancies (from Makiri's point of view) in some of their interactions. Once he and Chise establish their contract, he finally recognizes himself as a dog.

After their contract is in place, he has two forms: dog and human. Since he was originally a dog, he's not at all shy about touching her, but there's no particular romantic interest between them. If a comparison has to be made, it's something like "Chise sees Makiri as her little brother and he sees her as his mother."

Black Dog
(Based on the
Irish wolfhound)
Curly hair.

Takes human form

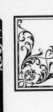

Early Designs
Silky

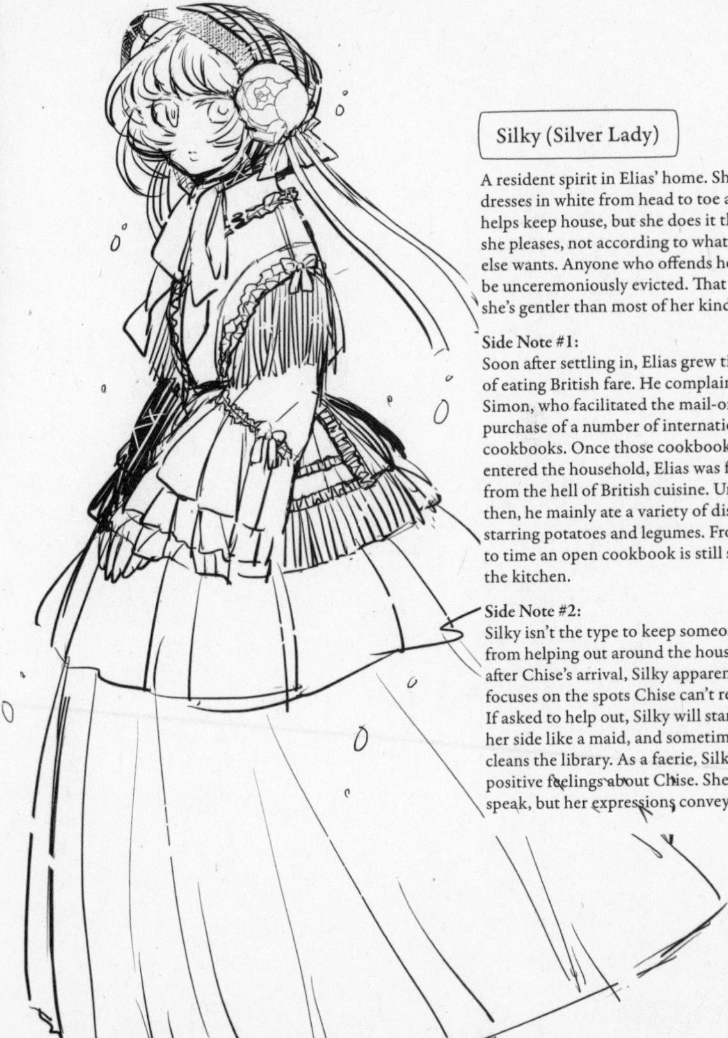

Silky (Silver Lady)

A resident spirit in Elias' home. She dresses in white from head to toe and helps keep house, but she does it the way she pleases, not according to what anyone else wants. Anyone who offends her will be unceremoniously evicted. That said, she's gentler than most of her kind.

Side Note #1:
Soon after settling in, Elias grew tired of eating British fare. He complained to Simon, who facilitated the mail-order purchase of a number of international cookbooks. Once those cookbooks entered the household, Elias was freed from the hell of British cuisine. Until then, he mainly ate a variety of dishes starring potatoes and legumes. From time to time an open cookbook is still seen in the kitchen.

Side Note #2:
Silky isn't the type to keep someone else from helping out around the house, so after Chise's arrival, Silky apparently focuses on the spots Chise can't reach. If asked to help out, Silky will stand at her side like a maid, and sometimes she cleans the library. As a faerie, Silky has positive feelings about Chise. She doesn't speak, but her expressions convey a lot.

Early Designs
Angelica Purley

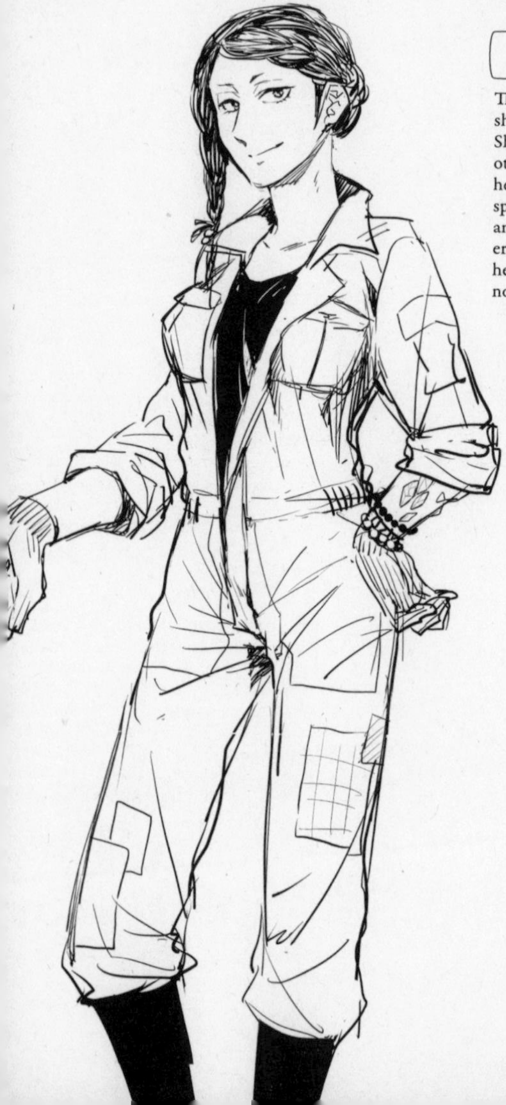

Angelica Purley

The owner of a Magus Crafts shop off Regent Street in London. She sells some items made by other artificers, but most of her stock is her own work. She specializes in working with stone and metal. Due to an alchemical error she made as a child, part of her left arm was transformed and now has scale-like stones.

Her husband is an ordinary human who works at a trading company. Her daughter, Althea, may have a little talent as an alchemist?

Althea

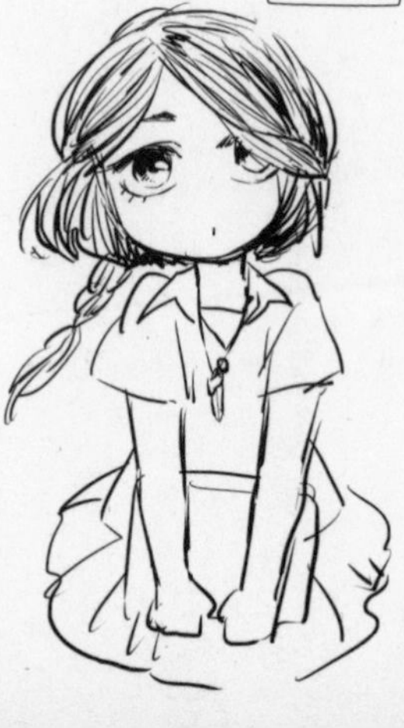

Early Designs
Mikhail Renfred

Mikhail Renfred

An alchemist who resents Elias. He despises mages in general, seeing them as unreasonable and unfair, but he has a particular hatred for Elias, who is neither fae nor human yet uses human magic. The scope of his skills as an alchemist is impressive, but for the past decade or so he's been studying how to make use of "blights," dark pockets of malice and intense human emotion that influence both the people and the land in their vicinity.

He knows that Elias purchased Chise. (He was at the auction house too, hoping to buy her himself.) He wants to take Chise with him, both for research and for revenge against Elias, but she flatly refuses.

He's kind enough to humans and animals, in an impersonal way, but comes close to hating everything else. It's a twisted expression of his appreciation for what he understands to be the natural order of things in a world he knows can never be fully understood. When he's envious of something, it overflows and makes his hatred vastly more intense. Again, he's magnanimous when it comes to humans, but anyone who's hostile to him will get the same in return.

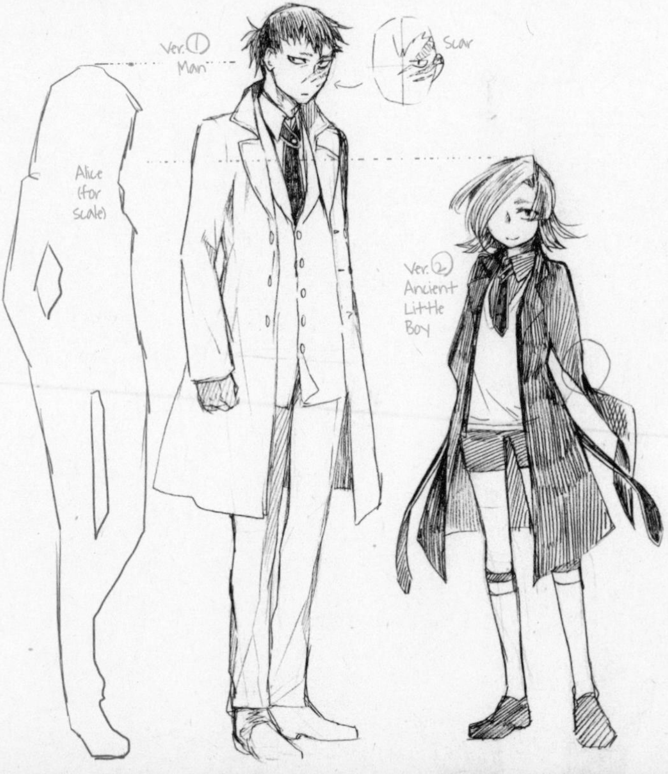
Ver.① Man
Scar
Alice (for scale)
Ver.② Ancient Little Boy

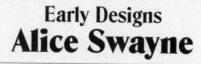

Early Designs
Alice Swayne

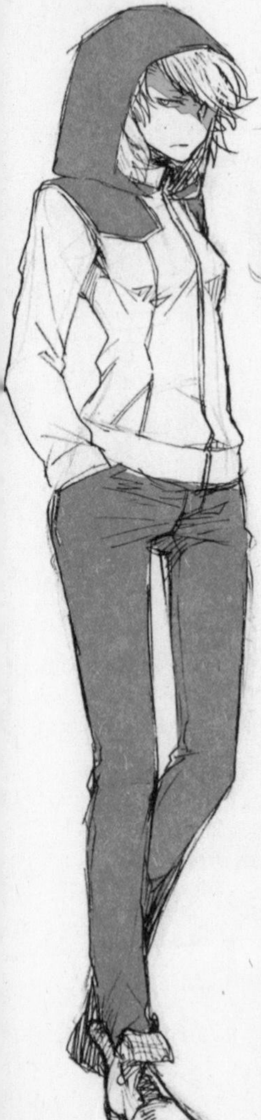

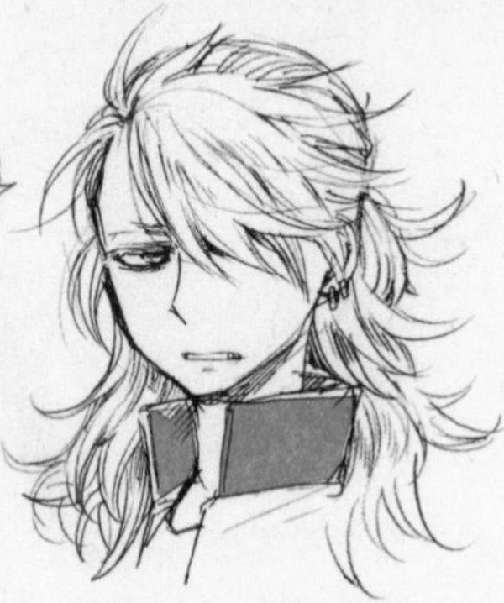

I think it would be cute if the mage and alchemist apprentices could get along, even though their masters don't. Maybe they could secretly meet up on weekends, and Alice could show Chise around London...

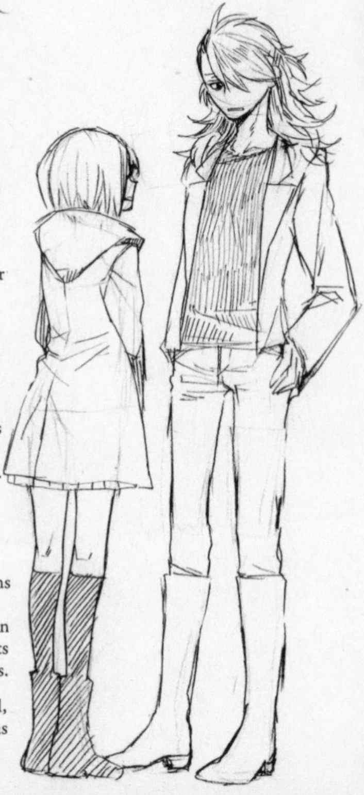

Alice Swayne

Seventeen years old. She grew up in the slums, then was saved by Mikhail when she was thirteen. She'd be cute with a jagged smile. At first she was wary and disliked Ullr, but then, after she made a mistake in an experiment and Ullr was injured protecting her, she opened her heart to him. Sometimes she can't follow his thought processes, but her affection for him means she'll still do exactly as he asks without questioning it. She loves him enough that she'd kill for him. (Although, given her upbringing, she doesn't really have that many qualms about crime anyway.)
A budding alchemist with an affinity for flame, which puts her rather at odds with Elias.

Right now, I see her as a girl, but she could also be good as an underfed, stunted boy.

Early Designs
Side Characters

Seth Noel

The person who found Chise in Japan and auctioned her off. He has no mage talent, but is capable of seeing and hearing fae, spirits, etc. He's protective of his sister, who is much younger. He's come to think of his ability simply as a profitable skill.

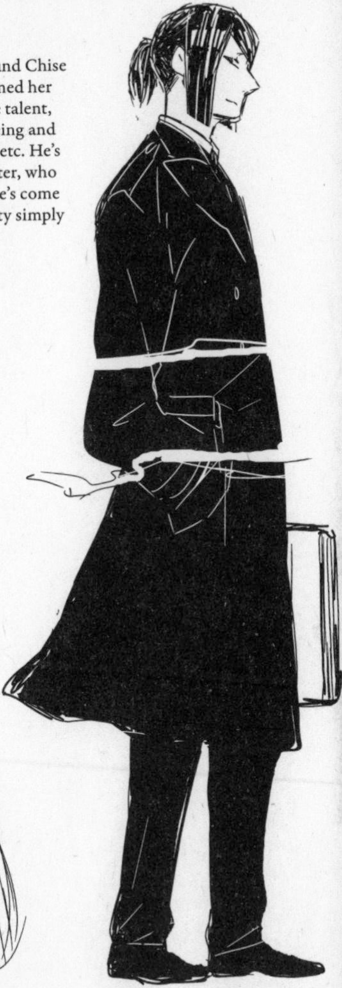

Hugo

Angelica's familiar. A vodyanoi (a type of water spirit). Before Angelica happened to find him and lectured him for his behavior, he worked a lot of mischief (wherever it is he came from). He fell for her and became her familiar. He's a masochist (with Angelica, anyway). Like all of his species, he has a weakness for gold, silver, and jewels, so he loves the things Angelica makes.

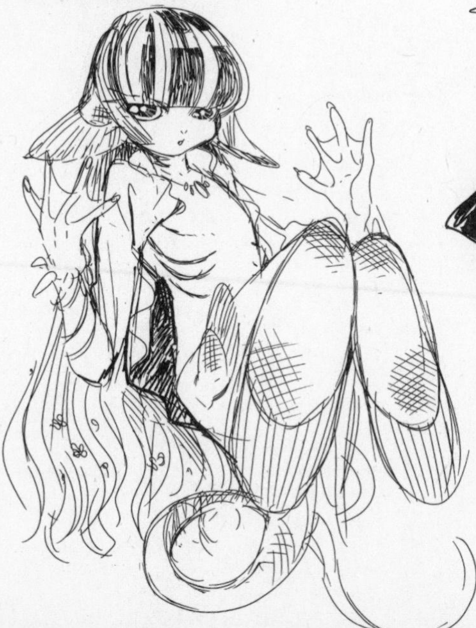

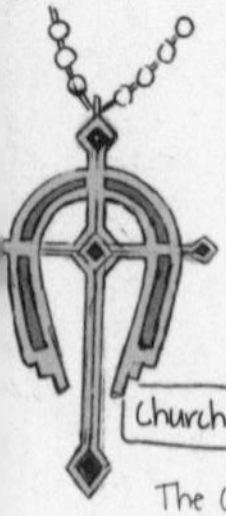
Church cross
The Church creed is basically the same as Christianity (Catholic/Protestant).

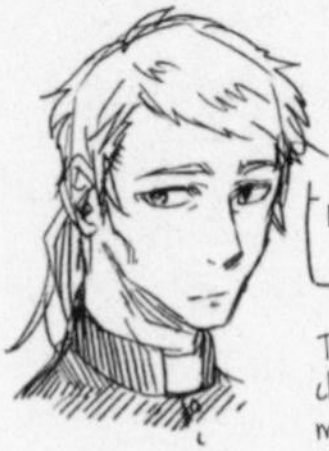
Father Simon
(Priest)
The Church has charged him with monitoring Elias. He's an observer, not any kind of fighter.

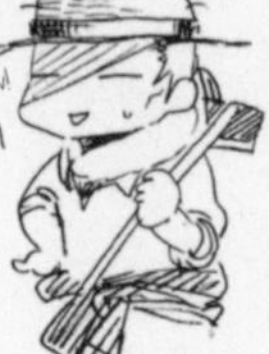
whew!
His hobby is growing vegetables behind the church, where there's a forest. He thinks his veggies are very tasty, if he does say so himself.

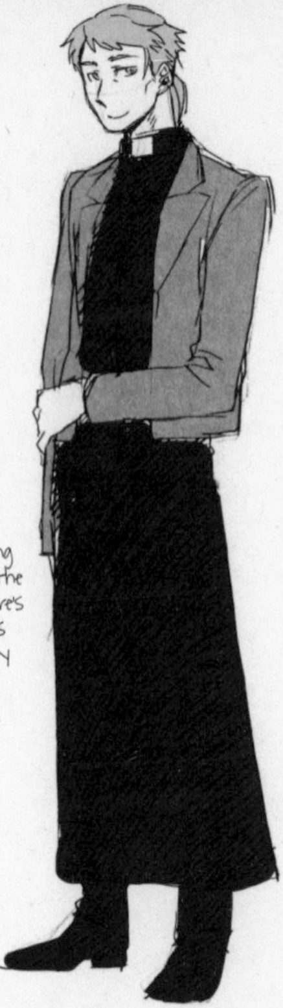

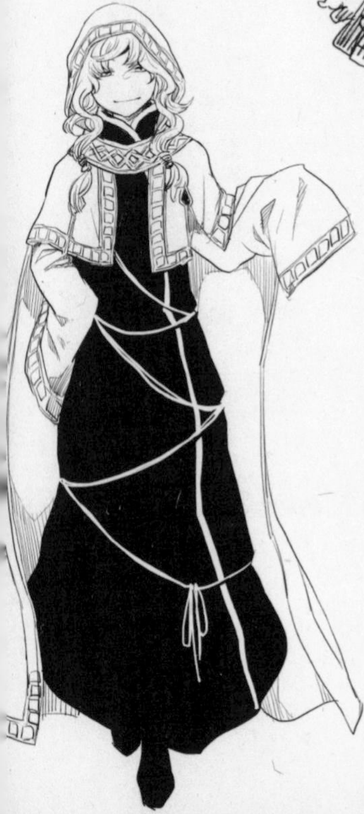

Lindel

A mage nicknamed Echos. He's lived for hundreds of years, but even he doesn't know his exact age.

He enjoys playing pranks and teasing people, but his playful ways are a reaction to the harshness of the many ages he's lived through. He has friends scattered all around the world. He met Ainsworth over a century ago, and for a time their relationship was much like that of a master and apprentice. But eventually, after years passed, they evolved into something more like colleagues.

He's one of the very few people who truly understands the nature of sleigh beggy.

◆ He has one apprentice (a student, technically) and works as an instructor (or high-level administrator) at the college.

His nickname comes from his habit of conversing with spirits in song to perform his magic. The name "Lindel" comes from the Old English for "linden."

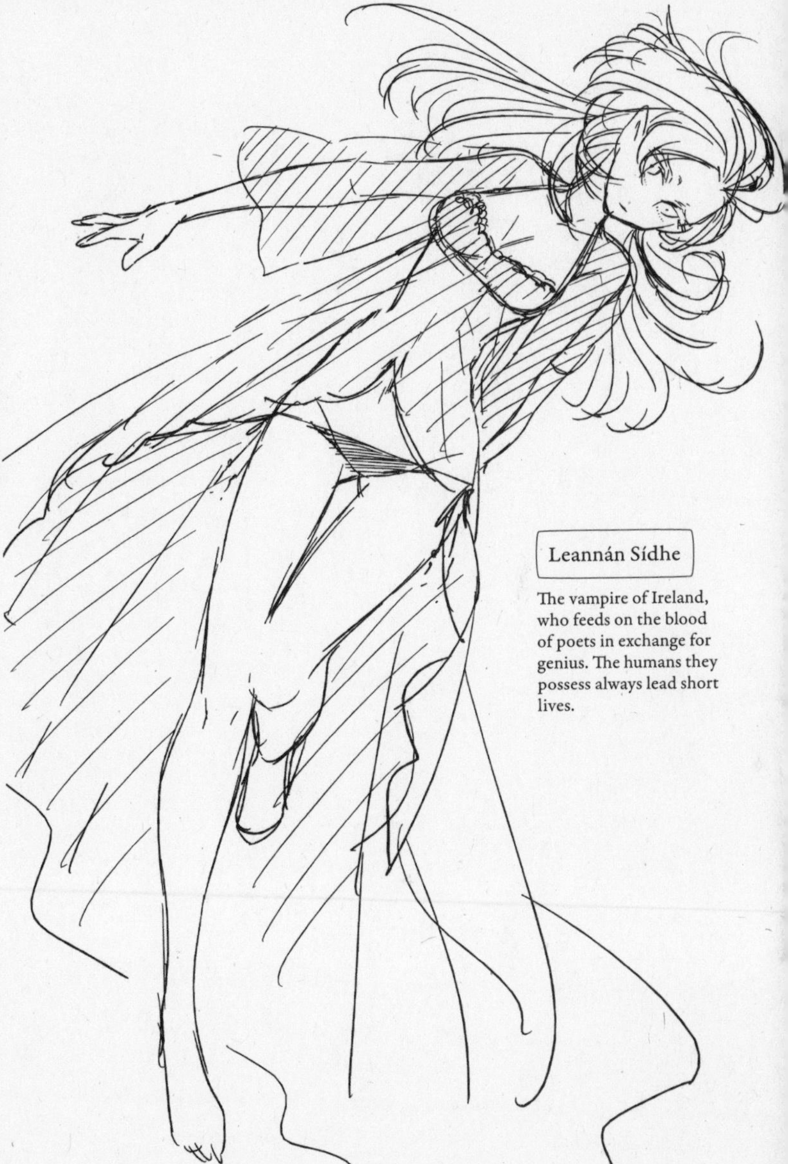

Leannán Sídhe

The vampire of Ireland, who feeds on the blood of poets in exchange for genius. The humans they possess always lead short lives.

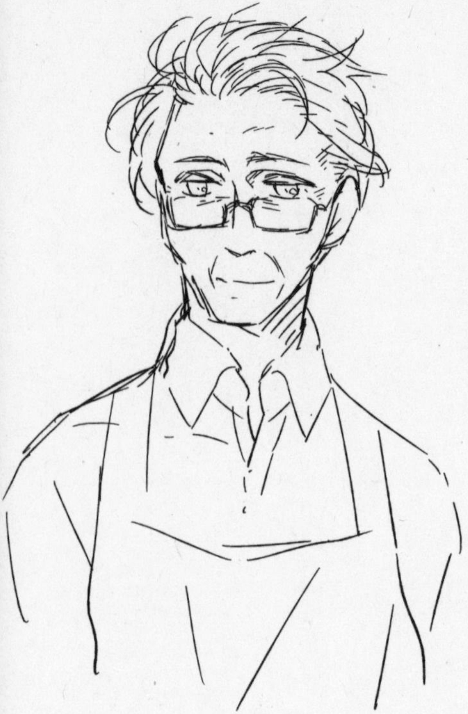

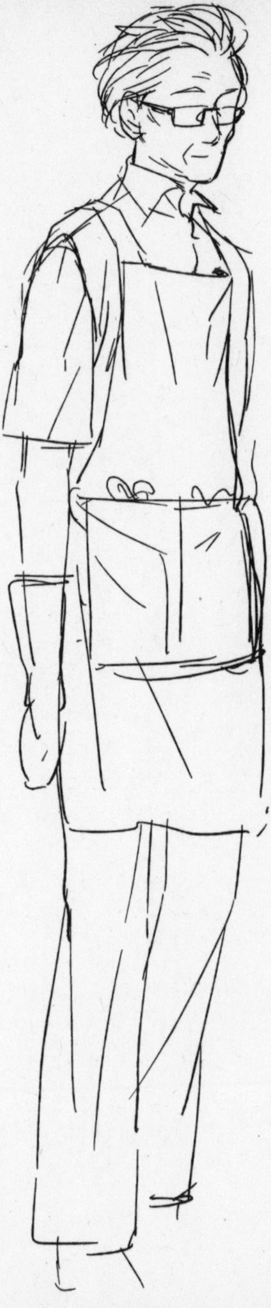

Joel Garland

A former postal worker who's lived comfortably at home and gardened since retirement. Tall and thin. Over ten years ago he saw a mysterious woman by his garden, and fell in love with her at first sight. He's been single ever since.

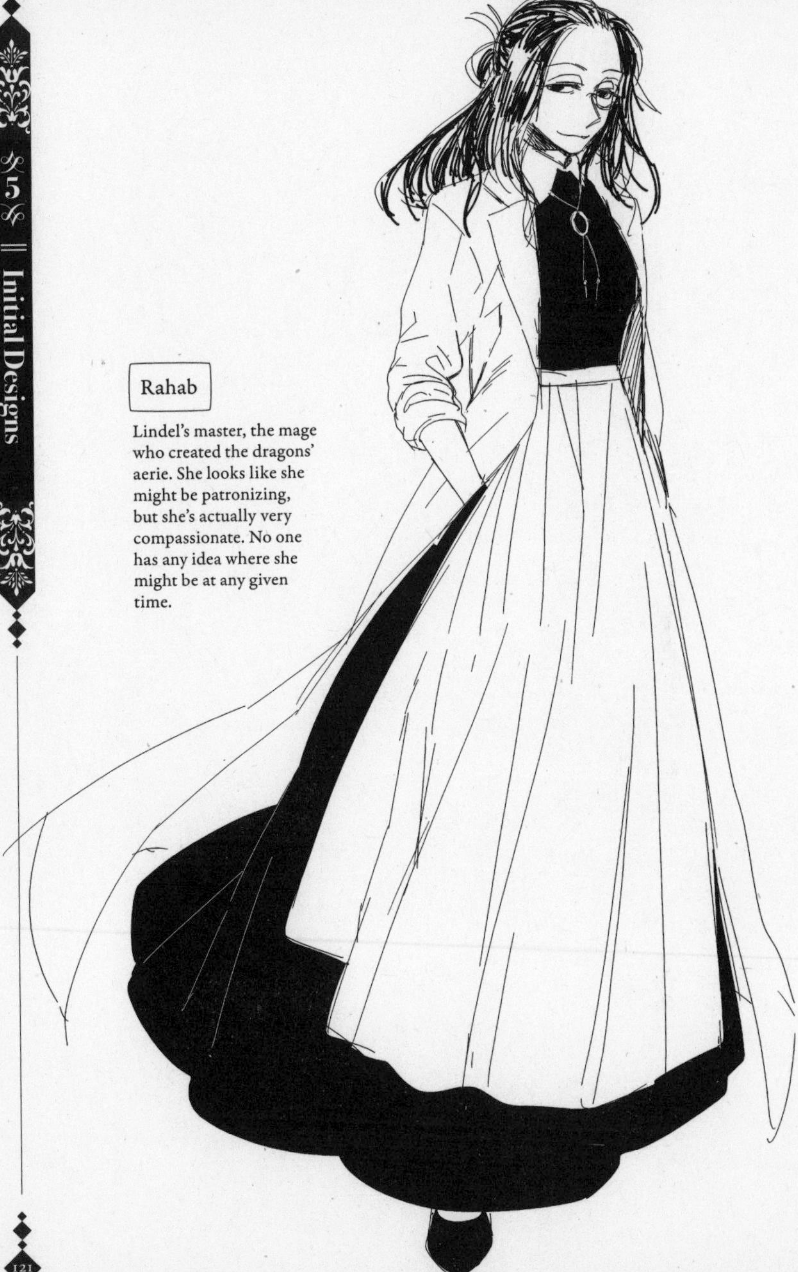

Rahab

Lindel's master, the mage who created the dragons' aerie. She looks like she might be patronizing, but she's actually very compassionate. No one has any idea where she might be at any given time.

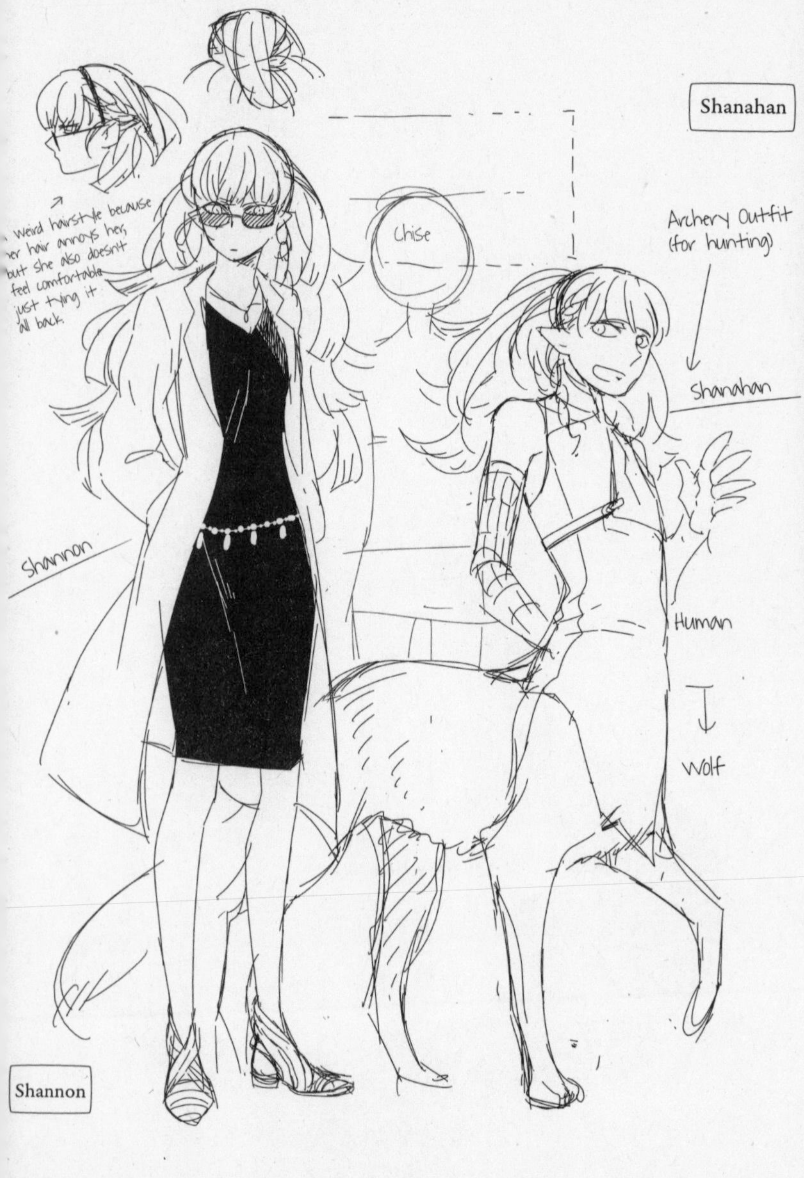
Shanahan
Chise
Archery Outfit
(for hunting)
weird hairstyle because
er hair annoys her,
but she also doesn't
feel comfortable
just tying it
all back.
Shanahan
Shannon
Human
Wolf
Shannon

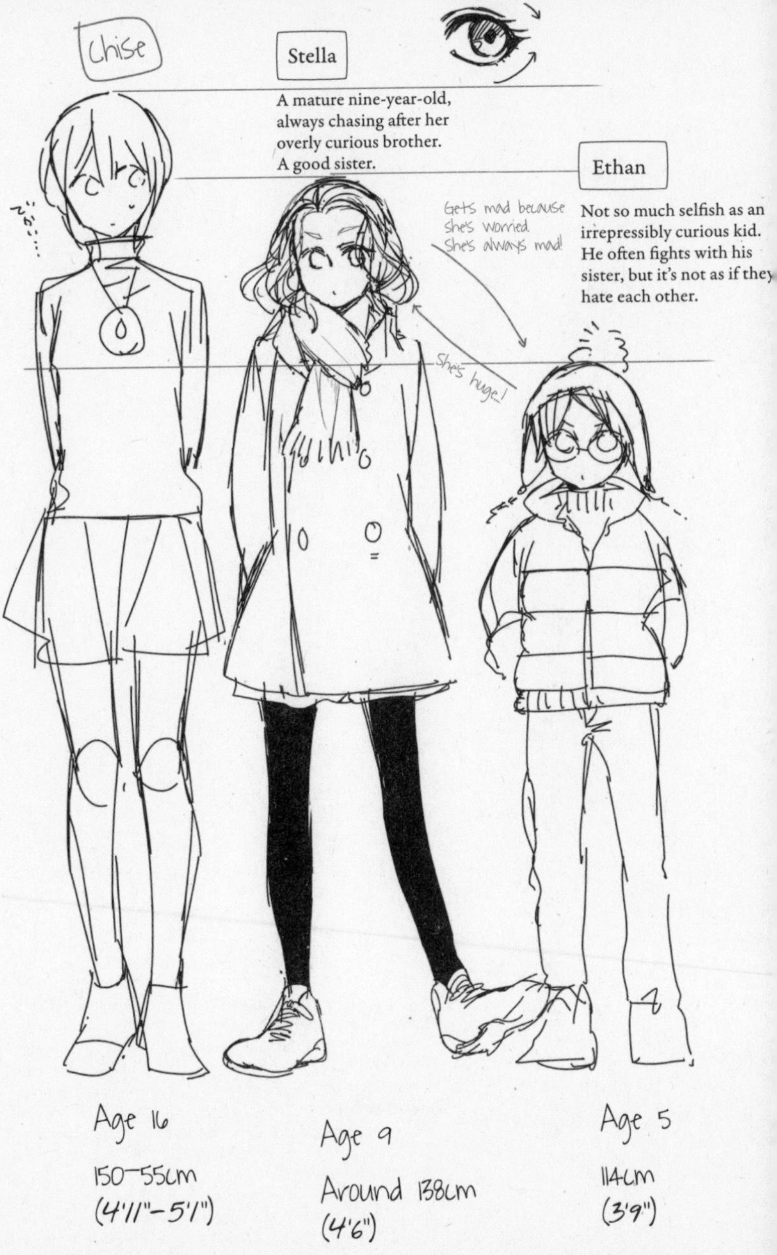
Chise
Gets mad because she's worried. She's always mad!
She's huge!
Age 16
150–55cm
(4'11"–5'1")
Age 9
Around 138cm
(4'6")
Age 5
114cm
(3'9")

Stella

A mature nine-year-old, always chasing after her overly curious brother. A good sister.

Ethan

Not so much selfish as an irrepressibly curious kid. He often fights with his sister, but it's not as if they hate each other.

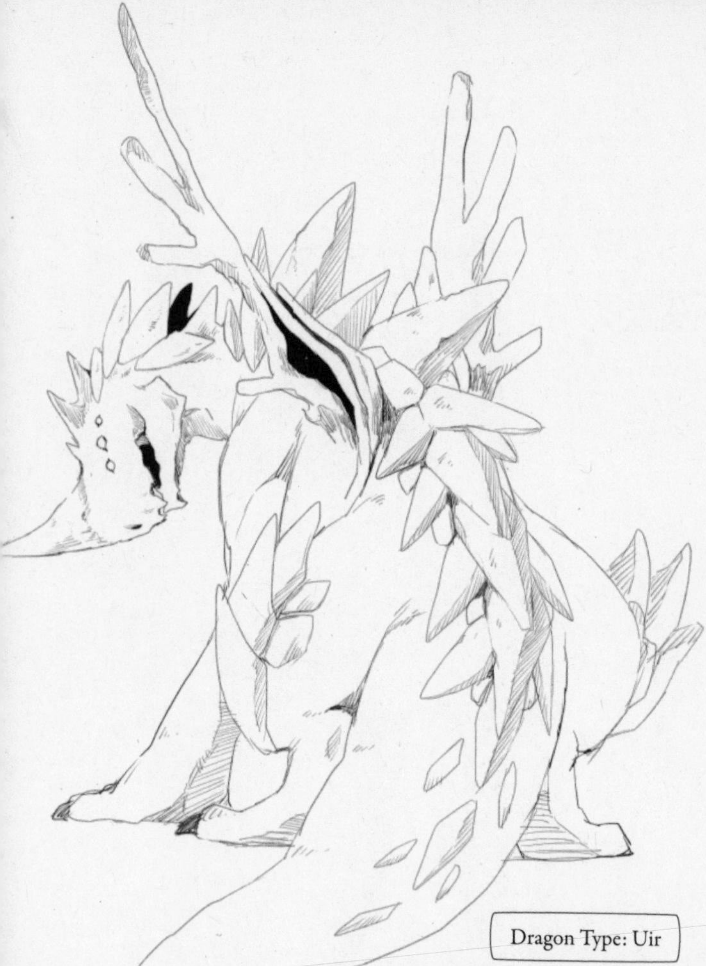

Dragon Type: Uir

(Gaelic for "Earth")

A massive species that once soared freely through the sky. In more recent generations they've lost the ability to fly and have begun changing from carnivores to herbivores. Dragons have the ability to drastically evolve to suit their environment within just two or three generations. Those of the uir variety live about 100-150 years. When they die, enzymes break down their bodies from within so that they return to the earth in about three days, leaving only their bones. Trees and moss grow from the seedbed of their remains, and the bones continue to contribute as fertilizer, so that a small forest grows around them.

Dragon Type: Gaoth

(Gaelic for "Wind")

The most common species that still has the power of flight. Also known as the "wyvern." A member of this species, which are small for dragons and have bird-like skeletons, can fly with a human or two on its back. They're rather simple in nature, and while they can quickly be enraged, they forget their anger just as quickly.

Individuals aren't terribly powerful, but a swarm is fearsome. (An individual is agile enough to bring down a single fighter jet.) They attack by breathing fire, using flammable mucus secreted from the back of their throats, which is similar to napalm. Their build is slight so that they can fly, but they also have a lot of muscle to support their size. Being hit by one of their flapping wings would kill you.

They're mostly carnivorous, but also enjoy fruit. The average lifespan falls between 50-100 years, but some rare specimens have lived past 300.

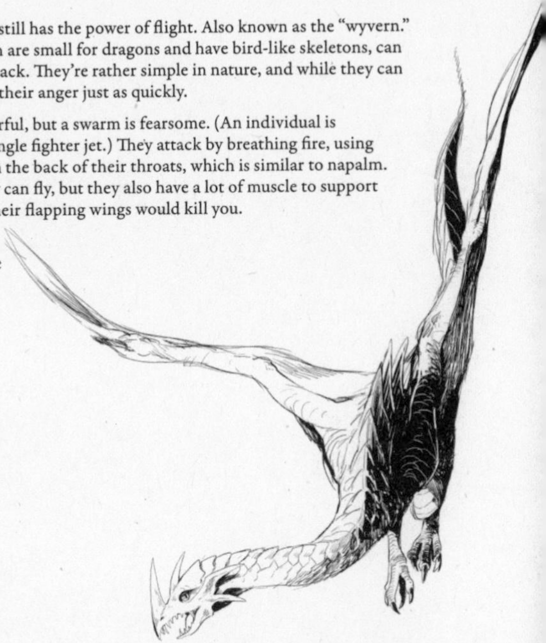

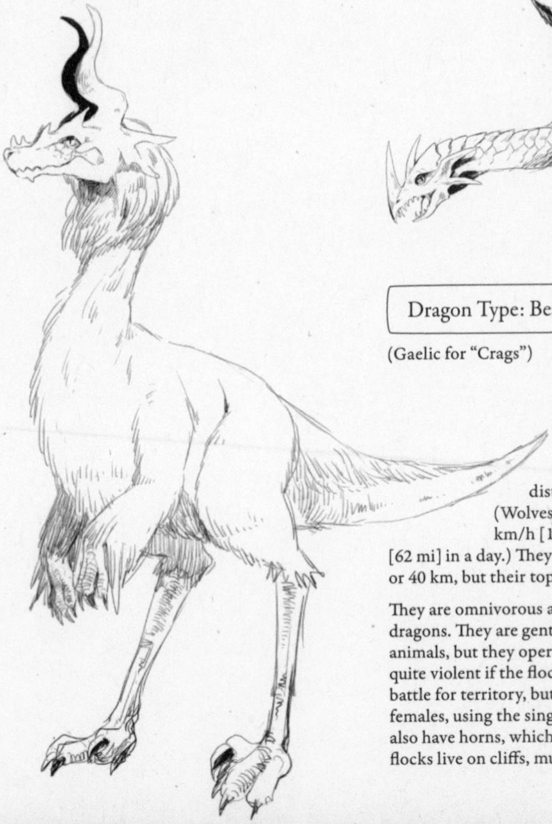

Dragon Type: Beanna

(Gaelic for "Crags")

A furry species made for running. Their legs bear vestiges of the dinosaurs (theropods). They're short-distance runners. Over long distances wolves are superior. (Wolves are capable of running at 30 km/h [19 mph] all night, over 100 km [62 mi] in a day.) They can only manage to run 30 or 40 km, but their top speed reaches 70-80 km/h.

They are omnivorous and the most fertile of all dragons. They are gentle compared to most wild animals, but they operate in flocks and can become quite violent if the flock is threatened. They no longe battle for territory, but at mating season males fight f females, using the single horns on their heads. Femal also have horns, which are similar but shorter. Some flocks live on cliffs, much like certain goats.

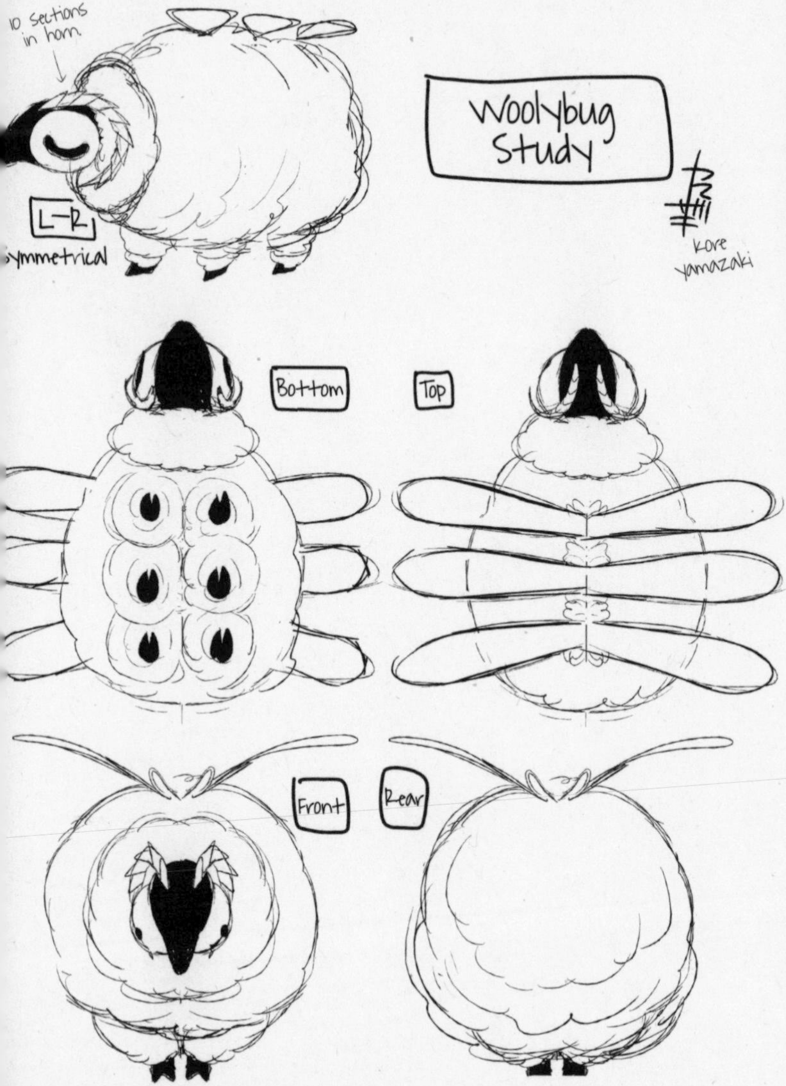
Woolybug Study
Kore Yamazaki
10 sections in horn.
L–R
ymmetrical
Bottom
Top
Front
Rear

Marielle

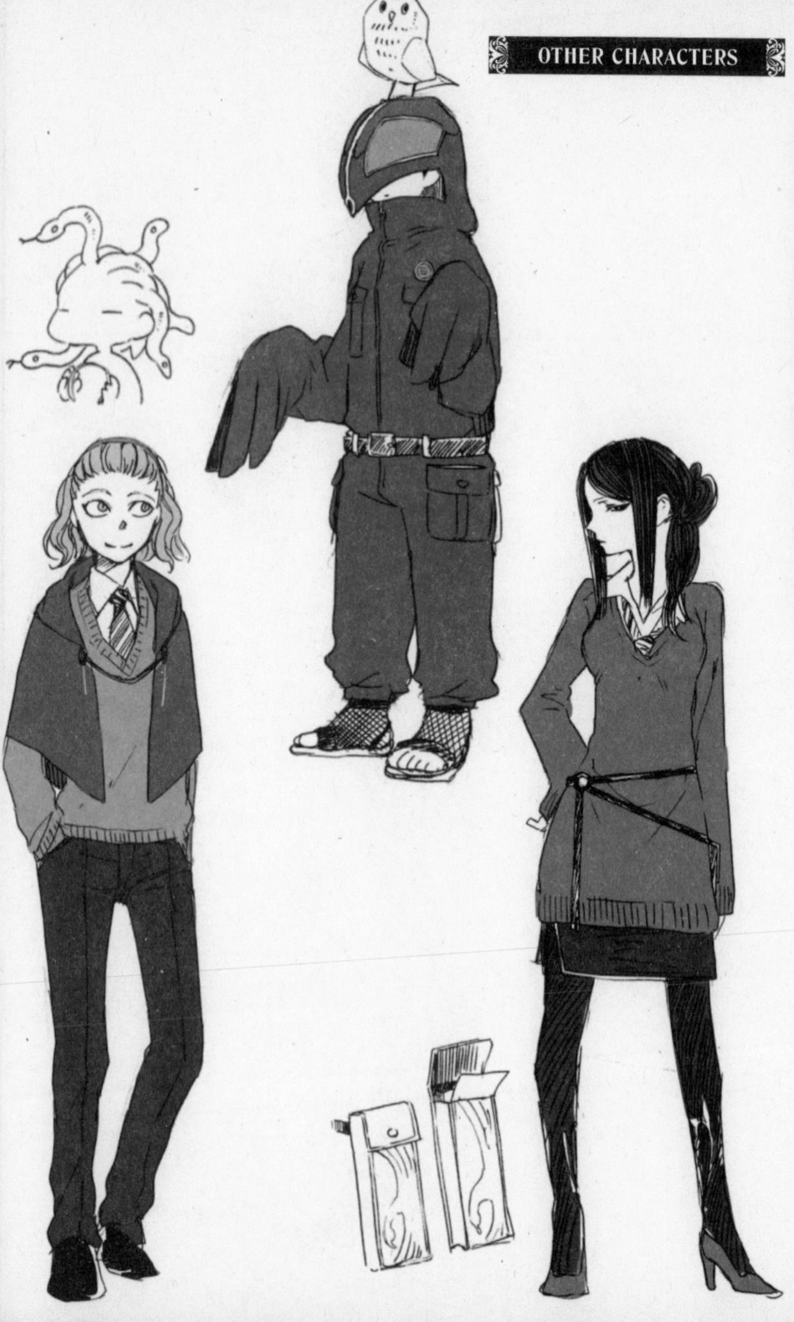

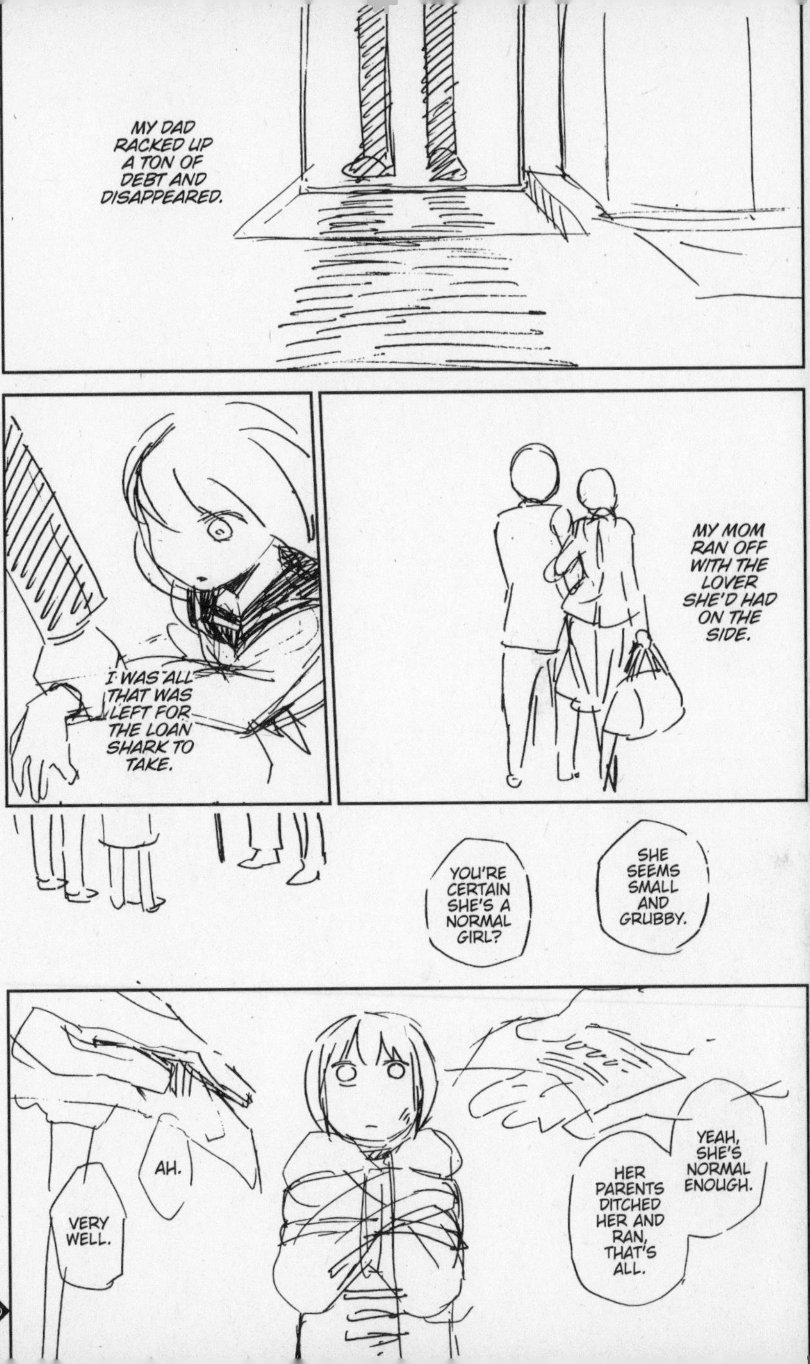
MY DAD RACKED UP A TON OF DEBT AND DISAPPEARED.
MY MOM RAN OFF WITH THE LOVER SHE'D HAD ON THE SIDE.
I WAS ALL THAT WAS LEFT FOR THE LOAN SHARK TO TAKE.
SHE SEEMS SMALL AND GRUBBY.
YOU'RE CERTAIN SHE'S A NORMAL GIRL?
YEAH, SHE'S NORMAL ENOUGH.
HER PARENTS DITCHED HER AND RAN, THAT'S ALL.
AH.
VERY WELL.

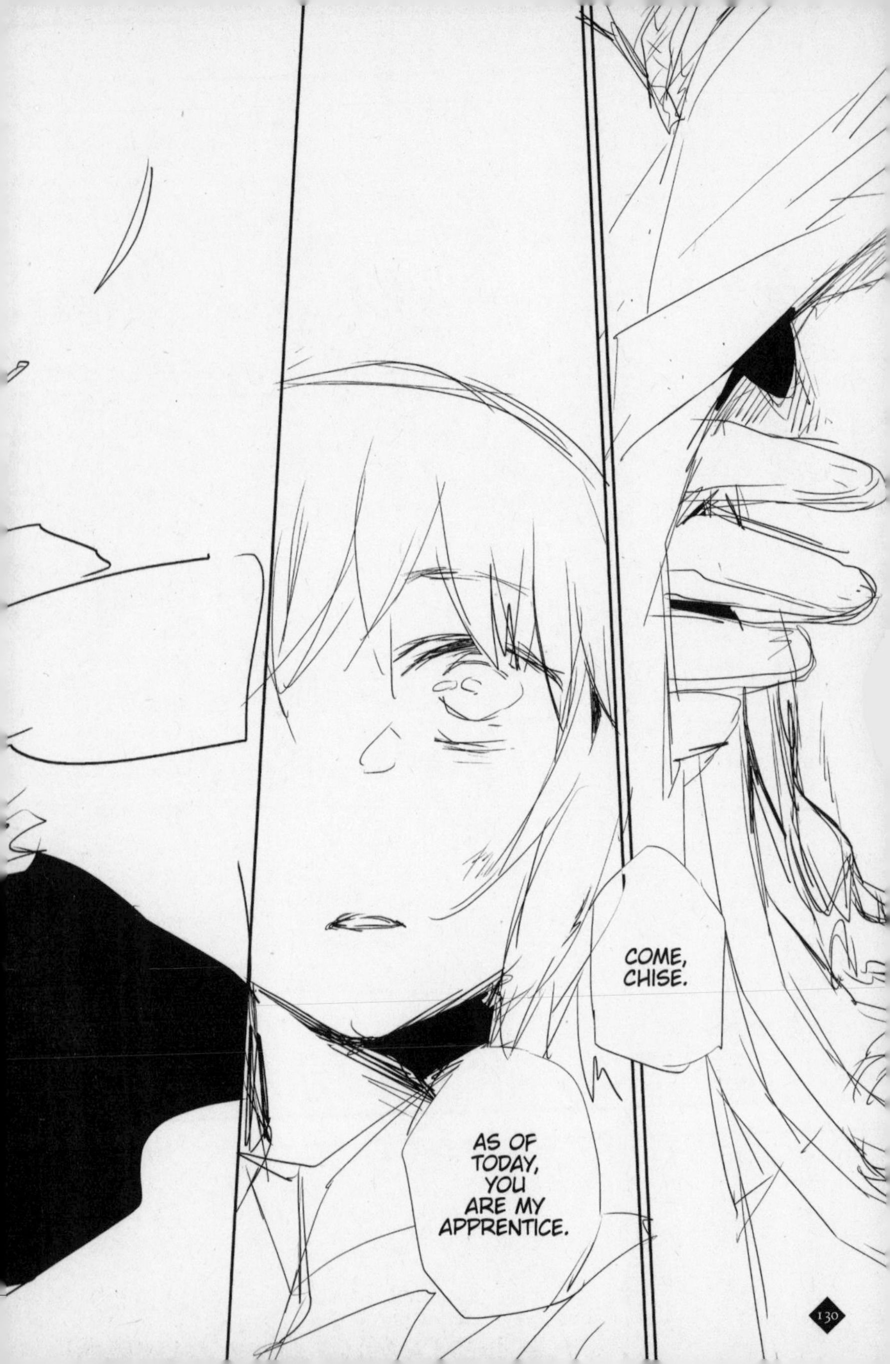
COME, CHISE.
AS OF TODAY, YOU ARE MY APPRENTICE.

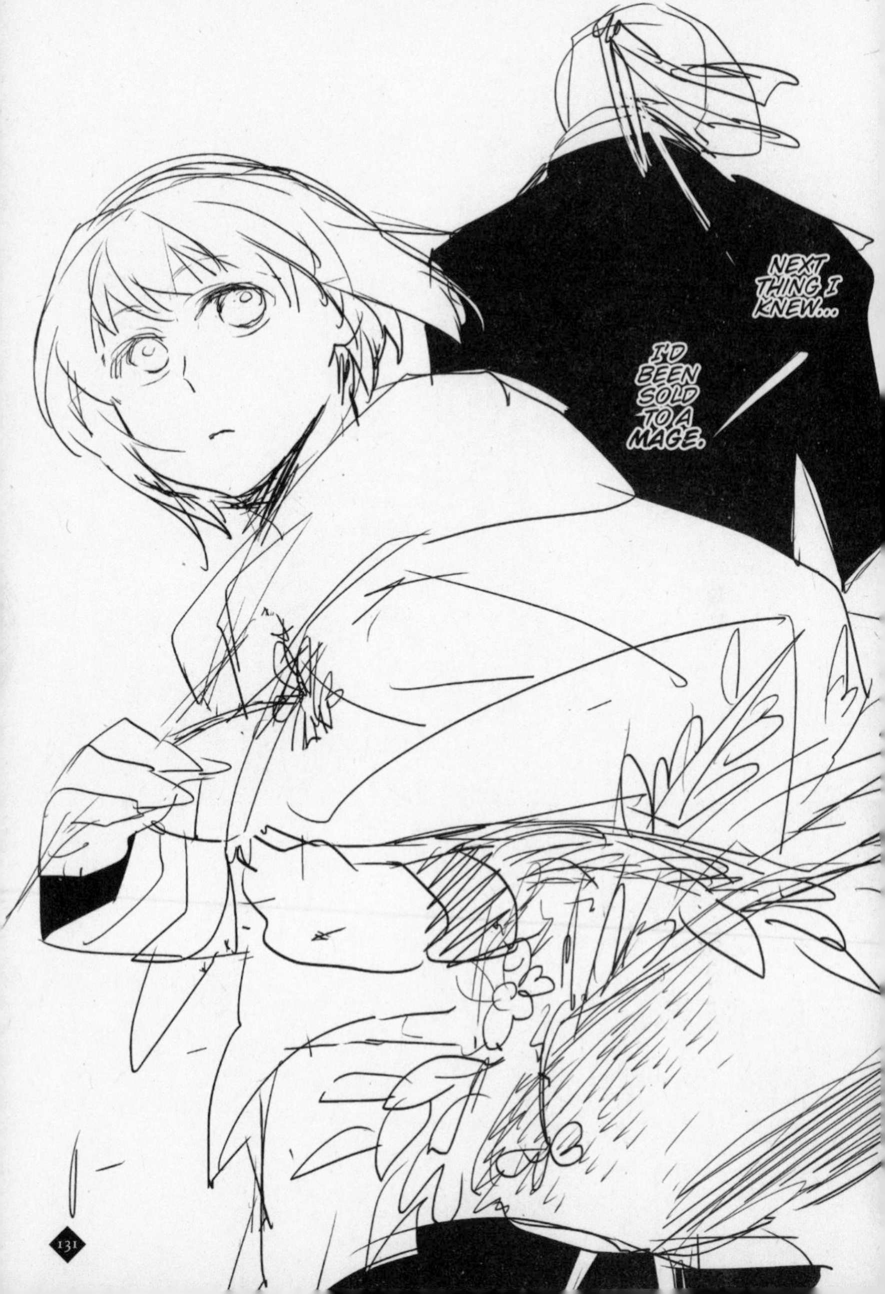
NEXT THING I KNEW...
I'D BEEN SOLD TO A MAGE.

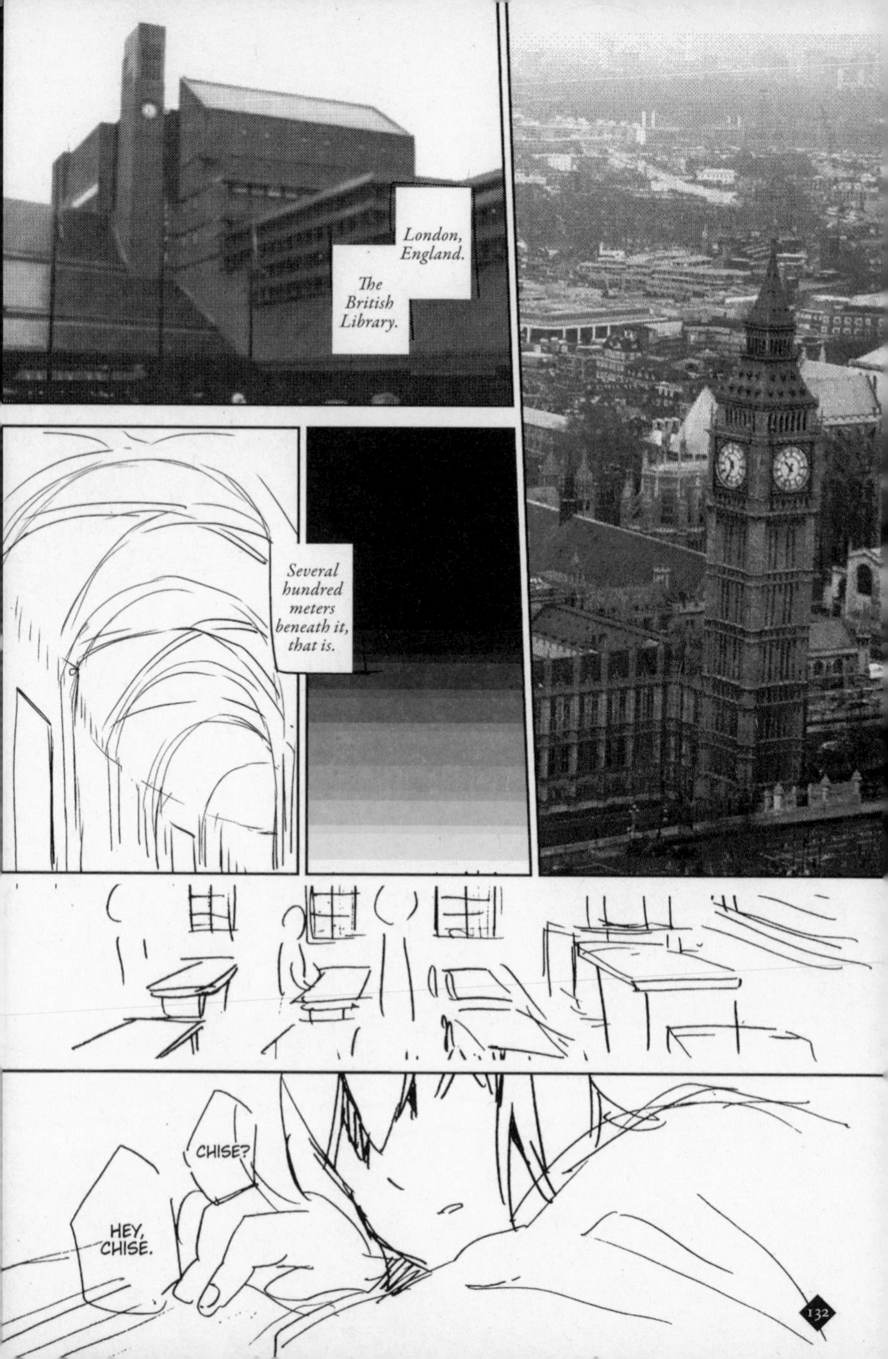
London, England.
The British Library.
Several hundred meters beneath it, that is.
CHISE?
HEY, CHISE.

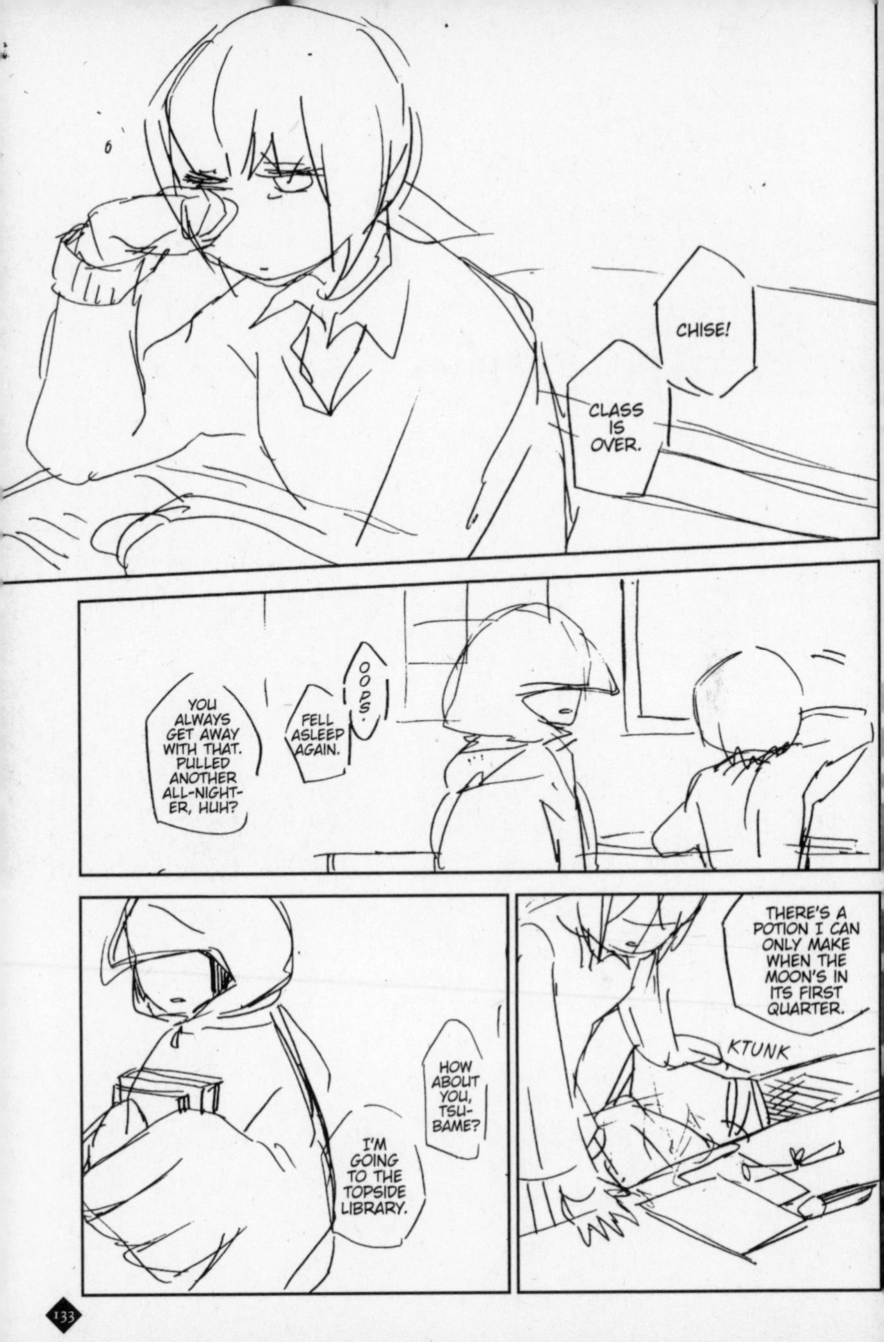
CHISE!
CLASS IS OVER.
OOPS.
FELL ASLEEP AGAIN.
YOU ALWAYS GET AWAY WITH THAT. PULLED ANOTHER ALL-NIGHTER, HUH?
THERE'S A POTION I CAN ONLY MAKE WHEN THE MOON'S IN ITS FIRST QUARTER.
KTUNK
HOW ABOUT YOU, TSUBAME?
I'M GOING TO THE TOPSIDE LIBRARY.

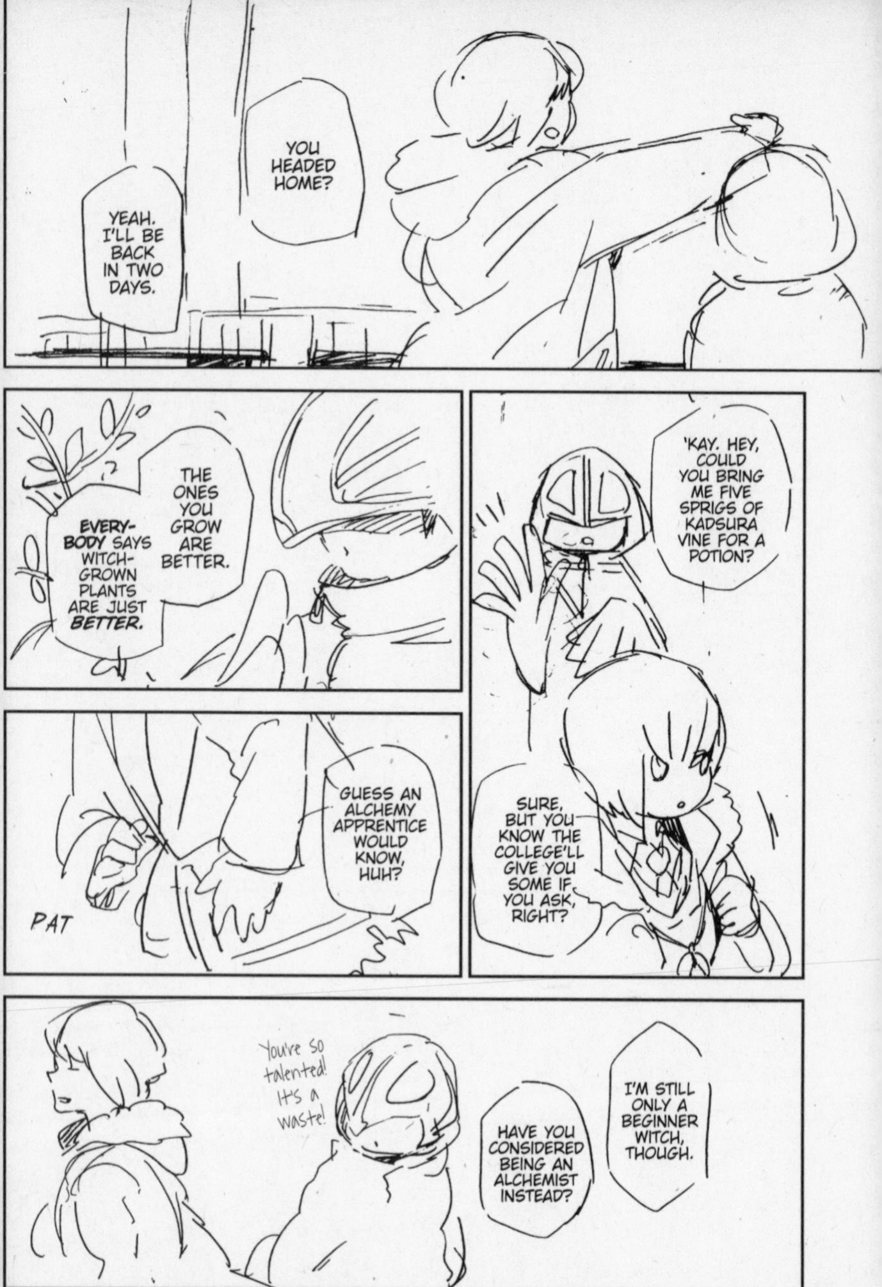
YOU HEADED HOME?
YEAH. I'LL BE BACK IN TWO DAYS.
'KAY. HEY, COULD YOU BRING ME FIVE SPRIGS OF KADSURA VINE FOR A POTION?
SURE, BUT YOU KNOW THE COLLEGE'LL GIVE YOU SOME IF YOU ASK, RIGHT?
THE ONES YOU GROW ARE BETTER.
EVERYBODY SAYS WITCH-GROWN PLANTS ARE JUST BETTER.
GUESS AN ALCHEMY APPRENTICE WOULD KNOW, HUH?
PAT
I'M STILL ONLY A BEGINNER WITCH, THOUGH.
HAVE YOU CONSIDERED BEING AN ALCHEMIST INSTEAD?
You're so talented! It's a waste!

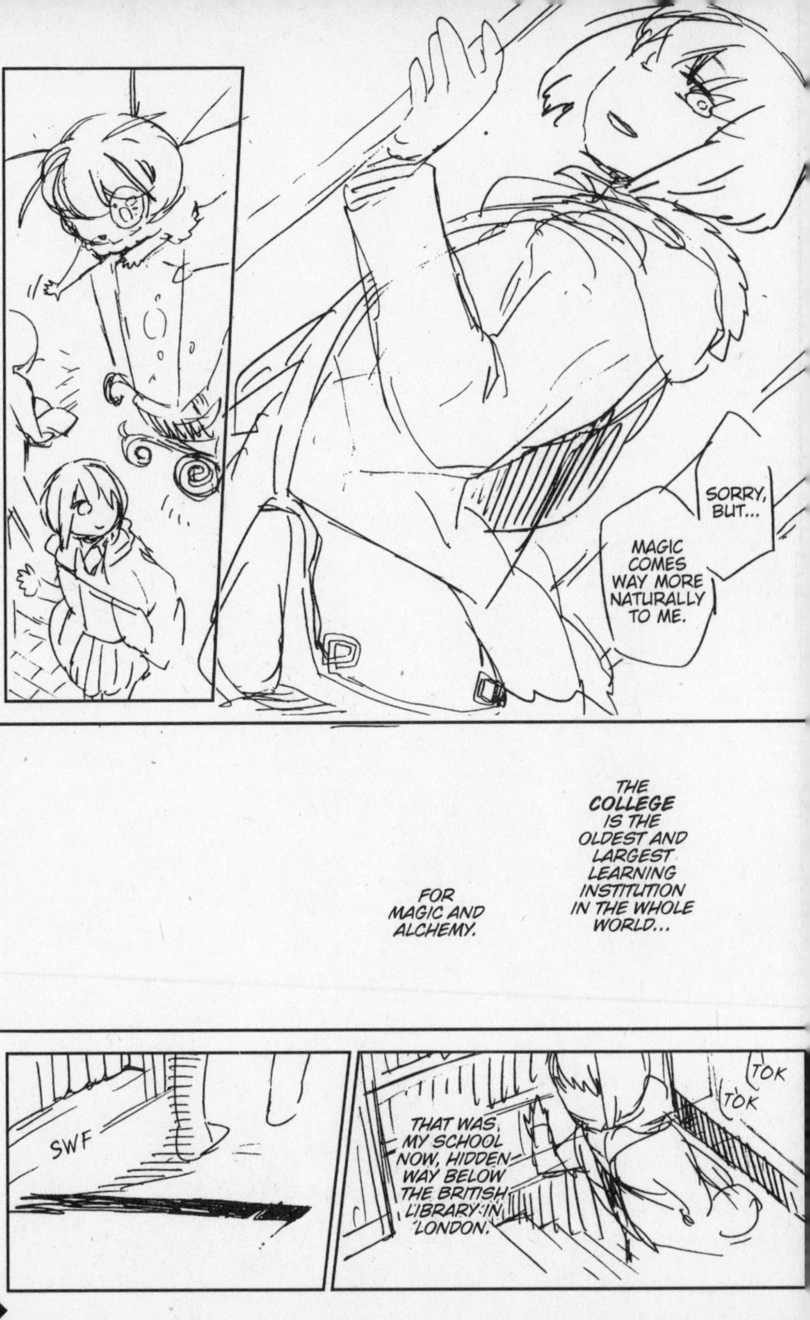
SORRY, BUT...
MAGIC COMES WAY MORE NATURALLY TO ME.
THE COLLEGE IS THE OLDEST AND LARGEST LEARNING INSTITUTION IN THE WHOLE WORLD...
FOR MAGIC AND ALCHEMY.
TOK
TOK
THAT WAS MY SCHOOL NOW, HIDDEN WAY BELOW THE BRITISH LIBRARY IN LONDON.
SWF

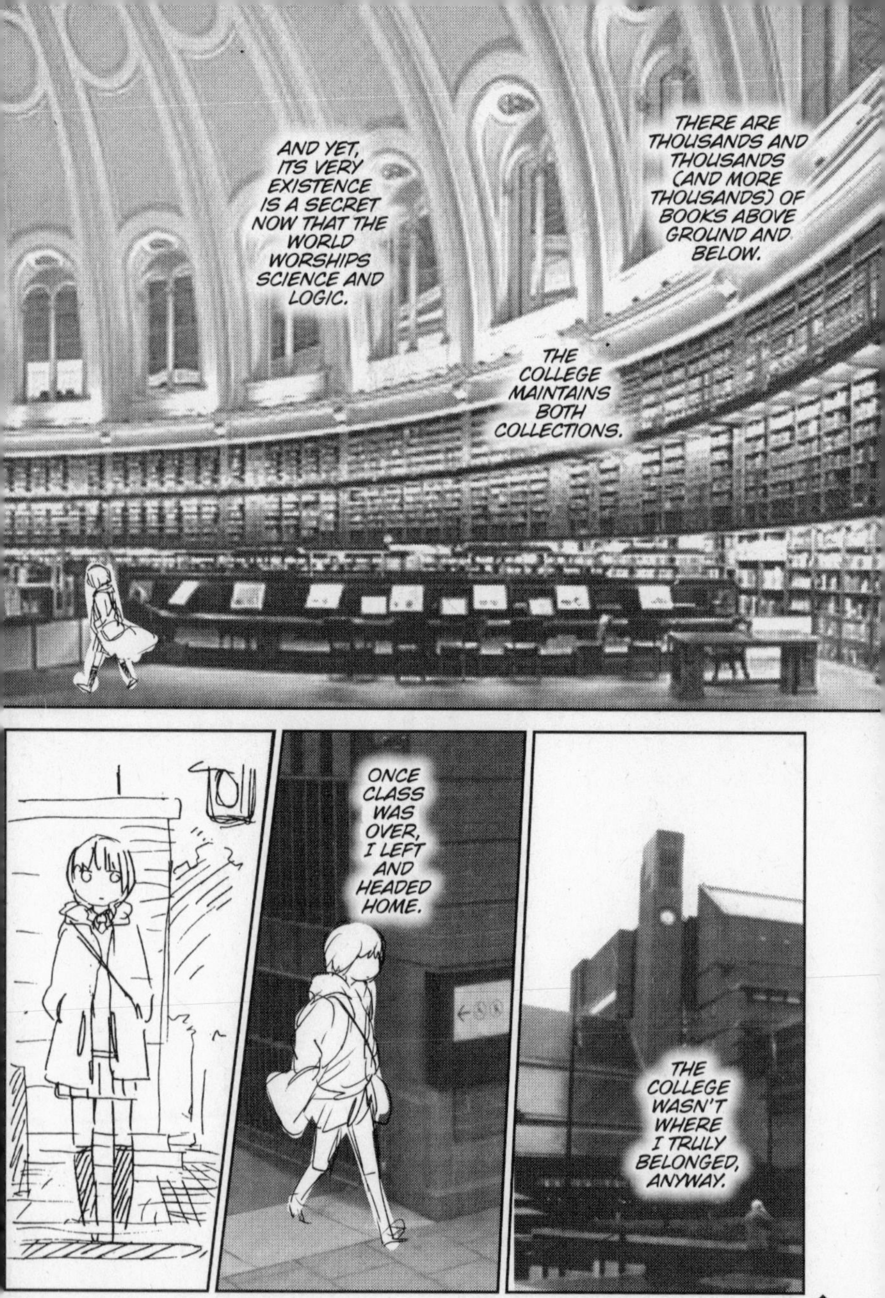
THERE ARE THOUSANDS AND THOUSANDS (AND MORE THOUSANDS) OF BOOKS ABOVE GROUND AND BELOW.
AND YET, ITS VERY EXISTENCE IS A SECRET NOW THAT THE WORLD WORSHIPS SCIENCE AND LOGIC.
THE COLLEGE MAINTAINS BOTH COLLECTIONS.
THE COLLEGE WASN'T WHERE I TRULY BELONGED, ANYWAY.
ONCE CLASS WAS OVER, I LEFT AND HEADED HOME.

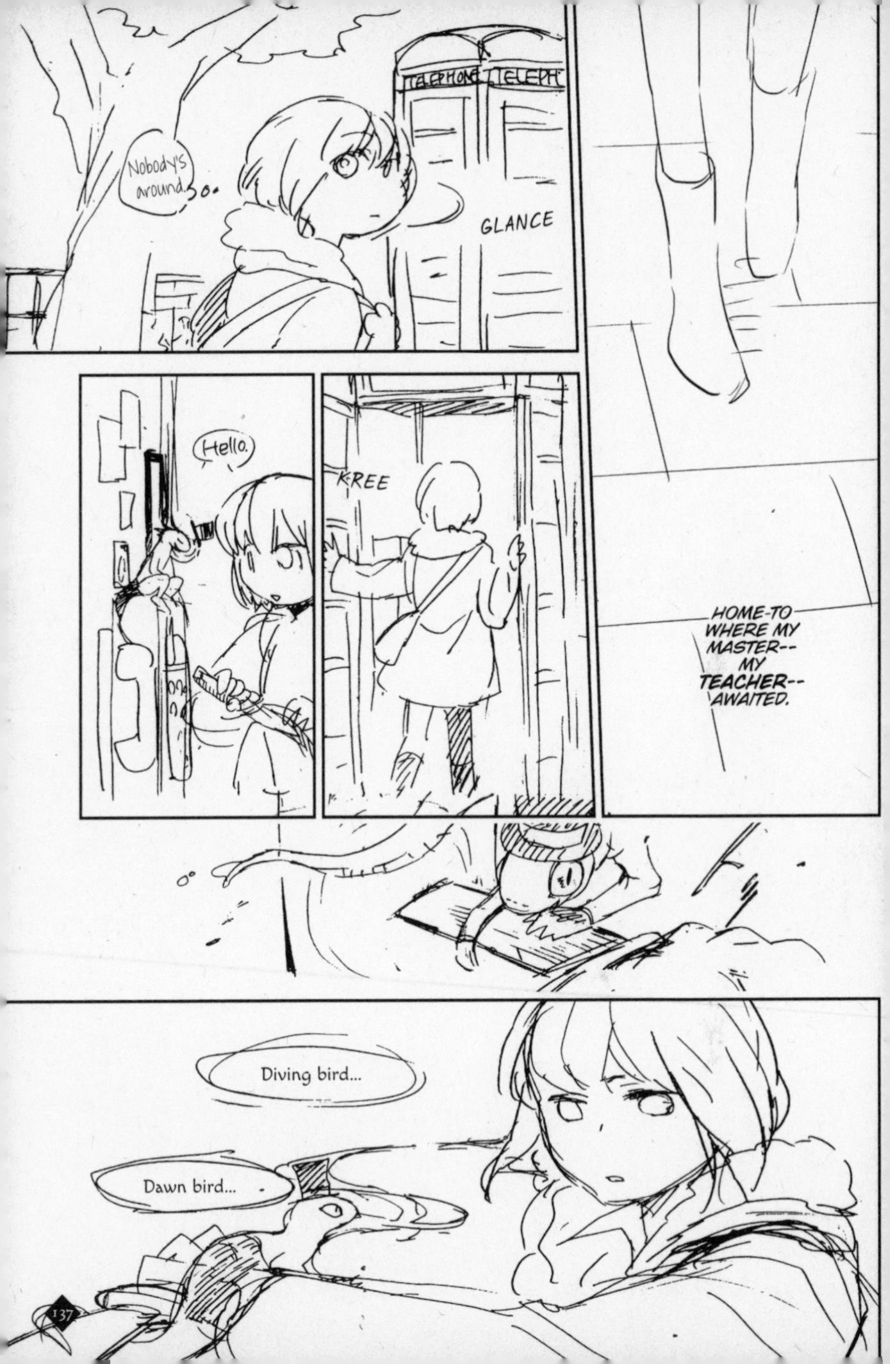
HOME-TO WHERE MY MASTER-- MY TEACHER-- AWAITED.
Nobody's around.
GLANCE
TELEPHONE TELEPH
KREE
Hello.
Diving bird...
Dawn bird...

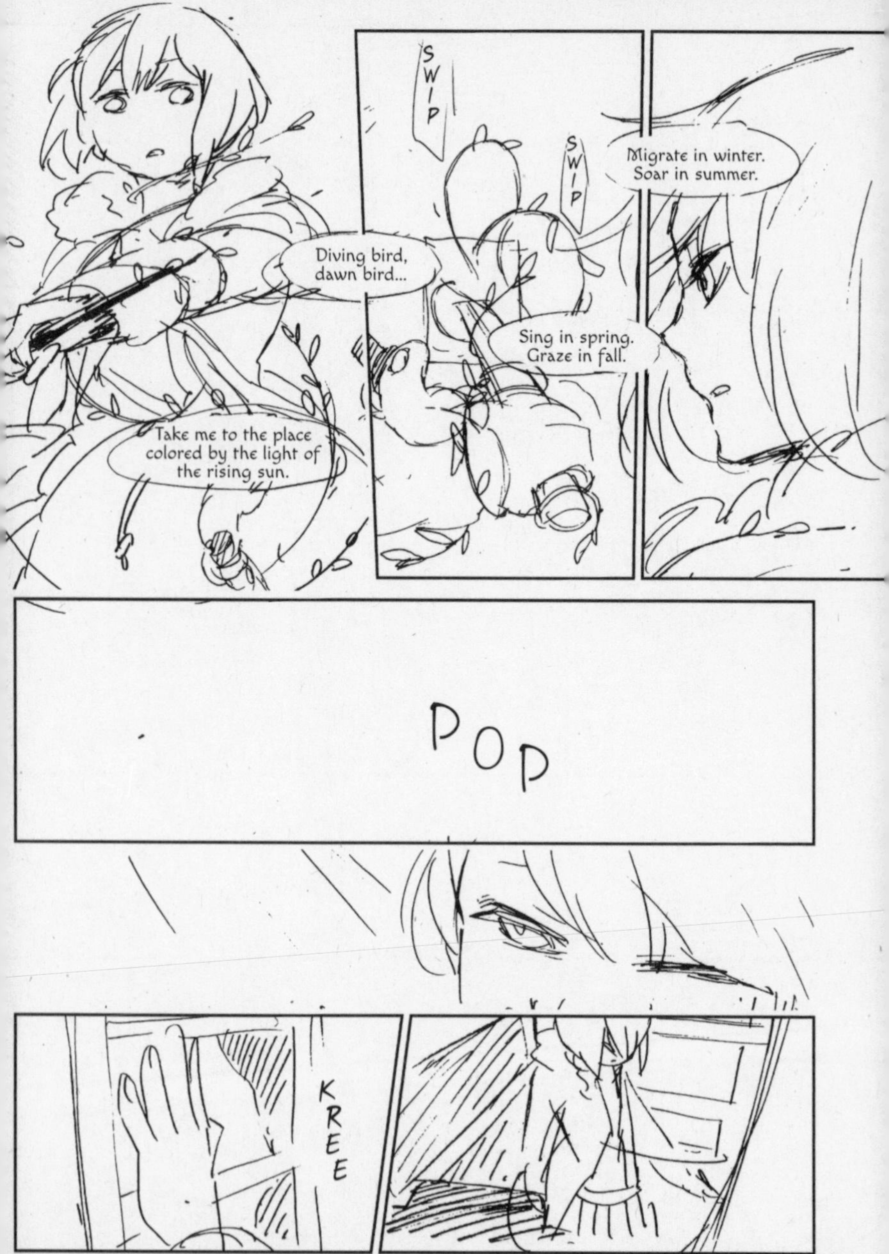
Migrate in winter.
Soar in summer.
SWIP
SWIP
Sing in spring.
Graze in fall.
Diving bird,
dawn bird...
Take me to the place colored by the light of the rising sun.
POP
KREE

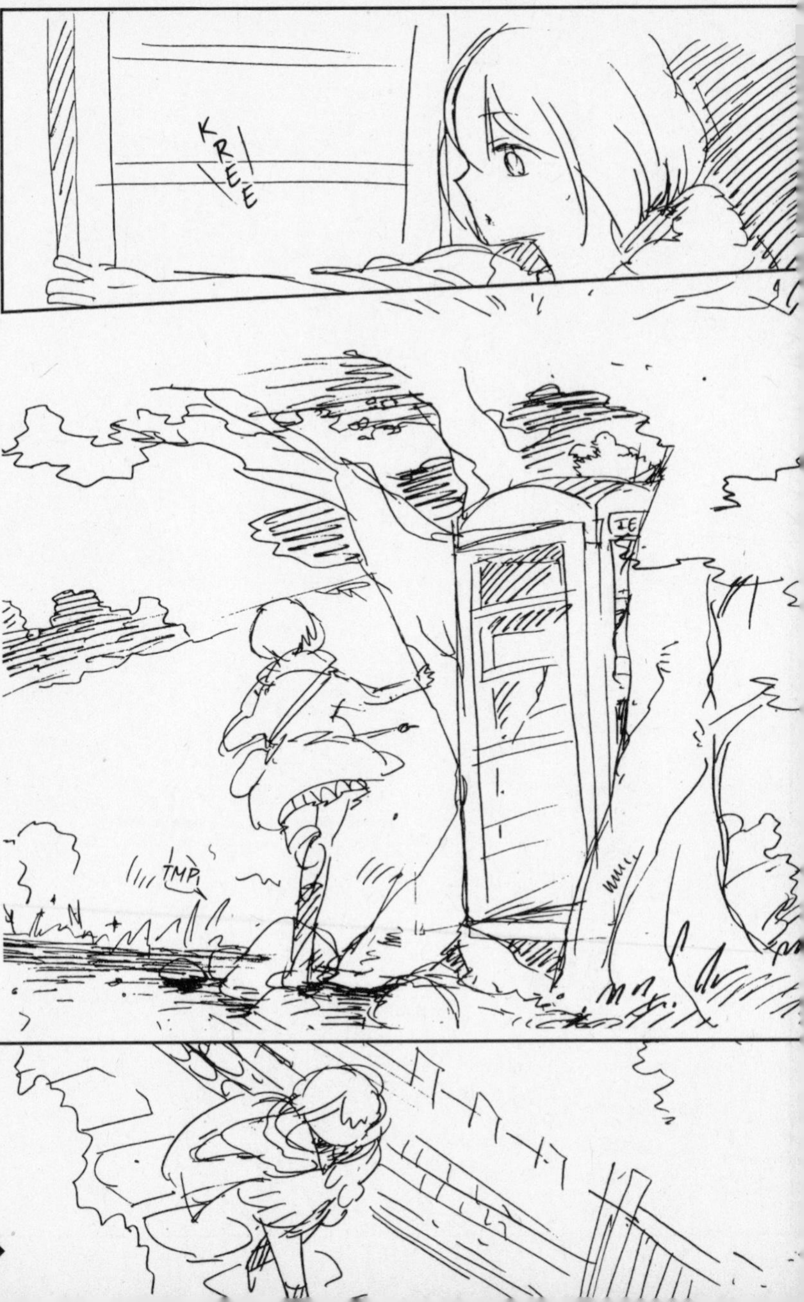
KREEE
TMP

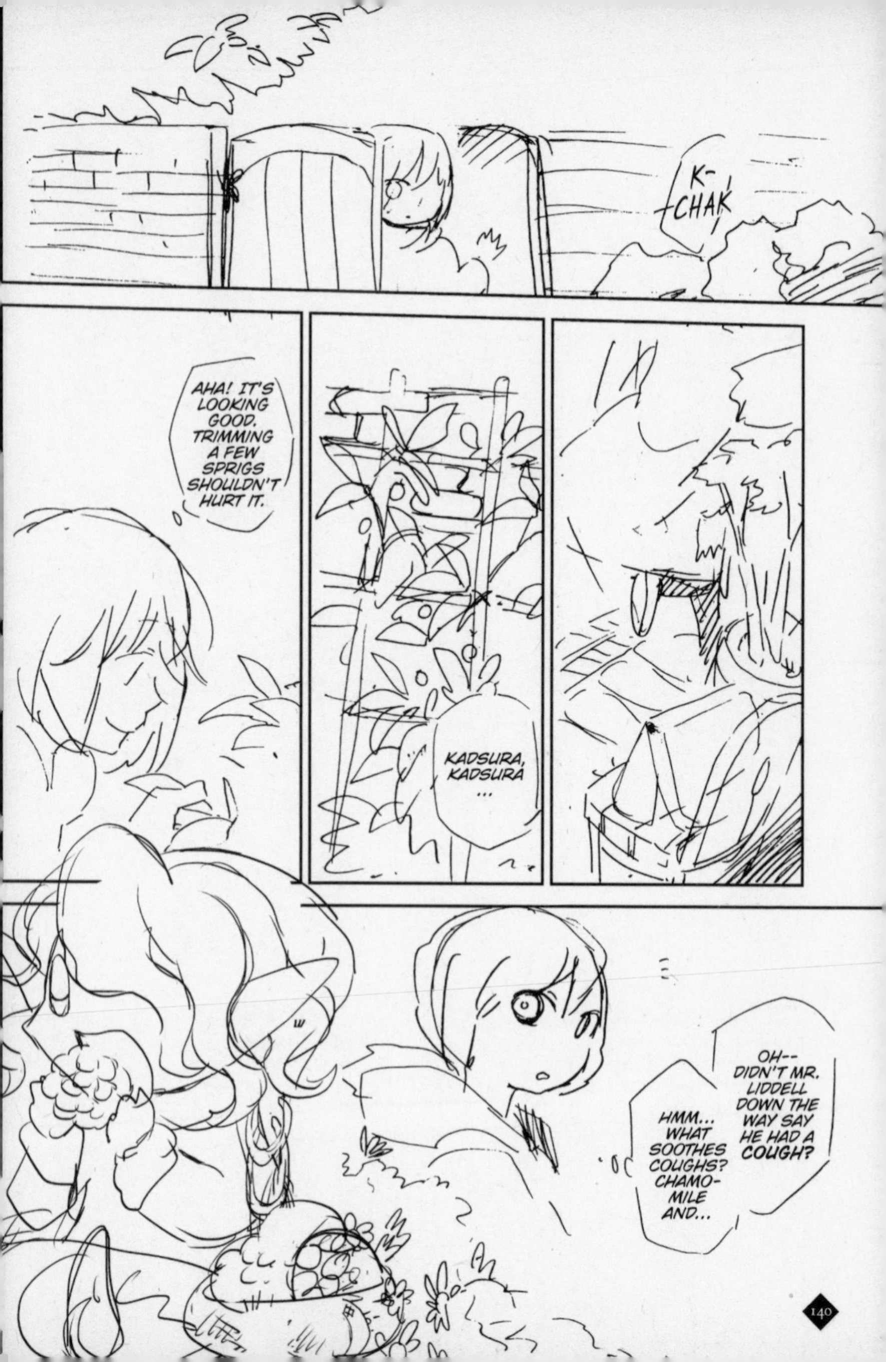

K-CHAK
KADSURA, KADSURA ...
AHA! IT'S LOOKING GOOD. TRIMMING A FEW SPRIGS SHOULDN'T HURT IT.
OH-- DIDN'T MR. LIDDELL DOWN THE WAY SAY HE HAD A **COUGH?**
HMM... WHAT SOOTHES COUGHS? CHAMOMILE AND...

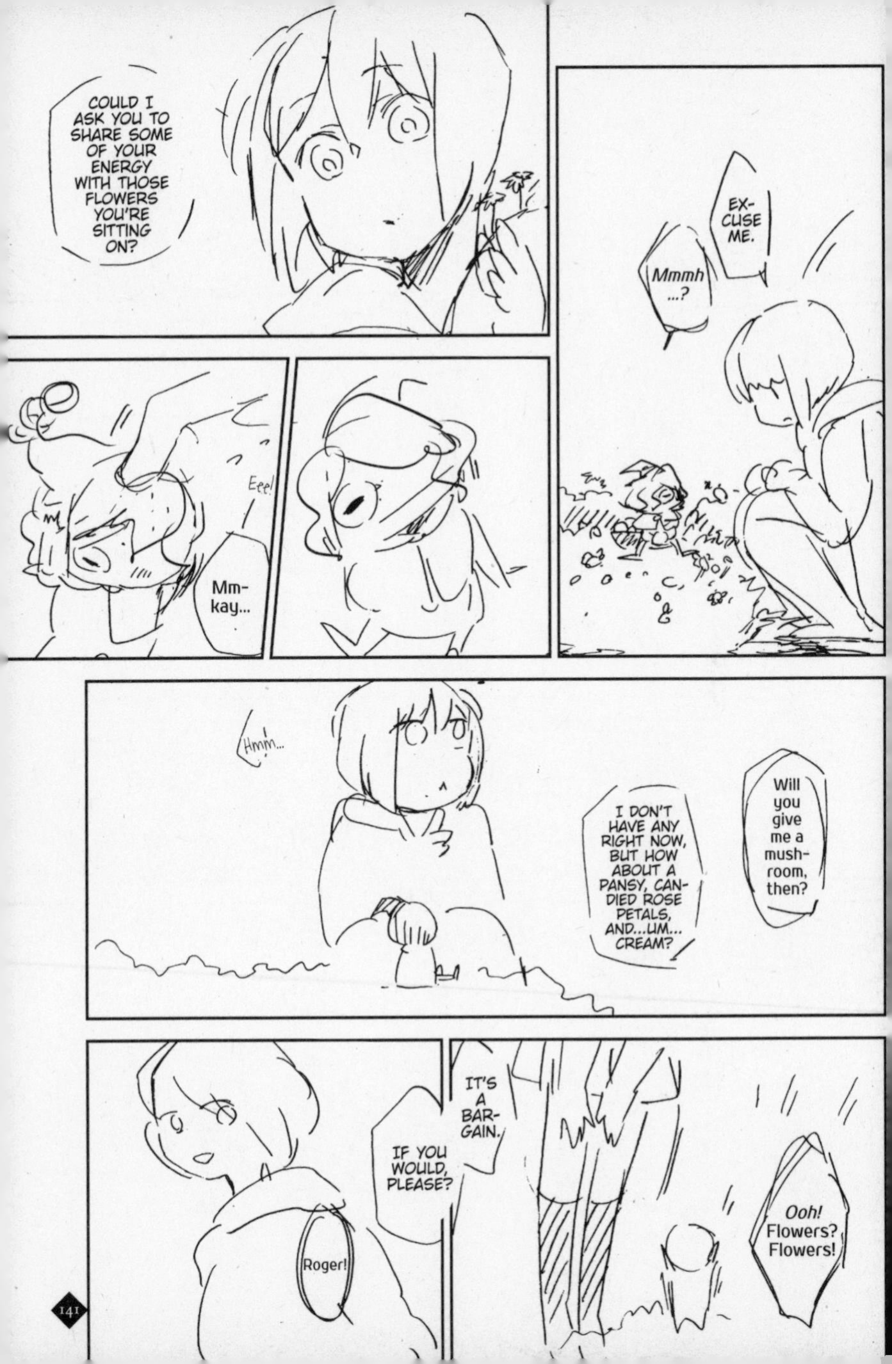
EX-CUSE ME.
Mmmh ...?
COULD I ASK YOU TO SHARE SOME OF YOUR ENERGY WITH THOSE FLOWERS YOU'RE SITTING ON?
Eee!
Mm-kay...
Will you give me a mush-room, then?
I DON'T HAVE ANY RIGHT NOW, BUT HOW ABOUT A PANSY, CAN-DIED ROSE PETALS, AND...UM... CREAM?
Hmm...
IT'S A BAR-GAIN.
Ooh! Flowers? Flowers!
IF YOU WOULD, PLEASE?
Roger!

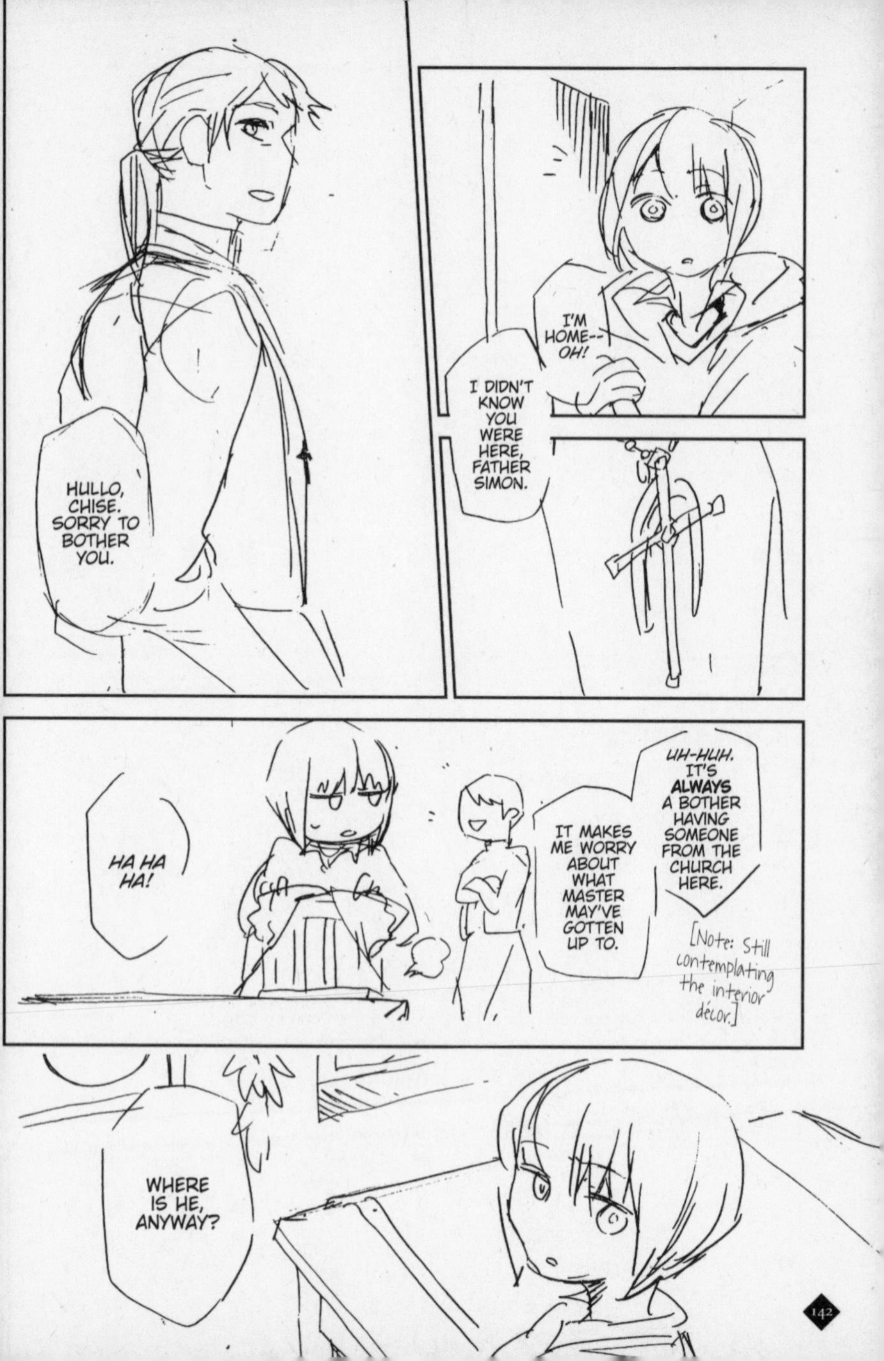
I'M HOME-- OH!
I DIDN'T KNOW YOU WERE HERE, FATHER SIMON.
HULLO, CHISE. SORRY TO BOTHER YOU.
UH-HUH. IT'S **ALWAYS** A BOTHER HAVING SOMEONE FROM THE CHURCH HERE.
IT MAKES ME WORRY ABOUT WHAT MASTER MAY'VE GOTTEN UP TO.
[Note: Still contemplating the interior décor.]
HA HA HA!
WHERE IS HE, ANYWAY?

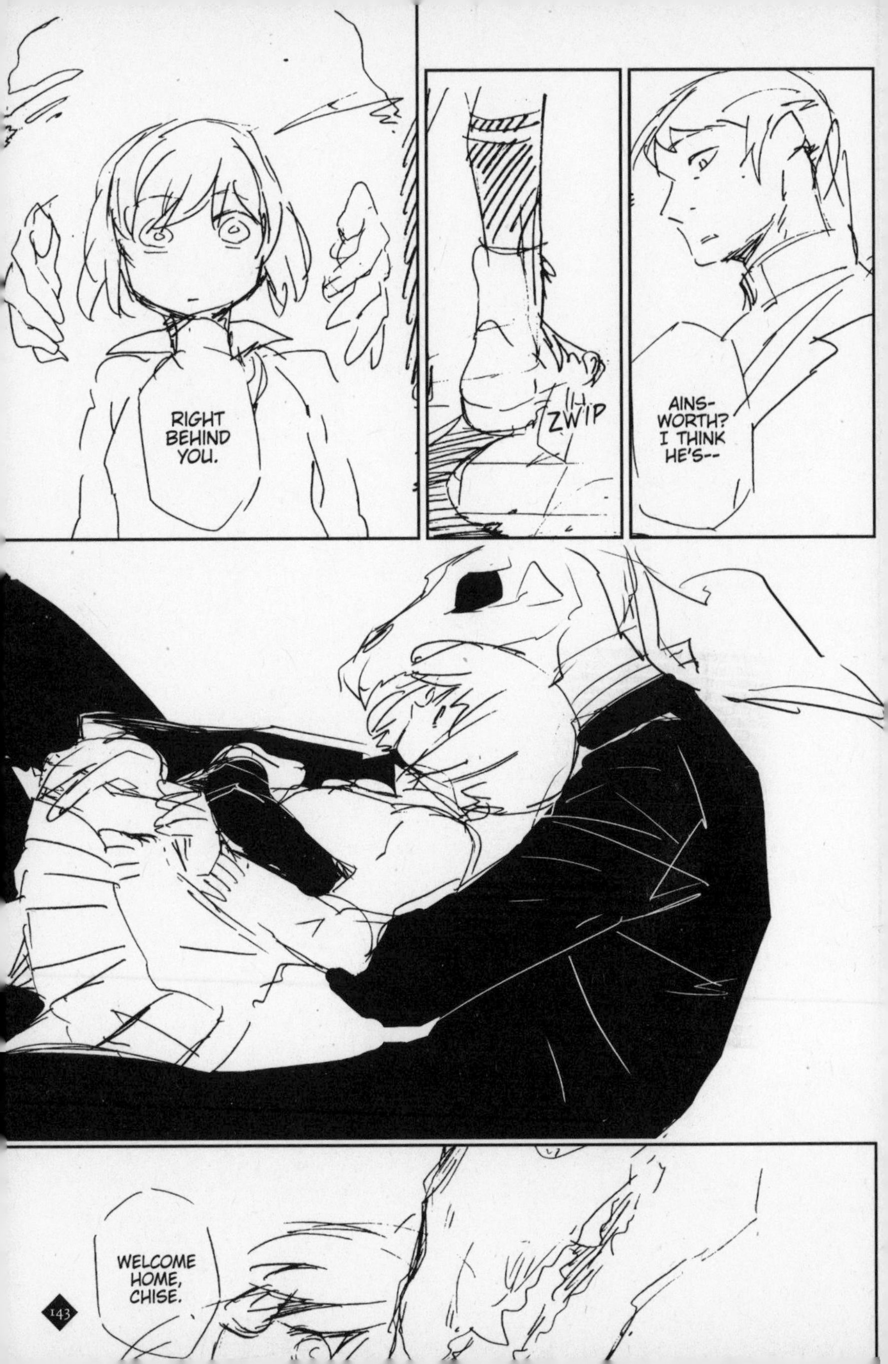
AINS-WORTH? I THINK HE'S--
ZWIP
RIGHT BEHIND YOU.
WELCOME HOME, CHISE.

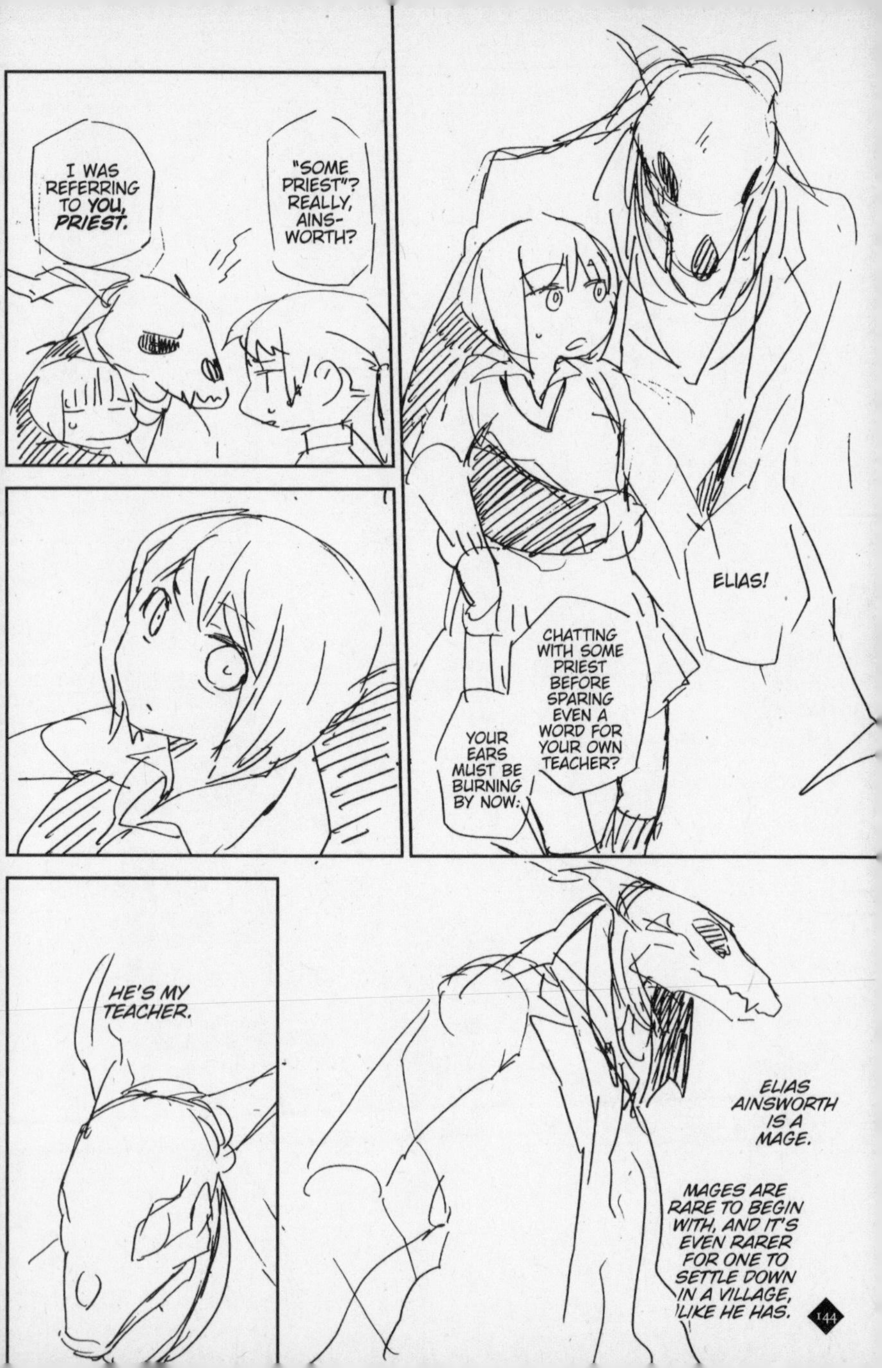
ELIAS!
CHATTING WITH SOME PRIEST BEFORE SPARING EVEN A WORD FOR YOUR OWN TEACHER?
YOUR EARS MUST BE BURNING BY NOW.
"SOME PRIEST"? REALLY, AINS-WORTH?
I WAS REFERRING TO YOU, PRIEST.
ELIAS AINSWORTH IS A MAGE.
MAGES ARE RARE TO BEGIN WITH, AND IT'S EVEN RARER FOR ONE TO SETTLE DOWN IN A VILLAGE, LIKE HE HAS.
HE'S MY TEACHER.

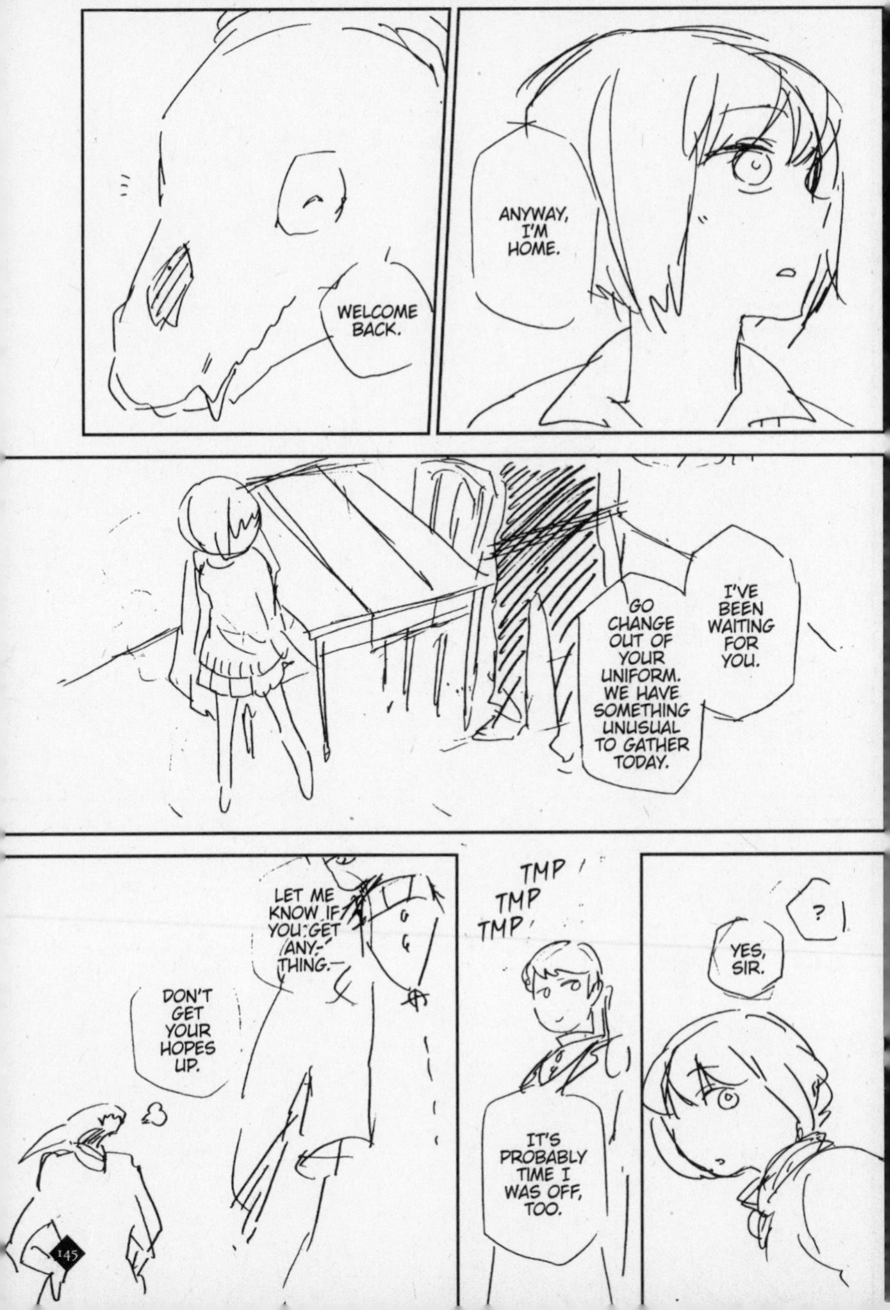

ANYWAY, I'M HOME.
WELCOME BACK.
I'VE BEEN WAITING FOR YOU.
GO CHANGE OUT OF YOUR UNIFORM. WE HAVE SOMETHING UNUSUAL TO GATHER TODAY.
?
YES, SIR.
TMP
TMP
TMP
IT'S PROBABLY TIME I WAS OFF, TOO.
LET ME KNOW IF YOU GET ANY-THING.
DON'T GET YOUR HOPES UP.

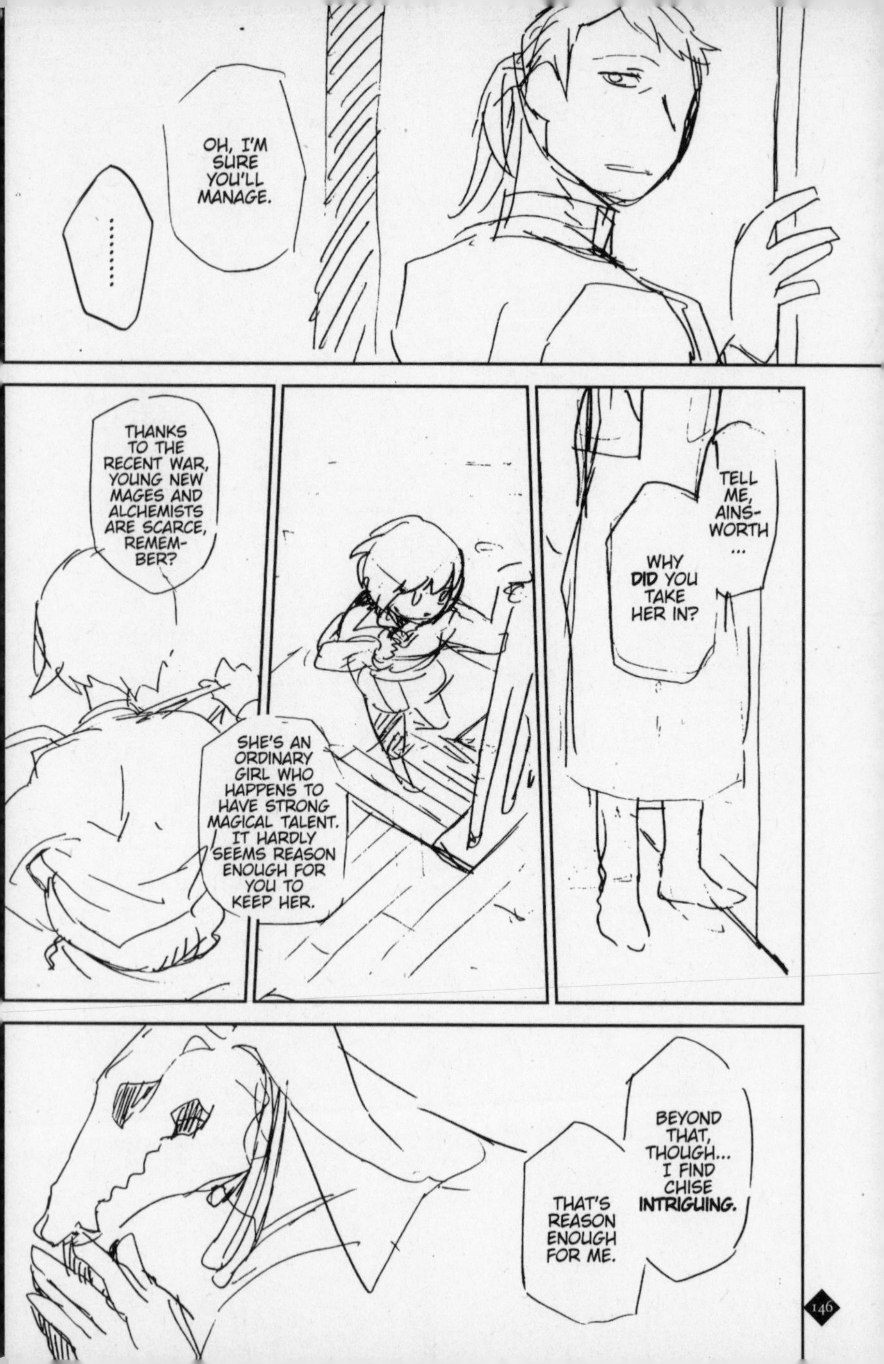
OH, I'M SURE YOU'LL MANAGE.
......
TELL ME, AINSWORTH...
WHY DID YOU TAKE HER IN?
SHE'S AN ORDINARY GIRL WHO HAPPENS TO HAVE STRONG MAGICAL TALENT. IT HARDLY SEEMS REASON ENOUGH FOR YOU TO KEEP HER.
THANKS TO THE RECENT WAR, YOUNG NEW MAGES AND ALCHEMISTS ARE SCARCE, REMEMBER?
BEYOND THAT, THOUGH... I FIND CHISE INTRIGUING.
THAT'S REASON ENOUGH FOR ME.

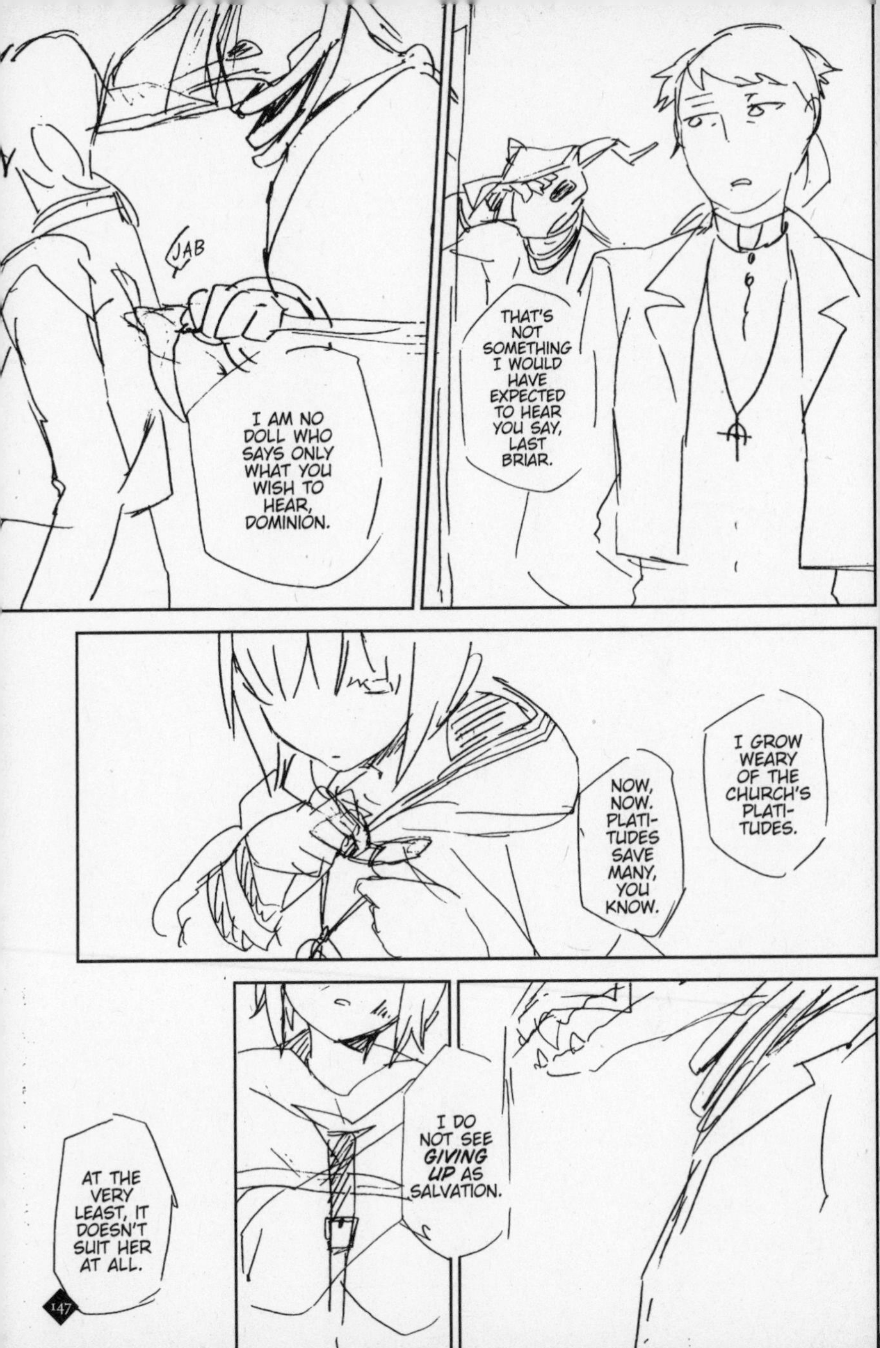
THAT'S NOT SOMETHING I WOULD HAVE EXPECTED TO HEAR YOU SAY, LAST BRIAR.
JAB
I AM NO DOLL WHO SAYS ONLY WHAT YOU WISH TO HEAR, DOMINION.
I GROW WEARY OF THE CHURCH'S PLATI-TUDES.
NOW, NOW. PLATI-TUDES SAVE MANY, YOU KNOW.
I DO NOT SEE *GIVING UP* AS SALVATION.
AT THE VERY LEAST, IT DOESN'T SUIT HER AT ALL.

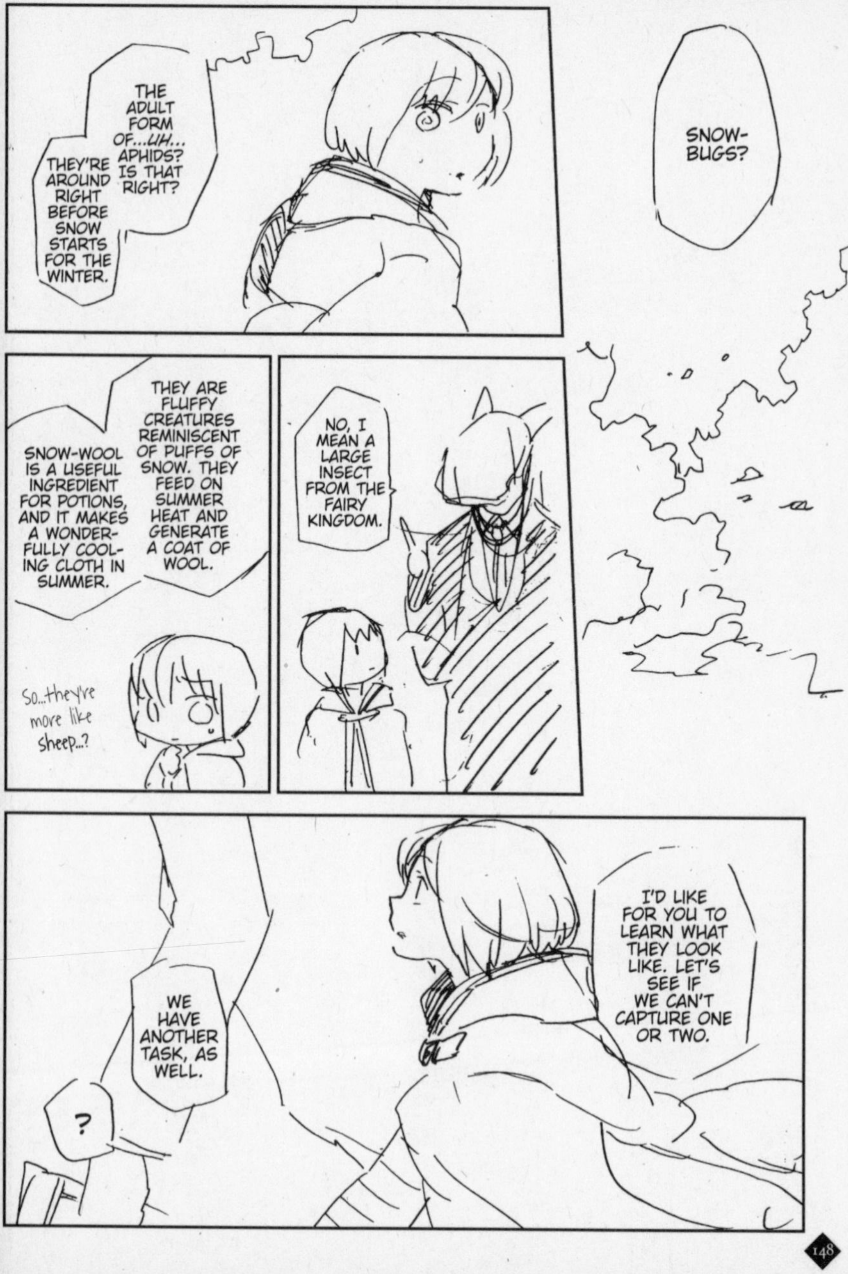
SNOW-BUGS?
THE ADULT FORM OF...UH... APHIDS? IS THAT RIGHT?
THEY'RE AROUND RIGHT BEFORE SNOW STARTS FOR THE WINTER.
NO, I MEAN A LARGE INSECT FROM THE FAIRY KINGDOM.
THEY ARE FLUFFY CREATURES REMINISCENT OF PUFFS OF SNOW. THEY FEED ON SUMMER HEAT AND GENERATE A COAT OF WOOL.
SNOW-WOOL IS A USEFUL INGREDIENT FOR POTIONS, AND IT MAKES A WONDERFULLY COOLING CLOTH IN SUMMER.
So...they're more like sheep...?
WE HAVE ANOTHER TASK, AS WELL.
I'D LIKE FOR YOU TO LEARN WHAT THEY LOOK LIKE. LET'S SEE IF WE CAN'T CAPTURE ONE OR TWO.
?

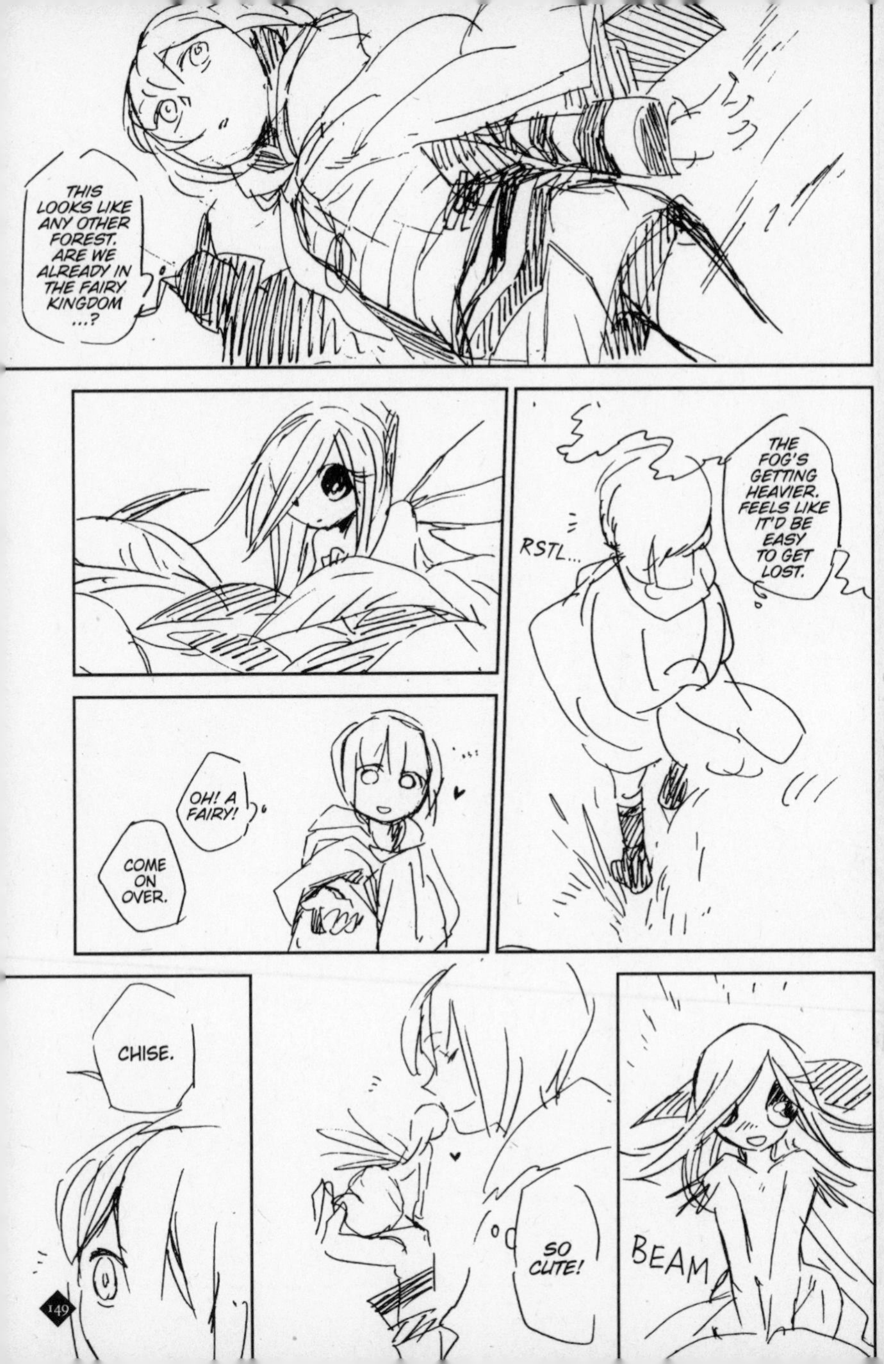
THIS LOOKS LIKE ANY OTHER FOREST. ARE WE ALREADY IN THE FAIRY KINGDOM ...?
THE FOG'S GETTING HEAVIER. FEELS LIKE IT'D BE EASY TO GET LOST.
RSTL...
OH! A FAIRY!
COME ON OVER.
BEAM
SO CUTE!
CHISE.

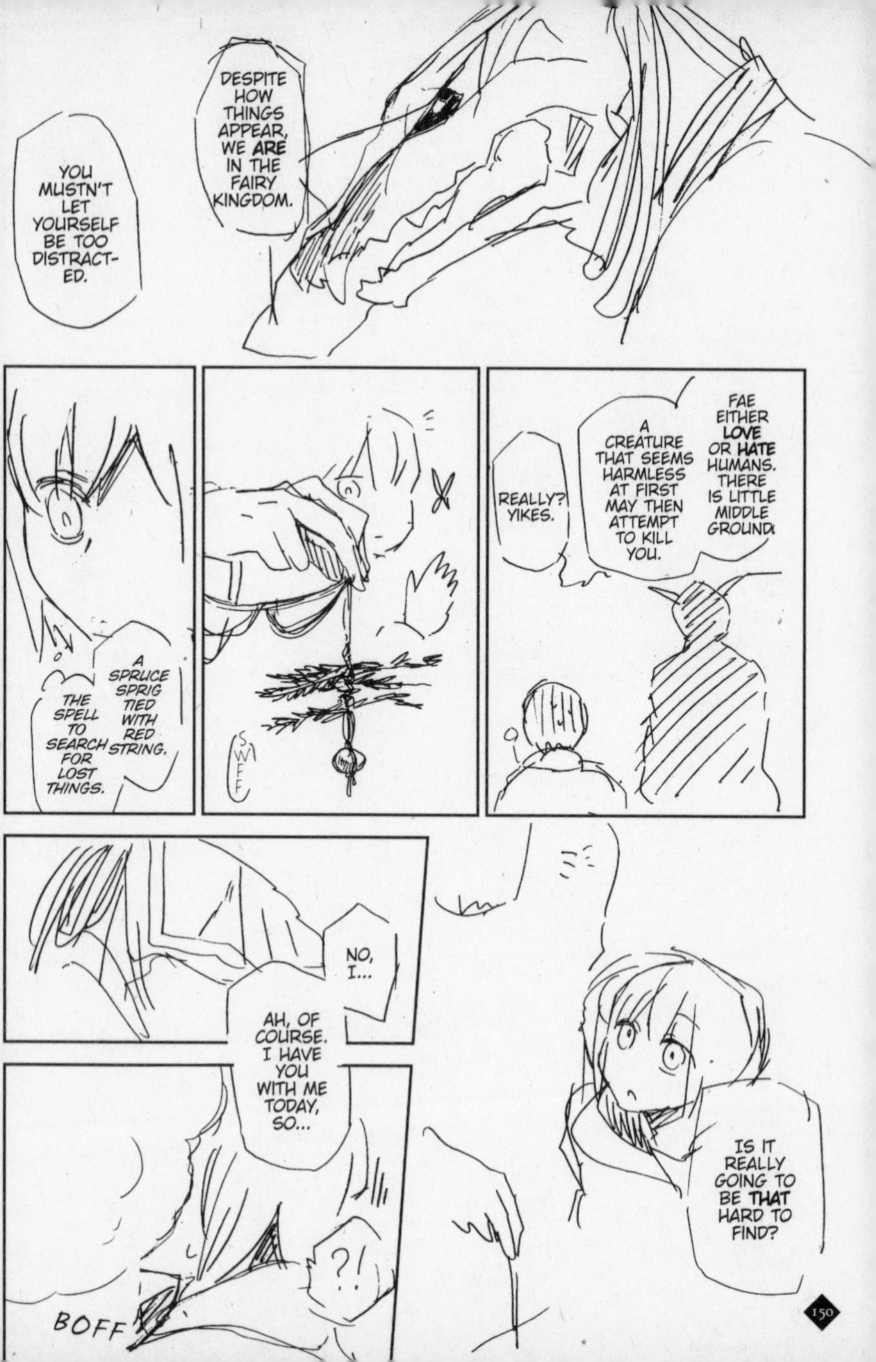
DESPITE HOW THINGS APPEAR, WE **ARE** IN THE FAIRY KINGDOM.
YOU MUSTN'T LET YOURSELF BE TOO DISTRACTED.
FAE EITHER **LOVE** OR **HATE** HUMANS. THERE IS LITTLE MIDDLE GROUND.
A CREATURE THAT SEEMS HARMLESS AT FIRST MAY THEN ATTEMPT TO KILL YOU.
REALLY? YIKES.
SWFF
A SPRUCE SPRIG TIED WITH RED STRING.
THE SPELL TO SEARCH FOR LOST THINGS.
IS IT REALLY GOING TO BE **THAT** HARD TO FIND?
NO, I...
AH, OF COURSE. I HAVE YOU WITH ME TODAY, SO...
?!
BOFF

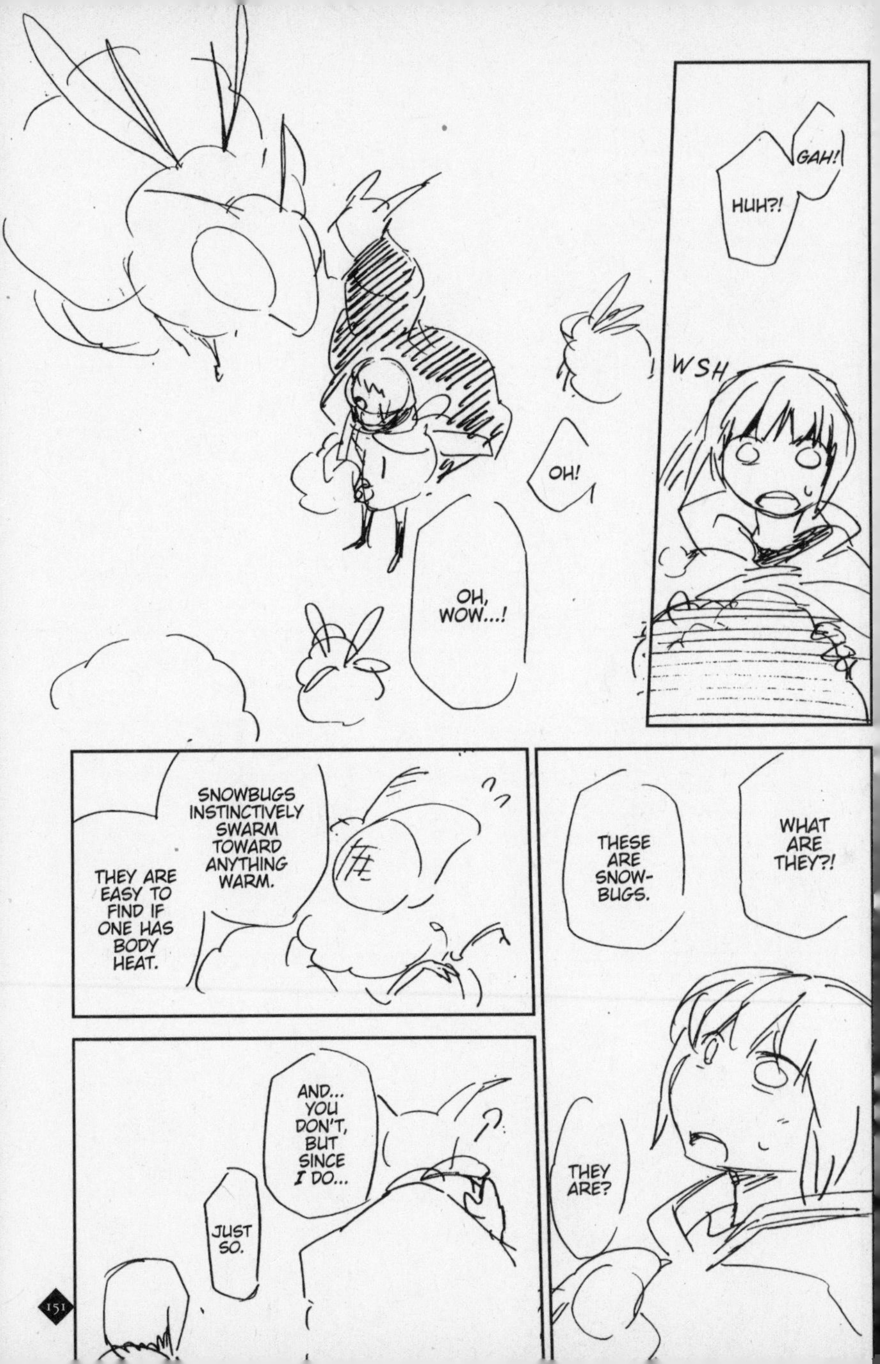
GAH!
HUH?!
WSH
OH!
OH, WOW...!
WHAT ARE THEY?!
THESE ARE SNOW-BUGS.
THEY ARE?
SNOWBUGS INSTINCTIVELY SWARM TOWARD ANYTHING WARM.
THEY ARE EASY TO FIND IF ONE HAS BODY HEAT.
AND... YOU DON'T, BUT SINCE I DO...
JUST SO.

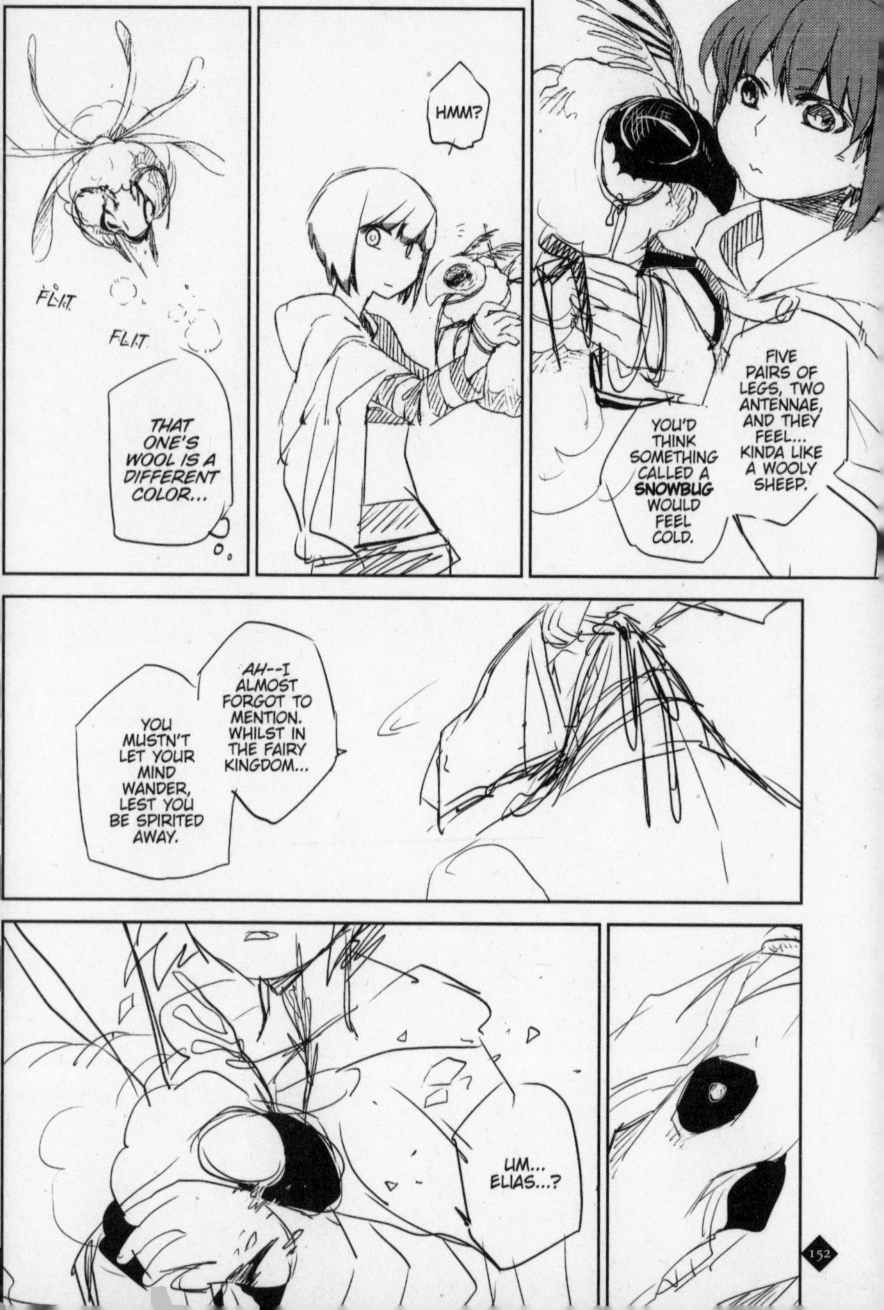
FIVE PAIRS OF LEGS, TWO ANTENNAE, AND THEY FEEL... KINDA LIKE A WOOLY SHEEP.
YOU'D THINK SOMETHING CALLED A **SNOWBUG** WOULD FEEL COLD.
HMM?
FLIT.
FLIT.
THAT ONE'S WOOL IS A DIFFERENT COLOR...
AH--I ALMOST FORGOT TO MENTION. WHILST IN THE FAIRY KINGDOM...
YOU MUSTN'T LET YOUR MIND WANDER, LEST YOU BE SPIRITED AWAY.
UM... ELIAS...?

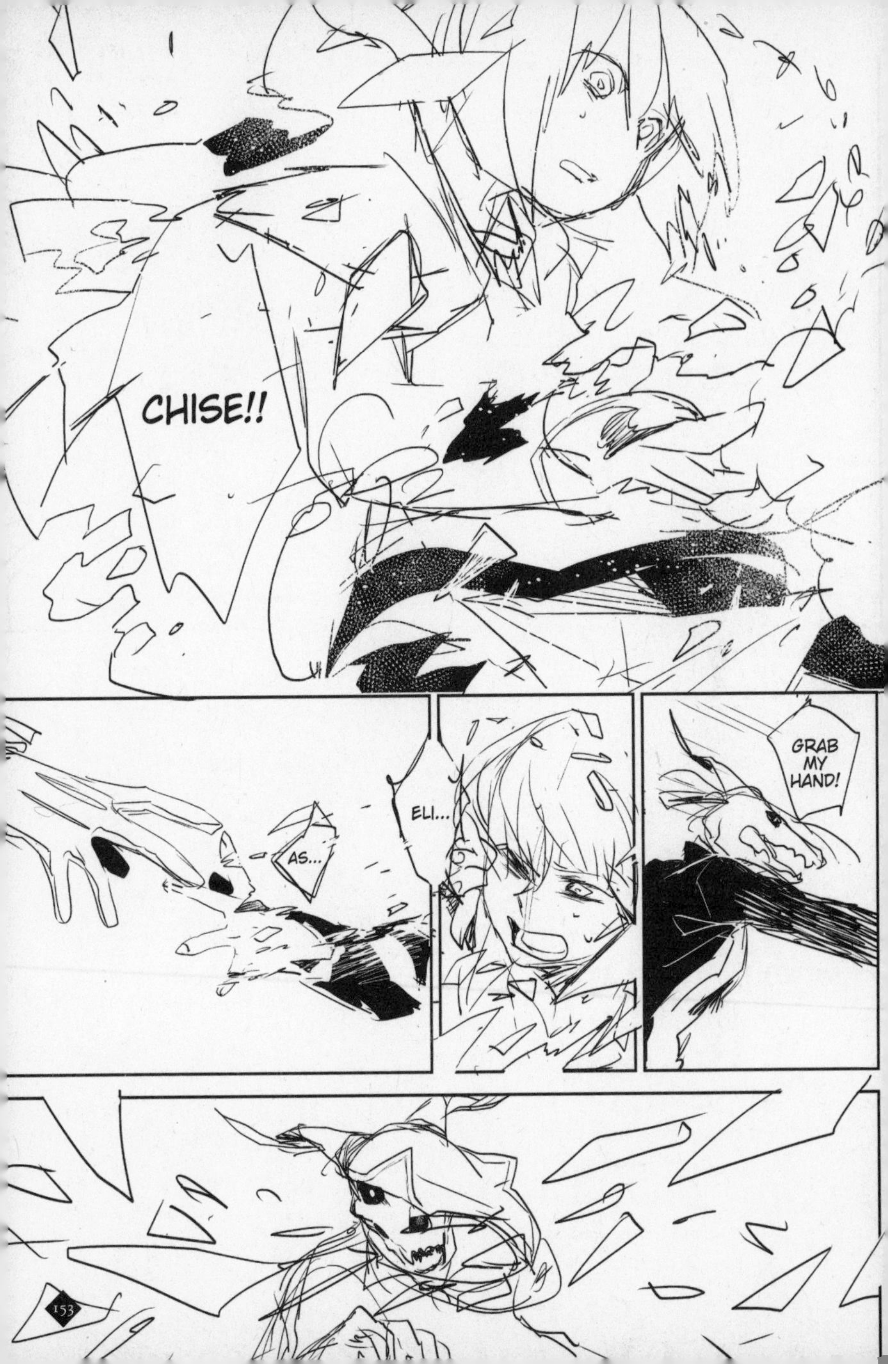
CHISE!!
GRAB MY HAND!
ELI...
AS...

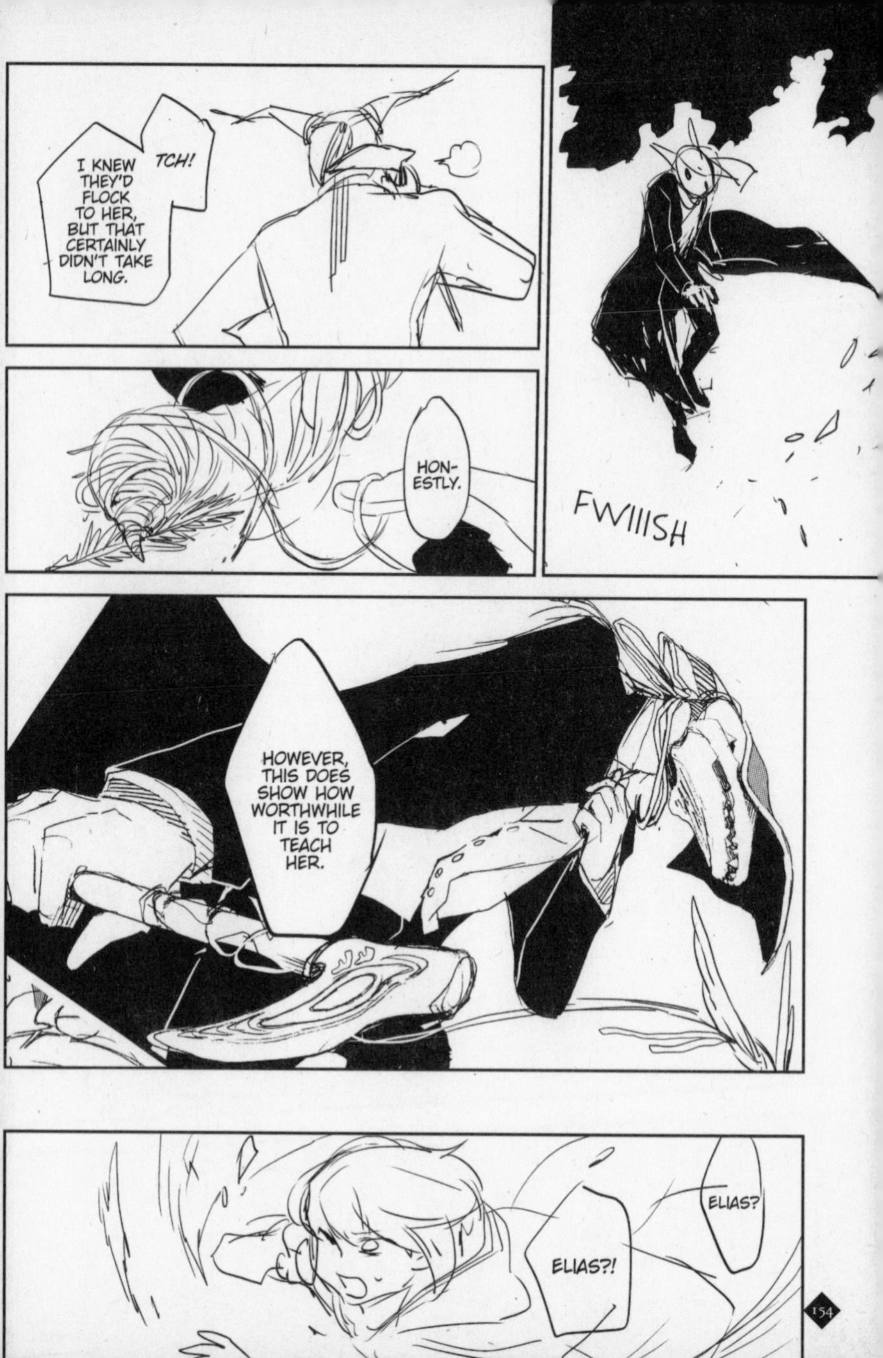
FWIIISH
TCH!
I KNEW THEY'D FLOCK TO HER, BUT THAT CERTAINLY DIDN'T TAKE LONG.
HON-ESTLY.
HOWEVER, THIS DOES SHOW HOW WORTHWHILE IT IS TO TEACH HER.
ELIAS?
ELIAS?!

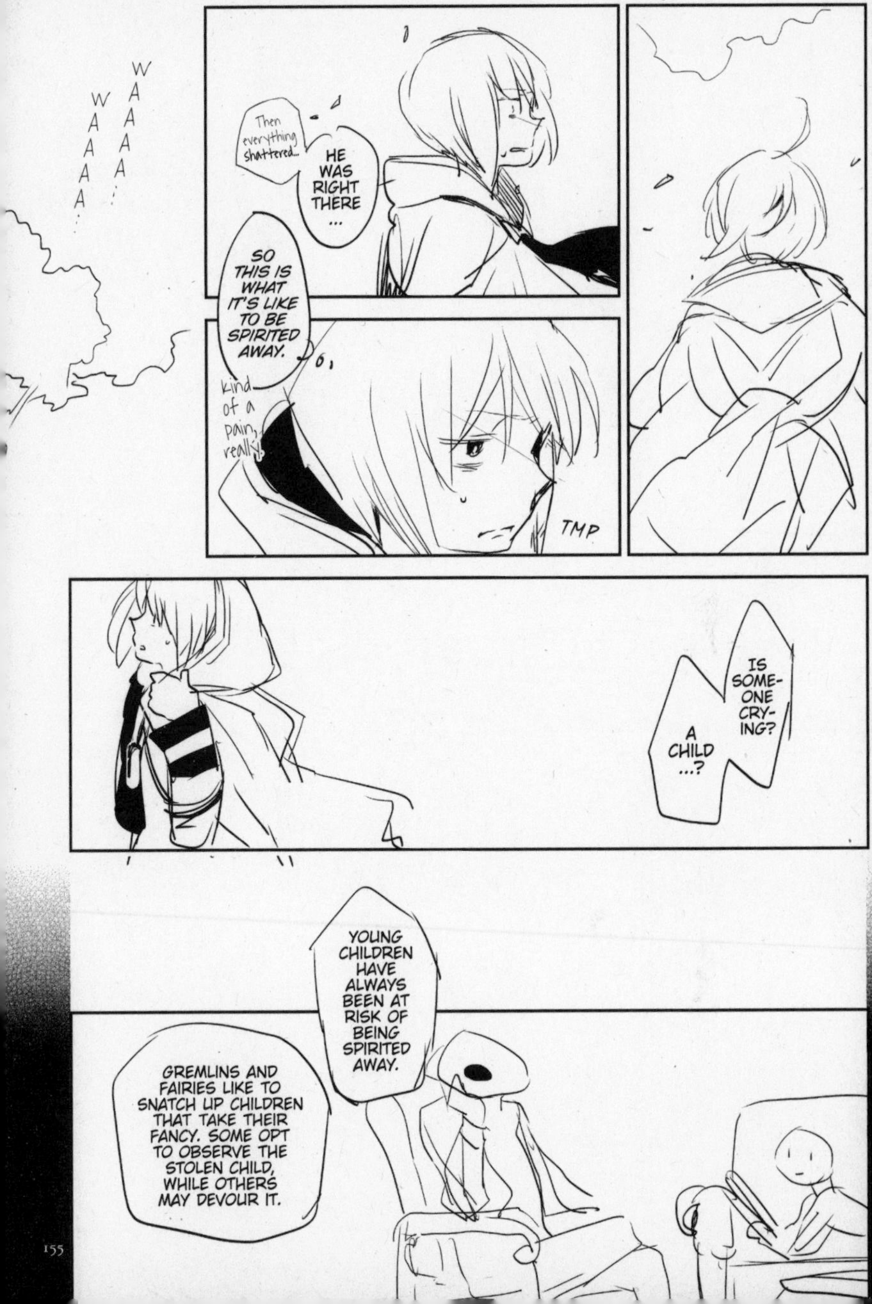
HE WAS RIGHT THERE ...
Then everything shattered...
SO THIS IS WHAT IT'S LIKE TO BE SPIRITED AWAY.
WAAAA...
WAAAA...
kind of a pain, really.
TMP
IS SOME-ONE CRY-ING?
A CHILD ...?
YOUNG CHILDREN HAVE ALWAYS BEEN AT RISK OF BEING SPIRITED AWAY.
GREMLINS AND FAIRIES LIKE TO SNATCH UP CHILDREN THAT TAKE THEIR FANCY. SOME OPT TO OBSERVE THE STOLEN CHILD, WHILE OTHERS MAY DEVOUR IT.

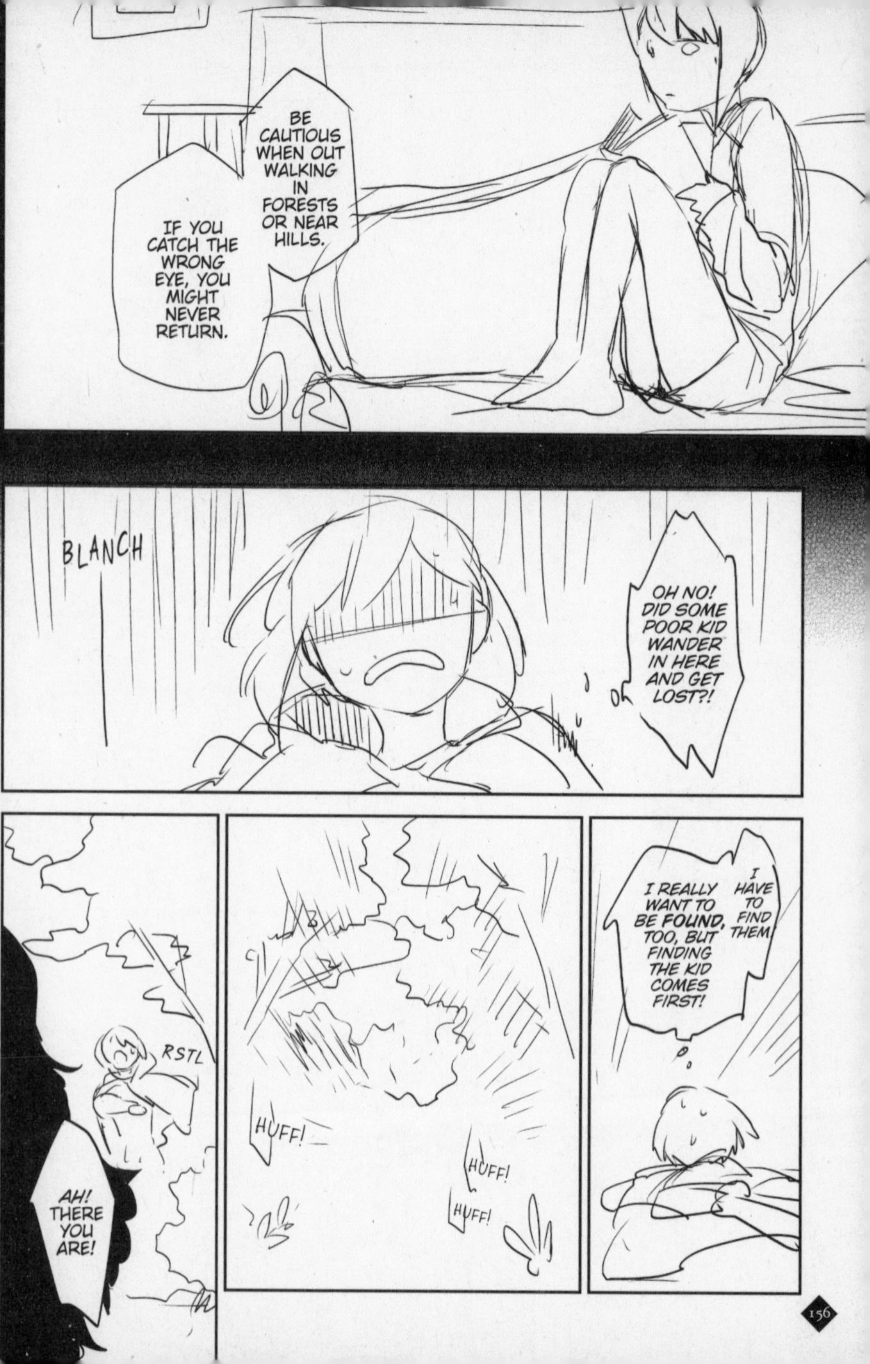
BE CAUTIOUS WHEN OUT WALKING IN FORESTS OR NEAR HILLS.
IF YOU CATCH THE WRONG EYE, YOU MIGHT NEVER RETURN.
OH NO! DID SOME POOR KID WANDER IN HERE AND GET LOST?!
BLANCH
I HAVE TO FIND THEM.
I REALLY WANT TO BE FOUND, TOO, BUT FINDING THE KID COMES FIRST!
HUFF!
HUFF!
HUFF!
RSTL
AH! THERE YOU ARE!

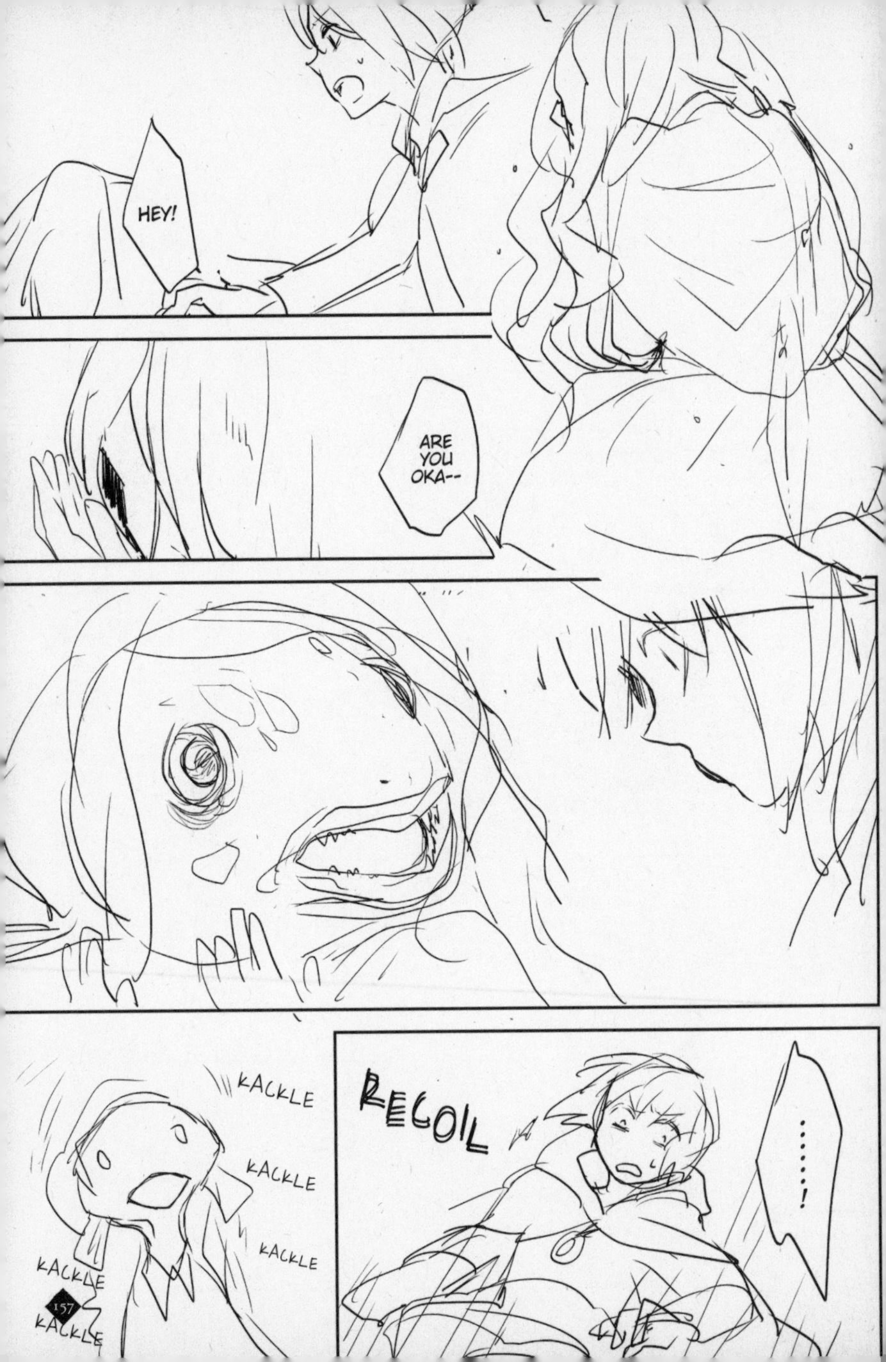
HEY!
ARE YOU OKA--
RECOIL
......!
KACKLE
KACKLE
KACKLE
KACKLE
KACKLE

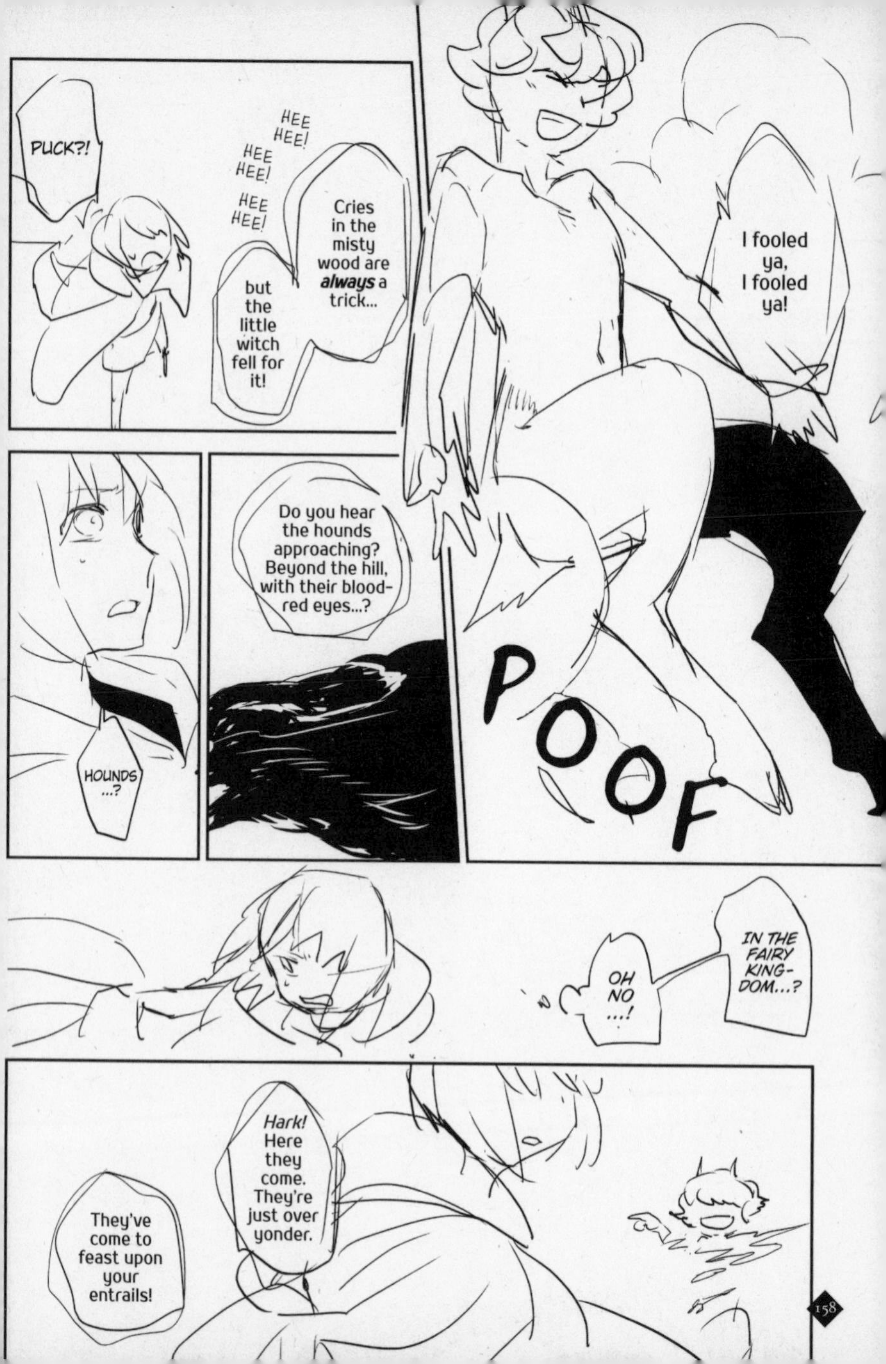

I fooled ya, I fooled ya!
POOF
Cries in the misty wood are *always* a trick...
but the little witch fell for it!
HEE HEE! HEE HEE! HEE HEE!
PUCK?!
Do you hear the hounds approaching? Beyond the hill, with their blood-red eyes...?
HOUNDS ...?
IN THE FAIRY KING-DOM...?
OH NO ...!
Hark! Here they come. They're just over yonder.
They've come to feast upon your entrails!

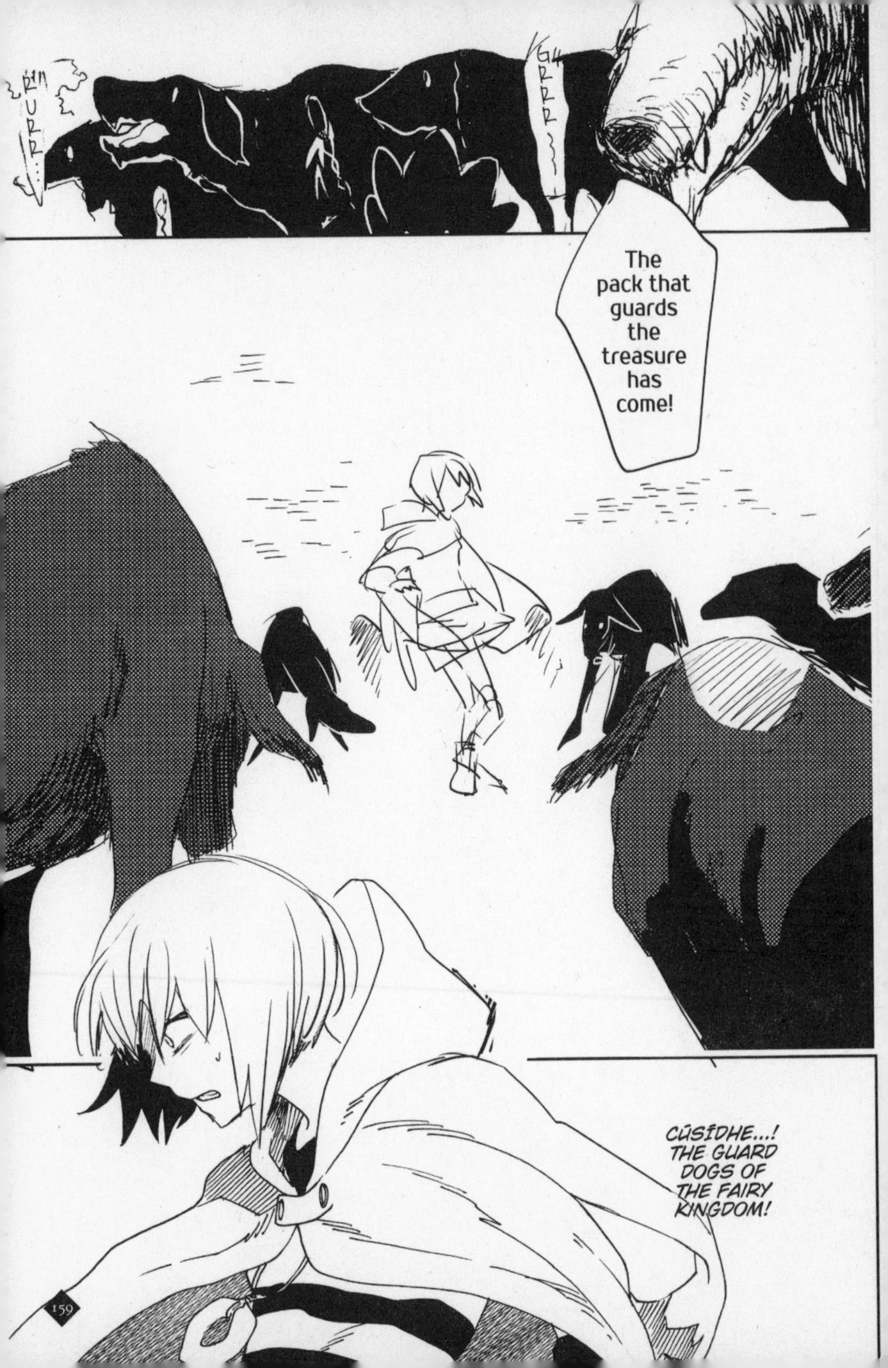
GRRR~
RURR...
The pack that guards the treasure has come!
CŪSÍDHE...! THE GUARD DOGS OF THE FAIRY KINGDOM!

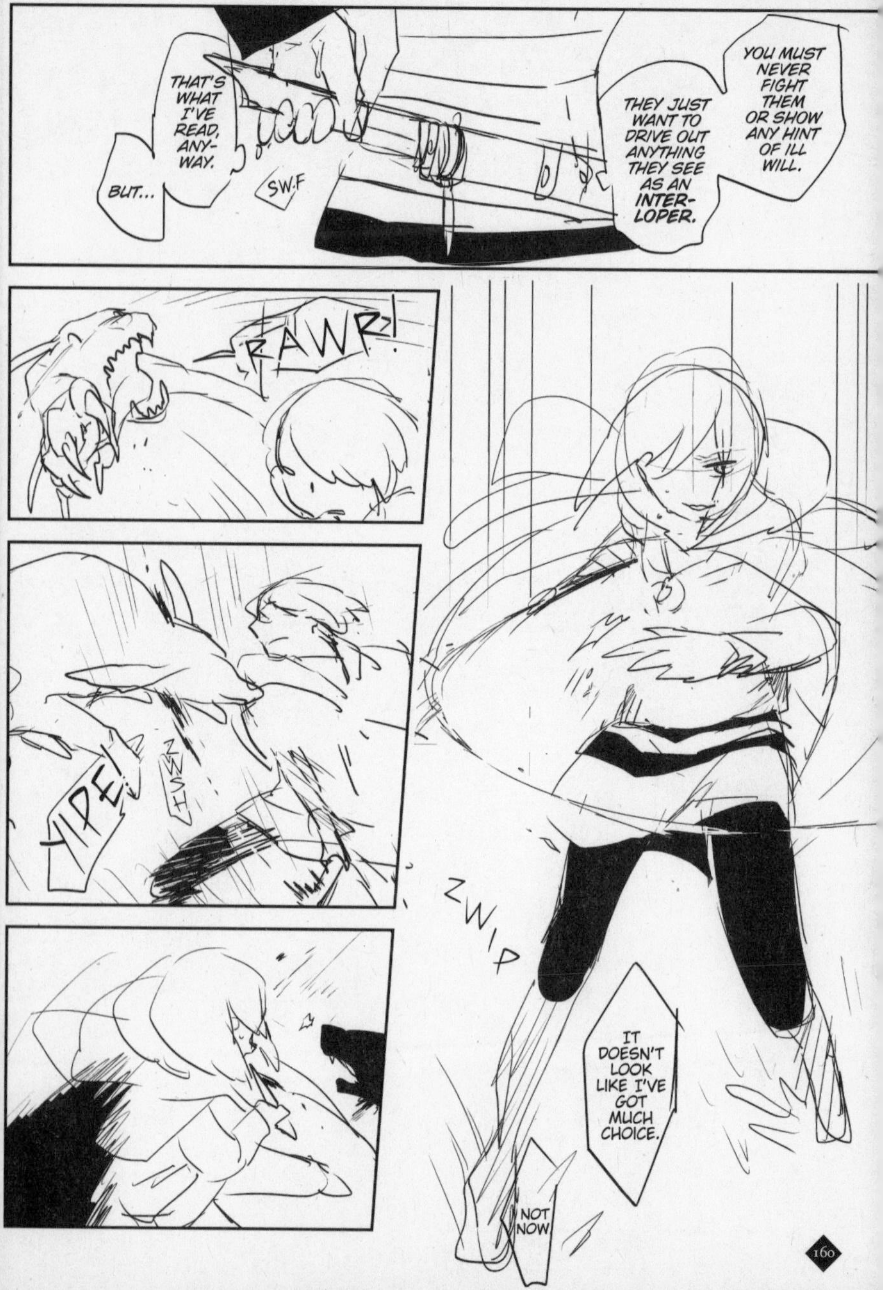
YOU MUST NEVER FIGHT THEM OR SHOW ANY HINT OF ILL WILL.
THEY JUST WANT TO DRIVE OUT ANYTHING THEY SEE AS AN INTER-LOPER.
THAT'S WHAT I'VE READ, ANY-WAY.
BUT...
SW.F
ZWIP
IT DOESN'T LOOK LIKE I'VE GOT MUCH CHOICE.
NOT NOW
RAWR!
ZWSH
YIPE!

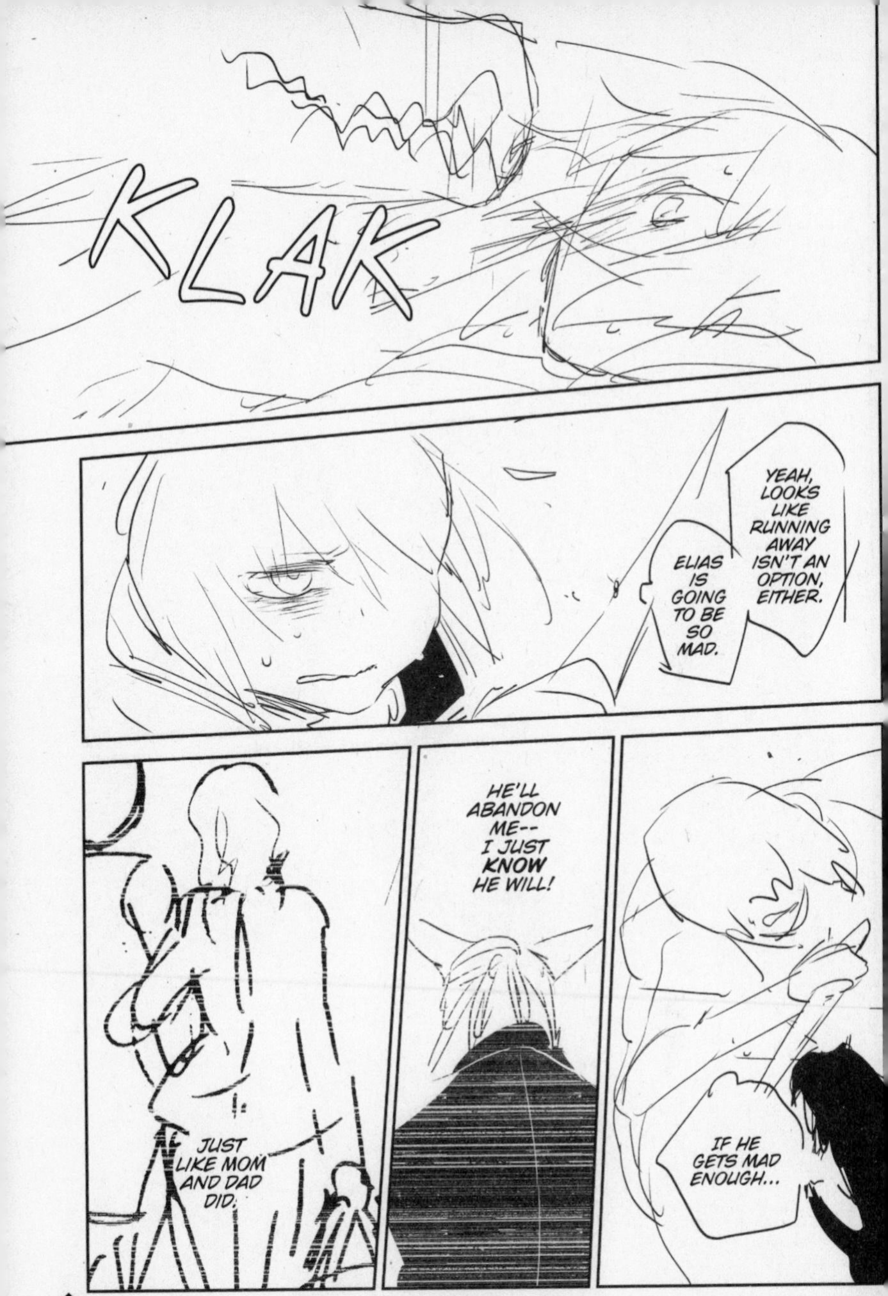
KLAK
YEAH, LOOKS LIKE RUNNING AWAY ISN'T AN OPTION, EITHER.
ELIAS IS GOING TO BE SO MAD.
IF HE GETS MAD ENOUGH...
HE'LL ABANDON ME-- I JUST KNOW HE WILL!
JUST LIKE MOM AND DAD DID.

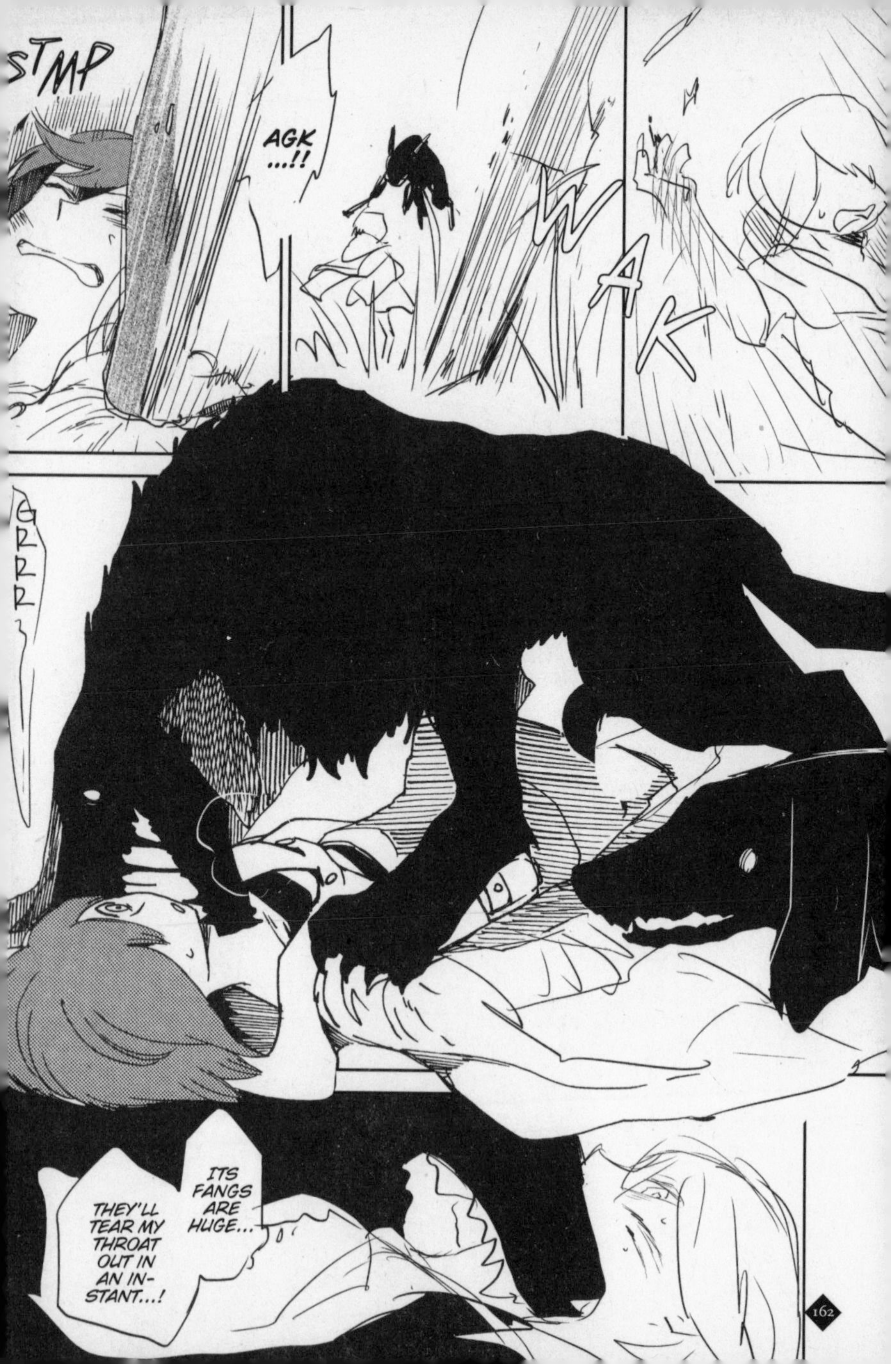
WAK
AGK ...!!
STMP
GRRRR
ITS FANGS ARE HUGE...
THEY'LL TEAR MY THROAT OUT IN AN IN- STANT...!

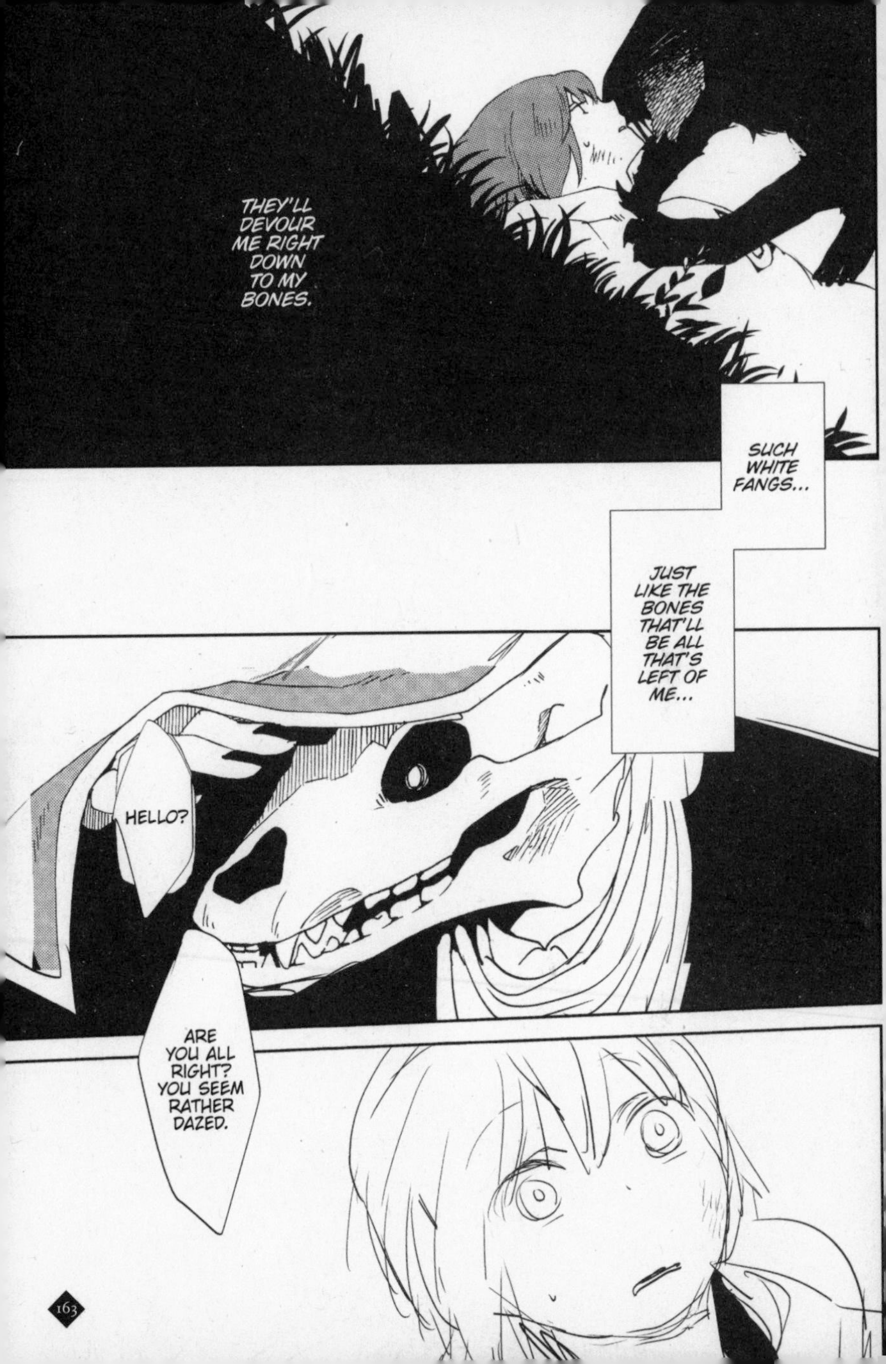
THEY'LL DEVOUR ME RIGHT DOWN TO MY BONES.
SUCH WHITE FANGS...
JUST LIKE THE BONES THAT'LL BE ALL THAT'S LEFT OF ME...
HELLO?
ARE YOU ALL RIGHT? YOU SEEM RATHER DAZED.

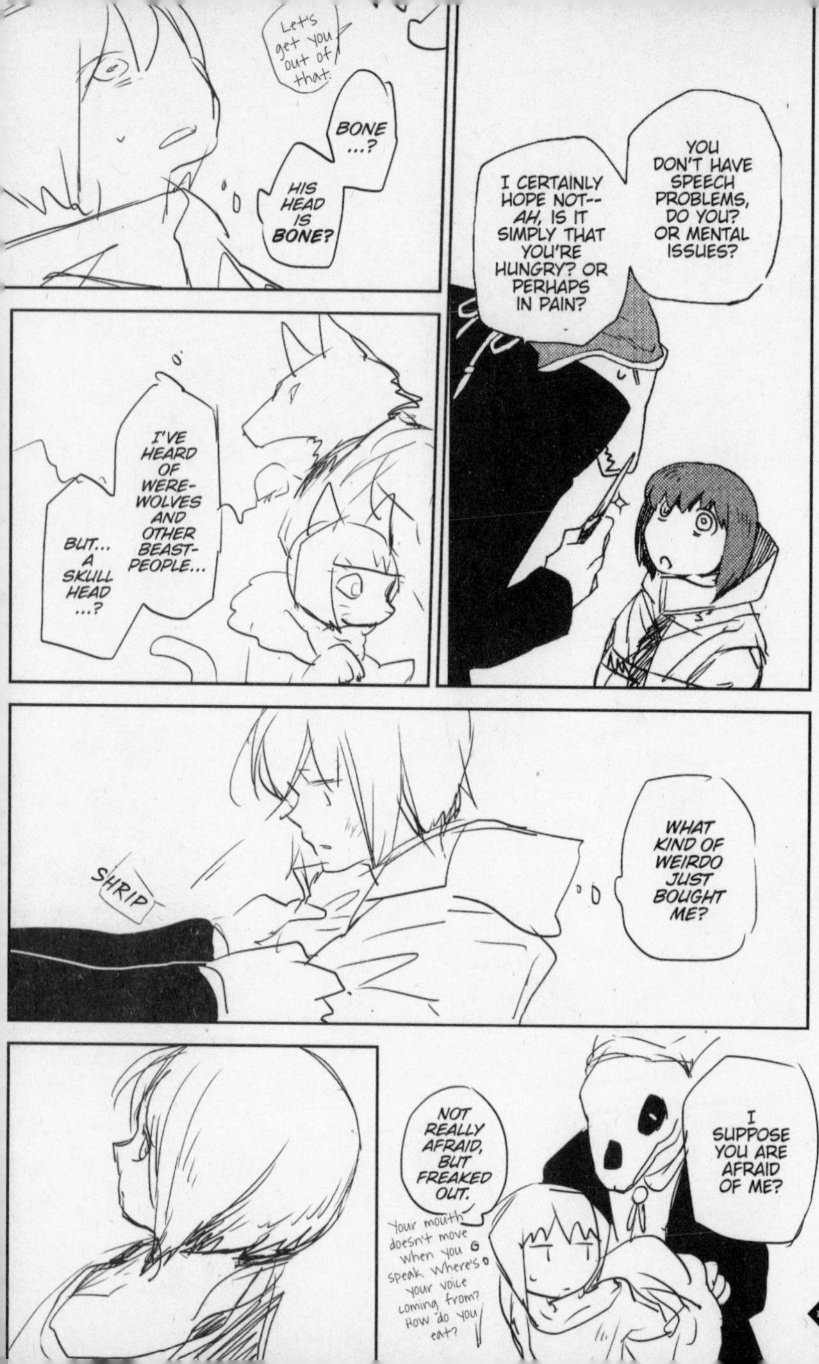
YOU DON'T HAVE SPEECH PROBLEMS, DO YOU? OR MENTAL ISSUES?
I CERTAINLY HOPE NOT-- *AH*, IS IT SIMPLY THAT YOU'RE HUNGRY? OR PERHAPS IN PAIN?
Let's get you out of that.
BONE ...?
HIS HEAD IS *BONE*?
I'VE HEARD OF WERE-WOLVES AND OTHER BEAST-PEOPLE...
BUT... A SKULL HEAD ...?
WHAT KIND OF WEIRDO JUST BOUGHT ME?
SHRIP
I SUPPOSE YOU ARE AFRAID OF ME?
NOT REALLY AFRAID, BUT FREAKED OUT.
Your mouth doesn't move when you speak. Where's your voice coming from? How do you eat?

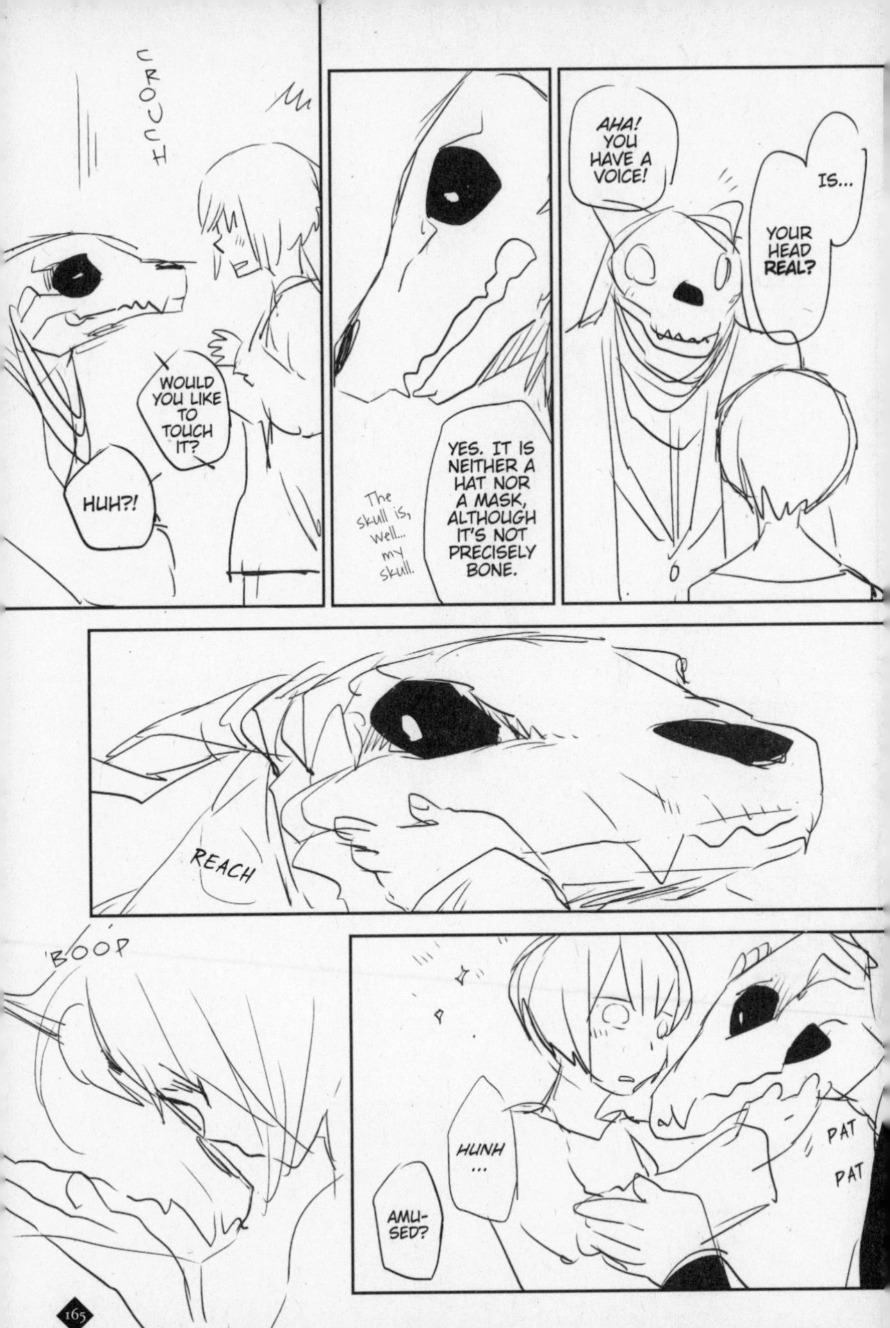
AHA! YOU HAVE A VOICE!
IS... YOUR HEAD REAL?
YES. IT IS NEITHER A HAT NOR A MASK, ALTHOUGH IT'S NOT PRECISELY BONE.
The skull is, well... my skull.
CROUCH
WOULD YOU LIKE TO TOUCH IT?
HUH?!
REACH
PAT PAT
HUNH...
AMU-SED?
BOOP

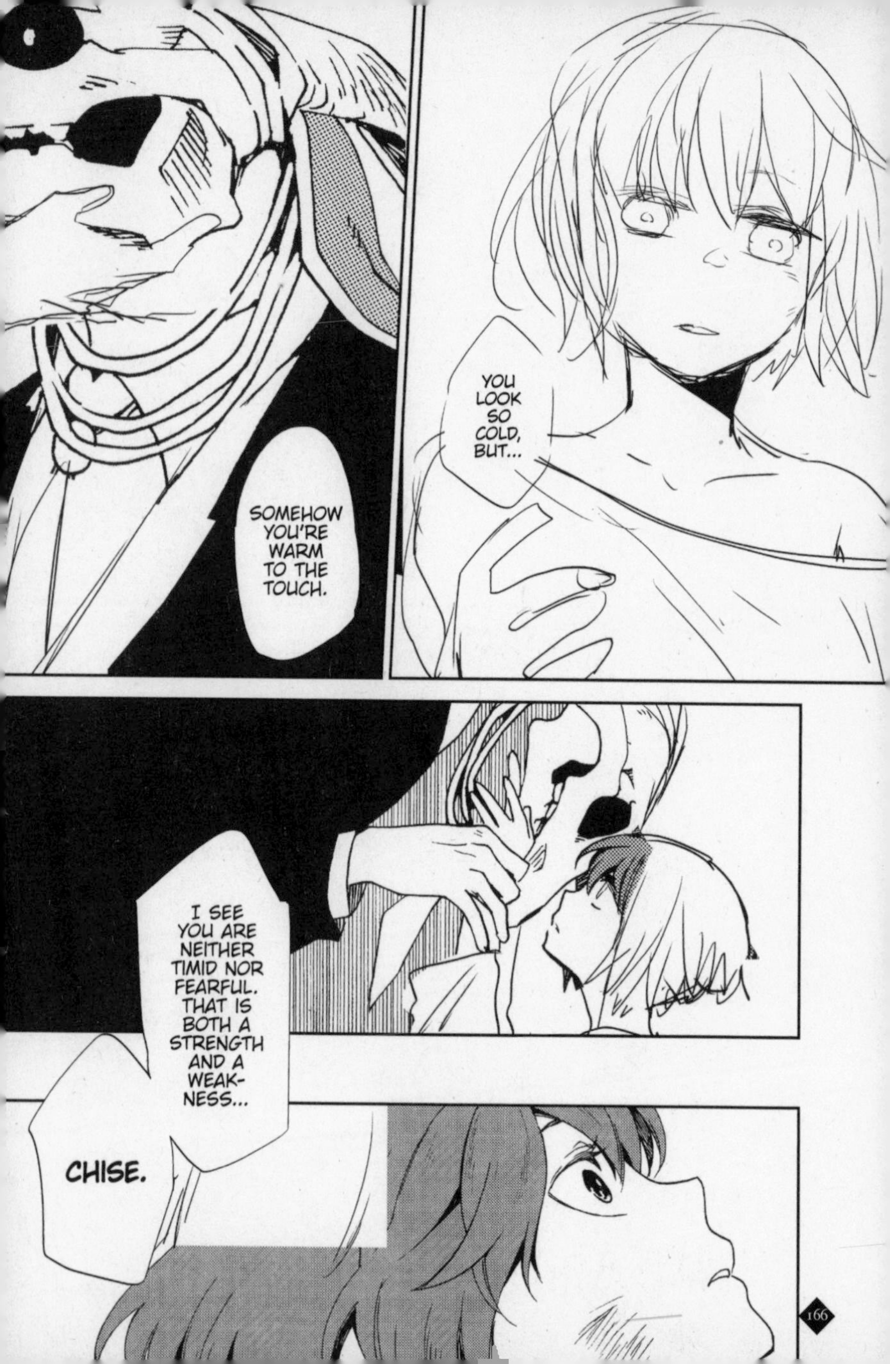
YOU LOOK SO COLD, BUT...
SOMEHOW YOU'RE WARM TO THE TOUCH.
I SEE YOU ARE NEITHER TIMID NOR FEARFUL. THAT IS BOTH A STRENGTH AND A WEAK-NESS...
CHISE.

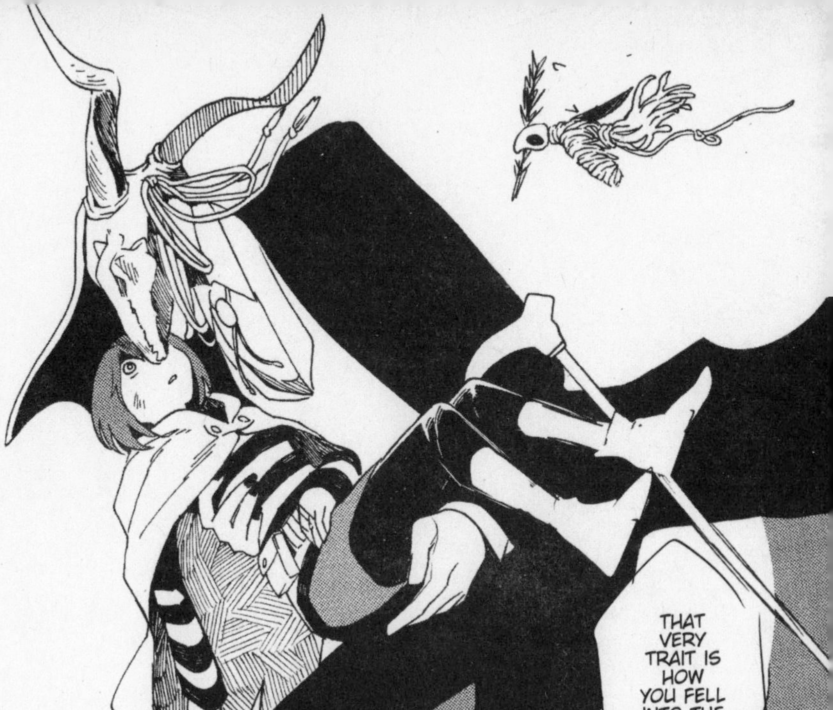
THAT VERY TRAIT IS HOW YOU FELL INTO THE HANDS OF A BEING LIKE ME.

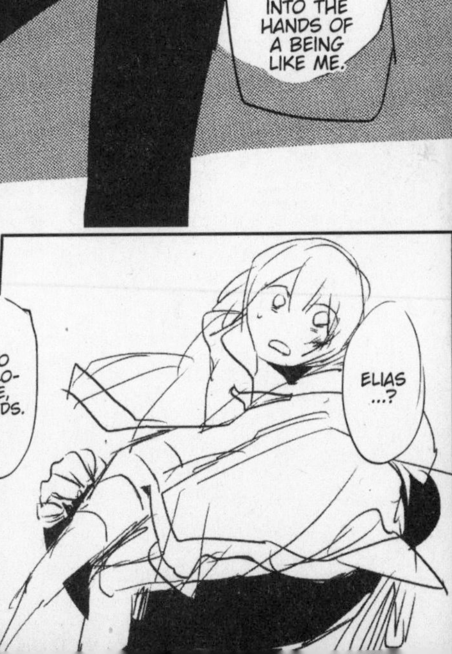
ELIAS ...?

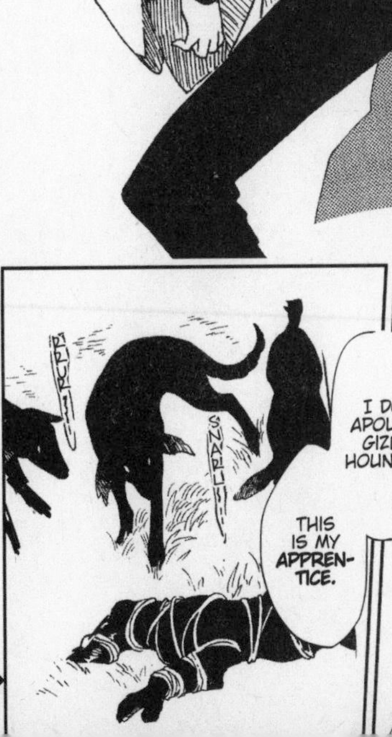
I DO APOLO-GIZE, HOUNDS.
THIS IS MY APPREN-TICE.
SNARL

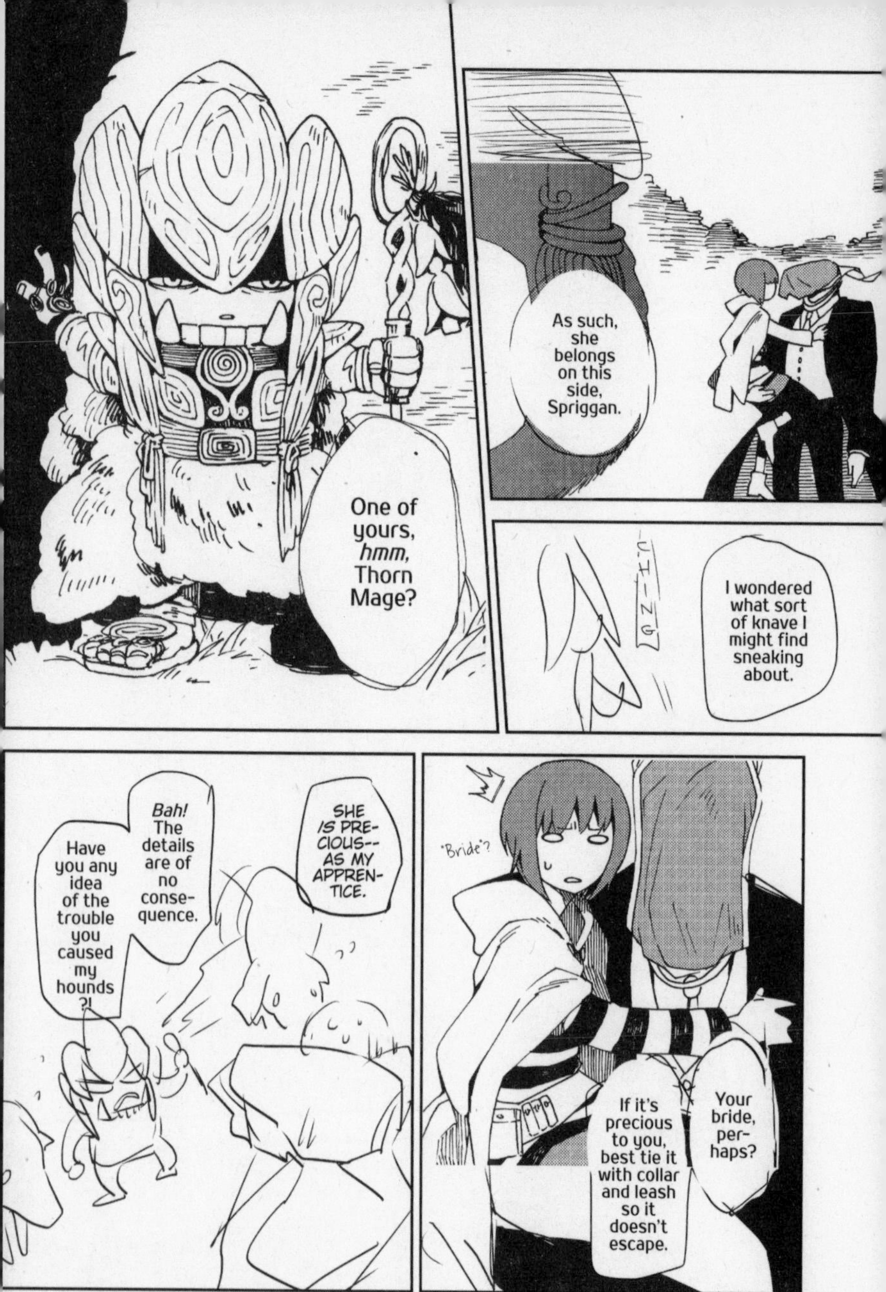
As such, she belongs on this side, Spriggan.
I wondered what sort of knave I might find sneaking about.
CHING
One of yours, *hmm,* Thorn Mage?
"Bride"?
Your bride, perhaps?
If it's precious to you, best tie it with collar and leash so it doesn't escape.
SHE *IS* PRECIOUS--AS MY APPRENTICE.
Bah! The details are of no consequence.
Have you any idea of the trouble you caused my hounds?!

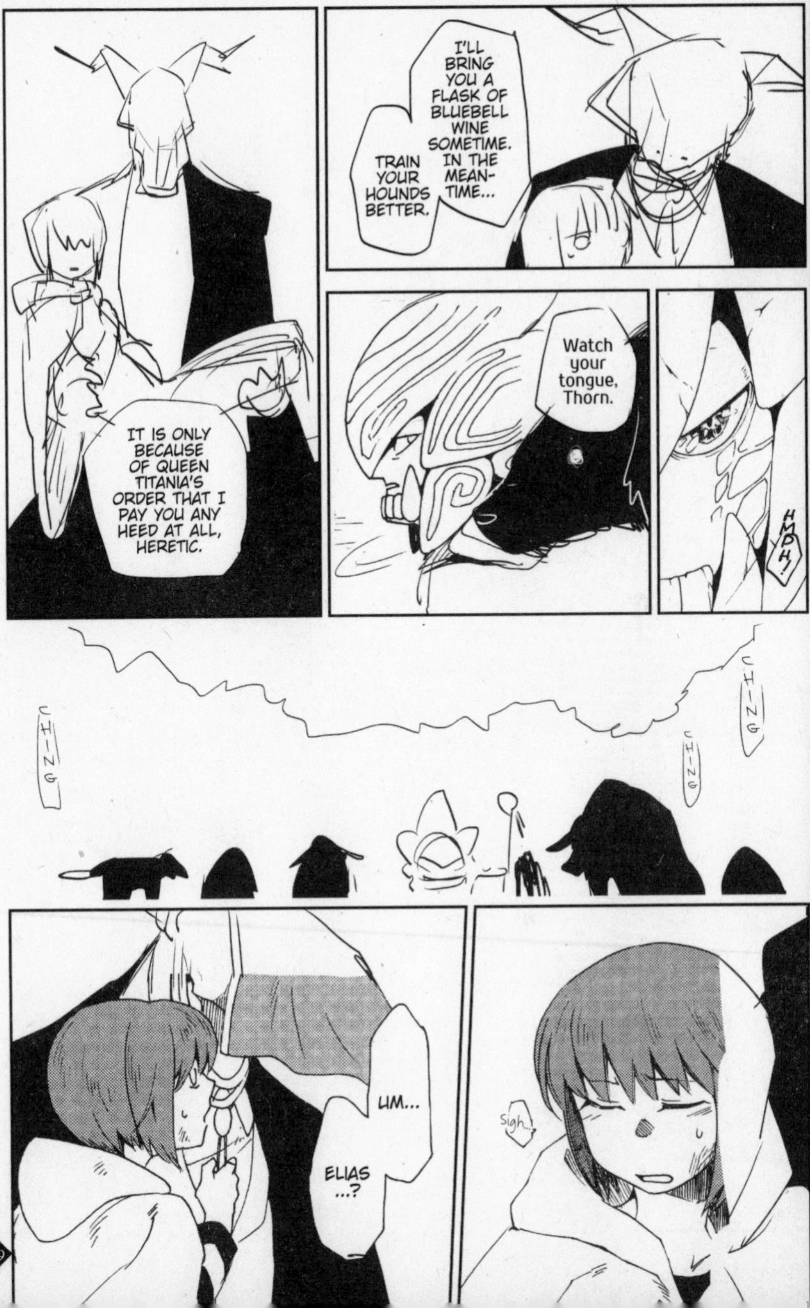
I'LL BRING YOU A FLASK OF BLUEBELL WINE SOMETIME. IN THE MEAN-TIME...
TRAIN YOUR HOUNDS BETTER.
HMPH!
Watch your tongue, Thorn.
IT IS ONLY BECAUSE OF QUEEN TITANIA'S ORDER THAT I PAY YOU ANY HEED AT ALL, HERETIC.
CHING
CHING
CHING
Sigh...
UM...
ELIAS ...?

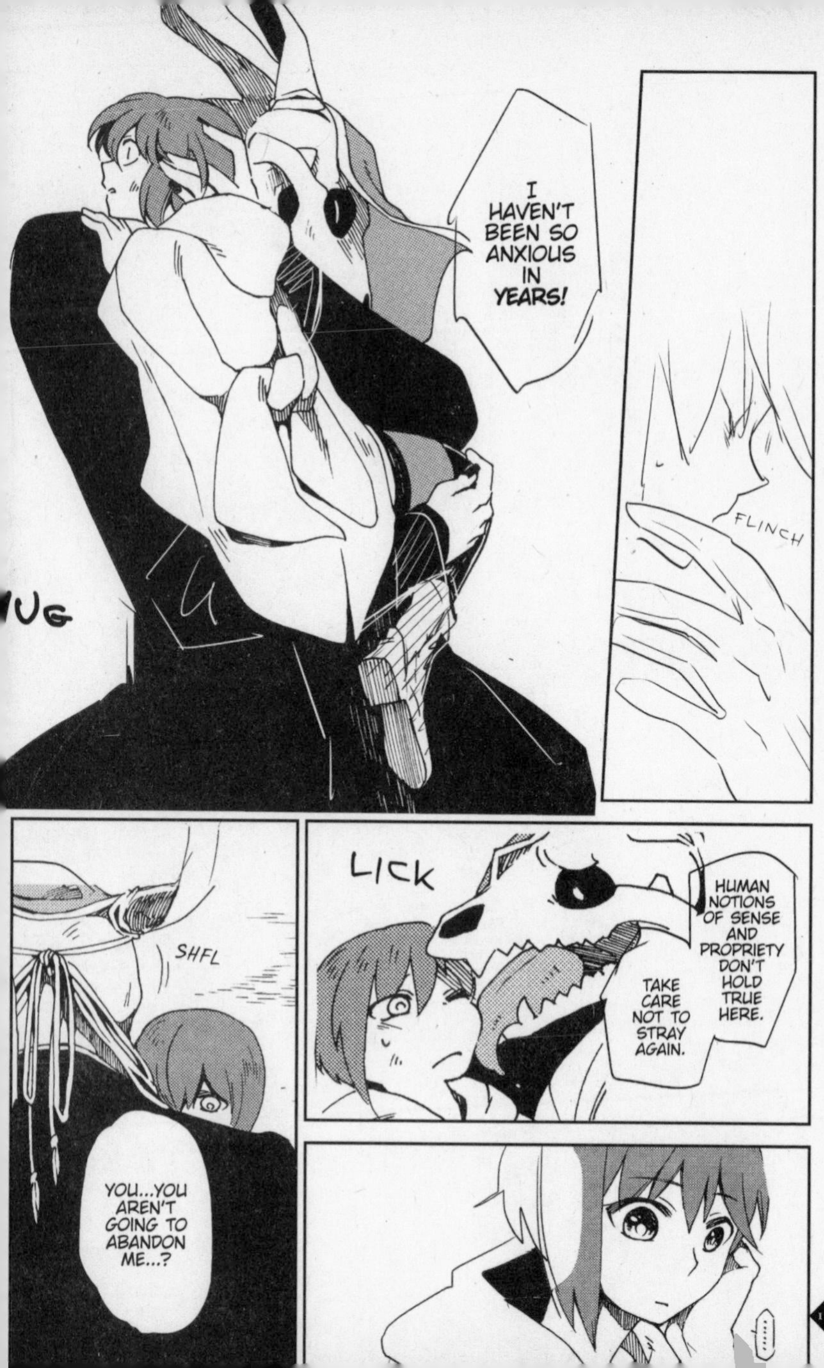
FLINCH
I HAVEN'T BEEN SO ANXIOUS IN YEARS!
UG
HUMAN NOTIONS OF SENSE AND PROPRIETY DON'T HOLD TRUE HERE.
TAKE CARE NOT TO STRAY AGAIN.
LICK
......
SHFL
YOU...YOU AREN'T GOING TO ABANDON ME...?

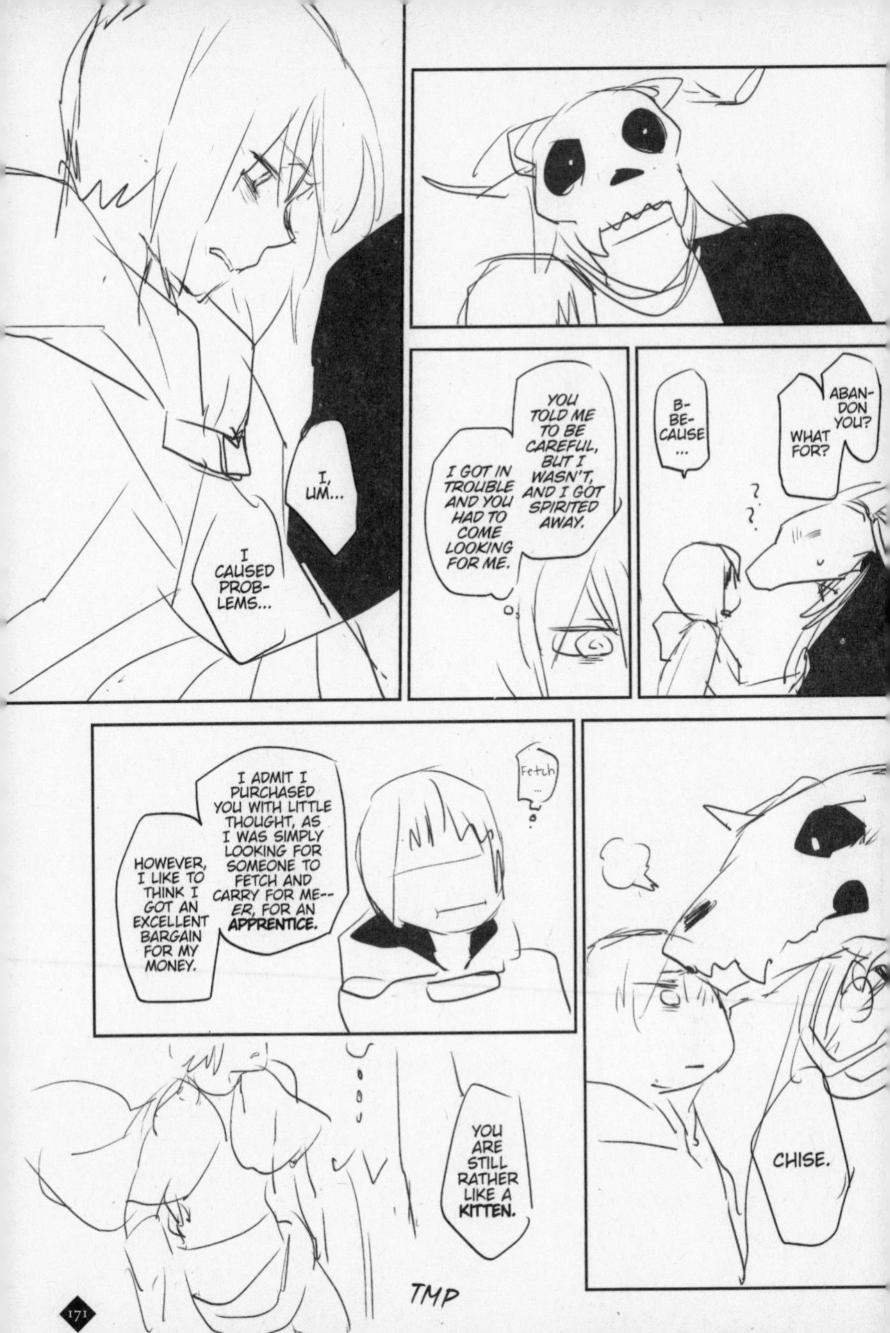
ABANDON YOU? WHAT FOR?
B-BE-CAUSE...
YOU TOLD ME TO BE CAREFUL, BUT I WASN'T, AND I GOT SPIRITED AWAY.
I GOT IN TROUBLE AND YOU HAD TO COME LOOKING FOR ME.
I, UM...
I CAUSED PROB-LEMS...
CHISE.
Fetch...
I ADMIT I PURCHASED YOU WITH LITTLE THOUGHT, AS I WAS SIMPLY LOOKING FOR SOMEONE TO FETCH AND CARRY FOR ME-- ER, FOR AN APPRENTICE.
HOWEVER, I LIKE TO THINK I GOT AN EXCELLENT BARGAIN FOR MY MONEY.
YOU ARE STILL RATHER LIKE A KITTEN.
TMP

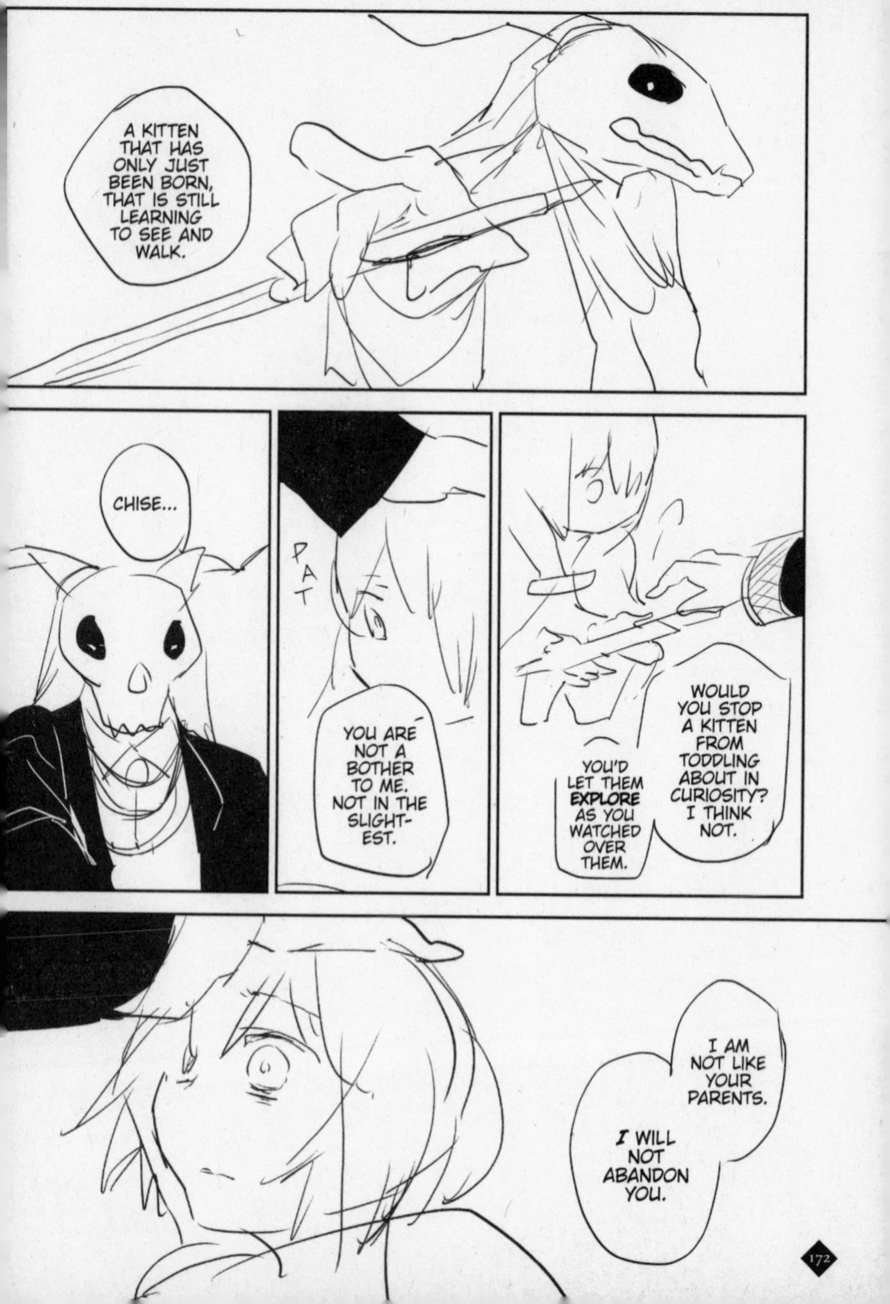
A KITTEN THAT HAS ONLY JUST BEEN BORN, THAT IS STILL LEARNING TO SEE AND WALK.
WOULD YOU STOP A KITTEN FROM TODDLING ABOUT IN CURIOSITY? I THINK NOT.
YOU'D LET THEM **EXPLORE** AS YOU WATCHED OVER THEM.
PAT
YOU ARE NOT A BOTHER TO ME. NOT IN THE SLIGHT-EST.
CHISE...
I AM NOT LIKE YOUR PARENTS.
I WILL NOT ABANDON YOU.

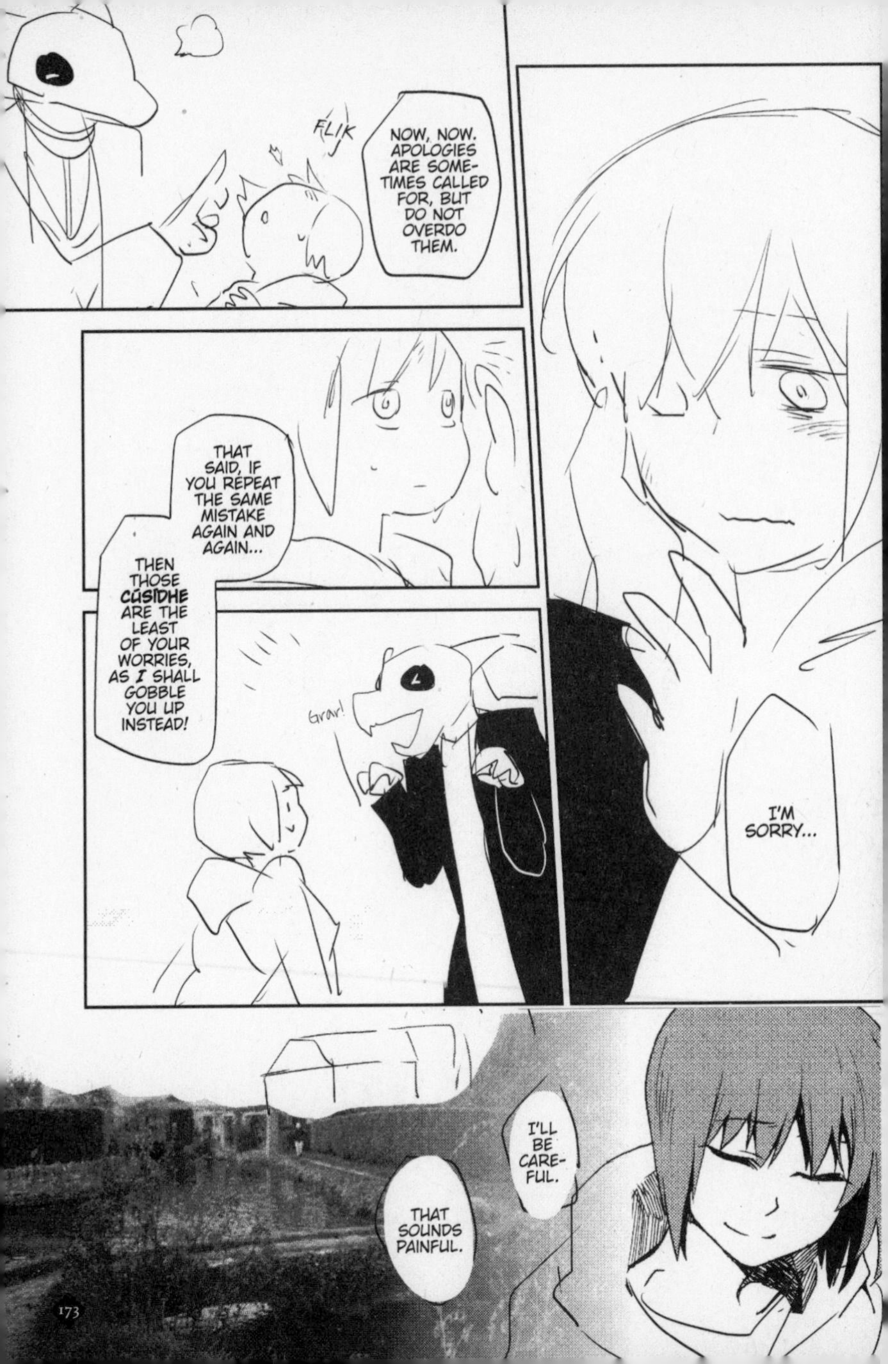
FLIK
NOW, NOW. APOLOGIES ARE SOMETIMES CALLED FOR, BUT DO NOT OVERDO THEM.
THAT SAID, IF YOU REPEAT THE SAME MISTAKE AGAIN AND AGAIN...
THEN THOSE **CÚSIDHE** ARE THE LEAST OF YOUR WORRIES, AS *I* SHALL GOBBLE YOU UP INSTEAD!
Grar!
I'M SORRY...
I'LL BE CAREFUL.
THAT SOUNDS PAINFUL.

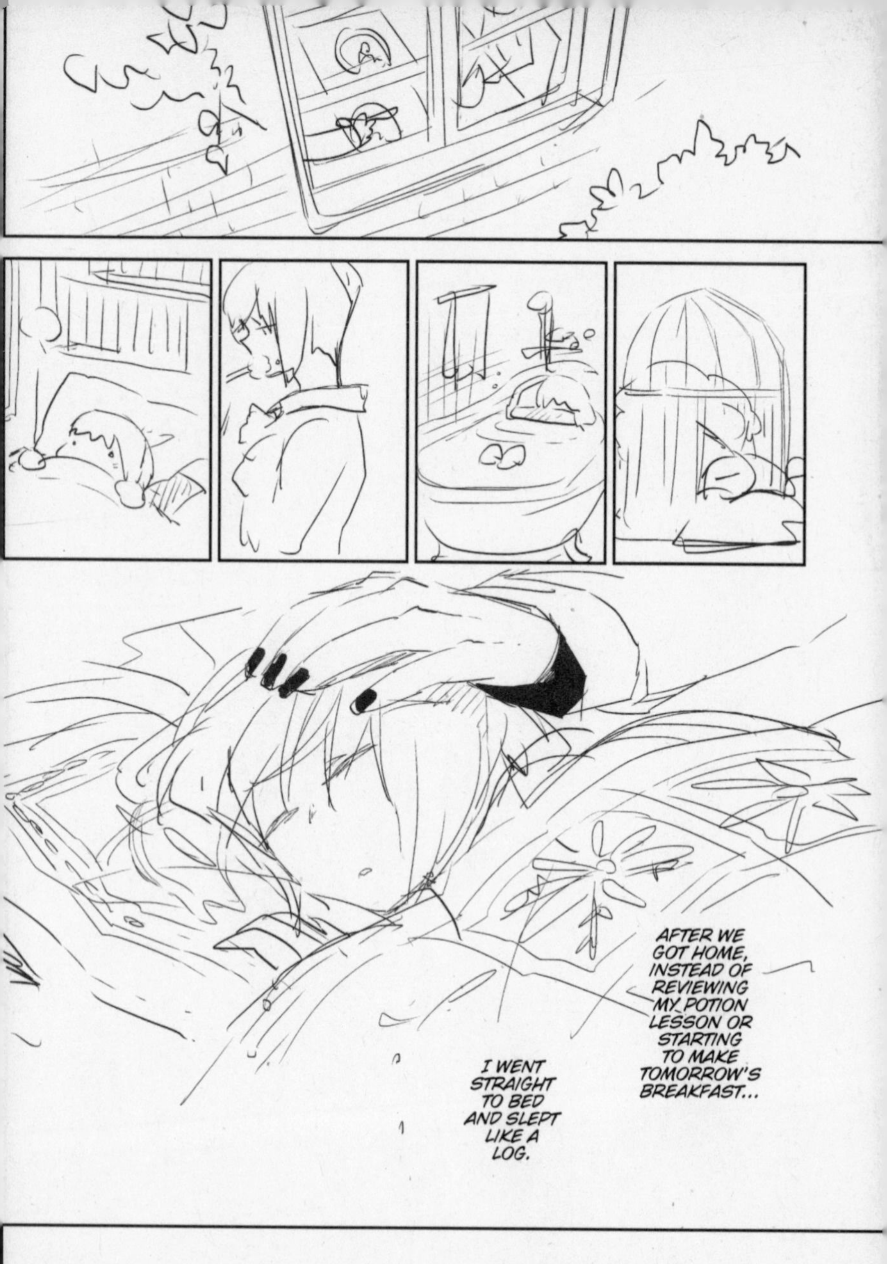
AFTER WE GOT HOME, INSTEAD OF REVIEWING MY POTION LESSON OR STARTING TO MAKE TOMORROW'S BREAKFAST...
I WENT STRAIGHT TO BED AND SLEPT LIKE A LOG.

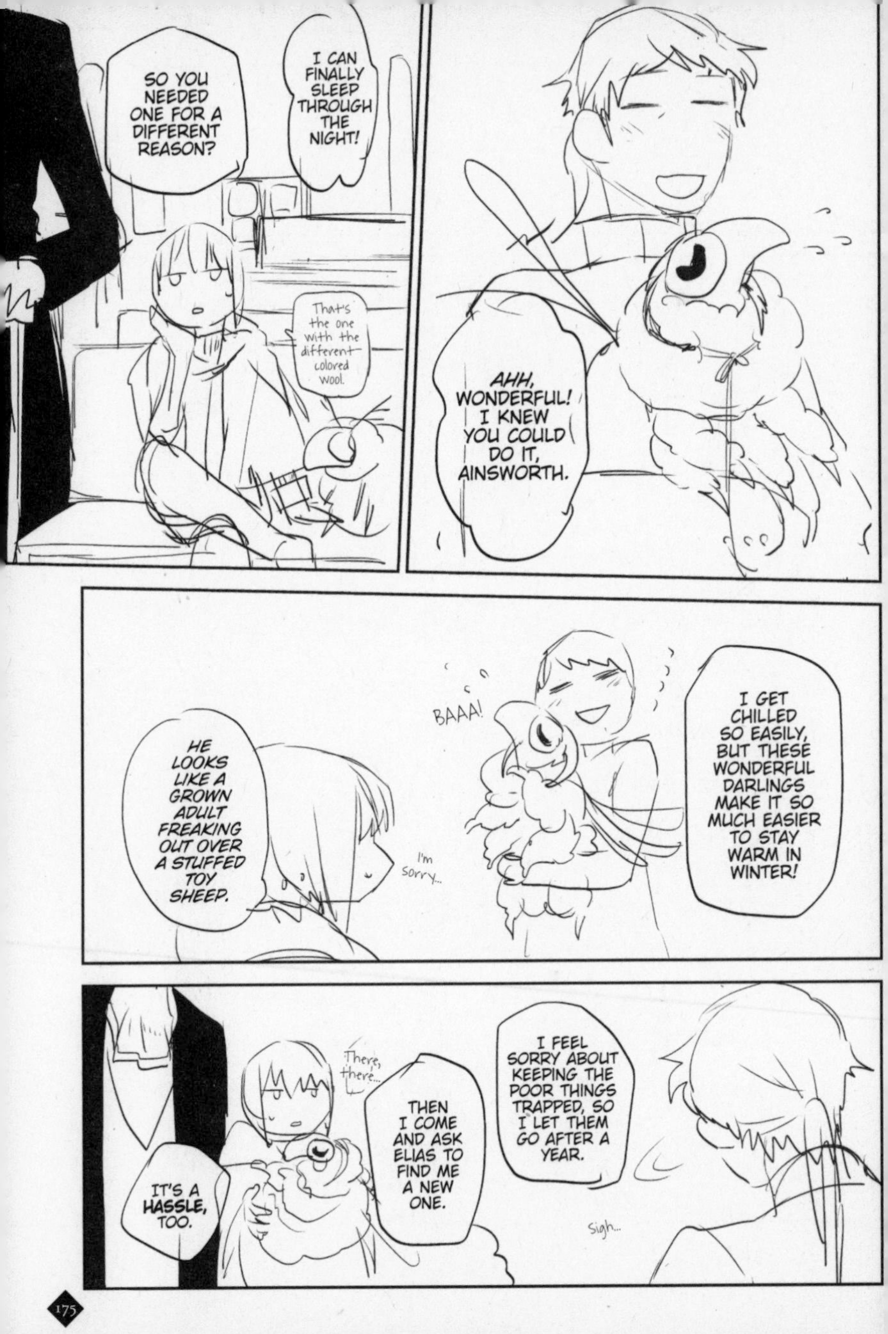
AHH, WONDERFUL! I KNEW YOU COULD DO IT, AINSWORTH.
I CAN FINALLY SLEEP THROUGH THE NIGHT!
SO YOU NEEDED ONE FOR A DIFFERENT REASON?
That's the one with the different colored wool.
I GET CHILLED SO EASILY, BUT THESE WONDERFUL DARLINGS MAKE IT SO MUCH EASIER TO STAY WARM IN WINTER!
BAAA!
I'm sorry...
HE LOOKS LIKE A GROWN ADULT FREAKING OUT OVER A STUFFED TOY SHEEP.
I FEEL SORRY ABOUT KEEPING THE POOR THINGS TRAPPED, SO I LET THEM GO AFTER A YEAR.
Sigh...
THEN I COME AND ASK ELIAS TO FIND ME A NEW ONE.
There, there...
IT'S A HASSLE, TOO.

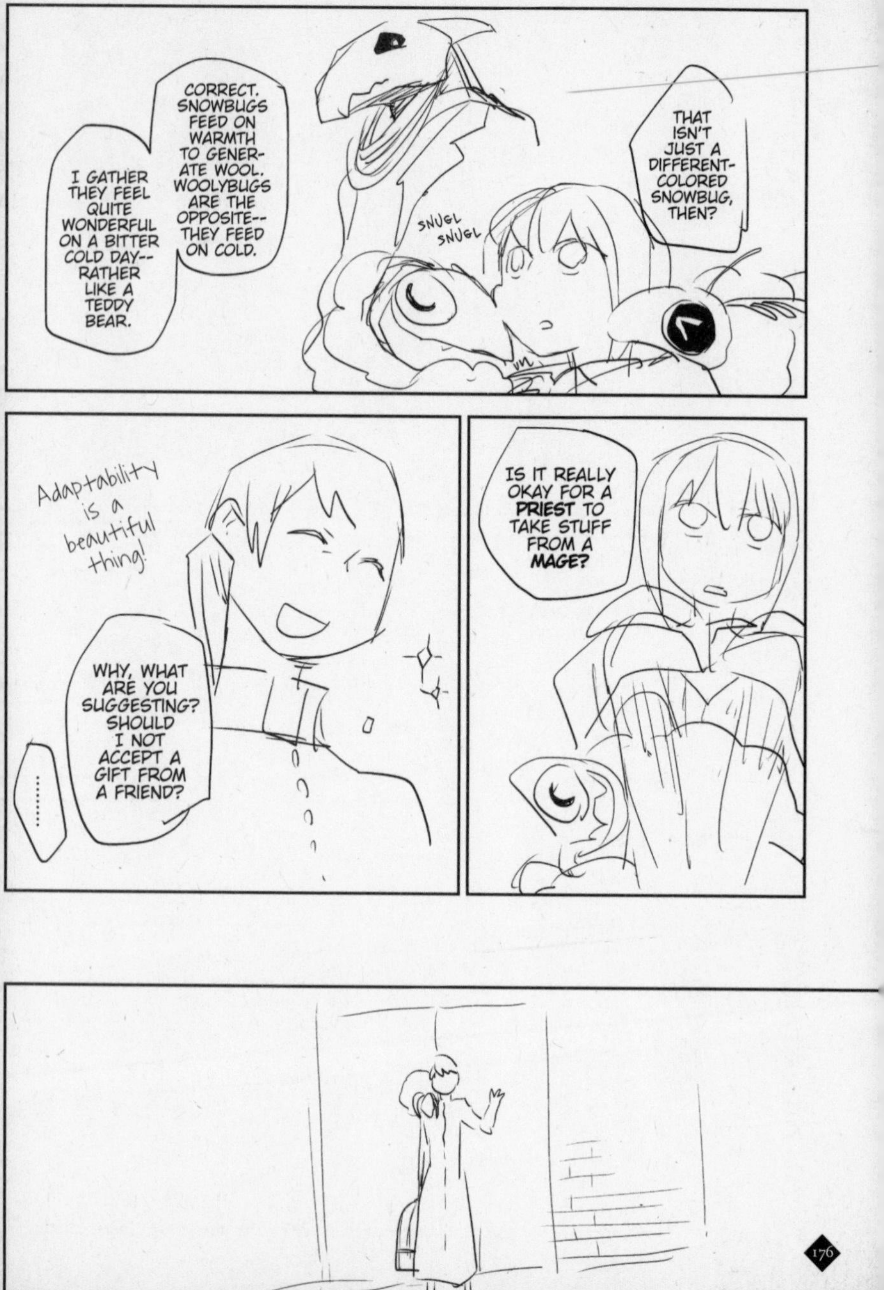
THAT ISN'T JUST A DIFFERENT-COLORED SNOWBUG, THEN?
CORRECT. SNOWBUGS FEED ON WARMTH TO GENERATE WOOL. WOOLYBUGS ARE THE OPPOSITE-- THEY FEED ON COLD.
I GATHER THEY FEEL QUITE WONDERFUL ON A BITTER COLD DAY-- RATHER LIKE A TEDDY BEAR.
SNUGL SNUGL
IS IT REALLY OKAY FOR A **PRIEST** TO TAKE STUFF FROM A **MAGE**?
Adaptability is a beautiful thing!
WHY, WHAT ARE YOU SUGGESTING? SHOULD I NOT ACCEPT A GIFT FROM A FRIEND?
......

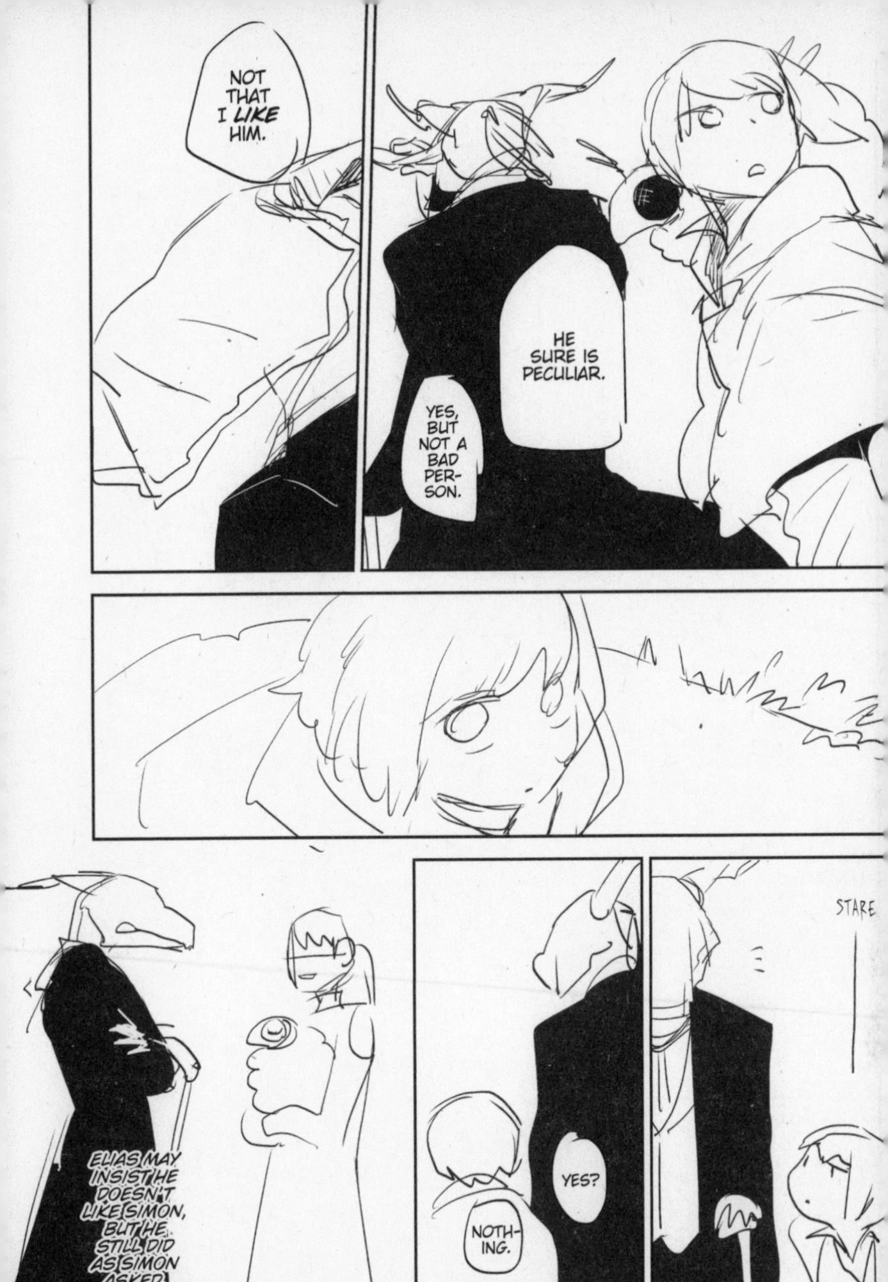
HE SURE IS PECULIAR.
YES, BUT NOT A BAD PER-SON.
NOT THAT I *LIKE* HIM.
STARE
YES?
NOTH-ING.
ELIAS MAY INSIST HE DOESN'T LIKE SIMON, BUT HE STILL DID AS SIMON ASKED.

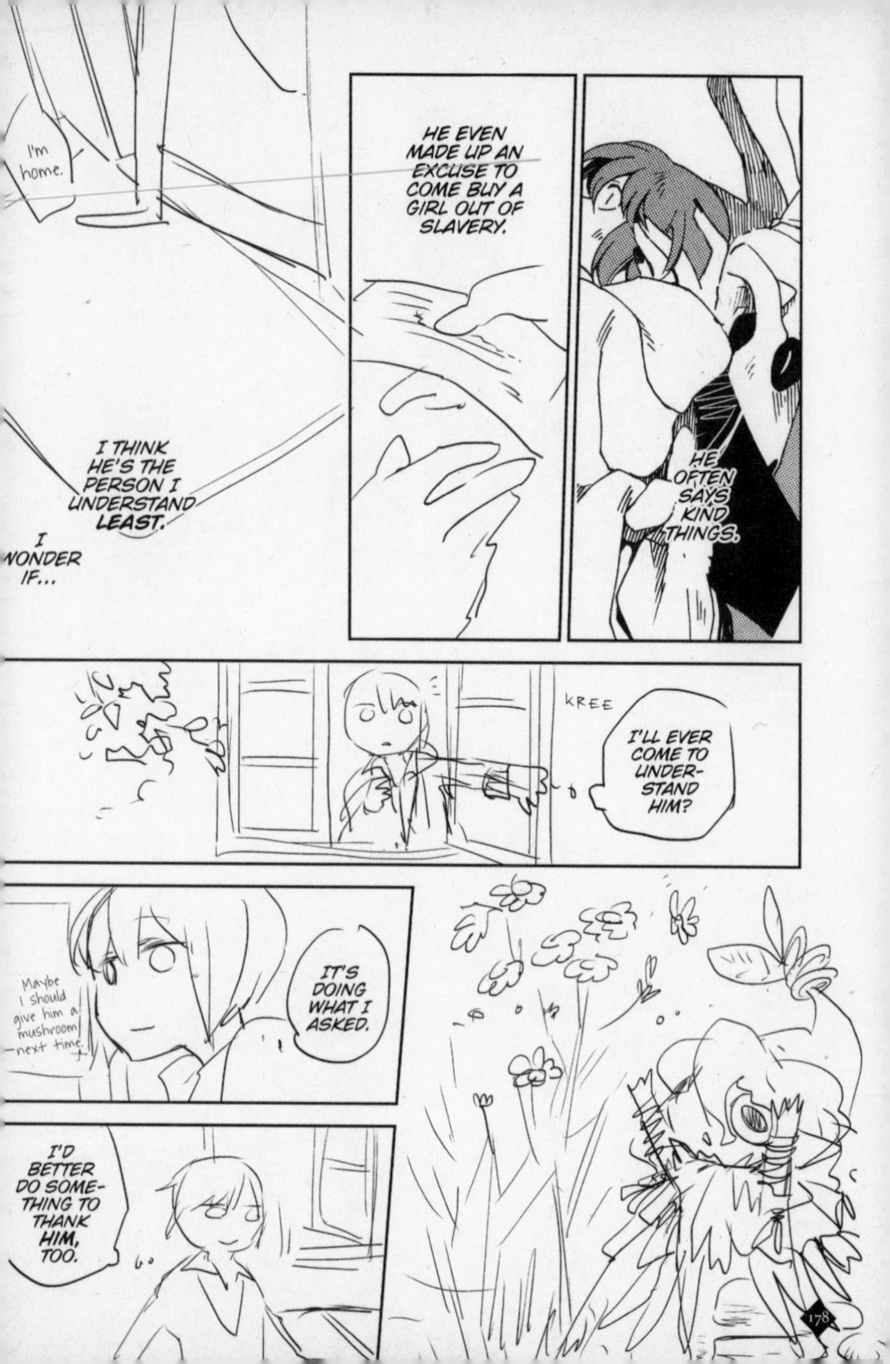
HE OFTEN SAYS KIND THINGS.
HE EVEN MADE UP AN EXCUSE TO COME BUY A GIRL OUT OF SLAVERY.
I'm home.
I THINK HE'S THE PERSON I UNDERSTAND LEAST.
I WONDER IF...
KREE
I'LL EVER COME TO UNDER-STAND HIM?
IT'S DOING WHAT I ASKED.
Maybe I should give him a mushroom next time.
I'D BETTER DO SOME-THING TO THANK HIM, TOO.

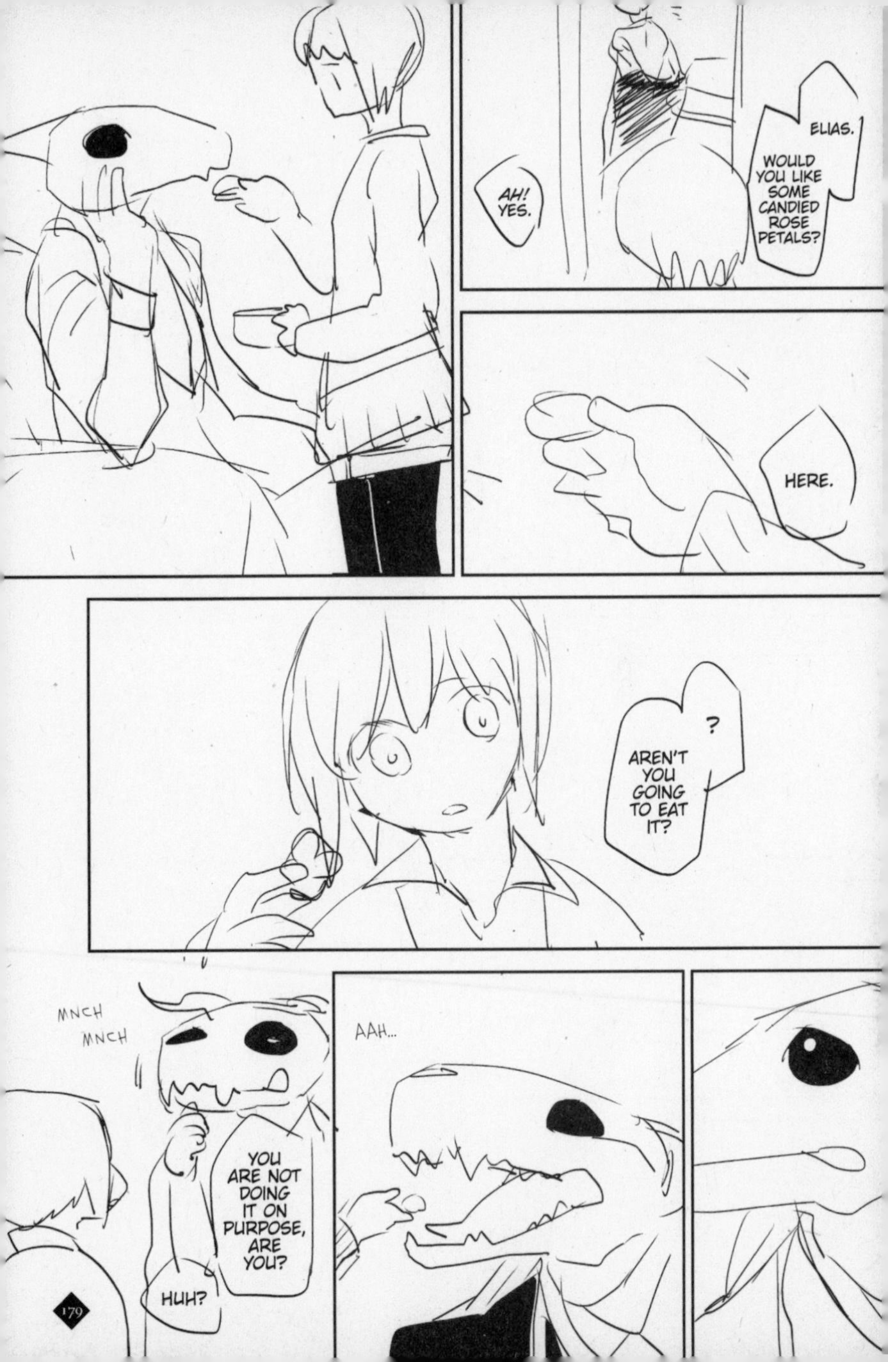
ELIAS.
WOULD YOU LIKE SOME CANDIED ROSE PETALS?
AH! YES.
HERE.
?
AREN'T YOU GOING TO EAT IT?
AAH...
MNCH MNCH
YOU ARE NOT DOING IT ON PURPOSE, ARE YOU?
HUH?

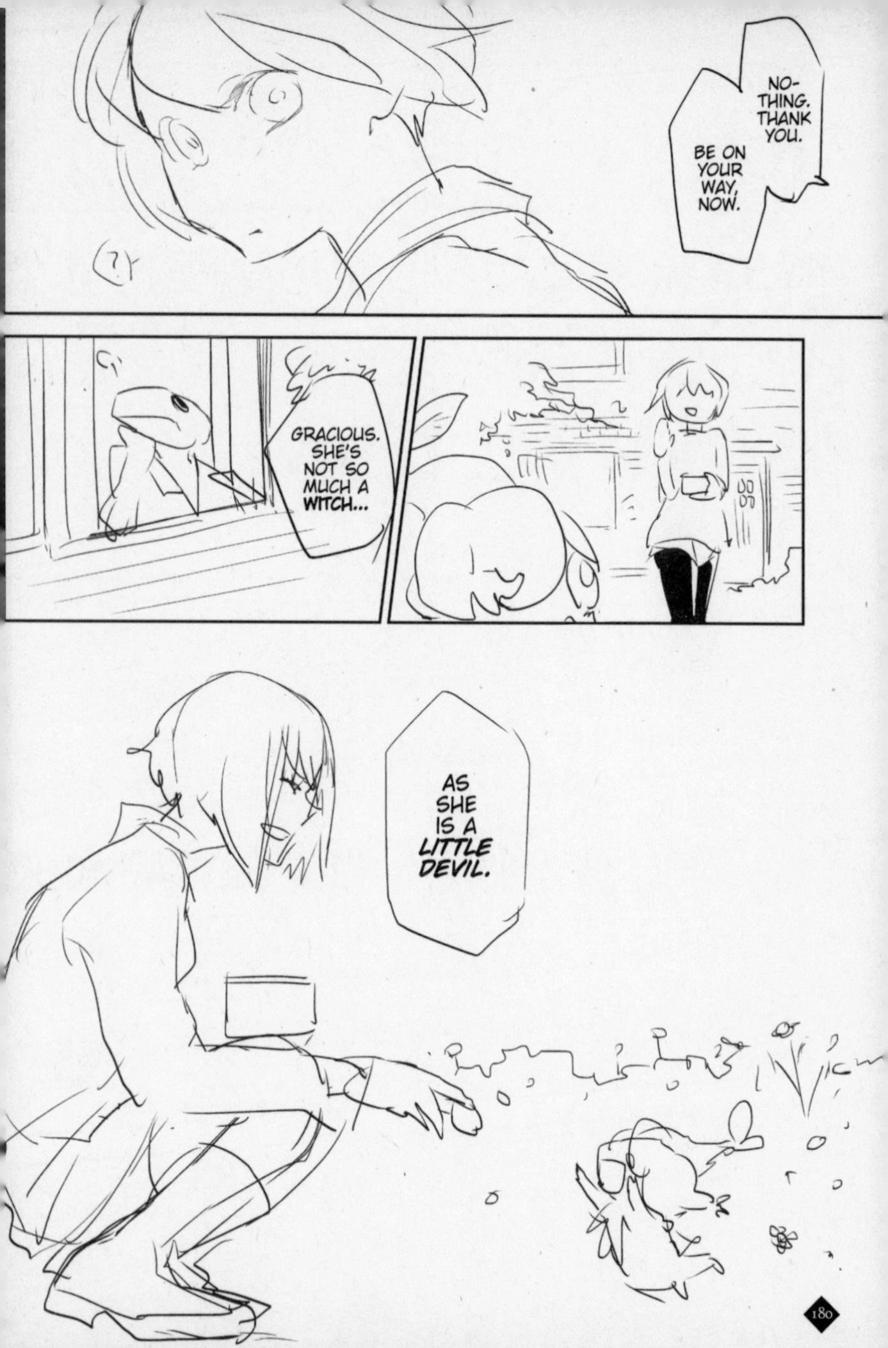
NO-THING. THANK YOU.
BE ON YOUR WAY, NOW.
?
GRACIOUS. SHE'S NOT SO MUCH A WITCH...
AS SHE IS A *LITTLE DEVIL.*

Illustration Gallery

魔法使いの嫁
1巻
喜久屋書店さまにて
お買い上げ
ありがとうございます!!

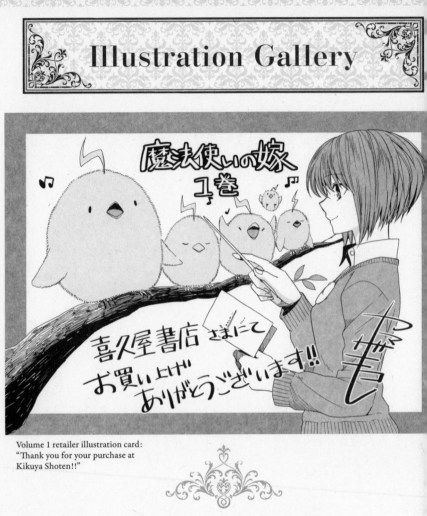

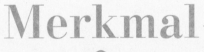

Volume 1 retailer illustration card:
"Thank you for your purchase at Kikuya Shoten!!"

Merkmal

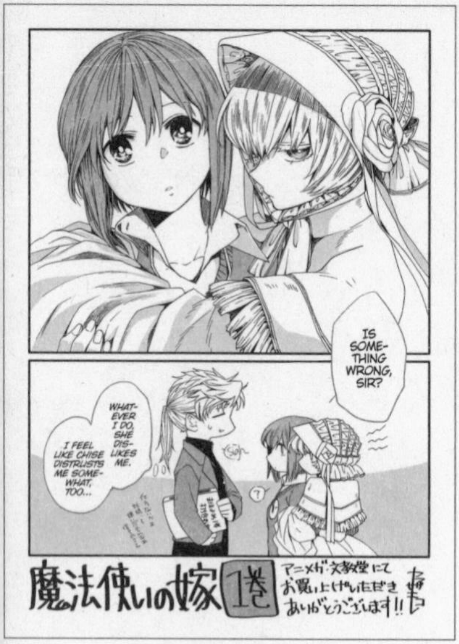
IS SOMETHING WRONG, SIR?
WHATEVER I DO, SHE DISLIKES ME.
I FEEL LIKE CHISE DISTRUSTS ME SOMEWHAT, TOO...
魔法使いの嫁 1巻
アニメガ・文教堂にて
お買い上げいただき
ありがとうございます!!

Volume 1 retailer illustration card: "Thank you for your purchase at Animega/Bunkyodo!!"

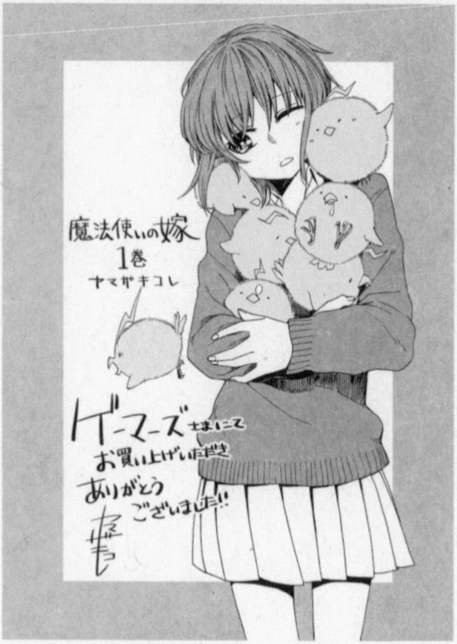
魔法使いの嫁
1巻
ヤマザキコレ
ゲーマーズ様にて
お買い上げいただき
ありがとう
ございました!!

Volume 1 retailer illustration card: "Thank you for your purchase at Gamers!"

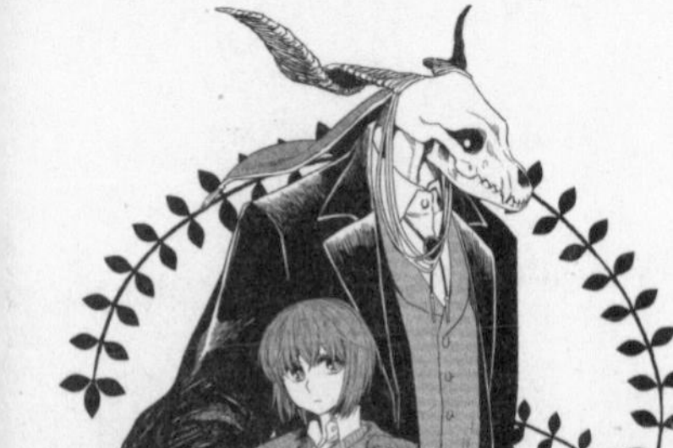

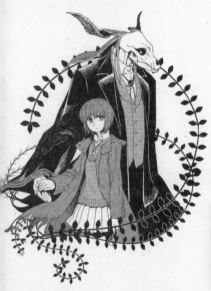

Illustration card for purchasers of *The Ancient Magus' Bride* Vol. 1 to celebrate 100,000 copies sold.

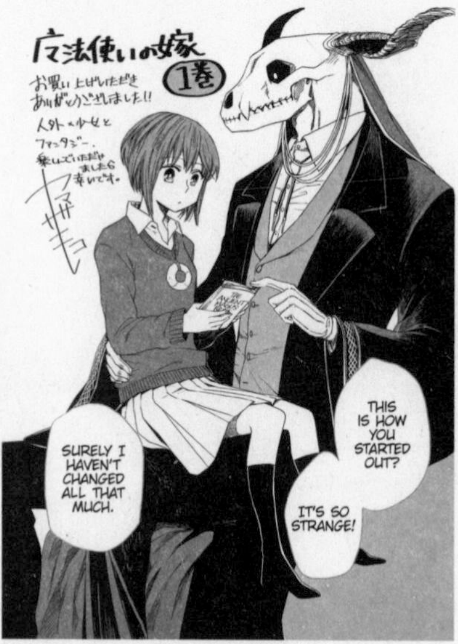
魔法使いの嫁
1巻
お買い上げいただき
ありがとうございました!!
人外と少女と
ファンタジー。
楽しんでいただけましたら
幸いです。
THIS IS HOW YOU STARTED OUT?
IT'S SO STRANGE!
SURELY I HAVEN'T CHANGED ALL THAT MUCH.

Volume 1 retailer illustration card: "Thank you for your purchase!! I hope you enjoy this human-inhuman fantasy."

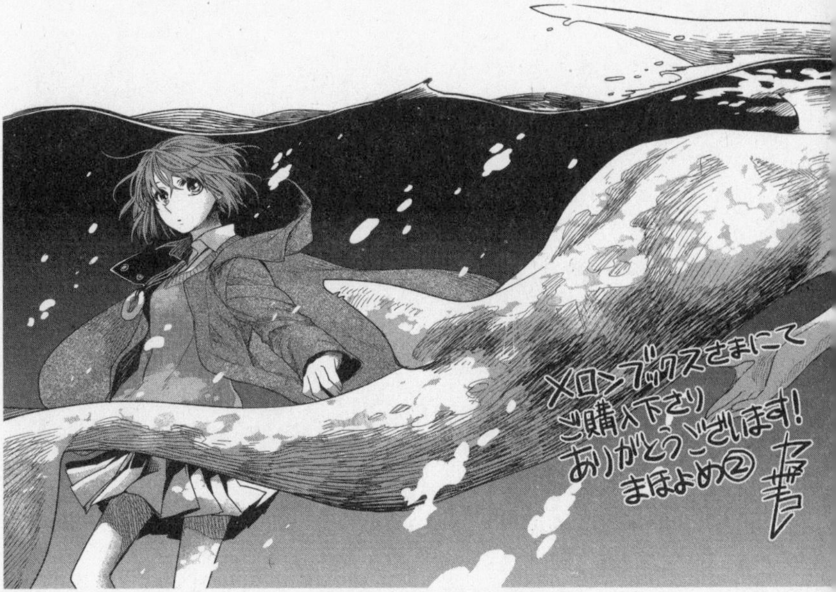
メロンブックスさまにて
ご購入下さり
ありがとうございます!
まほよめ②

Volume 2 retailer illustration card:
"Thank you for your purchase at Melonbooks!"

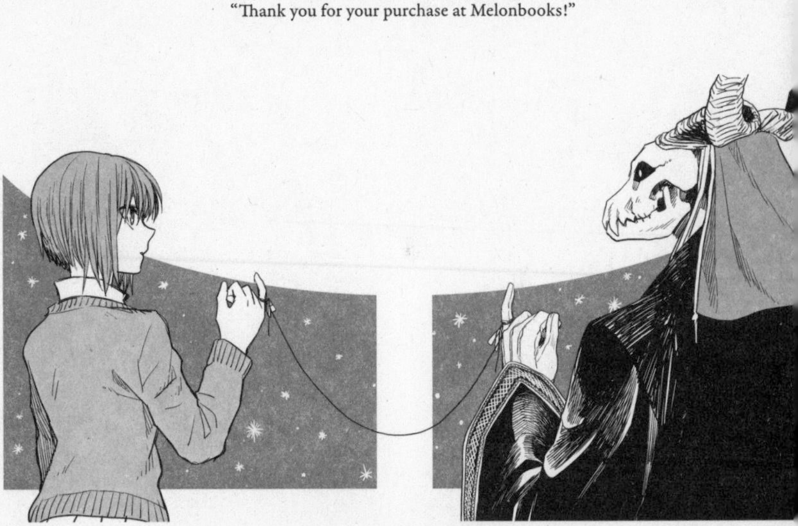

Coaster set for purchasers of
The Ancient Magus' Bride Vol. 2.

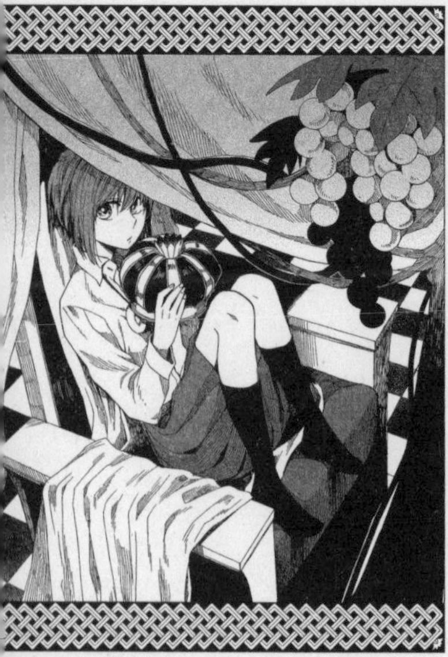

Clear file for purchasers of *The Ancient Magus' Bride* Vol. 2 at Toranoana.

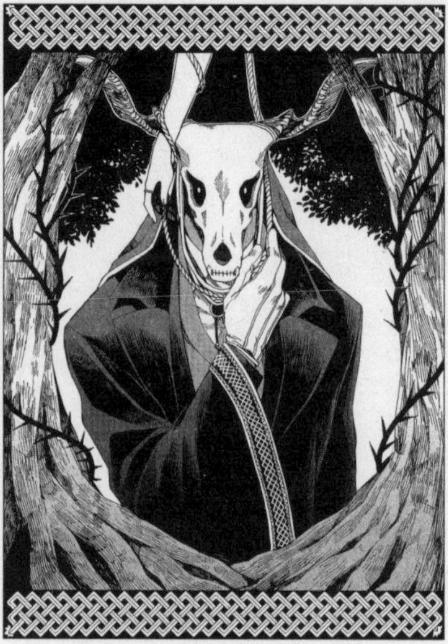

Clear file for purchasers of *The Ancient Magus' Bride* Vol. 2 at Toranoana.

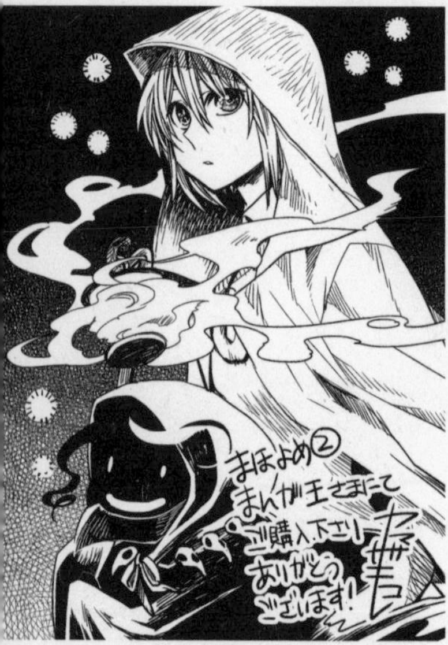
まほよめ②
まんが王さまにて
ご購入下さり
ありがとう
ございます!

Volume 2 retailer illustration card: "Thank you for purchasing *Magus' Bride* 2 at Mangaoh!"

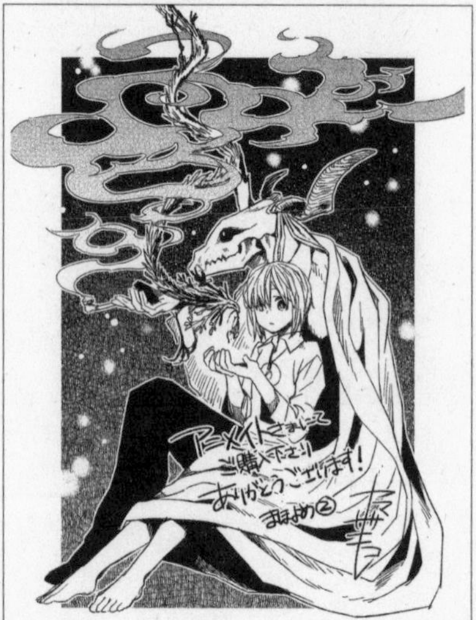
アニメイトさまにて
ご購入下さり
ありがとうございます!
まほよめ②

Volume 2 retailer illustration card: "Thank you for your purchase at Animate!"

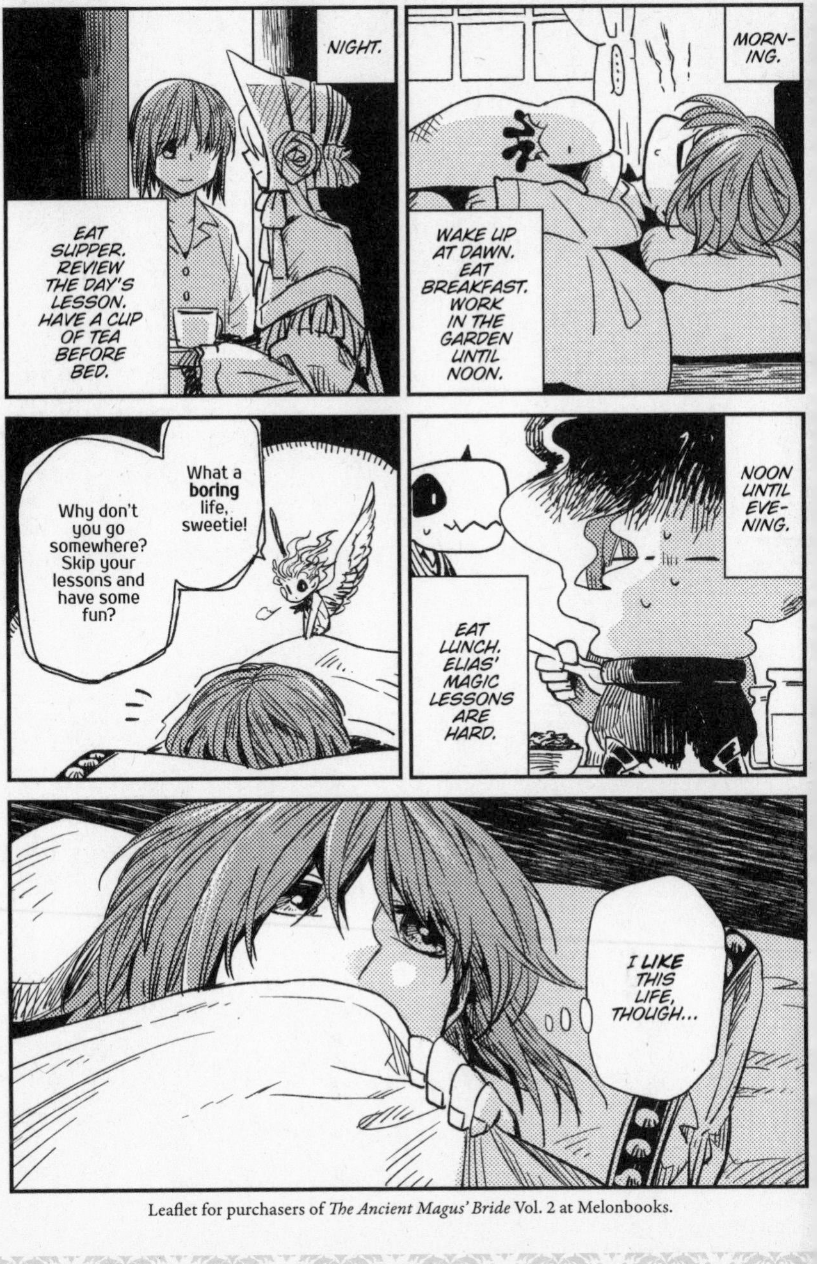
MORNING.
WAKE UP AT DAWN. EAT BREAKFAST. WORK IN THE GARDEN UNTIL NOON.
NIGHT.
EAT SUPPER. REVIEW THE DAY'S LESSON. HAVE A CUP OF TEA BEFORE BED.
NOON UNTIL EVENING.
EAT LUNCH. ELIAS' MAGIC LESSONS ARE HARD.
What a boring life, sweetie!
Why don't you go somewhere? Skip your lessons and have some fun?
I LIKE THIS LIFE, THOUGH...

Leaflet for purchasers of *The Ancient Magus' Bride* Vol. 2 at Melonbooks.

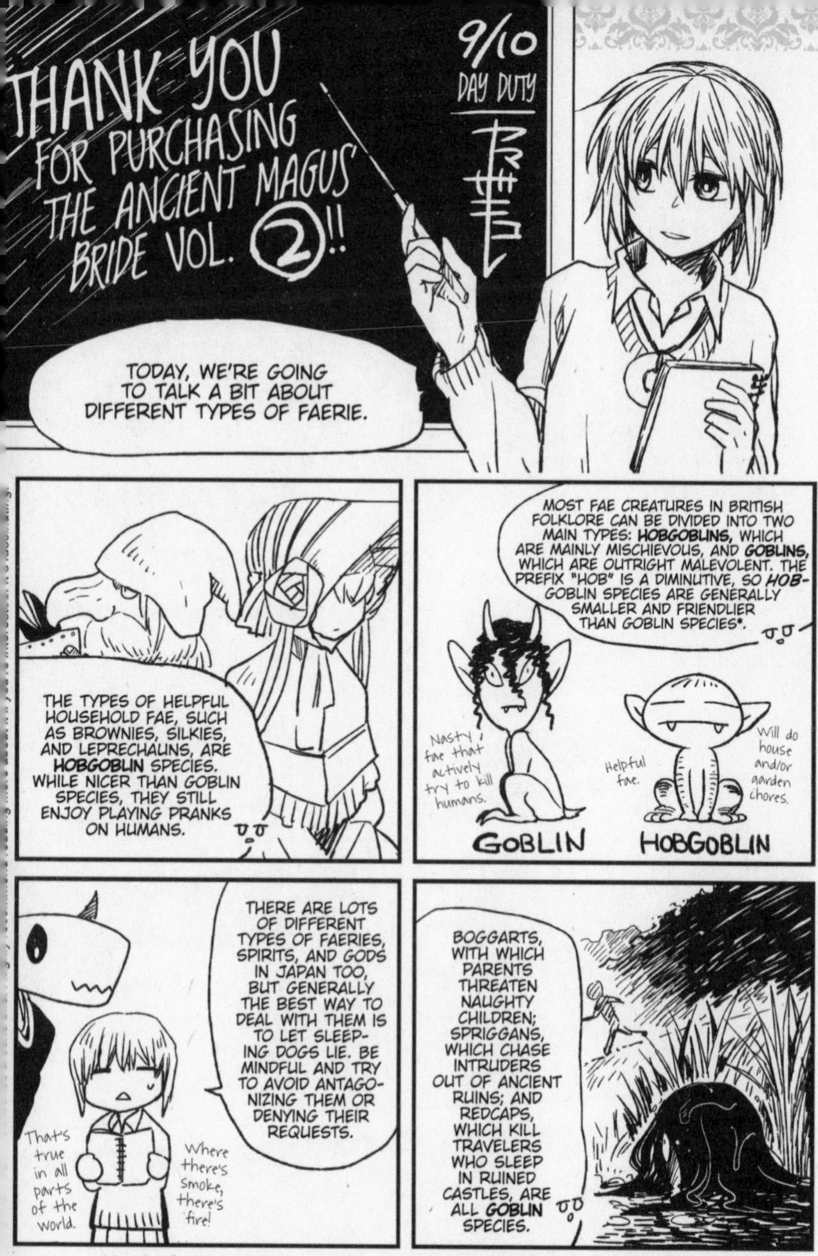
9/10
DAY DUTY
THANK YOU FOR PURCHASING THE ANCIENT MAGUS' BRIDE VOL. 2!!
TODAY, WE'RE GOING TO TALK A BIT ABOUT DIFFERENT TYPES OF FAERIE.
MOST FAE CREATURES IN BRITISH FOLKLORE CAN BE DIVIDED INTO TWO MAIN TYPES: HOBGOBLINS, WHICH ARE MAINLY MISCHIEVOUS, AND GOBLINS, WHICH ARE OUTRIGHT MALEVOLENT. THE PREFIX "HOB" IS A DIMINUTIVE, SO HOBGOBLIN SPECIES ARE GENERALLY SMALLER AND FRIENDLIER THAN GOBLIN SPECIES*.
Will do house and/or garden chores.
Helpful fae.
HOBGOBLIN
Nasty fae that actively try to kill humans.
GOBLIN
THE TYPES OF HELPFUL HOUSEHOLD FAE, SUCH AS BROWNIES, SILKIES, AND LEPRECHAUNS, ARE HOBGOBLIN SPECIES. WHILE NICER THAN GOBLIN SPECIES, THEY STILL ENJOY PLAYING PRANKS ON HUMANS.
BOGGARTS, WITH WHICH PARENTS THREATEN NAUGHTY CHILDREN; SPRIGGANS, WHICH CHASE INTRUDERS OUT OF ANCIENT RUINS; AND REDCAPS, WHICH KILL TRAVELERS WHO SLEEP IN RUINED CASTLES, ARE ALL GOBLIN SPECIES.
THERE ARE LOTS OF DIFFERENT TYPES OF FAERIES, SPIRITS, AND GODS IN JAPAN TOO, BUT GENERALLY THE BEST WAY TO DEAL WITH THEM IS TO LET SLEEPING DOGS LIE. BE MINDFUL AND TRY TO AVOID ANTAGONIZING THEM OR DENYING THEIR REQUESTS.
Where there's smoke, there's fire!
That's true in all parts of the world.

Mag Garden Special Designated Shop Bonus Strip for *The Ancient Magus' Bride*, Vol. 2.

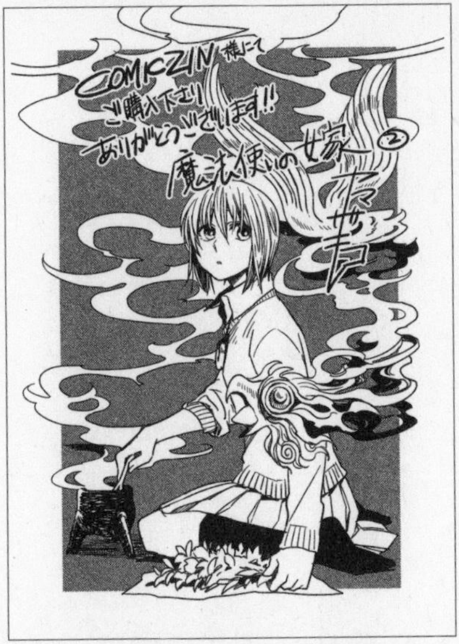
COMIC ZIN様にて
ご購入下さり
ありがとうございます!!
魔法使いの嫁②
Volume 2 retailer illustration card: “Thank you for your purchase at Comic Zin!!”

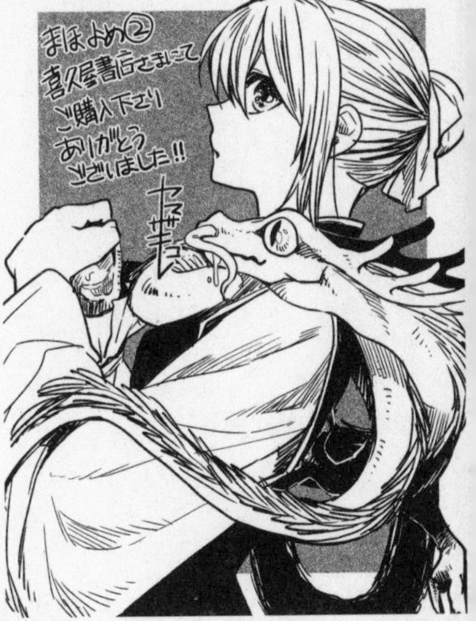
まほよめ②
喜久屋書店さまにて
ご購入下さり
ありがとう
ございました!!
Volume 2 retailer illustration card: “Thank you for your purchasing *Magus’ Bride* 2 at Kikuya Shoten!!”

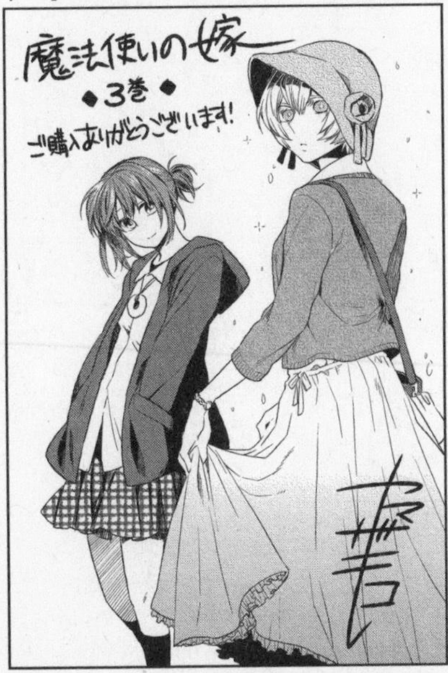
魔法使いの嫁
◆3巻◆
ご購入ありがとうございます!
Volume 3 illustration card: “Thank you for your purchase!”

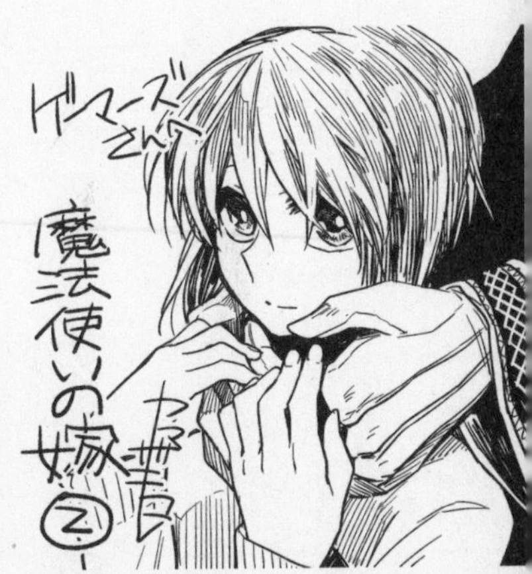
ゲーマーズさんへ
魔法使いの嫁
②
Mini-shikishi for purchasers of *The Ancient Magus’ Bride* Vol. 2 at Gamers. “For Gamers.”

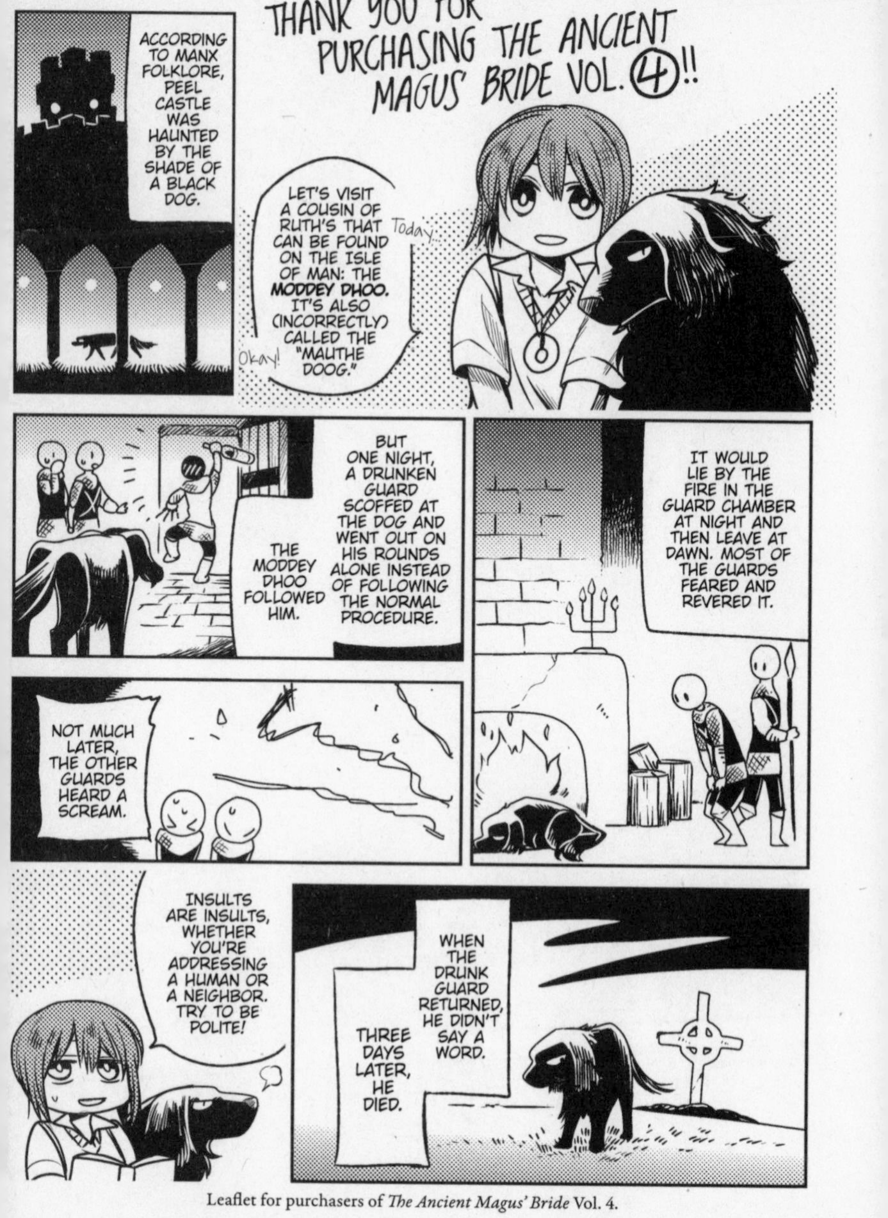
THANK YOU FOR PURCHASING THE ANCIENT MAGUS' BRIDE VOL. ④!!
LET'S VISIT A COUSIN OF RUTH'S THAT CAN BE FOUND ON THE ISLE OF MAN: THE **MODDEY DHOO.** IT'S ALSO (INCORRECTLY) CALLED THE "MAUTHE DOOG."
Today...
Okay!
ACCORDING TO MANX FOLKLORE, PEEL CASTLE WAS HAUNTED BY THE SHADE OF A BLACK DOG.
IT WOULD LIE BY THE FIRE IN THE GUARD CHAMBER AT NIGHT AND THEN LEAVE AT DAWN. MOST OF THE GUARDS FEARED AND REVERED IT.
BUT ONE NIGHT, A DRUNKEN GUARD SCOFFED AT THE DOG AND WENT OUT ON HIS ROUNDS ALONE INSTEAD OF FOLLOWING THE NORMAL PROCEDURE.
THE MODDEY DHOO FOLLOWED HIM.
NOT MUCH LATER, THE OTHER GUARDS HEARD A SCREAM.
WHEN THE DRUNK GUARD RETURNED, HE DIDN'T SAY A WORD.
THREE DAYS LATER, HE DIED.
INSULTS ARE INSULTS, WHETHER YOU'RE ADDRESSING A HUMAN OR A NEIGHBOR. TRY TO BE POLITE!

Leaflet for purchasers of *The Ancient Magus' Bride* Vol. 4.

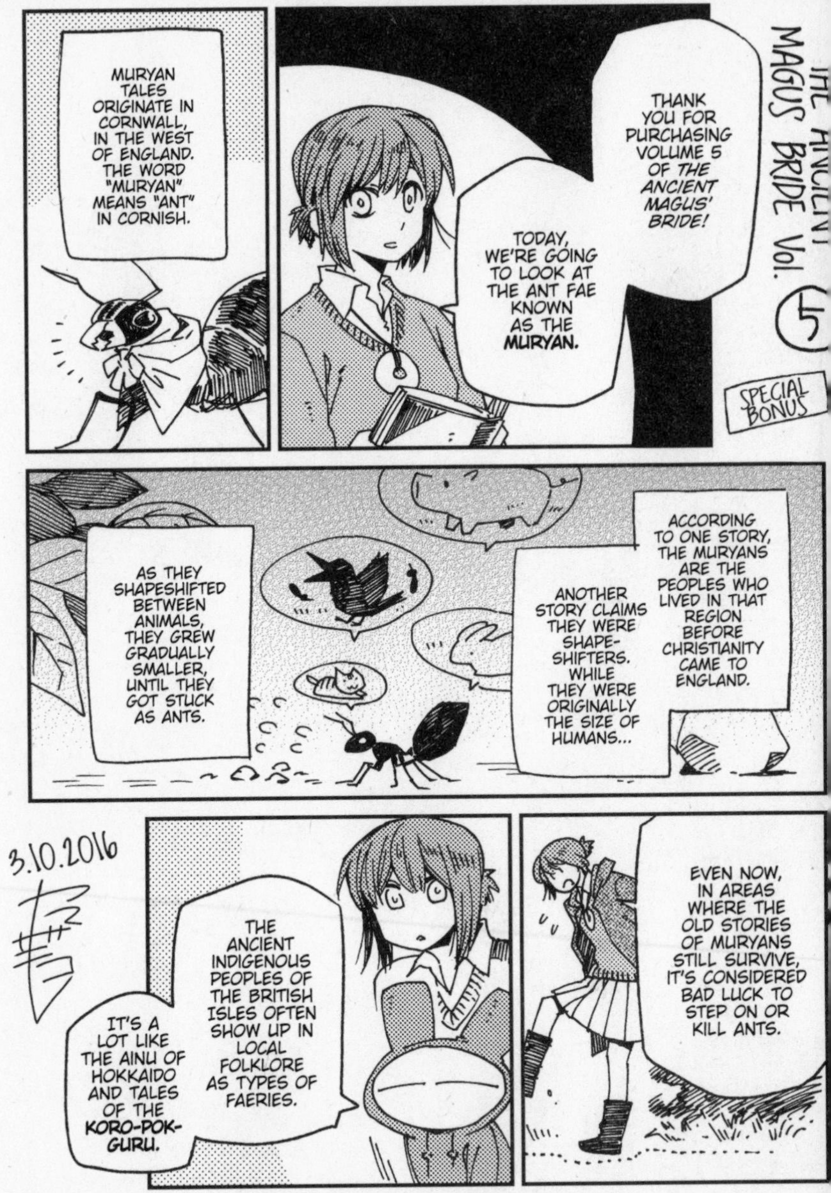
THE ANCIENT MAGUS BRIDE Vol. 5
SPECIAL BONUS
THANK YOU FOR PURCHASING VOLUME 5 OF THE ANCIENT MAGUS' BRIDE!
TODAY, WE'RE GOING TO LOOK AT THE ANT FAE KNOWN AS THE MURYAN.
MURYAN TALES ORIGINATE IN CORNWALL, IN THE WEST OF ENGLAND. THE WORD "MURYAN" MEANS "ANT" IN CORNISH.
ACCORDING TO ONE STORY, THE MURYANS ARE THE PEOPLES WHO LIVED IN THAT REGION BEFORE CHRISTIANITY CAME TO ENGLAND.
ANOTHER STORY CLAIMS THEY WERE SHAPE-SHIFTERS. WHILE THEY WERE ORIGINALLY THE SIZE OF HUMANS...
AS THEY SHAPESHIFTED BETWEEN ANIMALS, THEY GREW GRADUALLY SMALLER, UNTIL THEY GOT STUCK AS ANTS.
EVEN NOW, IN AREAS WHERE THE OLD STORIES OF MURYANS STILL SURVIVE, IT'S CONSIDERED BAD LUCK TO STEP ON OR KILL ANTS.
THE ANCIENT INDIGENOUS PEOPLES OF THE BRITISH ISLES OFTEN SHOW UP IN LOCAL FOLKLORE AS TYPES OF FAERIES.
IT'S A LOT LIKE THE AINU OF HOKKAIDO AND TALES OF THE KORO-POK-GURU.
3.10.2016

Leaflet for purchasers of *The Ancient Magus' Bride* Vol. 5.

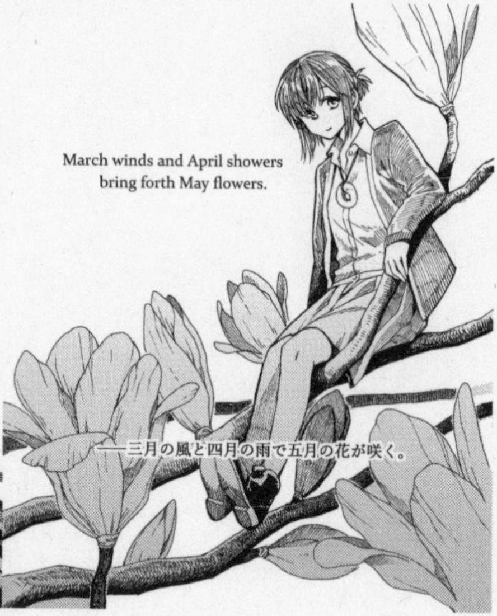
March winds and April showers
bring forth May flowers.
——三月の風と四月の雨で五月の花が咲く。

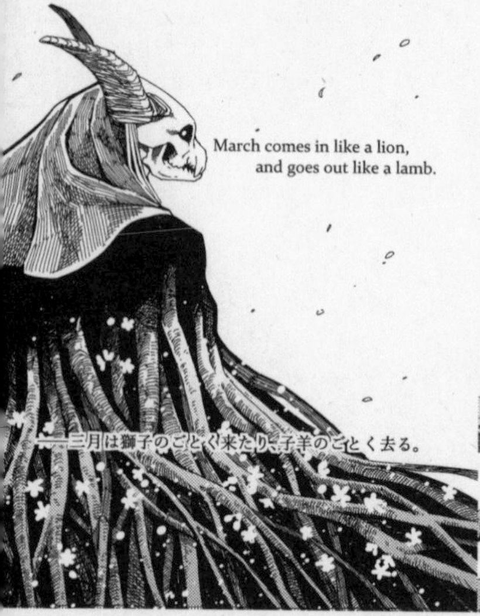
March comes in like a lion,
and goes out like a lamb.
——三月は獅子のごとく来たり、子羊のごとく去る。

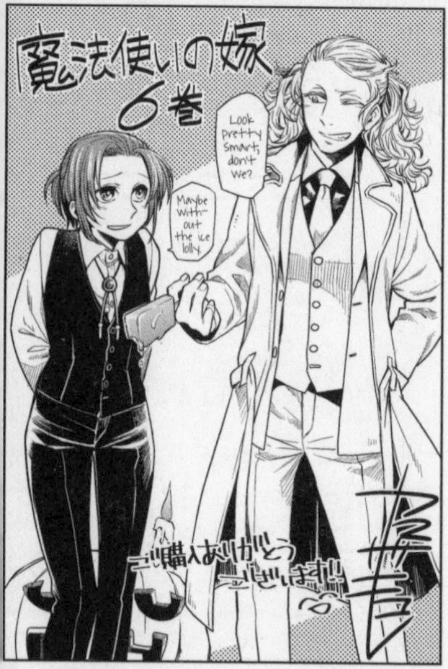
魔法使いの嫁
6巻
Look pretty smart, don't we?
Maybe with-out the ice lolly.
ご購入ありがとうございます!!

Merkmal

UPPER RIGHT
Folded card for purchasers of *The Ancient Magus' Bride* Vol. 5

UPPER LEFT
Folded card for purchasers of *The Ancient Magus' Bride* Vol. 5.

LOWER LEFT
Volume 6 illustration card: "Thank you for your purchase!!"

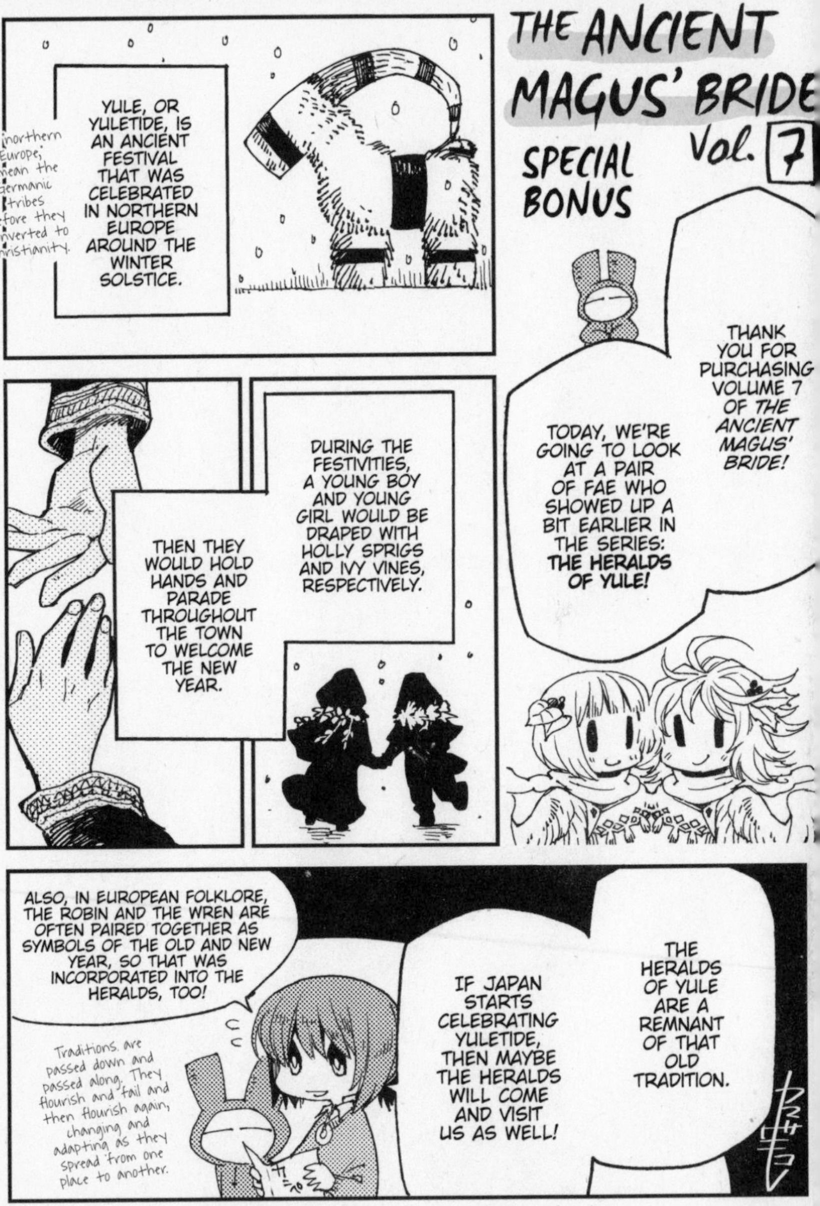
THE ANCIENT MAGUS' BRIDE Vol. 7
SPECIAL BONUS
THANK YOU FOR PURCHASING VOLUME 7 OF *THE ANCIENT MAGUS' BRIDE*!
TODAY, WE'RE GOING TO LOOK AT A PAIR OF FAE WHO SHOWED UP A BIT EARLIER IN THE SERIES: **THE HERALDS OF YULE!**
YULE, OR YULETIDE, IS AN ANCIENT FESTIVAL THAT WAS CELEBRATED IN NORTHERN EUROPE AROUND THE WINTER SOLSTICE.
By northern Europe, I mean the Germanic tribes before they converted to Christianity.
DURING THE FESTIVITIES, A YOUNG BOY AND YOUNG GIRL WOULD BE DRAPED WITH HOLLY SPRIGS AND IVY VINES, RESPECTIVELY.
THEN THEY WOULD HOLD HANDS AND PARADE THROUGHOUT THE TOWN TO WELCOME THE NEW YEAR.
THE HERALDS OF YULE ARE A REMNANT OF THAT OLD TRADITION.
IF JAPAN STARTS CELEBRATING YULETIDE, THEN MAYBE THE HERALDS WILL COME AND VISIT US AS WELL!
ALSO, IN EUROPEAN FOLKLORE, THE ROBIN AND THE WREN ARE OFTEN PAIRED TOGETHER AS SYMBOLS OF THE OLD AND NEW YEAR, SO THAT WAS INCORPORATED INTO THE HERALDS, TOO!
Traditions are passed down and passed along. They flourish and fail and then flourish again, changing and adapting as they spread from one place to another.

Leaflet for purchasers of *The Ancient Magus' Bride* Vol. 7.

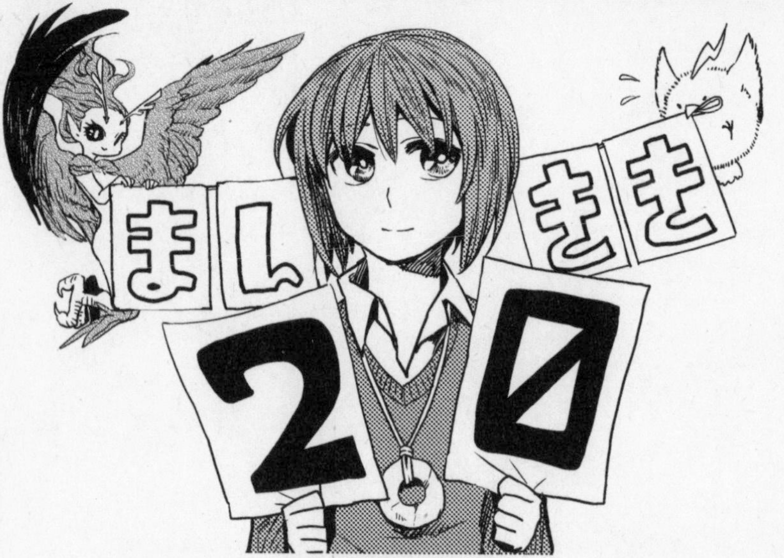
まんきき
20

Cover illustration for *Mankiki* Vol. 20.

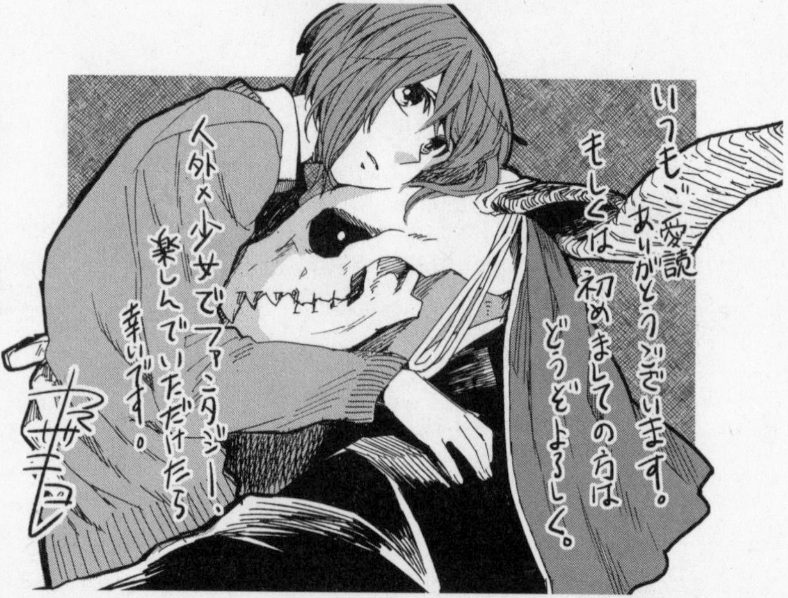
いつもご愛読ありがとうございます。
もしくは初めましての方はどうぞよろしく。
人外×少女でファンタジー。
楽しんでいただけたら幸いです。

Supporting art for the *Comic Garden Introduction Book*. "Thank you for reading faithfully! Or if you're just starting, pleased to meet you! I hope you enjoy this human-inhuman fantasy."

Clear bookmark illustration of Elias for the Mag Garden Comics Fair.

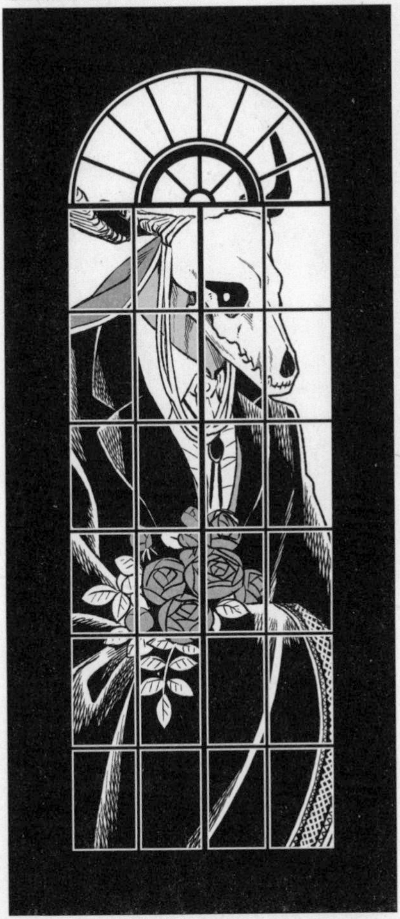

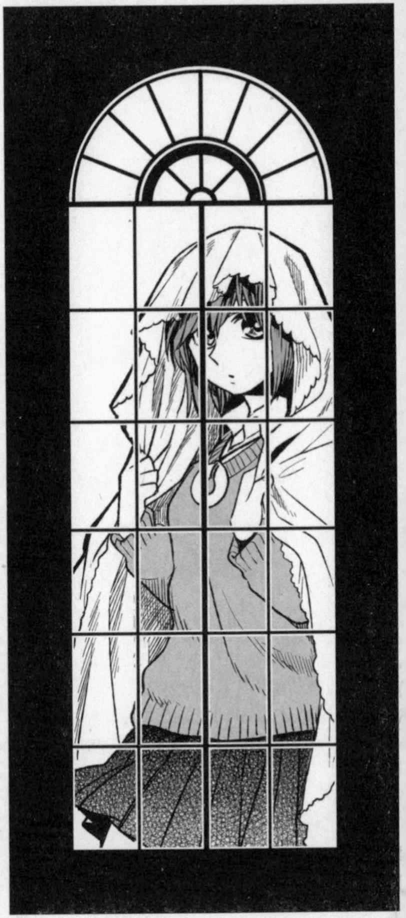

Clear bookmark illustration of Chise for the Mag Garden Comics Fair.

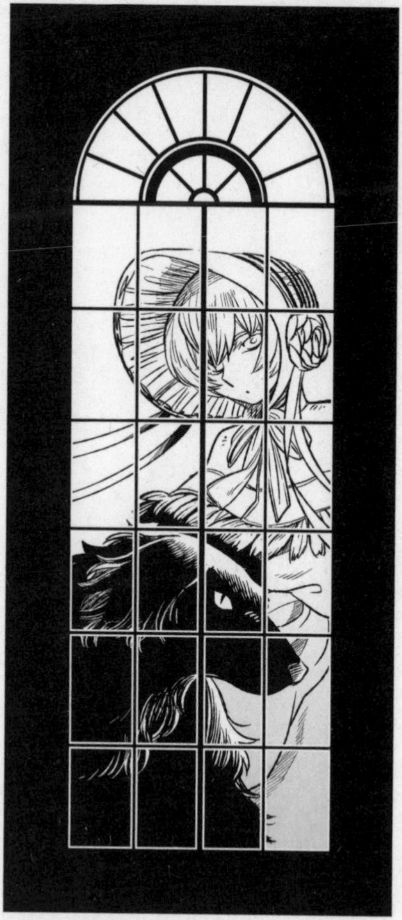

Clear bookmark illustration of Ruth & Silky for the Mag Garden Comics Fair.

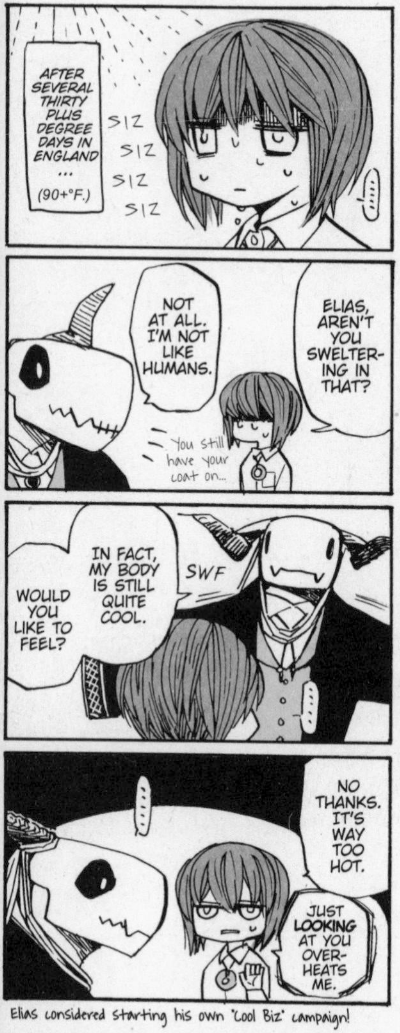
!......
SIZ SIZ SIZ SIZ
AFTER SEVERAL THIRTY PLUS DEGREE DAYS IN ENGLAND ... (90+°F.)
ELIAS, AREN'T YOU SWELTER-ING IN THAT?
NOT AT ALL. I'M NOT LIKE HUMANS.
You still have your coat on...
......
SWF
IN FACT, MY BODY IS STILL QUITE COOL.
WOULD YOU LIKE TO FEEL?
NO THANKS. IT'S WAY TOO HOT.
JUST **LOOKING** AT YOU OVER-HEATS ME.
!......
Elias considered starting his own "Cool Biz" campaign!

4-koma bookmark strip for the collaborative fair FANTASTIC3.

6

Interviews

This chapter includes reprinted interviews with Kore Yamazaki-sensei and also a new interview that offers insight into Yamazaki-sensei's personal life!

Reprinted Interviews

This is a collection of excerpts from previously published interviews with Kore Yamazaki-sensei. If you missed out on reading them in the magazines in which they originally appeared, you won't want to miss this section!

How *The Ancient Magus' Bride* Came to Be

■ **To begin, can you tell us how *The Ancient Magus' Bride* originally came to be? We've heard that it originated as a doujinshi you released at COMITIA, but how did that originate? And what changes did you later make for the serialized version of the story?**

When I was storyboarding my original idea, I kept thinking, "There's no way I can finish this on time, and it's not even that interesting." Thoughts like that made me freeze up, but the deadline was still looming. That original version of *The Ancient Magus' Bride* came from an idea that popped into my head, and it was realized in about half a day. The main characters' personalities changed a lot for the serialized version.

■ **A distinct element of *The Ancient Magus' Bride* is that magic doesn't come from nowhere; rather, it's something miraculous that's made possible by borrowing power from inhuman beings. What made you choose that sort of magical system for the story?**

I was thinking that everything had to have both causes and constraints. Animals require energy in order to act and think, so magic should also require some sort of power source. But the idea of simply treating it the same way— swapping in something like mana instead of caloric intake—seemed silly. As I imagine it, it's essentially that humans come up with the plans for something and faeries or spirits follow their lead to create the final product. It's inefficient but powerful. The way I see it, everything should have benefits and drawbacks, and it takes contributions from all kinds of people to create a single thing. That's how I think of it, anyway, so that's why I went that route.

—*Kikan S*, January 2017

■ **What inspired the concept of *The Ancient Magus' Bride*?**

I was racking my brains trying to come up with an idea to develop for COMITIA [a convention focused on original doujinshi]. A scenario and dialogue just popped into my head, and there were the two main characters. I'm not sure you'd call that an "inspiration." But those characters were slightly different in design from Elias and Chise as we know them now, and their relationship was the other way around.

■ What led to its commercial debut?

The manga was posted on an online art community, where it happened to catch the eye of the editor.

—*Katsukura*, vol. 13

■ What led to the serialization?

It was based on a doujinshi I published at a convention in February last year. I've always loved fantasy, and I was able to channel my desire to draw it into this series. The editor came across that original version, and the story began to be serialized last November. Chise originally had more attitude, but otherwise it was pretty much the same.

—*Entermix*, September 2014

Fictional Inspirations

■ What other works have inspired you?

I like foreign children's fantasy, especially the *Harry Potter* series, and weird myths and ghost stories, like *The Classic of Mountains and Seas* from China. I used to buy foreign grimoires and look at the magic circles even though I couldn't read English. When I was a kid, I wanted to be a novelist, but with prose you have to leave a lot to the reader's imagination, you know? So when I was in high school, I realized prose wasn't for me, and I worked toward expressing myself in comics. This story is set in the U.K., but honestly, I've never been there. I think that might mean I idealize it more. But I'm given to understand that folklore is still alive and well there, especially in Ireland and Scotland. I would definitely like to visit if I get time.

—*Entermix*, September 2014

■ What's the first book you remember?

White Fang. It was part of a children's hardcover series. It was sort of a digest edition for kids, but the pictures were really vivid, and the wolf-dog main character was really cool.

■ What books do you remember most clearly from your childhood?

For Japanese books, *Kamigami no Shima Mamuda*, *Jigokudou Reikai Tsuushin*, and *Denderaryuu ga Dete Kita yo*. For foreign books, the *Neschan-Trilogie*, the *Doomspell Trilogy*, the *Harry Potter* series, and *The Saga of Darren Shan*, to name a few.

■ As a fan of children's literature, can you recommend any books?

Kamigami no Shima Mamuda is the best among Japanese books. I can't really articulate why, though. The writing, the structure, the characters—I don't know, I just love every aspect of it. It's as if myth is rooted and alive, and you can still gaze on it. I still reread that book every year.

I suppose plenty of people have already read *Harry Potter* and *Darren*, so for foreign books, I recommend *The Doomspell Trilogy* and the *Neschan-Trilogie*. In *The Doomspell Trilogy*, first and foremost, the protagonist, Rachel, is just the coolest! All of the characters are amazing in their own way, and the system of magic and the world are so unique. In the *Neschan-Trilogie*, the Christian symbolism and relationships are exquisite, and again, it's as if I'm reading a legend being told for the first time. The books are thick, but you lose all track of time when you read them. It's also fascinating how the main character exists in two different worlds.

■ What work, be it a novel or a comic, would you say drew you in most deeply?

For novels, either *The Summer of the Ubume* or *Harry Potter*. For comics, I guess *Ashiaraiyashiki no Juunintachi* and *Sukkuto Kitsune*. I'm having trouble remembering.

■ What's your favorite genre of books to read lately? Has it changed?

Lately I've pretty much only managed to read reference books and comics. I don't pay too much attention to genres; I read what I like. But, yeah, I guess I skew toward fantasy. I like gun action and sci-fi, too.

■ What's your all-time favorite work, whether fiction or nonfiction?

The works I want near me until I die are the *Doomspell Trilogy*, *Kamigami no Shima Mamuda*, and *Ashiaraiyashiki no Juunintachi*, for the simple reason that I love them. That's all there is to it.

■ You've said that you like to look at the interior design and atmosphere of bookstores. Of all the bookstores you've been to, which is your favorite?

Bookhouse Jinbocho, in Jinbocho [closed February 20, 2017], and Kitazawa Bookstore on the second floor of the same building, up a spiral staircase, are my favorites. Bookhouse Jinbocho's long shelves all the way down both sides, the storytime space in the middle where kids can read...and the selection! I'm not that knowledgeable and I can't buy it all, but it thrills me. When you go up the spiral staircase to Kitazawa Bookstore, there are all these thick Western books crammed in there, and seeing all those leather spines makes my heart sing. I always visit when I go to Jinbocho.

■ **If you were to open your own bookstore, what would you want it to be like? Tell us about the interior design and selection.**

I'd only stock books I've read and liked. (*laughs*) The genres would be photography collections, children's literature, picture books, fantasy, plants and animals, and art. It would be nice if there were a café corner, too, overlooking a little garden, where you could sip tea while reading the books you just bought and eat things that are mentioned in famous books. It strikes me that this might be a fun thing to do when I get old.

■ **Why would you say reading appeals to you so intensely?**

Because it lets you travel to another world. A picture is worth a thousand words and all, so it can never compare to seeing something in person, but I think it's a great starting point.

—Katsukura, vol. 13

Favorite Fantasy Works

■ **You've said that you began reading foreign children's literature as a child. Did you start to draw fantastic images and inhuman characters based on those books then? Also, are there any inhuman beings that you especially like?**

I did like to draw back then, but it was almost all copying and imitating manga. It wasn't until junior high or high school that I really started to draw original things or characters from children's books. I drew a lot of fantasy creatures, but I'd say I was mostly drawing humans. As for inhuman beings I like... It's hard to even know where to start.

■ **The appeal of inhuman beings lies in how different they are from us—a mysterious aura or a clash between their personality and how we see them, things like that. What would you say appeals to you personally about inhuman creatures?**

Fundamentally, what gets me most is that their appearance is so different from ours, but as I keep drawing a manga, they stop seeming strange to me at all. Anyway, I like to imagine them living with very different rules than we have in everyday human society, and then, if I like the story, it doesn't matter so much. Inhuman beings seem so mysterious to us because they have their own rules, which humans don't know or understand and can't empathize with. But to them, it's all perfectly natural. Maybe they see us as equally mysterious.

■ **How do you come up with the chants Elias and Chise use to perform magic? Is there something in particular you're aiming for? Are there rules?**

When they call on a specific fae, they use phrases that match its lore. This takes a good bit of inspiration from *Ashiaraiyashiki no Juunintachi* by Tokuichi Minagi-sensei, actually. It's kind of like meta tags, or like a word association game. Other than that, I consider the rhythm, the euphony, the number of characters and how it will look in the speech bubble, and things like that. When Elias chants, I gird it with plants that have thorns, and when Angie chants, I use stuff related to Hugo. When Chise opens a lock, she establishes a relationship in which she is the key. That's the kind of chant anyone can use if they're a mage.

■ **The series features fae and inhuman beings that figure in Irish lore, such as selkies and banshees. Is there anything you pay extra attention to when designing or characterizing such traditional beings?**

I try to give them features that make sense for where they live. In the sea, they should have fish or snake features; in the forest, they should have plant or insect features. In general, they should be like animals adapted to their environment. If they live near humans, they'll tend to have a look that fits into human civilization more.

■ **You also included dragons. How did you want to represent them? It was impressive how you showed the natural cycle of life and death with Nevin, the dragon at the end of his life, turning into a tree and returning to the earth.**

Dragons are animals that share our world in the story, so I really wanted to integrate them into that cycle. I was also thinking it would be romantic if what we were looking at wasn't just stone crags but the body of a long-dead dragon or something like that.

■ **In the scene in which the Dark Lady and the Horned God pass by in the forest, Elias and Chise hide with bated breath, and Elias says, "There's no predicting what will please or anger them. That's what makes them so frightening." That was very striking. What did you have in mind when you drew these gods? It's fascinating that the Dark Lady appears to be pregnant.**

I wanted to make them so they could be *both* or they could be *neither*. Endearing, scary, cold, warm, eerie, divine. Good or evil, or neither—they're not meant to fit in any of the boxes humans have set out. They're just there. They're just themselves, and it's humans who try to assign reasons. That's what I had in mind when I conceived of and drew them. The Lady is pregnant with the goddess of spring, who is born at the winter solstice, grows up, and becomes like her mother as winter approaches. Then, at the next winter solstice, she gives birth to the next goddess of spring. That's more or less the story, inspired by how the Celts explained the cycle of the seasons.

■ **Elias and Chise's way of life is very rich and appropriately mage-like. It's full of seasonal customs and knowledge, like how they decorate with certain plants for the winter solstice. It seems as though you've paid a great deal of care to the representation of the seasons and a life close to nature. Can you comment on this?**

The story assumes that mages live by borrowing the products of nature, so I want to represent nature as much as I can. But I wouldn't say I've paid a huge amount of care to it; it's more that I've incorporated the feelings I normally have about the seasons and drawn the things I like. I do like to think about the story and its background and think, "So this means this!", but then I don't have the skill as an artist to easily express it.

■ **The world of *The Ancient Magus' Bride* also includes alchemists, who use science to get their results. What led you to factor in alchemy as a second force that's both similar and dissimilar to magic?**

In the manga, magic and alchemy are the same thing done in different ways. The effects and the constraints are different, and there are different advantages and disadvantages. There are cases where something was once considered occult, but was later proven scientifically. I was hoping to represent that kind of diversity in ways of looking at things.

—*Kikan S*, January 2017

■ **We understand that you like fantasy, but is there anything you're especially concerned about in creating the kind of fantasy you like?**

I'm trying to create a world that feels nostalgic to both me and my readers and makes us wonder whether there really is a world like this one right beside us that we just don't know about.

■ **What aspects of fantasy offer special pleasures or present challenges as a creator?**

It's a pleasure to be able to draw what I like, and I suppose it's a frustrating challenge not to be able to draw what I like well enough. I don't have enough skill; I don't have enough time; I don't have enough of anything.

■ **Do you have any clear internal rules for your world, to the effect that you won't let such-and-such type of object or entity appear in it, or won't let such-and-such kind of action be taken?**

Not really, but I've avoided showing magic or alchemy being directly used for combat. The characters can fight using the objects that result from magic or alchemy. I don't have specific rules for action, either, but if I think to myself, "This character wouldn't do that or say that," then I won't have them do it—or they won't say it even if I ask.

■ What do you enjoy most about drawing inhuman beings?

The faeries and monsters in folklore exist right alongside humans, so they often imitate human form, and sometimes they even emulate human culture. However, their beliefs, lifestyles, and thoughts are all rather different from ours. Once you realize they have their own set of rules to follow, it's very easy to understand. If I'm able to express that, it pleases me.

■ What do you find most difficult?

It's very difficult to find all the detailed information I need about skeletons and musculature and then draw it, but all I can do is keep working at it. I wish I knew more about biology.

—*Katsukura*, vol. 13

Character Relationships

■ You've said that you're a fan of human/inhuman relationships. What is it about them that appeals to you?

I suppose I like how they tear down each other's values and rebuild them, and then empathy develops out of that. It's pretty intense for people who'd normally never interact at all to put in the effort needed just to coexist. They can say things to each other that you'd never feel comfortable discussing with another human precisely *because* they're so different. It's actually easier than talking to another human. You can also extend that to aliens from different worlds, with different cultures and all that.

■ In the flashback to when Elias and Lindel first met, when Elias has no memory, Lindel accepts Elias into his life as an "acquaintance," and they travel together. They're master and apprentice, and they're friends, and they're also like father and son. It's a striking relationship. What were you aiming for?

I'm not very good at defining a relationship in just one way. If both parties are on the same page, then lovers can be like friends, friends can be like couples or relatives, couples can be like business partners... I don't think it's necessary to shove how we relate to others into boxes. I want to portray this kind of relationship that can be interpreted however you want.

■ **Elias and Chise have a very appealing relationship, too. Magically speaking, they're master and apprentice, but at the heart of it, they look like lovers, or even parent and child. Is there anything in particular you have in mind with them?**

When you look at two people, I think one is always ahead and the other is behind in certain areas. I want to portray that dynamic. It's a given that Elias, in some ways, is very different from humans, and that in some ways Chise can't understand him. But that's okay! That's the idea.

■ **From early on, Elias doesn't seem to have much sense of personal space when it comes to Chise. He's often nuzzling her or picking her up. Do you have any particular thoughts regarding how he touches her?**

When kids trust someone—at least, judging by the kids around me—they hug that person and ask to be hugged back. They'll take your hand whenever they feel like it, or ask you to draw with them, or try as hard as they can to explain things that have happened. So on the one hand I'm depicting Elias as if he's a child in a large body, but on the other hand, given how he comes across, I'm also trying to add in some more mature attraction.

—*Kikan S*, January 2017

■ **The love between Elias and Chise seems to be one of the story's major themes. It's heartwarming to watch the two of them growing closer after each being so alone, and to see their feelings deepening. Could you tell us what you particularly like about their relationship, or what you especially enjoy as you bring it to life? Is there a kind of love between them that can really only exist between a human and an inhuman?**

Elias' frame is sharp and shocking, and when you stop and think about it, seeing him should be frightening. After all, death is what usually makes you look like him! At any rate, while Elias bears some resemblance to a human, he's a monster who doesn't know how to empathize with humans. In comparison, Chise is a girl at the age when she should be full of hope and starting to figure out who she is, but she has no interest in life. So their interests align; they're together, but not especially interested in each other at first, and then they gradually become closer. This is a relationship that really does it for me, so I have tons of fun depicting it, even though neither of them is anywhere near ready for romance.

The human/inhuman thing is something I'm really into, but I don't think the love that springs from it is any different than the love between humans, whether it's the love of lovers or spouses, familial love, or love between friends. The experience of cherishing someone, or of hating and despising someone, is the same regardless of what kind of creature they are. I think what makes it different between humans and inhumans is that it's easy to conclude that the other person is something *other,* someone you feel you can't understand, based their appearance or on what you can perceive of their inner life. Because of that, it feels more moving than a dynamic between humans. That's my serious analysis, but really, I just adore the drama of love and hate between humans and inhumans. I could go on and on about reasons and distinctions all day, but it doesn't add up to much.

—*Da Vinci*, March 2015

■ **Is there anything in particular you focus on or think about when you're depicting Chise and Elias' relationship and their degree of distance from each other?**

They don't get too close and comfortable, but they also don't back off too much. They aren't tremendously friendly, but they clearly don't dislike each other. It's a delicate dynamic that isn't really like that of friends or lovers or even master and apprentice. All I can say is I'm doing my best with it.

—*Katsukura*, vol. 13

■ **How did you develop Chise and Elias as characters?**

This could be because I like buddy stories so much, but I always think of characters in pairs, so I came up with the concepts for these two at the same time. My original idea was actually that Elias had once been human, and that Chise was a specter in human form, but after many twists and turns I wound up with the characters you see. I was born and raised in Hokkaido, but *"chise"* actually means "house" in Ainu. My hope is that Chise can be like a home to Elias—independent, but bound by trust. I like that comfortable-spouse kind of relationship.

—*Entermix*, September 2014

The Characters of *The Ancient Magus' Bride*

■ **What do you like most about Elias and Chise, respectively?**

Chise is being raised almost from scratch by Elias, and she's like a dry flower sipping up water and gradually filling back up with life. I see that clearly as I'm drawing, and it blows my mind. For better or for worse, she has a powerful ability to absorb what's around her, yet at heart she's deeply stubborn. She has a lot of good traits and also a lot of room for improvement, and in that respect, she's very appealing.

As for Elias, I like that he looks like something that would hunt and feed on people, but on the inside he's really just a child. He's something of a failure.

He imitates humans as best he can, but in some ways even a toddler would see him as emotionally stunted. We get to watch him grow and develop thanks to meeting Chise, and that is precious.

■ **Since Elias' head is a skull, he doesn't really have facial expressions, but he looks so handsome when you read the manga! Chise herself says that the light in his eyes makes her think of a child. It feels like Elias displays so many expressions, from sadness to benevolence.**

Please tell me the tricks to making Elias handsome and showing his emotions! I'm awestruck that you think he's handsome. I'm always telling myself to get it together. I mean, his head's a skull, so there isn't much you can do with that. Maybe it's his big hands or his gestures? I draw the light in his eyes the same way I do with humans, so don't ask me what the trick is.

—*Da Vinci*, March 2015

■ **What do you focus on or enjoy when you draw Chise?**

I try to draw Chise so that you can feel the wind or moisture or light or texture. It's enjoyable to draw her eyes, her hair, her expression, her body—all of it! It's frustrating if I can't make her charming.

■ **What about Elias?**

He's got quite the build. When he's next to Chise, I need to really work hard on the art. My heart skips a beat to see his big body next to her little one. The one problem is that it's hard to fit them both into the same frame.

—*Katsukura*, vol. 13

The Story of *The Ancient Magus' Bride*

■ **The first two volumes of the manga have so many memorable events! Elias and Chise meet, they visit the last home of the dragons, they go to "Ulthar, the town where cats congregate," we meet the faerie queen and king, and so on. The stories set at the dragon aerie and Ulthar both wound up making me cry.**

Do you have a favorite storyline, or is there one that's the most memorable for you? If so, could you explain why?

The dragon story. I really wanted to draw dragons in the modern age, so I'm glad I got the opportunity, even if it was brief. I used a linden tree because Lindel brought the seed, but later I discovered that lindens used to be planted at meeting places in Europe, so I think it's perfect.

—*Da Vinci*, March 2015

■ **Is there any storyline (or scene) you've drawn so far that was particularly memorable for you?**

Yes. There's the part where Chise falls into the water and then makes eye contact with a dragon. That scene, where two utterly different beings face each other, is my favorite.

■ **What storyline or scene has elicited the strongest response from readers?**

The dragon story. You'd think by now dragons have been done to death, but here we are. I admire how, generation after generation, dragons never fail to excite and inspire us.

—*Katsukura*, vol. 13

Character Design

■ **Looking at Elias and Chise, it's Elias who really jumps out visually, but Chise is a girl with a very special nature. She feels very fresh. It seems that Chise's nature as a sleigh beggy may be the key to the story. How did you come up with the concept?**

It wouldn't be interesting if there were only advantages to her nature. I wanted there to be downsides, too. If it were just like, oh, this girl got picked up and everything about her life improved, it wouldn't be so poignant. I wanted to utterly exhaust her both mentally and physically. That's the plain truth.

There's a saying that's my guiding light for this: "Children belong to the gods until age seven." The thing is, sleigh beggy aren't actually *that* rare, but they usually end up dying before they're discovered, for whatever reason—including being eaten or dragged off into the darkness. That's what I imagine.

■ **What was your process for developing each of the characters?**
● *Chise Hatori:*

I thought to myself, "I'm presumably going to draw her the most, so I should make her the simplest,"—but then somehow she became the most difficult character, with her expressions and all. Her eyes are characteristic of a sleigh beggy; the most important thing is that I try to give them a translucent look. She's meant to have a balanced, all-purpose look so that she seems natural whether she's in pants or a skirt.

● *Elias Ainsworth:*

○ *Head Design–*

It just came to me intuitively, like it fell from the sky. At first he had bull horns, but I went with the version you see now. I started out with a canine skull, but that wouldn't let him eat (since he'd need the flesh of the face), so I changed it so there was less of a gap. That makes him easier to draw, too.

○ *Costume–*

The strings [that hang under his chin from his horns] are a visual association with his nature—by which I mean that I figured he should have a lot of strings. You expect a mage to wear a robe, but that's just too obvious, so I tried to give him a little more of a "modern suit" look.

○ *Expression–*

I exaggerate it a little bit, but otherwise I keep it at a level where readers can just pick up on what he's feeling, with the context and pauses and such.

○ *Human Form–*

I initially conceived of him as inhuman, so I didn't want to make him look too much like us. But then I decided that, yeah, he actually would need that kind of mimicry to live in the modern world, so I went ahead and let him do it.

○ *Speech–*

I try to make him sound like a mild-mannered child pretending to be an adult. One reason for that is simply that if he acted too cool or dark or prickly, it would piss me off.

● *Silky:*

Silky appeared to me fully formed as I was reading folklore. Her costume isn't just a dress; it draws some inspiration from ladies' coats from old times. She had long hair as a banshee, so I made it short now for visual contrast.

● *Ruth:*

I've loved curly-coated black dogs since I first read about them in folklore. I always hoped to have a chance to draw one. The idea was, "A familiar who'd be drawn to Chise... She'll be in a strange, scary situation... I want her to have some sort of animal, since it'd be therapeutic... Oh!" At first Ruth was going to be an older man, but I wanted keep the number of huge guys to a reasonable level, so when he became her familiar, I shrank him down.

● *Lindel:*

I envisioned him as the very picture of a mage—or rather, a kind of goofy wise man. When I first drew him, he didn't volunteer any information about things like his birthplace, but as I keep writing, his background's gradually being filled in. Now we know he's from Finland—that kind of thing. He was the first character to demonstrate that, yes, mages are powerful, but they also have their share of suffering.

● *Angelica Purley:*

She's an embodiment of my ideal woman. She's meant to be strong and warm, but sometimes she's wrong. She has some regrets. A normal woman, in other words.

● *Mikhail Renfred:*

He's another character who didn't tell me anything about himself when he first appeared, but he slowly opens up as I draw him. In terms of appearance, he's another one who appeared fully formed. At first his only real role was meant to be having his arm taken, but next thing I knew he'd become a regular character, there to offer a contrast to Elias.

● *Alice:*

I tried to make her the polar opposite of Chise. She's tall, with boyish, damaged wavy hair. She behaves in a way that's very easy to understand, so putting her into action is a blast. She's the go-to character when something needs to be done, and she'll bluntly say whatever needs saying, so she's really useful.

● *Simon Cullum:*

I do have a backstory for Simon, but you'll have to wait and see.

● *Ashen Eye:*

Ashen Eye doesn't live by human rules at all, and thinks of humans the way we might think of a kitten or puppy—it's delightful to play with them for the fun of seeing what they do. This offers the perspective of an observer who knows that they themselves are safe no matter how things play out.

● *Cartaphilus:*

I thought that a child would be creepier—acting so innocent, like in a horror movie—so that's how I developed his appearance. I hope you'll enjoy learning more about what's going on inside him.

■ **By living with Chise, Elias develops humanlike feelings. This is especially striking when he becomes jealous of Chise's closeness to Stella, when he's like a child who can't comprehend his own emotions. It's somehow cute when he's in such a bizarre form and holding Chise tightly, even nipping at her. Events and interactions like that seem to be the essence of the human/inhuman relationship. Is that part of what you intended for *The Ancient Magus' Bride*?**

I'd say it's not so much that he develops "humanlike feelings" as that he develops emotions that are adapted to life in human society. Elias is a mage with 999 MP and 999 HP, so if he's going to develop, it *has* to be his heart, or something inside him. If you imagine a human of the same age doing the exact same things Elias does, that's really bad—and not in the good way. We can only forgive that behavior because he isn't human. Is that the essence of that kind of relationship, then? Maybe it's more of a perk. Human or not, what I ultimately want to depict is an equal relationship. I think it'll take them a while to get there.

—*Kikan S*, January 2017

■ **There are so many great characters: Ariel, Silky, Angelica, Simon, Echos, Renfred and Alice, Titania the faerie queen, Oberon the faerie king—they're all wonderful. Who are your favorite characters other than Elias and Chise, and why?**

I love them all, but I can explain why in some cases better than others. Alice and Renfred, Lindel (Echos), and Angelica are probably the most explicable ones. I like Silky and Spriggan, too. Alice is the most emotionally turbulent over the course of the story, and she's very honest, so I have a lot of fun with her as I draw her. She's the kind of girl I want as a granddaughter.

—*Da Vinci*, March 2015

Work Environment

■ **What is your process for drawing the manga?**

Outline, storyboard while revising, pencil, ink the lines and fill concurrently, and then do the backgrounds and tones concurrently. I allocate about a week for the outline and storyboard, about three or four days for penciling—depending on how many characters appear and how complicated the scenes are—and then three or four days for inking and two or three days for backgrounds. But that's all theoretical. In reality, penciling and storyboarding kill me.

■ **Can you tell us about your tools and environment for color and black-and-white art?**

For both manga and color illustrations, I use digital and analog tools. I'll even switch between digital and analog for the same step, depending on my mood. The one thing I always do in analog is line art. (The disadvantage there is that you can't correct it, but it's faster.)

ANALOG

Paper: The publisher gives it to me. Otherwise, 110-kilogram paper is best.
Nibs: Tachikawa G and Maru.
Ink: Kuretake bottled ink.

Other: 0.28 to 0.38 permanent ballpoint pens, brush pen, Mckee, Prockey, etc. I have a bad habit of always buying new black pens when they come out. I press on them hard enough to reliably destroy even advanced technology.

DIGITAL

Clip Studio Paint: I use this for almost everything except line art.
Photoshop CS5 and Photoshop CC: I use this for coloring. I stick to the brushes that are included.
Wacom tablet
Epson A3 multifunction scanner
Google Search (for colors and references)

■ Is there anything you need in order to draw besides those tools?

Well, music and videos that match the scene I'm drawing are important, but the most important things are references—lots of references. I can't rely on my own memory, so I have to look at photos I took or other references. Oh, and stamina. Stamina is absolutely vital!

—*Kikan S*, January 2017

■ Do you keep your own notes and references on the series?

Yes, I make notes. I have to make the time to organize them.

■ What do you tend to center your thinking on as you create? Scenes, lines, characters…?

Scenes. It starts with visions and conversations coming to me like daydreams, and then I work to fill in the blanks—or rather, I have the characters talk and do things to bridge the gaps.

■ What are the best conditions for coming up with ideas?

If I'm at my desk and nothing's coming, I go on a meandering walk. If I'm still not getting anything, I sleep. That lets any hazy ideas start to take shape in my head, and I pull them in little by little. As for where the ideas come to me, it could be outside, inside, at my place or my family's, or in the bath. It's totally random.

■ What are your favorite and least favorite steps in the process of drawing manga?

My favorite is inking. I love watching all that white space get filled in! My least favorites are storyboarding and penciling. They suck up my soul.

■ Is there anything you absolutely must have when you draw, such as music or little indulgences?

I like my tea, and a few snacks. I also need a window with a good view of the changing seasons, one that I can open when I want to. I need music sometimes, but other times I make more progress in silence.

■ **For you, what is a nonnegotiable requirement for art—maybe something you hold dear in the process of creation?**

I worry about the wording of the lines at any given time, even when I'm working on a different step. I mean, it takes both the scenery and the dialogue to make manga, so I worry right up to the last minute about whether the text fits the pictures and whether a character's dialogue is plausibly something they'd say. I cut things I definitely don't need, but there's always some worry. It's hard to generalize.

■ **What do you do if you start feeling burned out?**

I go as far away as I can or do something different. I often end up making something. I also clean, air out my place, cook, or do laundry and other chores.

—*Katsukura*, vol. 13

Republished in Its Entirety! Recollections of France

On the plane back from Japan Expo 2015.

Editor S: Well, time to just sit tight until we get back to Japan, hmm?

Yamazaki: What a crazy trip!

Editor S: No kidding. Now, I know you're tired, but shall we get started?

Yamazaki: Sure, why not?

Question 1: What did you think of this trip to France?

Yamazaki: It was so great! It was my first time visiting Europe, and always having an interpreter there made things so much easier. It took all the stress off.

Editor S: That's true. The interpreter dealt with all the red tape for us, from checking in at the hotel to returning to the airport.

Yamazaki: And calling taxis for us everywhere we went. What a lifesaver.

Editor S: Yeah, especially since I wound up having so many problems to deal with.

Yamazaki: Right! A new crisis every day!

Editor S: I mean, I had no idea what to do when the leg of my bed broke!

Yamazaki: I'm so sorry, but that really was hilarious. (*laughs*)

Editor S: I was there like some kind of amulet to draw all the bad luck away from you!

Yamazaki: (*laughs*) All right, but at least nothing in particular happened to me.

Editor S: Wait, wait—there was something, wasn't there?

Yamazaki: What? There was?

Editor S: The thing at the Métro, and the reference books.

Yamazaki: Oh! Yeah, you mean when we got separated at the subway gate, and when I bought too many reference books in Paris!

Editor S: Exactly. I'll explain the Métro incident: we'd made it as far as the vicinity of the Arc de Triomphe, and then we couldn't get a taxi. So we unexpectedly had to take the Métro.

Yamazaki: The interpreter gave us tickets, but none of my tickets worked, including the spare ones...

Editor S: You almost got left behind at the ticket gate!

Yamazaki: I finally found a new ticket and made it through. It was scary, though! Apparently, in France no one collects your tickets when you're finished using them, so if you just tuck them into your wallet "for now," they get mixed in with your unused ones. I guess this happens a lot.

Editor S: Apparently so. It was pretty unfortunate, though!

Yamazaki: It was. (*laughs*) And the buying-too-many-reference-books incident was...well, just what it sounds like.

Editor S: That was today [July 7, 2015], just a little while ago.

Yamazaki: Right. Just now.

Editor S: You kept buying reference material until the very last minute, and then you couldn't fit it all in your luggage, and it was getting so close to our flight time!

Yamazaki: I ended up buying a whole new bag at the airport to ship them in. I'm very sorry about that.

Editor S: Don't worry about it. But how about the books themselves? Did you get anything good?

Yamazaki: I got so many things I couldn't get in Japan! It's perfect!

Editor S: Well, that's good, then. Can we assume they'll help you make the manga even better going forward?

Yamazaki: Ha ha! Sure, if I ever find the time to actually read them all!

Editor S: No problem, then! All you have to do is stick to your schedule, since it allows for so much spare time!

Yamazaki: Oh, of course it does. (*eyeroll*)

Question 2: What did you think of Japan Expo?

Yamazaki: Hmm... The first thing that comes to mind is how everyone seemed to be having such a good time. There was...how should I put this? An atmosphere or a sense of power, like, "We're here to party!"

Editor S: It did seem to have a subtly different vibe from our doujinshi conventions in Japan.

Yamazaki: You're right. There were even families with kids. It felt domestic.

Question 3: What did you do there, professionally speaking?

Yamazaki: My French publisher, Komikku, had a booth, and I did signings.

Editor S: How many of those did you do?

Yamazaki: Uh, there were two per day, and I signed for about fifty people in each session... Oh, but on the last day I'd gotten the hang of it, so I got through sixty people.

Editor S: You also signed at the bookshop Komikku ran the day before the expo, so that was nine sessions total, with about 450 people. Good work!

Yamazaki: It was hard work, you know! But now I can dash off the word *"Merci"* really smoothly!

Editor S: Good job! (*laughs*) Now, could you describe how the event seemed to you?

Yamazaki: Everyone just looked so glad to be there, which makes me happy. Some people gave me art that they'd drawn, and some of them came a really long way to be there.

Editor S: Yeah. I think the person who came the farthest was from Israel.

Yamazaki: And there were people actually from the U.K., where *Magus* is set. Wasn't there at least one Spaniard, too?

Editor S: I think the person you're thinking of was a Catalan. Catalonia is in Spain, but apparently they don't like to be lumped in together. You really get a sense of Europe's history.

Yamazaki: Yeah. Oh, another thing—there were lots of kids at the event in general, but there were even kids under ten at my autograph sessions.

Editor S: It was interesting to see that a lot of them were boys, not girls. Oh! Oh yeah, speaking of boys!

Yamazaki: Oh, Elias-kun!

Editor S: We've got to talk about him. He was probably the most memorable fan of all the autograph sessions.

Yamazaki: We're talking about a boy who couldn't actually make it to the autograph session.

Editor S: That's right. He couldn't make it to the autograph session at the Komikku shop.

Yamazaki: He came up to us afterwards, though, once we were all done.

Right in front of all the grown-ups, he said, "I couldn't make it to your signing, so I don't need an autograph. But I love *The Ancient Magus' Bride*, and my name is Elias. That's all!" And he ran back to his mom.

Editor S: That was surprising and adorable! (*laughs*)

Yamazaki: It sure was! Other than that...I did lots of media interviews. I lost track of how many.

Editor S: Mmm, I think it was about five a day, so altogether...twenty or so? So many different kinds of media, too: TV, print magazines, radio, websites...

Yamazaki: I remember someone saying that they were starting an interview for French public TV, and I didn't have the first clue what was going on.

Editor S: Then it was actually on the French national evening news! Freaky, wasn't it?

Yamazaki: I was thinking, "Are you serious, France?" (*laughs*)

Editor S: (*laughs*) So, how did those interviews go?

Yamazaki: Well, they didn't ask me any awkward questions that went beyond the scope of the work. One way I felt they differed from Japanese interviewers was that they seemed more into fantasy overall. I felt like they asked me a lot of really deep questions.

Editor S: Interesting! Can you think of any examples?

Yamazaki: Things like, "The portrayal of nature in *Magus' Bride* is powerful. What sort of spot does nature hold in your worldview?"

Editor S: Do you remember how you answered?

Yamazaki: Um, I think I said something like, "Nature is so easy to destroy, but building it up takes so much time and effort, so we can't afford to lose it."

Editor S: Wow, that's a good answer! It's like saying nature is like trust. You lose it once, it's gone!

Yamazaki: Okay, sure. (*eyeroll*)

Editor S: (*laughs*) Was that the most penetrating question?

Yamazaki: No, there were more, but it was so hot that it took all I had just to think of answers, so I don't remember it terribly well. But seriously, some of these people were into way more than just manga! They knew tons about folklore and mythology and all of these massive fantasy tomes from Tolkien on up.

Oh, wait—I do remember one more question someone asked. They wondered if the ariels were inspired by harpies! The answer is no, they weren't, but I wasn't expecting harpies to come up!

Editor S: Interesting! Now I'm thinking of how Ruth's name comes from the Bible. Did anyone ask you if there's some religious significance to that?

Yamazaki: Not that, exactly, but they asked, "Is there a Christian backbone to the story? Do you intend to focus on any religious aspects in the future?"

Editor S: Were they asking about Christian values?

Yamazaki: Christian values, racial issues, stuff like that.

Editor S: What did you say?

Yamazaki: I said my hope was that the manga would be accessible and enjoyable for everyone without making anyone think about things like that, so I probably wouldn't go there.

Editor S: Hmm, yes. It would be a totally different story if it ended up having a focus on religion.

Yamazaki: Besides, I'm Japanese. My frame of reference is fundamentally different from Westerners'. Maybe there's a tiny bit of that sort of thing, but only a dash—just enough that people who pick up on it can be pleased about catching it.

Editor S: Now, what were the reporters themselves like, generally speaking?

Yamazaki: It was overwhelming. You could really tell that all these people had become manga and anime journalists because they loved manga so intensely.

Editor S: I could see that, too. How do I put it? It's like they weren't there because they wanted journalism experience—rather, it was like they'd become journalists so that they *could* be there.

Yamazaki: I also have to say that they all seemed very professional and responsible as journalists.

Question 4: What did you do at Japan Expo when you had free time?

Yamazaki: Let's see. When I had free time I'd go walking around, or else I drew in the greenroom. I sketched things that caught my eye.

Editor S: Oh, and remember how there were some local creators who visited our booth?

Yamazaki: Oh! That was so much fun! I got to talk to local artists and other Japanese artists who were published in France. We traded autographs and stuff.

Editor S: Indeed. I was just an old man on the sidelines.

Yamazaki: Poor you, stuck just watching. (*laughs*)

Editor S: I told Komikku that I felt anxious about not having any work to do, and they told me I had a problem.

Question 5: How was your stay in Paris?

Yamazaki: I loved every second of it! The only thing was, it was *so* hot.

Editor S: I've heard that France only gets as hot as Japan one week a year, but it seems like we managed to be there that exact week.

Yamazaki: It was a heat wave blowing in from the Sahara. The day we arrived, it was 38 degrees [100 °F], and the next day it was 40 [104 °F]. I was dying.

Editor S: It was 40 degrees when we went to the Louvre... At the Louvre Pyramid, I felt like a "steamed elderly Japanese man" or something.

Yamazaki: Like the pyramid was a pressure cooker? It hardly even gets that hot in Japan!

Editor S: Speaking of cooking, though, wasn't the food fantastic?

Yamazaki: We got to eat lots of traditional food, like *pâté de foie gras*. That was amazing! And you could order duck anywhere!

Editor S: The fish was great too, and so were the salads. And that dessert, *baba*?

Yamazaki: The sponge cake you pour brandy over before eating!

Editor S: Komikku's director said, "Baba is even more delicious with more brandy!" We poured brandy on it until the sponge blew up! (*laughs*)

Yamazaki: I was like, "Oops, we overdid it." That was funny. (*laughs*) Oh, and we had *escargots*, didn't we? They were kind of like shellfish, and the meat didn't actually seem to have that much taste.

Editor S: Escargots were better than I expected. We really lucked out, in that the director was such a connoisseur. Everything we ate was delicious.

Yamazaki: And you tried so many different wines!

Editor S: Hey, he was drinking more than I was, all right? And you know how it is for a businessman; I have no choice. Oh, alcohol. It's so frightening.

Yamazaki: Well, you looked like you were having a good time!

Editor S: Right, right. (*eyeroll*)

Question 6: What did you think of the city and the architecture?

Yamazaki: Awesome.

Editor S: Could you be more specific? (*laughs*)

Yamazaki: It wasn't like it was just all clean and tidy, but everything had its own history. I could really feel the weight of it.

Editor S: I believe you took quite a few pictures. Of course, every place we went was photo-worthy, but can we expect any of them to find their way into *Magus*?

Yamazaki: I don't have any plans to use the cityscape for now. I mean, sure, it's in Europe, but I don't think England and France have that much in common. Some of the little details will be very useful, though.

Question 7: What was your impression of the people of Paris?

Yamazaki: Hmm. Well, this is all just from looking, so I'm not saying this is necessarily accurate, but I felt an air of impatience everywhere, like with born-and-raised Tokyo folks.

Editor S: Paris is crowded, and there are a lot of cars, so maybe people get irritable. I did have to laugh at the rhythm of the car horns during traffic jams. (*laughs*)

Yamazaki: It was pretty extreme on the last day when we were heading to the airport. There was this chic young lady who barged across the street against a red light. This taxi barely stopped before it hit her—and she smacked the window hard, flipped the finger, and carried on her way.

Editor S: Really? I totally missed it. That's pretty extreme.

Yamazaki: It was also amazing how the taxi driver just shrugged and laughed it off.

Editor S: I suppose this is obvious, but the world really is full of people who think and live in totally different ways than we do in Japan.

Yamazaki: Exactly. It really hits you.

Question 8: How were the attractions in Paris?

Yamazaki: There was an herbalist that had been around since the nineteenth century, and beautiful courtyards in the middle of apartment complexes where ordinary people lived. At the herbalist shop there was a woman in a white coat in the midst of all that herbal fragrance, and it was so picturesque. The apartment complexes each had their own unique gardens, and that was beautiful, too.

Editor S: The interpreter showed us a lot of places like that that aren't touristy.

Yamazaki: We also saw the Sacré-Cœur Basilica on Montmartre, the Notre-Dame Cathedral, and the Louvre Museum. We went from the Seine River and saw a bunch of places.

Editor S: We saw the Arc de Triomphe and the Obelisk, too. This was your first time seeing Western architecture in person, wasn't it? Especially those churches—what did you think?

Yamazaki: It was just majestic. All I could think was, "Humans really built this?" That was my overwhelming impression.

Editor S: It was like a magnificent theater set where people could experience the greatness of God, or something like that. Even unbelievers were awed. It must really be tremendous for those who do believe.

Yamazaki: No kidding!

Editor S: Speaking of impressive things, what did you think of the Louvre Museum?

Yamazaki: The Louvre? It was...*damn!*

Editor S: Language! (*laughs*)

Yamazaki: I mean, like, the *Nike of Samothrace*. No matter how many photos I've seen... A sculpture is a three-dimensional artwork, you know? In person you can look at it from all angles, not just the best one, and then you can look from the best angle again. The sense of presence that the real thing has just can't be captured. Just...damn.

Editor S: I must concur. Maybe it's just me, but I think the *Nike of Samothrace* has allure and attracts people because it's broken. It's as if the missing parts give us room to fill in its beauty.

Yamazaki: Yeah. If she had a face and hands, her emotions or the sculptor's intent would probably be clearer, and yet in a way that would limit it. It would be better defined, but there'd be people who wouldn't like how it was defined. I think maybe it's the *Nike*'s incompleteness that gives it the power to draw people in the way it does, because it leaves room for everyone to interpret it in their own way.

Editor S: Maybe that goes for Elias, too. Climbing to the top of the Arc de Triomphe was also wonderful. We could see all of Paris. I felt like Napoleon!

Yamazaki: That was a hard climb, though! (*laughs*)

Editor S: Everyone was out of breath. (*laughs*)

Question 9: Did you get any inspiration for your work?

Editor S: Frankly, I can't see how any of that could *not* be inspiring, but I'd like to hear what you think.

Yamazaki: Well... Yes, pretty much everything...really, everything was inspiring. It was all a completely new experience for me! But I'd say the people were the most inspiring part. I mentioned this earlier, but I think that everyone's mentality must be deeply affected by their culture, which is rooted in the land and in their history. Their views on religion and nature are so influential, too. I think being able to really see that for myself is significant.

Editor S: I see. Well, it looks like our plane is taking off, so we're about to start our twelve-hour flight. Shall we take a moment to reflect on *The Ancient Magus' Bride* itself, since so many kind people are reading it in France that you were invited there? Take it away!

Yamazaki: Um... Gosh, that's an open-ended question! (*laughs*) Every month, I focus hard on the chapter at hand, and I've only gotten started. At any rate, it's trial and error each time...

Editor S: Well, yes. It's the kind of thing you can reflect on when you're old.

Yamazaki: Exactly, it's too early for me to reflect on it! (*laughs*) I mean, there are still only four volumes!

Editor S: I suppose so. (*laughs*) All right, we're in the air now, and we can see Paris at night from our window—it's like *The Spirit of St. Louis*. To wrap up, please tell us something about Volume 4.

Yamazaki: All right. Sorry that this isn't a terribly original thing to say, but the distance between Chise and Elias is going to dwindle, bit by bit, and I hope everyone will enjoy watching that happen!

Editor S: Can't miss that gradual progress of their relationship. Everyone should buy the regular editions, the limited editions, and the magazines! How about three copies of each? (*laughs*)

Yamazaki: Don't say that! They'll go bankrupt if they do that!

Editor S: (*laughs*) Three copies or not, we've included an insert with a very special notice in Volume 4, so don't miss that!

Yamazaki: Thank you, everyone!

Editor S: Well, good work, Yamazaki-san.

Yamazaki: Yes, you too.

Editor S: It seems they're going to serve food soon!

Yamazaki: Really? Already?

Editor S: I know. Either way, this old man's gonna drink.

Yamazaki: You sure like drinking!

—*Gekkan Comic Garden*, October 2015

Merkmal

New Interview with Kore Yamazaki
Looking to the Past & Future

Since The Ancient Magus' Bride *has been running for three and a half years,*
we did a brand-new interview with Kore Yamazaki-sensei for this book!
It's a roundtable discussion including both an interviewer and Editor S,
who conducted the "Recollections of France" interview.

Reflecting on Three and a Half Years of Serialization

—The manga has been running for three and a half years now. How have
those years been for you?

Yamazaki: I moved around a lot. I moved to Tokyo ahead of my professional
debut. The first place I ever lived in Tokyo was Kita-Senju, and the abrupt
change to such an urban area was a shock to the system.

Editor S: You moved back to Hokkaido in order to change your work
environment, is that right?

Yamazaki: Yes, and I don't regret that. Hokkaido and the U.K. have some
visual similarities, so it's relatively easy for me to get reference photos, and
there are lots of places I can go when I need a breather. So my environment
hasn't changed that much.

Recent Mysterious Happenings

—Have you had any more mysterious experiences since the things you
wrote about in the Afterword of Volume 3?

Yamazaki: Yes! I was sleeping at my desk because my deadline was so close,
and I felt this presence appear behind me—but it wasn't a bad presence. I
had the feeling it was a man standing there. And then I woke up. It felt like
someone telling me to go sleep in an actual bed. (*laughs*)

Editor S: Or at least to sleep lying down. (*laughs*)

Yamazaki: Oh, also, there was this thing that happened when I was out for
a walk one foggy night. I like fog, so I was enjoying it. The lights were all
too hazy to even make out their outlines, and I was thinking, "Wow, this
is the best." There was no one else around—not even any cars. It was about
11 P.M. Anyway, I walked by this stream that runs behind a hospital. I
remember wondering if all the mist might be coming from it, although
obviously that's impossible. (*laughs*) But then I looked at the stream, and

someone—or something—was there. At first I thought it might be a flag, but I couldn't remember there ever being a flagpole there.

Editor S: This is starting to sound like *Silent Hill* or *The Mist*.

Yamazaki: There was some fabric hanging where a flag should be, but even though the wind was blowing pretty hard, the fabric didn't move. I was so scared that I ran away, but when I went back later to check, there wasn't a flag there at all.

Editor S: Did you consider taking a closer look at the time?

Yamazaki: Oh, no, I was far too scared. (*laughs*)

No Changes to the Storyline?

—The manga is up to thirty-seven chapters so far [as of this interview]. Have you been sticking to the storyline you'd planned, or have you made changes?

Yamazaki: I did wind up cutting some things I'd wanted to have happen, due to the constraints of serialization. But I don't think I've made any plot-level changes. I mean, even with those cuts it's still this long... (*sweats*)

—Have you made any structural changes, like rearranging the planned sequence of events?

Yamazaki: This isn't a plot issue, but I did change the characters of Alice and Renfred a lot. It was as if the characters taught me better as we went. When I looked back at Renfred at the beginning, I went, "He's such a villain!" (*laughs*)

Editor S: His face does have a pretty evil look in the first chapter of Volume 2.

Yamazaki: He looks evil, and when I look at it now, it makes me think, "So, this is how this jerk smiles." (*laughs*) But no, I don't think I've changed the plot. The characters I planned on initially didn't change, either.

Editor S: It's pretty close to the original plan, but there are a lot of little bits that got cut. It would be nice if we had a chance to stick them in somewhere, wouldn't it?

Yamazaki: It would. Things are going according to plan, but I've been thinking some things up as I go.

Editor S: I think that's just how it is with serialization. I think the nature of serialization has special value for you, Yamazaki-san.

—What do you mean?

Editor S: Yamazaki-san has so much side material she wants to include, it threatens to overshadow the main plot. She seems to enjoy exploring side paths like that, but early on, it made me worry that the main plot might get lost. (*laughs*)

Yamazaki: He's right. I love little side trips too much. (*laughs*)

Editor S: Sometimes it feels as if you're going to take a little "side trip" and wind up deep in the mountains.

Yamazaki: That actually happened once during the serialization, remember? What I drew when Angelica-san reappeared.

Editor S: I remember that! It gave me chills. (*laughs*)

Yamazaki: We ended up discarding that part entirely and pretending it had never happened. (*laughs*)

Editor S: While there was some digression, I think we ultimately managed to pack so much into the first volume *because* we had someone like that addressing the constraints of serialization, and the fact that a series that doesn't sell well is going to get cancelled. That's what I mean when I say she benefits from serialization.

Yamazaki: So the whole thing was improved by not allowing unnecessary content. Maybe I'm overstating, but I suspect for a lot of manga-ka, the scenes they really want to include aren't necessary. (*laughs*)

—**Interesting.** (*laughs*) **How does it look from an editorial standpoint?**

Editor S: I think that may be taking it too far. (*laughs*) But she has a point. I think it's not so much that the scenes aren't necessary, but that you have to wait for readers to get to the point where they're excited for those scenes, too. The problem comes when you throw that material out there at the beginning.

Yamazaki: Yeah, it's a matter of timing.

Editor S: Right. By the time a series begins, the author's been wrestling with the story for a long time, so for them, the characters already feel like friends by chapter one. The reader, on the other hand, is meeting the characters for the first time, so the reader still needs to get to know them, empathize with them, and get invested. If you go ahead and include a diversion that works for the author based on their deep familiarity with the characters, it's not going to click emotionally for the audience. I think the first step is to carefully build rapport with the reader, and then, once the reader is all fired up, you can include those diversions and the reader will appreciate them. You have to be in sync with the reader to get good results.

Yamazaki: Something like that, yes. Something else to think about is how the lines the manga-ka *wants* the character to say aren't necessarily things the character *would* say. I think that most of the things we want a character to say are unnecessary. Maybe I'm taking it too far again, but I think the character has to truly feel what they're saying for it to work. I mean, we all write things early on that we really want to include, but that we ultimately can't make work. The character just refuses.

Editor S: You can give directions, like, "I'd like you to say this line," but if you force them, it ends up being something the author is saying, not the character.

Yamazaki: That's right. Actually, I just had something like that. I threw it away. (*laughs*)

Editor S: Right. (*laughs*)

A Peek at the Future

—Is there anything you're planning for the story's future that you can drop even a little hint about?

Yamazaki: I'm planning a College Arc. We informally call the current storyline the Honeymoon Arc, after which I'm planning to address the main plot and the various stories of the young people.

Editor S: She starts by going on her first errands, and now she'll be going to school for the first time, hmm?

Yamazaki: That's right. It's the Starting Elementary School Arc. (*laughs*)

—I imagine some readers will hear "College Arc" and wonder, "But what will happen to Elias and the others?"

Yamazaki: Oh, we have to have them! I'm pretty sure they'll appear. There are a lot of things I still want to cover, but no matter what, the heart of this story is about Elias and Chise. They both need to mature emotionally to a certain point before we can really do romance.

Editor S: So, they each have to experience a lot of different feelings. We're just getting started, aren't we?

Yamazaki: Yes. Even a child can have a crush, but when we're talking about love, there's a certain amount of maturity you need to... Oops, I'd better stop before I tell you everything! (*laughs*)

A Gift from the Author to Chise and Elias

—Yamazaki-san, do you have a gift you'd like to give to Chise or Elias?

Yamazaki: Maybe a camera? A camera is a tool that lets you objectively capture something subjective. I'd like them to learn the difference.

Editor S: Yeah, photographs look different depending on how you take them. It all varies depending the choice of subject, the composition, the lens— things like that.

Yamazaki: Yeah. I'd like them to both get their hands on a camera, so that they could each see what the other is looking at.

Editor S: Even if they both photographed the same thing, it would probably look completely different.

Yamazaki: Hey, let's do that in the manga! (*laughs*) That sounds cool. Polaroid or digital? Maybe Polaroid would be better. A camera with a limit on the number of pictures you can take, so they'd really have to consider each one. Then they could each take like thirty pictures and show them to each other.

Editor S: That's good. You should do that.

—**So that's your answer? A camera?**

Yamazaki: Yes. I'd give them a camera.

Franchise Dreams

—**Starting in October, there's finally going to be a TV anime, and we've already had a drama CD, bundled OVAs, and novels. Are there any other media into which you'd like the franchise to expand?**

Yamazaki: Hmm... A game would be cool. Not one where you play as Elias or Chise, but one where you're someone else entirely, having fun in the world of *The Ancient Magus' Bride*. The player's face would never appear. It would be an open-world game where you could just enjoy exploring.

Editor S: Ambitious! So, it would be like *Skyrim*?

Yamazaki: It wouldn't have to be on the scale of *Skyrim*. You could just stay around Elias and Chise's house, or maybe you could go to the next village. You'd be one of the villagers or something. Play with the kids, gather ingredients for potions and then take them to Chise or Elias to prepare for you, take a walk around the village. That would be nice.

Editor S: I see. That *does* sound nice. Anything else?

Yamazaki: I'd like to hear a live orchestra performance—maybe of the anime score.

Editor S: If we're thinking along those lines, how about a live performance of the TV anime score along with a live reading?

Yamazaki: Awesome! I'd love that!

Awaiting the Anime in the Same Way

—**We've mentioned the TV anime. There's going to be a preview screening of the first episode, along with the final part of *Those Awaiting a Star*. How do you feel while you're waiting to see it?**

Yamazaki: Probably the same way as the readers! (*laughs*)

—**You think so?**

Yamazaki: It's based on my work, but the animators are the ones pouring their lives into making the anime come to life, aren't they? I mean, I'm doing the same thing with the manga, but they're different people, and of course animation offers different possibilities. That's why I imagine I'll feel the same way the readers do when I see it—like, "Ohhh, so this is how it can look!" I imagine readers also have opinions on how their favorite scenes should look or who should voice a certain character. So yes, it's the same. I'm looking forward to it as one of many viewers.

Editor S: For a viewer, you've been pretty involved, though. (*laughs*)

Yamazaki: That's true. (*laughs*) From that perspective, I think I can assure everyone who loves the original that they're going to enjoy the way it's turning out.

The Characters of The Ancient Magus' Bride

—**Is there any character in *The Ancient Magus' Bride* who reminds you of yourself, Yamazaki-san?**

Yamazaki: A friend said, "Chise gets her submissiveness from you, doesn't she?" (*laughs*) I think maybe the closest in personality is Torrey. I'm not that shameless, but I guess we're both curious. I couldn't ask about what I want to know the way he does, but I really wish I could. So I guess you could say our curiosity is similar on the inside. I'd also say I'm similar to Adolf. But then, my indecisiveness does make me like Chise. Even so, I see Chise as her own distinct person.

—**Is there any character who you think isn't like you at all?**

Yamazaki: Elias. He pisses me off. (*laughs*)

Editor S: That was quick. Could you please not talk like that? (*laughs*)

Yamazaki: I don't think I have anything in common with Cartaphilus, either. And Angelica is a far cry from me. But in the end, I'm their creator, so I suppose there must be a little of me in each of them.

Editor S: You don't have any of Angie's "kick ass and take names" attitude?

Yamazaki: Damn, I wish! (*laughs*)

Editor S: I see. (*laughs*) Elias gets a lot of flak from women, but I think he's kind of like a naïve teenage boy or young man. I suppose it depends on the person, but I feel like this is pretty much what happens when a man with a personality like Elias' falls in love for the first time.

Yamazaki: What, really? That's good.

Editor S: Personally, I suspect that men can identify a lot with his possessiveness and uncertain feelings.

Yamazaki: I hope so. Some people have said that Elias embodies a certain type of female wish fulfillment, but not for me. Not in a million years. (*laughs*) Like hell I'd fall for a guy like that. There, that's what the author herself thinks. (*laughs*) Anyway, Elias pisses me off, but he's just like a troublesome child. He's not like me.

Likes and Dislikes in Drawing Characters

—Is there any character you came to like as you drew them?
Yamazaki: Maybe Cartaphilus? There wasn't any character I outright hated to begin with. I'm drawing them because I like them. The way I've treated Cartaphilus has changed as I've drawn him more. At first he was fairly opaque, but gradually you're starting to get inside his head. I did have him defined as a character, but as I've drawn him, I guess he's getting better defined in some respects. Also, the selkie (Merituuli). At first I didn't expect to draw him so much, but after I started, I really enjoyed it.

—Is there any character who is just hard to draw?
Yamazaki: All the guys! (*laughs*) I don't know if it's okay for me to say this, but it's just hard. It's fun to draw characters like Torrey and Adolf who show their emotions, but the kind of guys who suppress their feelings? That's really hard. (*laughs*)
Editor S: Is that because it's difficult to figure out what they're thinking?
Yamazaki: It's simpler than that. Just physically and psychologically. Girls are fun to draw. (*laughs*) You know who's really hard? Lindel-san. First of all, he's supposed to be beautiful, and he's also supposed to take the grown-up role sometimes, and yet deep down he has trouble dealing with other humans. Showing all of those layers is hard. He's like an unfathomable depth, and I imagine he's still got a lot to be unearthed.
Editor S: Sounds like if you linger and pay attention to him, it'll make the story that much longer.
Yamazaki: Yeah. Like, "Hey, Lindel had this mage friend, and here's how they interact," or something like that. And I'd love to show how he and Rahab met, if people are interested.

"It Won't End Even if You Do It" & "Escape Is Victory"

—Do you have a saying that you try to live by?
Yamazaki: Uh...
Editor S: Maybe a motto or something? Like, "It will end if you do it, and it

won't if you don't"?

Yamazaki: I had that on my wall for a while, but recently I added, "It won't end even if you *do* it." (*laughs*)

Editor S: If you get like that, all you can do is get some sleep. (*laughs*) Sleep and then work hard the next day.

Yamazaki: Yeah, when I sleep and then get up early to get back to work, I make some progress.

—Perhaps just certain words that have stayed with you?

Yamazaki: There's the saying, "Escape is victory." I was the youngest sibling, so I often had to deal with my siblings treating me unreasonably, and I didn't have the vocabulary to push back. That's when my mother told me, "Escape is victory." She said it a lot, actually.

Editor S: You can't escape your deadlines, you know.

Yamazaki: No, that's not what I meant! I'm fully aware that if I tried to run, you'd chase me to the ends of the earth. (*laughs*) It's more like, when you *can* run, you need to run for all you're worth; and when you can't run, you need to stand tall.

This isn't exactly a saying, but I often tell myself, "Doubt yourself." It's bad to assume that you're always right! That's true for both manga and everyday life.

Kore Yamazaki's Weakness

—What do you consider your weakness?

Yamazaki: Being lazy. I'm the type of person who does what she wants and then brags about it.

Editor S: But people say there are good things about being lazy too, like finding more efficient ways to do things.

Yamazaki: That's true. I do that with drawing. I look for ways to reduce the number of steps or shorten them. I pick the shortest route. I mean, look— I've dropped out of normal society! (*laughs*) I can't even imagine swaying on that train every morning. All of you people who commute every day blow my mind. I just had the incredible luck to be good at this—which doesn't change the fact that drawing manga is a gamble. I always have to remember that I depend on readers for my survival. Anyway, if I tried to make a full list of my own weaknesses, it would never end.

—What about your strengths?

Yamazaki: My strength is that even when someone bashes what I've worked to create, I can just shrug it off. (*laughs*) If even one or two people say my work is interesting, that's enough motivation for me. I think it's important not to get caught up in that stuff.

Editor S: In some ways, it's best to always have people around who'll tell you your work's boring.

Yamazaki: Yeah, that's healthier.

Editor S: I think it's scariest either to get nothing but praise or to not be read by anyone.

Yamazaki: I think you're totally right. Oh, but I should say how much I appreciate all the encouraging letters I get from readers. If I ever have time, I want to write back! Someday I will!

What Pride Won't Allow

—Is there anything your pride won't allow you to do, or that you just don't think you can do?

Yamazaki: A normal job.

Editor S: (*laughs*) Maybe stick to the topic of creative work here.

Yamazaki: Well, I see characters as different people who are living within the story, so I don't want to portray them as saying or doing things they wouldn't. We touched on this earlier, but I wouldn't be able to step outside of the mindset of, "I give them direction, but in the end I let the characters have their say." It's kind of like I'm peeking into the same world the readers are. As a creator, I do think, "I want this character to say this line," but ultimately I won't force it on them. That's not so much a matter of pride as honestly just being unable to do it.

—On a similar note, are there any genres or such you don't think you could work in?

Editor S: I couldn't do mystery. My mind's not flexible enough. I'd like to try occult or horror, although I'm a scaredy-cat. (*laughs*) As far as manga goes, I don't think you really need to have pride when your primary focus is to always make it better. It's not as if you're always right; in fact, you're often wrong! You can't see your own work from the outside, so you have to value outside perspectives. And you're always learning new information, so over the years the way you think will change. You don't need to be stubborn about sticking to the plot.

Where to Visit

Editor S: If you had a chance to travel somewhere for research, where would you go?

Yamazaki: Finland. I'd like to go back to the U.K., too—stay in the Cotswolds for two or three nights and take plenty of pictures. I'd also like to visit Canada and Switzerland. Oh, and Bosnia-Herzegovina and Croatia. I saw them on TV recently. Oh, and Iceland. I want to go someplace where there's nothing. (*laughs*)

Editor S: You love your moors and wilds. (*laughs*)

Yamazaki: I sure do! Also, I'm not good with hot climates, so I like visiting cold places.

—**What about the Middle East or Africa?**

Yamazaki: I'd like to visit Morocco.

Editor S: What about Turkey?

Yamazaki: That, too! (*laughs*)

Editor S: Turkey would be nice. That lamp in Part 2 of *Those Awaiting a Star* looked like a Turkish lamp. Don't you want to go buy one?

Yamazaki: Yeah. Oh, and Mongolia might be fun. Sorry, I guess my answer ended up being "everywhere in the world." But I really do want to visit most countries. (*laughs*)

A History Without Career Dreams

—**Moving on, is there any job you ever aspired to other than being a manga-ka?**

Yamazaki: I don't know if this counts, but when I was a kid I dreamed of being a photographer. My first dream was being a novelist, though, as I mentioned in a previous interview. I gave up on it. The thing is, it's not so much that I liked taking pictures as that I liked to travel. I was thinking I could see lots of different places and that photography would let me capture all their fun and beautiful aspects. My elementary-school self thought being a photographer sounded great.

—**I see. So, what did you think once you were old enough to realistically contemplate your future?**

Yamazaki: I thought it sounded really hard to have a normal job. My siblings are a lot older than me, and they were always so exhausted when they came home.

Editor S: Are you saying you didn't have any hopes or dreams about work?

Yamazaki: There was no way I could have those dreams, watching my siblings. I thought it sounded horrible. I figured I had no choice but to work if I wanted to eat, so I got a desk job, but after one year, I was like, "I can't do this anymore." It wasn't even so much the work itself as it was my boss. The work itself I liked, I just couldn't get along with the other people. After that, I did a bunch of odd jobs, like working as a farmhand and at a used bookstore. I stuck out a bit everywhere except at that bookstore. I really enjoyed the work itself, but somehow I simply couldn't manage to work with people.

Editor S: Was it because you found it hard to stay in step with the others, or because you didn't get along with your bosses?

Yamazaki: In my experience, it was more the latter. Maybe I was just unlucky, but I had so many unreasonable bosses. At my last job, though, at that bookstore, my boss and coworkers were all nice. It was the best.

—What made you quit that last job, then?

Yamazaki: The shop went out of business. By that point, I'd already made my commercial debut, but the manga wasn't selling, so that went down the drain, too. Then I just goofed off, took walks, read books, and drew doujinshi, and eventually I met you. (*laughs*)

Editor S: I see. (*laughs*) People eventually arrive where they're meant to be, don't they?

Yamazaki: You could also say they "wash up." (*laughs*) Looking back on it, I guess it was a good experience. I'm not saying I'm so worldly now, but I suppose it's good that I got a bit of experience in the real world before I became a manga-ka. After all, once you start drawing manga, you don't have much opportunity to interact directly with society anymore.

Where to Find Love

—Given that you have experience in the self-published comics scene, Yamazaki-sensei, what would your advice be for how to enjoy a convention?

Yamazaki: It's the best! You create something with your circle, you see someone take it in their hands, you see their expression, and you're surrounded by creative comrades. It's like everyone is your friend. It's so much fun! Like, "I'm not in the minority!" (*laughs*) It makes you feel like you're not alone. Of course, everyone there probably sees things differently, but when you experience the joy of creating something with your circle, it's weird—you feel like you're all in it together. That's fun, and it's great. Comitia is all original works, so I think that lends itself even more to what I described. If you're doing secondary works, you might actually find it a bit hard to get along with the people in the next booth if they have a different interpretation of the characters. (*laughs*)

Editor S: There's a lot of diversity in secondary works, isn't there? (*laughs*) So, that's all about self-publishing at a convention, but what if you're a reader?

Yamazaki: Good question. I think commercial manga tends to be made for a mass audience, you know? But at Comitia, most people are just creating whatever they enjoy, so I think it's best to just approach it with an attitude of, "I am in a place full of love. I am going to find love." You go look for the expression of love that someone's created, and you get to touch that love. That's the fun part. And then there's the joy you get when that love matches what you're looking for! You find something that makes you go, "I just love this so much," and your eyes fill with tears... It's just, whoa. I think everyone there has so much love in their hearts. It's so great. I want to go again.

Treasure Every Feeling You Have

—Please give us a final message for the readers.

Yamazaki: This is the hardest part! (*laughs*) I mean, I'm already scratching down everything I want to convey, everything I want people to feel in my manga. But okay... I'd like you all to treasure every feeling you get from reading the manga or watching the anime. Whether you think something is good or you think something is off, either way, your feelings are valuable. No matter what anyone else says, your feelings are *yours.* I want you to value your own feelings about it over what other people say. If you do that, and you enjoy the manga we're making, I'll be so incredibly happy.

—Thank you for the interview!

Merkmal

SEVEN SEAS ENTERTAINMENT PRESENTS

The Ancient Magus' Bride
Merkmal

TRANSLATION
Daniel Komen
Adrienne Beck

ADAPTATION
Ysabet Reinhardt MacFarlane

LETTERING
Clay Gardner
Karis Page

COVER DESIGN
Nicky Lim

PROOFREADER
Shanti Whitesides
Jade Gardner

ASSISTANT EDITOR
Jenn Grunigen
J.P. Sullivan

PRODUCTION ASSISTANT
CK Russell

PRODUCTION MANAGER
Lissa Pattillo

EDITOR-IN-CHIEF
Adam Arnold

PUBLISHER
Jason DeAngelis

THE ANCIENT MAGUS' BRIDE OFFICIAL GUIDE BOOK MERKMAL
© Kore Yamazaki 2017
Originally published in Japan in 2017 by MAG Garden Corporation, Tokyo.
English translation rights arranged through TOHAN CORPORATION, Tokyo.

Seven Seas books may be purchased in bulk for promotional, educational, or business use. Please contact your local bookseller or the Macmillan Corporate and Premium Sales Department at 1-800-221-7945, extension 5442, or by e-mail at MacmillanSpecialMarkets@macmillan.com.

Seven Seas and the Seven Seas logo are trademarks of Seven Seas Entertainment, LLC. All rights reserved.

ISBN: 978-1-626928-86-2

Printed in Canada

First Printing: May 2018

10 9 8 7 6 5 4 3 2 1

FOLLOW US ONLINE: *www.sevenseasentertainment.com*

READING DIRECTIONS

This book reads from *right to left*, Japanese style. If this is your first time reading manga, you start reading from the top right panel on each page and take it from there. If you get lost, just follow the numbered diagram here. It may seem backwards at first, but you'll get the hang of it! Have fun!!

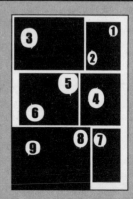